Bill Bright &
Campus Crusade for Christ

JOHN G. TURNER

Bill Bright &

The Renewal of

Evangelicalism in

Postwar America

Campus

Crusade

for Christ

The University of
North Carolina Press
Chapel Hill

© 2008 The University of North Carolina Press

All rights reserved

Designed by Heidi Perov

Set in Bembo

Manufactured in the United States of America

The paper in this book meets the guidelines for permanence
and durability of the Committee on Production Guidelines for
Book Longevity of the Council on Library Resources.

Library of Congress Cataloging-in-Publication Data

Turner, John G.

   Bill Bright and Campus Crusade for Christ : the renewal of
evangelicalism in postwar America / John G. Turner.

   p. cm.

   Includes bibliographical references (p.   ) and index.

   ISBN 978-0-8078-3185-4 (cloth: alk. paper)

   ISBN 978-0-8078-5873-8 (pbk.: alk. paper)

1. Bright, Bill.   2. Campus Crusade for Christ—History.
3. Evangelicalism—United States—History.   4. United
States—Religious life and customs.   I. Title.

   BV3785.B73T87 2008

   267'.61—dc22   2007035930

cloth   12 11 10 09 08   5 4 3 2 1

paper   12 11 10 09 08   5 4 3 2 1

Contents

Illustrations

Acknowledgments

That this book carries the name of a single author obscures the fact that its successful completion has depended on innumerable archivists, librarians, and readers. For searching their collections and sending me valuable documents, I am grateful to the helpful staff at the John Vaughan Library of Northeastern State University in Tahlequah, Oklahoma; the Flower Pentecostal Heritage Center of the Assemblies of God in Springfield, Missouri; the United Methodist Church Archives in Madison, New Jersey; the Hoover Institution Library in Stanford, California; the National Archives and Records Administration in College Park, Maryland; the Jimmy Carter Presidential Library in Atlanta, Georgia; the Ockenga Institute in South Hamilton, Massachusetts; the City of San Diego (California) Archives; and the University of Notre Dame Archives in Notre Dame, Indiana. Several institutions and individuals displayed particular hospitality and devoted considerable time to this project: Bob Shuster, Paul Ericksen, and Wayne Weber at the Billy Graham Center Archives in Wheaton, Illinois; Mike Knox at the Campus Crusade for Christ headquarters in Orlando, Florida; Christie Deming and Robert Benedetto at the Princeton Theological Seminary Archives in Princeton, New Jersey; David Bundy at the Fuller Theological Seminary Archives in Pasadena, California; Mark Sidwell at the Bob Jones University Fundamentalism File in Greenville, South Carolina; Janna Berezkina at the Gospel Light Archives in Ventura, California; Mark Roberts at the Holy Spirit Research Center in Tulsa, Oklahoma; and Robert Krapohl at the Trinity International University Archives in Deerfield, Illinois. A number of individuals graciously allowed me to photocopy material or reproduce photographs from their private collections, including Spencer Brand, Peter Gillquist, Bob Kendall, Joanne McClurkin, Ralph Hamburger, Frank and Judy Kifer, Curt and Lois Mackey, Ted and Gwen Martin, Jerry and Sharyn Regier, Kent Hutcheson, and Dorothy Hauser Graham.

I would also like to thank several people who carefully read the entire manuscript, including George Marsden, Gail Bederman, James Turner, John McGreevy, Kathryn Long, Margaret Bendroth, Darren Dochuk, John Ferguson, Mike Hamilton, Joel Carpenter, Jason Bivins, and Grant Wacker. They saved me from embarrassing errors and recommended many courses of fruitful inquiry and analysis.

This book represents the interpretation of an outsider to Campus Crusade for Christ; it is in no way endorsed or authorized by the organization. I remain grateful for the opportunity to interview numerous current and former Campus Crusade staff members, and scores of interviews not cited in this book provided helpful background information. Several insiders, including Bailey Marks, Vonette and Brad Bright, Frank Kifer, Gordon Klenck, Stan Oakes, Kent Hutcheson, and Swede Anderson, read either the entire manuscript or selected portions. They did not agree with all of my interpretations and conclusions—and in some cases vehemently disagreed—but I appreciate their willingness to provide feedback and engage in dialogue. Former staff members Bob Kendall and Peter Gillquist also read portions of the manuscript.

I am very thankful to many colleagues at the University of Notre Dame, Colorado State University, and the University of South Alabama, all of whom supported me during the years I worked on this project. Julius Burke and Victoria Garrett deserve a special mention for their friendship and encouragement. My parents, Mike and Sally Turner, unswervingly provided steadfast support—both moral and financial—for the decades of education that made it possible for me to pursue an academic career. Finally, my wife, Elissa, contributed to this project in both large and small ways, all invaluable. She helped me choose a topic that still retains my interest, listened to hundreds of stories about Bill Bright and Campus Crusade for Christ, joined me on a two-thousand-mile research trip, and carefully proofread a draft of the manuscript. Most of all, she enabled me to more fully enjoy these years of research and writing.

Bill Bright &

Campus Crusade for Christ

Introduction

In June 1972, eighty-five thousand college and high school students converged for a weeklong festival. They lived in a "tent city," listened to rock music, played in mud formed by downpours, and enjoyed being away from their parents. Yet this throng of students was different from the youthful gatherings more often associated with the late 1960s and early 1970s. These young people were in Dallas for Campus Crusade for Christ's "Explo '72"—at "Godstock" rather than Woodstock.[1] The students spent the mornings listening to Bill Bright, Billy Graham, and other evangelical luminaries talk about Jesus Christ, the Holy Spirit, and evangelism. On several afternoons, they visited Dallas neighborhoods, knocked on doors, and shared the contents of a small booklet entitled *Have You Heard of the Four Spiritual Laws?* They visited the booths of agencies that sought to convince them to devote their postcollegiate lives to foreign missions. In the evening meetings, the assembled students applauded a large contingent of military personnel and cheered the South Vietnamese flag. Graham read a telegram from Richard Nixon, and a survey conducted by a local newspaper reported that the students favored Nixon over George McGovern in the upcoming election by a margin of more than five to one. On the final night of the event, tens of thousands of other Dallas residents joined the students for a "Jesus Music Festival," featuring the music of Johnny Cash and Kris Kristofferson. The young people in attendance swayed and danced to the music and pointed their index fingers to the sky in the "one way" symbol of the Jesus Movement. Explo '72 revealed an evangelical youth culture—in some ways conservative and traditional, in other ways modern and innovative—often overlooked in accounts of the late 1960s and early 1970s.

This book presents the history of Campus Crusade for Christ as a window into the world of American evangelicalism since 1945. Campus Crusade, founded by Bill Bright (1921–2003) at the University of California at Los Angeles in 1951, grew by century's end into a global evangelical empire. The ministry's staff talked about Jesus Christ at fraternity meetings, evangelized students from Daytona to Balboa on spring break trips, organized evangelistic advertising campaigns in American cities, brought a film about Jesus to remote overseas villages, and hosted conferences designed to "rekindle the fire" of Christian marriages. Alongside Billy Graham, Oral Roberts, Pat Robertson, and Jerry Falwell, Bright was one of the most influential evangelical power brokers of the late twentieth century, able to mobilize large coalitions of conservative Christians for both evangelistic and partisan ends. He recruited an army of evangelists who gathered donations from increasingly affluent supporters and aggressively marketed the evangelical message in the United States and around the world.

With the passage of several decades since the public resurgence of evangelicalism in the 1970s, it is easy to forget that the vitality of evangelicalism constitutes one of the more surprising developments in the recent history of the United States. For much of the twentieth century, many educated Americans shared H. Richard Niebuhr's characterization of fundamentalist Christianity as rural, backward, uneducated, and irrational, an appraisal that suggested conservative forms of Protestantism in America would disappear as the country progressed further into an urban, industrial, and modern future. By the 1960s, some cultural elites suggested that religion itself was passing away in America, leading *Time* magazine to ask on a 1966 cover, "Is God Dead?" Few reading *Time* in 1966 would have predicted that only ten years later, *Newsweek* would proclaim the nation's bicentennial to be "The Year of the Evangelicals."[2] Evangelicals reasserted their presence in America through the steady and sometimes spectacular growth of suburban churches and greatly increased political clout. Since the rediscovery of evangelicals by politicians, journalists, and scholars in the mid-1970s, historians have researched and chronicled the broad contours of the post–World War II evangelical movement.[3] This history of Campus Crusade emphasizes one reason for the vitality of evangelicalism in modern America: the ability of evangelical parachurch organizations to creatively adapt and market their faith to modern culture.

Campus Crusade is a prominent example of what evangelicals refer to as parachurch organizations. The word "parachurch" is not in most dictionaries—it refers to organizations that exist alongside (from the Greek *para*) the institutional church (i.e., denominations and congregations). "Parachurch groups," writes evangelical editor Stephen Board, "are religion gone free enterprise." Over the past half century, the continued rapid growth of denominations such as the Southern Baptist Convention and Assemblies of God has greatly increased evangelical numbers, but the impetus for cultural adaptation and innovative evangelistic techniques has come from nondenominational megachurches and parachurch agencies. Since parachurch organizations are normally dependent upon only their donors and the charismatic leadership of their founders, they alter their policies and strategies more quickly than denominations, which typically have thicker layers of decision making and bureaucracy. Because they cross denominational lines and transcend individual megachurches, parachurch organizations shape much of modern evangelicalism's character and public agenda. Moreover, according to sociologist Robert Wuthnow, the proliferation of parachurch organizations helped fracture American Protestants across denominational lines into politically and theologically conservative and liberal wings.[4]

It is difficult to overstate the significance of parachurch organizations in contemporary American evangelicalism, as they structure and direct billions of evangelical dollars toward humanitarianism, political advocacy, and evangelism. World Vision (founded in 1950 by Bob Pierce) spends nearly $1 billion annually on disaster relief, community development, and developing-world child sponsorships. James Dobson's Focus on the Family raises more than $125 million annually for radio broadcasts and lobbying efforts, and Pat Robertson's Christian Broadcasting Network disperses over $400 million per year for a variety of purposes, from the *700 Club* to Regent University. Above all, evangelicals form parachurch organizations to carry out the task of evangelism. These range from ministries revolving around individual evangelists (such as the Billy Graham Evangelistic Association and Benny Hinn Ministries) to missionary-sending organization such as Serving in Mission (SIM) and Youth with a Mission (YWAM). Young Life, founded by Jim Rayburn in 1938, spent $180 million in 2006 evangelizing high school students in local communities and at camps, and Charles Colson's Prison Fellowship expended over $50 million ministering to prisoners and their families.[5] Parachurch organizations sometimes come into conflict with denominations and local churches, which accuse them of diverting energy, individuals, and funds from congregational and denominational enterprises.[6] Evangelical parachurch organizations also compete with each other, as evangelicals rarely survey the religious landscape and conclude that it is too saturated to support a new ministry.

Parachurch organizations have long played a key role in American evangelicalism. The American Board of Commissioners for Foreign Missions, the American Sunday School Union, and the Tract Society provided avenues for nineteenth-century evangelicals from various denominations to join together in common evangelistic and benevolent missions.[7] The growth of evangelical parachurch organizations since World War II, however, has been particularly noteworthy, as parachurch ministries proliferated and their budgets grew explosively. During these decades, American parachurch foreign missionaries began to outnumber their denominational counterparts. Evangelical political-action organizations amassed far more political influence than their mainline competitors. Yet despite their prominence in the world of modern American evangelicalism, scholars have produced few sustained histories of these organizations.[8]

Although the National Association of Evangelicals provides some direction and leadership to evangelical institutions, evangelicalism has no central authority. Instead, as George Marsden has observed, evangelicalism functions like "the feudal system of the Middle Ages"—an array of sometimes competitive and sometimes cooperative fiefdoms.[9] As might be expected given this loose and dynamic structure, evangelicals exhibit considerable diversity, theologically and otherwise. In the United States, evangelicalism comprises a broad "mosaic" or "kaleidoscope" that at various times has included separatist fundamentalists, moderate fundamentalists remaining in mainline denominations, Holiness denominations, Pentecostals, and charismatics.[10] With these definitional caveats in mind, "evangelical" in this study refers to Protestant Christians who readily talk about their experience of salvation in Jesus Christ, regard a divinely inspired Bible as the ultimate authority on matters of faith and practice, and engage the world in which they live through evangelism and other forms of mission.[11]

It is hazardous to make generalizations about such a diverse and sprawling movement, especially through the history of a single organization. This endeavor is even more hazardous because until the early 1970s, Campus Crusade was a relatively small organization and Bill Bright was not yet a member of the evangelical pantheon that then included figures such as Graham, Carl Henry, and Harold Lindsell. Moreover, like any organization, Crusade exhibits its own distinctive characteristics. Crusade's staff members, for instance, spend much more time actively practicing evangelism than the average American evangelical. Also, Crusade's institutional character was strongly influenced first by Bob Jones University and later by Dallas Theological Seminary, two institutions with their own unique places on the conservative Protestant landscape. Nevertheless, Crusade provides an excellent lens into the recent history of evangelicalism for several reasons. First, as discussed above, parachurch groups are central to the modern evangelical enterprise, and Crusade has become the largest non-philanthropic evangelical parachurch organization in the United States. By the early twenty-first century, Crusade's annual revenues approached $500 million, and Crusade staff members around the world numbered nearly thirty thousand.[12] Unlike individual megachurches or seminaries, Crusade's influence in the United States is truly national, with campus chapters and other ministries spread across the country. Also, Crusade throughout its existence has positioned itself squarely in the middle of the evangelical mainstream. Bright and Campus Crusade participated in most of the major trends and controversies that shaped the trajectory of evangelicalism in the years following World War II: the revivals of the late 1940s, the divorce between evangelicals and fundamentalists in the 1950s, the embrace of popular music in the 1960s, the romance between evangelicals and conservative politicians, and the increasing prominence of ministries and political campaigns devoted to protecting the "biblical institutions of marriage and family."[13]

Finally, Campus Crusade provides a cogent example of the ability of parachurch organizations to creatively market their message and adeptly respond to cultural change. In the following chapters, I frequently employ language about "marketing" and "selling" in my description of Crusade's activities. Such language is not meant to imply that Crusade staff members are merely a sales force gaining either money or power by marketing their gospel. I take at face value the statements of Crusade staff about their heartfelt desire to share with others the spiritual experiences that have transformed their own lives. Moreover, Bill Bright lived modestly compared to most evangelical leaders and did not amass a fortune because of Crusade's success or from the sale of his own publications. Instead, I utilize the language of "selling" for two reasons. First, Bill Bright himself was a businessman and a salesman before he converted to Christianity and founded Campus Crusade for Christ. Also, Crusade has long been a leader in the evangelical world at adapting the lessons of marketing to the business of evangelism. Bright asked his early staff to read books on sales techniques, developed his *Four Spiritual Laws* in part on the advice of a salesman, and required his staff to record their contacts and conversions along the lines of a sales organization. Bright—and later many of his followers—also exhibited a striking ability to "sell" his ministry, becoming a fund-raiser par excellence among American evangelicals.

Among American religious movements, evangelicals have long displayed a distinctive talent for promoting their faith, their organizations, and themselves. In what became known as the Great Awakening, George Whitefield developed a complex and effective system of advance publicity, featuring pamphlets, manufactured controversies in newspapers, and advertisements. Evangelists from Charles Finney to Dwight L. Moody to Billy Graham all relied not only on the Holy Spirit to effect conversions but also on innovative preaching methods, barrages of publicity, and the use of emerging media. Bill Bright was a pragmatic evangelist in this tradition, trying and refining countless ways of spreading the evangelical gospel throughout his more than fifty years at the helm of Campus Crusade. Bright borrowed from the techniques of Hollywood, the counterculture, and even the GOP in order to further his vision of reaching the entire world with his message. Evangelicals are hardly alone in their use of marketing techniques to promote their faith—today, denominations such as the Presbyterian Church (U.S.A.) and the United Church of Christ purchase airtime to market their own brands of Protestant Christianity, and a host of both Christian and non-Christian movements also engage in the creative promotion of their beliefs. Evangelicals, however, continue to be among the most vigorous and resourceful religious marketers in the United States. In the twentieth century, evangelicals took the greatest advantage of new media like radio, television, and the Internet, and evangelicals proved themselves the most eager to change their forms of worship to attract rising generations of Americans.[14]

This effort to keep their spiritual wares attractive in an increasingly complex religious marketplace continually encourages evangelicals to remain in the cultural mainstream. Although fundamentalists in the early 1900s were hardly uniformly antimodern and untouched by mainstream culture, evangelicals since 1945 have visibly moved toward the center of American society. As D. G. Hart has commented, evangelicals now seek to "baptize rather than reject American popular culture."[15] Yet despite this adaptation to and even baptism of culture, evangelicals have never become entirely at ease in their American Zion. Evangelical leaders throughout the second half of the twentieth century voiced jeremiads about the dangers of communist subversion, the influence of secular humanism, and the decline in traditional sexual morality. Even as evangelicals made peace with rock music and fashion trends, they waged cultural war against feminism, homosexuality, and political liberalism. Evangelicals no longer exhibit the marked tension with American culture that in part characterized the fundamentalist movement of the early 1900s. Instead, their combination of adaptation and alarm mirrors the medium, or "optimum," tension that Rodney Stark, Roger Finke, and Armand Mauss believe characterizes successful religious movements. To apply an observation of Stark and Finke, evangelicals provide a faith for Americans who "want religion that maintains some moral reservations vis-à-vis secular life, but not too many."[16]

Scholars have long perceived elements of declension in the adaptation of religion to its surrounding culture. As H. Richard Niebuhr wrote in 1935, "faith loses its force" when it becomes "tied to the culture which it sponsored," and he identified capitalism and nationalism as the modern idols of the church. William McLoughlin criticized American revivalists from Finney to Graham for having diluted the theological and social content of evangelicalism in their "engineering of mass consent," and D. G. Hart alleges that parachurch organizations in particular have vitiated evangelical theology and church discipline by promoting a "lowest common denominator theology." R. Laurence Moore gently strikes a Niebuhrian tone when he suggests that the entrance of religion into the vulgar marketplace robbed religion of its "transformative power." The meaning of "transformative power," however, depends on one's own vantage point. Over the past few decades, evangelicals have moved closer to mainstream American culture, but they have also expended tremendous amounts of organizational energy in attempts to transform society, if not in the direction prescribed by liberal Protestants like Niebuhr. More significantly for this study, the creative marketing of evangelical culture and its gospel has helped evangelicals retain if not grow their share of the ever more diverse American religious marketplace. Campus Crusade has been one of the market leaders in this process. By experimenting with techniques in college evangelism, by attracting couples to FamilyLife conferences, and by hosting conferences geared toward executives, Campus Crusade has continually found new ways to gain an audience for its message about Jesus.[17]

What follows is a mostly chronological history of Campus Crusade's ministries within the United States. Although Campus Crusade in recent decades has sent a major portion of its resources and personnel overseas, the size and scope of Crusade's international activities permit only a brief overview within these pages. While chronicling the history of Campus Crusade, moreover, I concentrate on three areas of intersection between evangelicalism and American society. First, I examine the place of evangelical religion on the American campus since the middle of the twentieth century. By the time of Crusade's founding, most public universities had divested themselves of all but the vestiges of their Protestant heritages. The YMCA, a major evangelical influence on many campuses in the early twentieth century, dwindled as it shifted its focus from evangelism and Christian discipleship to recreation and service. Already a faint influence in the classroom, mainline Protestantism repositioned itself on the margins of university life.[18] Christianity was displaced but not eradicated, however, as evangelical ministries like InterVarsity Christian Fellowship, Campus Crusade, and the Fellowship of Christian Athletes carved out niches for themselves on campuses across the country. The place of evangelical student ministries on the periphery of university life places some constraints on evangelicalism's influence on the academy. On campuses with few evangelical professors, for instance, explicitly evangelical ideas rarely penetrate the classroom. Moreover, while the charge would not be true of all evangelical student ministries, Campus Crusade has self-consciously privileged evangelistic activism over the contemplative and intellectual pursuits typically considered the warp and woof of university life. Nevertheless, Crusade's approach has dovetailed effectively with the evolution of American higher education since World War II.[19] The marginalization of Christian belief inside the classroom did not create insurmountable obstacles for parachurch organizations conducting their ministries in cafeterias, dormitories, and locker rooms. For many students, Greek life and college sports were the central foci of their university years, and Crusade tapped an underserved religious marketplace by taking its evangelical message to sororities, dormitories, and athletic teams. If Campus Crusade, by any reasonable standard, failed in its quest to "win the campus for Christ," the secularization of the American university has not continued unabated, and evangelical subcultures thrive on most public university campuses.

Second, I use Campus Crusade's fund-raising literature and Bright's activities to trace the political evolution of evangelicalism since 1945. Scholars have not fully appreciated the relationship between evangelicalism and conservative politics in the decades before the mid-1970s,[20] largely because evangelicals were not well organized politically in those years. Crusade contributed to the grassroots anticommunism of the 1950s and 1960s, and Bright supported evangelical participation in precinct-level political efforts to oppose communism and protect free enterprise. Before the 1970s, however, politicians paid scant attention to evangelicals, partly because there were few well-known evangelical organizations and leaders beyond Billy Graham. By the 1970s, politicians took note of increasingly large evangelical organizations—like Campus Crusade—supported by increasingly affluent donors. Partly because evangelical leaders considered themselves outsiders who deserved greater political and cultural influence, conservative politicians found that they could readily gain the support of evangelical leaders by meeting with them privately and attending their conferences. These relationships reshaped the American political landscape, as evangelicals gradually became a reliable Republican voting bloc. In Bright's mind, the political and religious spheres could never be separate realms. For example, Campus Crusade evangelized politicians in the nation's capital, hoping to impact their eternal destinies while also shaping the direction of American policy on issues like abortion, school prayer, and same-sex marriage. When criticized for explicit and implicit partisanship by the press, left-leaning evangelicals, and even members of his own staff, Bright often minimized the extent of his political interests and denied the partisan implications of his rhetoric and activities. He, like many evangelicals, never resolved the tension between his evangelistic vision and a custodial impulse to reform American society through campaigns that awkwardly blended the spiritual and the political.

Finally, I analyze the changing ways that evangelicals have understood and prescribed gender roles since 1945. In the immediate postwar period, evangelicals reemphasized traditional roles for women and dwelt on the need for stronger male leadership. By the 1970s, the nation as a whole—and particularly intellectuals and journalists—had gradually embraced a more egalitarian conception of gender roles. As one response to that change, Campus Crusade organized FamilyLife marriage conferences at which speakers articulated the need for Christians to recognize the divine roles that God had assigned to men and women, respectively. On issues of gender, evangelicals appeared to resist rather than accommodate themselves to mainstream culture. By the end of the century, however, most conservative evangelicals made at least a pragmatic accommodation to a more egalitarian understanding of gender, paying lip service to ideals of male headship and female submission but encouraging women to assume positions of leadership and encouraging men to be sensitive leaders who respect their wives' opinions. A notable gap emerged between evangelical reality and evangelical rhetoric, with the latter sometimes serving as a symbolic protest against modern culture without necessarily shaping the everyday lives of evangelicals.[21] While intra-evangelical disagreements over female leadership and gender roles within church and family became pronounced, most evangelicals joined together in opposition to the slowly growing acceptance of homosexuality in modern America. Thus, evangelicals accommodated themselves gradually to one aspect of modern culture while simultaneously rallying themselves in opposition to another development.

Evangelical engagement with gender issues in late-twentieth-century America illustrates the broader relationship between evangelicalism and modern American society. American evangelicals are both cultural outsiders and insiders at the same time. They selectively embrace and resist modern American culture. Their evangelistic objectives push them toward mainstream culture, and in many respects—education, wealth, and politics—evangelicals are much closer to mainstream culture in the early twenty-first century than they were in 1945. At the same time, the desire of evangelicals to refashion American culture in their own image leads them to construct at least symbolic barriers between themselves and the culture they wish to transform.

I wrote this history of Campus Crusade for Christ as an outsider to the organization, but my own background and preconceptions have influenced my interpretations. Though I have never had any personal connection to Campus Crusade, as a high school and college student I participated in the world of parachurch evangelicalism through Young Life and InterVarsity. I occupy a religious space between mainline and evangelical Protestantism, appreciating the piety of evangelicalism while lamenting its politicization and obsession with numbers and "success." While I respect Campus Crusade for boldly and aggressively pursuing its objectives, I also highlight the ministry's periodic anti-intellectualism, its infatuation with large crowds and statistics, and the messy ways Bright connected his mission to partisan politics. I do not render judgment on the merits of Crusade's theology or mission; in any event, readers' opinions will likely hinge on their own relationship to that theology and mission.

When I began this project, I knew little about Bill Bright, who emerges in the following pages both as a hard-nosed autocrat and as a tenderhearted evangelist. When Bright practiced evangelism, he evidenced a patient concern for individuals, a concern frequently displayed to the members of his staff. As Crusade's president, on the other hand, Bright brooked no devia-tion from his vision, drove his followers to exhaustion, and questioned their loyalty when they questioned his decisions. More so than previous studies of Campus Crusade, I shed light on Bright's "feet of clay": the demand-ing nature of his leadership, his missteps, and his organizational hubris. Like most evangelical leaders, Bright felt the tug of conservative politics. Through a mixture of confusion, naïveté, or misdirection, he never admit-ted the rather obvious political implications of his activities and rhetoric. Yet despite such faults, it was impossible to complete this project without admiring Bright's persistence and, on balance, the fealty of his commit-ment to evangelism. At a time when scandal and hypocrisy are once more tarnishing evangelicalism's public image, Bright's authenticity is notewor-thy, as is Crusade's positive history of financial stewardship. His transparent commitment to his faith and to evangelism inspired tens of thousands of individuals — in the United States and abroad — to join his Crusade.

The adaptability and marketing prowess of parachurch organizations like Campus Crusade for Christ are not the only reason for the post-1945 vitality of American evangelicalism. No amount of cultural adaptation and aggressive salesmanship would produce success if the basic evangelical message had little appeal in the United States. The heritage of pre-1945 fundamentalism, the influx of Christian immigrants from Asia, Africa, and Latin America,[22] the high birth rates of conservative Protestants,[23] and the persistence of an American civil religion at least partly congruent with evangelicalism all helped evangelicals retain their hold on a substantial seg-ment of the American population into the twenty-first century. Amidst that backdrop, however, parachurch ministries have been the consummate marketers of the evangelical gospel in modern America through their in-novative use of technology, their open stance toward popular culture, and their aggressive fund-raising practices. First and foremost, evangelicals have sold large numbers of Americans on the need to personally initiate a relationship with God through Jesus Christ. They have also sold self-help books, study Bibles, and radio and television programs to both nurture that faith and grow their ministries. Evangelicals have attempted to sell their followers on a traditional understanding of gender roles and, finding it a tough sell, have repackaged those beliefs into a trimmed-down version of patriarchy and a practical embrace of egalitarianism. Finally, evangelicals have sold their constituents a particular understanding of American society and their role in it. Not all evangelicals have bought into this conception of the United States, but the evangelical version of manifest destiny continues to shape evangelical political rhetoric and has helped fashion evangelicals into a key voting bloc in modern American politics. Through their willingness to retain only a small number of theological essentials and continually adapt themselves to modern culture, evangelicals have kept their gospel an attractive product in the marketplace of American religions.

God May Choose a Country Boy

William Rohl Bright was born on 19 October 1921, the sixth child and fifth son born to Forrest Dale and Mary Lee Rohl Bright. Since her last pregnancy had ended in a stillbirth, Mary Lee worried that she would not be able to carry her next child to full term. When she became pregnant again, she "made a commitment to God that the next child would be dedicated to him." Earlier that year, the Brights had settled on a ranch located on the outskirts of Coweta, Oklahoma. Coweta was—and still is—a small town situated on the railroad line running southeast from Tulsa to Muskogee. Sam Bright, Bill Bright's grandfather, had made a small fortune in the Oklahoma oil business shortly after the federal government officially opened the old Indian Territory to white settlement. Aiming to provide his children with a source of stable income, he bought sizable ranches for Forrest Dale and his other three sons. Dale, as he was known, occasionally bought and sold horses and other livestock, but cattle were the heart of his ranching operation. He employed several hired hands, who helped the family raise cattle and grow crops for feed. Although the Brights never became wealthy, they were prosperous by comparison with most Coweta families.[1]

As a child, Bill Bright's main activities were ranching and reading. His first chores were collecting eggs and gathering dry corncobs and wood to heat the family's stove. Throughout his entire childhood, the ranch did not have electricity, but running water was provided by a windmill that pumped water into an elevated tank, from which it was fed by gravity into the house. The family installed gas lights after Dale Bright hit gas while drilling for oil on the property. As he grew older,

Bill Bright "took his place alongside his four brothers and other hired men in milking the cows, feeding the hogs, caring for the horses and cattle, working in the fields, plowing, cultivating, harvesting, threshing the grain and baling hay for the cattle." The family rose well before sunrise each morning, and the boys took kerosene lanterns to the barn to milk the cows and feed the hogs and chickens before breakfast. The Brights cranked their own cream and on Saturdays traveled by horse or wagon on the narrow five-mile gravel road that led to Coweta, where they traded eggs and cream for groceries and other necessities.

Mary Lee had taught school briefly before marrying Forrest Dale, and she devoted herself to her children's intellectual formation, instilling in them a love for literature and books. On days when it was his responsibility to herd cattle, Bright would put a book in his saddlebag and read "whenever precious moments allowed." "There are also vivid recollections," he wrote about days devoted to reading, "of those special days when in the providence of God it rained, and it was impossible to work outside." In the evenings, Mary Lee would read to the family Walter Scott novels and poetry by James Whitcomb Riley, a distant cousin and popular early-twentieth-century poet. Bright's mother, who had a conversion experience in a Methodist church at age sixteen and whose brother became a Methodist minister, read her Bible every morning and evening, sang hymns while doing housework, and took her children to Coweta's Methodist Church. "I can remember seeing her kneeling at her bed and praying," remembers Charley Bright, Bill Bright's nephew who came to live with his grandparents in 1935. Bill Bright later recorded that his mother "gathered the children of neighborhood families together in her home to teach the Bible." Following her example, he joined the Methodist Church at the age of twelve. Bright always maintained an especially close relationship with his mother, whom he would later refer to as his "saintly mother" or "Godly Christian mother." "When it came to his mom," comments Bright's own son Brad, "there was a spot in his heart that nothing else could touch."[2]

Bright's father was hard-driving, domineering, and less pious than his wife. When Mary Lee disciplined her children, she sent them to bed. Dale employed the "strap." He expected his children to follow his instructions. "He was always the boss in any circumstance," comments Charley Bright. Dale would sometimes escort Mary Lee to church, but often he would only bring her to the church door and then find somewhere in Coweta to talk business and politics. He was active in local and county Republican politics and at one point became chairman of the Wagoner County Republican Party. During these years, the Oklahoma Republican Party displayed a Protestant commitment to Prohibition, probusiness sentiment (partly due to the strength of the state's oil lobby), vitriolic opposition to the New Deal, and almost complete political impotency.[3] Dale Bright's partisan affiliation was unusual for his environs, as Coweta, like most of Oklahoma, was solidly Democratic territory. Partly because of that political reality, Dale would "usually get in a fight on election day." Bill Bright never deviated from his father's choice of political parties, and as a boy and young man he sometimes envisioned a career in politics. He also absorbed his father's indifference to religion. Given the spiritual dynamics of his own family, Bright later wrote that he "thought Christianity was for women and children but not for men."[4]

After eight years in a rural "one-room schoolhouse," Bright attended Coweta's high school. While the Works Progress Administration completed a new building, the school's lower grades met in church basements and classrooms. Most of the school teachers also taught Sunday school in Coweta's churches, and school days included a blend of Christianity and patriotism alongside reading, writing, and arithmetic. Curtis Zachary, Bright's brother-in-law, describes the atmosphere at Coweta's school. "You had prayer in schools, you sure did," Zachary remembers, "and the recitation of the Lord's Prayer and oftentimes individual prayer . . . even in high school." "We would always sing the Star Spangled Banner and have a flag salute," Zachary continues, "and then the pastor would give an invocation."

Alongside thirty-two classmates, Bright graduated in 1939. He enrolled at Northeastern State College in Tahlequah, Oklahoma, a former normal school that still primarily trained teachers. Now anticipating a career in medicine, Bright explored other academic options after he earned a C in chemistry during his first semester.[5] A solid B student for the rest of his collegiate years, Bright juggled academics, social events, several part-time jobs, and extracurricular activities with the boundless energy he would maintain for most of his life. He pledged the Sigma Tau Gamma fraternity chapter, performed in plays, and won first prize in an intercollegiate Prohibition oratorical contest sponsored by the Anti-Saloon League. In his junior and senior years, respectively, Bright served as student body vice president and president. He also managed to find time to enjoy campus social life, attending and organizing several dances during his years in Tahlequah. In the spring of 1941, he drummed up publicity for Northeastern's annual Sadie Hawkins dance; the *Northeastern*, the college's newspaper, described Bright's ideal consort as a "tall, lean freckled thin girl."

He also cooked, waited tables, and washed dishes in the college dining hall to pay for his meals, cleaned a dormitory to pay for his room, and became the campus representative for a local laundry and dry cleaner. He neither attended church nor gave much thought to religion. "There was no challenging Christian organization on campus," he later lamented, and he was "not disposed to seek such fellowship in the local churches."[6]

By 1942, the headlines of the *Northeastern* reported on Tahlequah students and alumni serving in the armed forces during the early months of American involvement in World War II. In November, Bright enlisted in the naval reserve and planned to assume active duty status following his graduation the following May. He left Northeastern with a bachelor's degree in education and considered becoming a rancher, lawyer, and politician after the war. There were only nine men among Northeastern's thirty-six graduating seniors in 1943. After he graduated, Bright learned that a burst eardrum he had sustained playing high school football rendered him ineligible for military service. While three of his brothers and a brother-in-law served in the military, Bright returned home to Coweta. Oklahoma A&M College hired him as an agent for Muskogee County, and Bright traveled around his home county meeting with farmers and agricultural students to discuss state and national programs on such topics as commodities futures and fertilizers. Perhaps because he was missing out on the war and unsure of his future vocation, Bright decided to search out new horizons. Like many other Oklahomans in the 1930s and 1940s, he moved to California.[7]

Bright's early years in Oklahoma left enduring marks on his outlook and personality. He was always reserved in personality and demeanor, suspicious of intellectuals from elite universities, and devoted to small-town "values." Admiring the success of his grandfather and father in the oil and ranching businesses—and adhering to his father's politics—Bright maintained a lifelong commitment to free markets and small government. Ironically, even though Bright claimed to have had no personal Christian faith as a young man, he clung to the way Coweta's public schools combined faith, patriotism, and education. For example, Bright later traced America's ills to the early 1960s Supreme Court decisions that ruled that public schools could not lead students in prayer and other religious devotions. Several other leaders of the evangelical movement that emerged after the war came from small towns across the American South and Midwest, many of which roughly resembled Coweta. Billy Graham grew up on a farm outside Charlotte, North Carolina, Oral Roberts on the Oklahoma sawdust trail, and Rex Humbard near Little Rock. Jimmy Swaggart, Jim Bakker,

*Bill Bright as a student at
Northeastern State College, 1942.
Courtesy of the Northeastern State
University Archives, Tahlequah, Okla.*

and James Robison—all younger than Bright—haled from the backwaters of the American South and Midwest. Pat Robertson, though he experienced a more cosmopolitan upbringing as the son of a U.S. senator, spent much of his childhood in rural Virginia. By contrast, the very first cluster of evangelical leaders in the 1940s had come from major metropolitan centers: Harold Ockenga from Chicago and Carl F. H. Henry from New York City. The rising generation of evangelical leaders—Graham, Bright, and Roberts—displayed a fascination with modernity, particularly with technology and popular culture. Yet their conception of what America should be always remained linked to the small towns and farms where they had come of age.

Mears Christianity[8]

When Bright arrived in Los Angeles in 1944, he again sought entrance into the military. He knew that another rejection was a distinct possibility, but he had also come to California with other aspirations. "There were several career options open to me," Bright later chronicled, "but the most attractive was a move to Los Angeles." Richard Quebedeaux, who wrote a biography of Bright in the 1970s, suggests that Bright was simply another Oklahoma migrant seeking wealth in the Golden State during an explosive wartime boom. "He was seeking his fortune," confirms Bright's friend Esther Brinkley. An admirer of Clark Gable, Bright planned to seek acting jobs in local theaters. He hoped to make money quickly and parlay his fortune into a political career.[9]

Bright, who at the time had no particular interest in religion, met several fervent Christians on his first night in Los Angeles. As he drove around town, he picked up a young man thumbing a ride. The hitchhiker worked for the Navigators, a ministry founded by Dawson Trotman in 1933 that evangelized servicemen, involved them in Bible studies, and encouraged them to memorize large caches of Bible verses. The Navigator brought Bright to Trotman's home, where Bright received an invitation to spend the night. After dinner, Bright accompanied his hosts to a birthday party for Dan Fuller, the son of the famous radio evangelist Charles Fuller, whose *Old-Fashioned Revival Hour* was among the most popular radio programs in America.[10]

Spiritually unchanged from these encounters with Bible-believing Christians, Bright visited the local draft board but was again disqualified because of his burst eardrum. He worked for a short time as an electrician's assistant for a contractor at a local shipyard but quit when he ascertained that his employer was billing for unperformed work. A new friend invited him to become a partner in a specialty food business, and after several weeks Bright bought out his friend and established Bright's Epicurean Delights, later renamed Bright's California Confections and Bright's Brandied Foods. Initially, the business was successful. Since wartime rationing had largely eliminated the chocolate industry, Bright's confections—containing, he once told a reporter, "brandy by the hogshead"[11]—sold well and caught the notice of distributors and department stores, such as Neiman-Marcus and B. Altman. Bright soon drove a convertible and had enough money for fine clothing and horseback riding in the Hollywood Hills. He rented an apartment from an elderly couple in Hollywood, undertook an amateur radio spot, and studied drama at the Hollywood Talent Showcase.

Bright's landlords attended the First Presbyterian Church of Hollywood, and they encouraged their new tenant to join them on Sundays. In the 1940s, Hollywood Presbyterian was the nation's largest Presbyterian church, and it attracted upwardly mobile businessmen and Hollywood stars. Lauralil Deats, daughter of Louis H. Evans Sr., then Hollywood Presbyterian's pastor, recalls "millionaires falling out of every pew." Bright's landlords introduced him to affluent businessmen who both modeled the life of material success that Bright desired and simultaneously insisted that a relationship with Jesus Christ was more important than worldly wealth and success. Initially reluctant, he eventually sampled a few services at the church, where he listened to the preaching of Evans and the Bible teaching of Henrietta Mears. One of the young women from Mears's thriving "College Department" invited Bright to attend a party held at the ranch of a movie star, and, impressed with the caliber of young people at the gathering, he began attending the church on Sundays and Wednesday evenings. The testimonies of these Christian peers and the evangelistic Bible lessons of Mears agitated Bright spiritually and convinced him to investigate scriptural accounts of Jesus Christ. One night Mears taught a lesson on the eighth chapter of Acts, which chronicles Paul's conversion experience on the road to Damascus. Mears encouraged her listeners to return to their homes, get on their knees, and pray as Paul had done: "Lord, what wilt Thou have me to do?" Bright followed Mears's advice and later identified this moment as the first major spiritual turning point in his life. "The dollar was no longer his [Bright's] god," he later wrote in an autobiographical account, "the materialistic philosophy had been abandoned for the Christ Who died for his sins." Bright experienced no "cataclysmic emotion," but he was convinced that Jesus was the son of God.[12]

Henrietta Mears exerted a strong influence on Bright's theology and the later shape of Campus Crusade for Christ; hence, it is necessary to explain at some length the shape and significance of her ministry at Hollywood Presbyterian. Reared in fundamentalist kingpin William B. Riley's First Baptist Church of Minneapolis, Mears taught high school chemistry following her graduation from the University of Minnesota. She also remained active at First Baptist, where scores of high school girls attended her Bible study class. In 1928, Hollywood Presbyterian's minister, Stuart MacLennan, recruited Mears to be his church's director of Christian Education, and within a few years several thousand children and adults attended the weekly programs she organized. Mears herself taught the College Department, which by the mid-1930s attracted several hundred young adults to a mixture of Bible teaching and social events. She encouraged her "boys" to become ministers, and she soon had a network of College Department alumni installed in Presbyterian pastorates across California. During the 1930s, Mears also launched two ventures that established Hollywood Presbyterian as a regional fundamentalist force. She wrote her own age-graded Sunday school curriculum and founded Gospel Light Press to publish it. Gospel Light became one of the most popular publishers of fundamentalist Sunday school curricula. Charles and Grace Fuller joined

Lake Avenue Congregational Church in large measure because they respected its Christian Education Department, which used Mears's materials. In 1938, Mears arranged the purchase of Forest Home, a resort in the San Bernardino Mountains, which she turned into a Christian retreat center. Forest Home became an important conduit for fundamentalist networking and growth in Southern California, as "Forest Home churches" of various denominations sent delegates to retreats and teacher training conferences organized and often hosted by Mears.[13]

Mears's career illustrates both the possibilities and limitations women encountered when they pursued careers in ministry within the context of midcentury fundamentalism. Mears, who was single and lived with her sister Margaret, worked hard to avoid transgressing fundamentalist gender norms. She officially served under a male superintendent and insisted her expository lessons were "teaching" rather than "preaching." Yet adherence to such standards masked her true authority and power. Her superintendent was a figurehead, and Mears ran the church's Christian Education program, Gospel Light Press, and Forest Home. Mears always served under male pastors who were renowned in their own right, but those connected with the church in these decades recall her as "the power behind the throne." "All the elders of the church and all the pastors of the church were men," explains longtime Hollywood Presbyterian member Anna Kerr, "and there were forty-five men on the session that seemed to be all delighted to eat out of her hand." With the prominent exception of herself, Mears wished to preserve traditional patterns of gendered leadership in the church. Citing the church's difficulty in attracting sufficient numbers of men, she claimed to select women as leaders as a matter of last resort. She argued for this course not as a matter of doctrine or Scripture but on the basis of pragmatic expediency. Both men and women, she believed, would find male leadership in the church more attractive. "I know that if I can get the best examples of young men to attend," she asserted, "I can always get the beautiful young women to follow!"[14]

Mears operated in the theological borderlands between early-twentieth-century fundamentalism and what became known as "evangelicalism" after the war. In many ways, she was a prototypical fundamentalist, participating in the creation of periodical literature, a retreat center, and a network of clerical followers and supporters. Theologically, Mears was decidedly conservative. "I learned all my theology by sitting at Mount Hermon," she once told Daniel Fuller, "and hearing speakers like Lewis Sperry Chafer from Dallas Theological Seminary." Mears accepted the entire Bible as the

*Henrietta Mears, director of Christian
Education at the First Presbyterian
Church of Hollywood, ca. 1945.
Courtesy of Forest Home Ministries,
Forest Falls, Calif.*

Word of God and concentrated on leading her students to a conversion experience and a decision to place their faith in Jesus as Savior. "Our teachers,"
Mears explained to Fuller Theological Seminary professor Wilbur Smith,
"are men and women who are willing to sign a declaration of faith stating
their acceptance of Christ as Saviour and Lord, the Bible as the infallible
Word of God, and the Deity of our Lord and Saviour Jesus Christ that he
is very God." "Every lesson," Mears told her teachers, "should always contain the WAY OF SALVATION!" (emphasis in original). Yet while operating
primarily in conservative Protestant circles, Mears had no interest in raising the typical battle banners of fundamentalism. She invited more liberal
speakers such as Princeton Seminary president John MacKay and German
theologian Helmut Thielecke to Forest Home. Mears contended for the
inspiration of Scripture, but her focus was on winning converts to Christ,
not to her understanding of the Bible. Like an increasing number of evangelicals in the 1940s, she focused her energy on galvanizing forces for evangelistic revivals rather than on internecine, intra-Protestant struggles. As a
Baptist-turned-Presbyterian (she termed herself a "Bapterian") with little
interest in the particulars of either denomination, Mears felt free to form
her own institutions and ignore denominational concerns.[15]

Devoted to evangelism, Mears's College Department created a setting
that competed effectively with other youth activities. During the war,

Mears asked the most attractive "girls" in the group to drive downtown and invite servicemen to the church. Mears and her students visited the campuses of UCLA and USC and witnessed to student body presidents and star athletes, as the conversion of a few campus leaders often led to scores of new students coming to the church regularly. Mears did not take issue with Greek life on campus, fashionable clothing and makeup, or popular music. Whereas many fundamentalists eschewed movies and considered the entertainment industry inherently corrupt, Mears took her students to the cinema, though not on Sundays. She was more comfortable than most fundamentalists with popular culture, and her openness foreshadowed the path evangelicalism would travel in subsequent decades. After his conversion, Bill Bright still went to dances, enjoyed movies, and occasionally smoked a pipe. Hollywood evangelicalism evidenced little of the cultural and ecclesiastical separatism associated with American fundamentalism.

At this time, conservative Protestantism in America was at a turning point, as the line between "evangelical" and "fundamentalist" was beginning to emerge. In the early 1940s, conservative Protestants referred to themselves with a variety of labels: fundamentalist, evangelical, Bible-believing, and orthodox. In 1943, a number of conservative Protestant individuals and denominations founded the National Association of Evangelicals (NAE). J. Elwin Wright and Harold Ockenga, two prominent New England fundamentalists, provided most of the early leadership. Wright and Ockenga envisioned a coalition that would function as a conservative counterweight to the Federal Council of Churches (FCC), promote evangelism, and defend the right of fundamentalist Christians to purchase radio airtime. At the same time, the NAE distanced itself from the American Council of Christian Churches (ACCC), a coalition of separatist fundamentalists organized by Carl McIntire in 1941. The ACCC insisted that revival would only come when fundamentalists separated themselves from denominations controlled by modernists or moderates. With the founding of the NAE, more moderate fundamentalists increasingly began to refer to themselves as "evangelicals," although such labels remained very fluid well into the 1950s. Hollywood Presbyterian, a member of a denomination belonging to the mainline FCC, was not officially linked to the NAE. Henrietta Mears, however, provided leadership in the NAE-affiliated National Sunday School Association, which promoted an evangelical Sunday school movement grounded in evangelism, biblical instruction, and spiritual power.[16]

In addition to elite-level excitement over the formation of the NAE, there were glimmers of widespread revival. Jack Wyrtzen, a radio preacher who targeted young audiences in New York City, began holding youth rallies in New York during the war. In early 1944, Wyrtzen on several occasions attracted upwards of twenty thousand young people to Madison Square Garden. Other fundamentalists, excited by Wyrtzen's success, held "Youth for Christ" rallies in cities across the country. Torrey Johnson, a pastor in Chicago and treasurer of a local NAE chapter, invited a young evangelist named Billy Graham to headline a Youth for Christ campaign in May 1944. Twenty-eight thousand heard Graham speak in Chicago Stadium. By the summer of 1945, Youth for Christ leaders estimated that over three hundred thousand young Americans were attending such rallies every week. The rallies mixed wartime patriotism, popular music, star athletes, and fervent evangelistic preaching, and Youth for Christ received extensive and positive coverage in major newspapers. At a time when American adults expressed considerable worry about the problem of juvenile delinquency, the success of Youth for Christ suggested that rising generations of Americans might embrace a religious message that incorporated popular culture and emphasized patriotism and clean living alongside traditional Christianity.[17]

Thus, Bill Bright embraced fundamentalist Christianity at a time when it was inching closer to mainstream American culture. The founding of the NAE and the crowds attracted by Youth for Christ suggested that Bible-believing Christians could reach a wider segment of the American population with their message of salvation. Madison Square Garden and Chicago Stadium were a long way from Hollywood Presbyterian, but at his own church Bright saw college athletes, movie starlets, and young businessmen flocking to hear the Bible teaching of Henrietta Mears. Bright found his evangelical faith in a congregation in large part defined by its affluence. Throughout his life, he would celebrate America's material abundance and form close connections with wealthy Christian businessmen, asking only that they channel a portion of that abundance toward the cause of evangelism.

The Fellowship of the Burning Heart

Following his conversion, Bright continued to expand his candy business and his involvement at his church. The College Department introduced Bright to the regular practice of evangelism. Members of the department wrapped evangelistic tracts in cellophane and then kept a few of these

"Gospel bombs" stuffed in their pockets to give to strangers they encountered. Henrietta Mears wanted to hear weekly reports from her students on attempts to witness at UCLA, USC, and other area campuses. She also took her followers to towns across Southern California to practice street evangelism. Bright was initially "scared to death" to talk with others about Jesus Christ. With "mouth dry and heart pounding," Bright wrote later, "I spoke with Bob [a visitor to Hollywood Presbyterian] about inviting Jesus Christ into his life . . . I told him my story, and showed him some Scriptures that highlighted man's need for God and how to receive Christ as one's personal Savior and Lord." Bright's effort was successful, and the recipient of his first attempt at personal evangelism eventually went to seminary. Instead of business or politics, Bright became convinced in August 1945 that God was calling him into the ministry. He did not, however, intend to immediately give up his business plans. Instead, he still hoped to earn a small fortune while he pursued theological education.[18]

In the summer of 1946, on the advice of Mears, Bright traveled across the country, enrolled at Princeton Seminary, and entered the ordination process of the Northern Presbyterian denomination. At Princeton, Bright enjoyed the lectures, especially those on the Bible, but he was unwilling to devote himself to biblical languages and systematic theology. That fall, he recruited the entering class at the seminary to "Gospel bomb" Princeton University, utilizing the strategy employed by Hollywood Presbyterian's College Department. They placed cellophane-wrapped tracts on every desk and table they could find. The university president angrily summoned John MacKay, president of the seminary, for an explanation. It appears that the bombs inflicted little damage on the alleged secularity of the Princeton campus. Princeton Seminary's erudite professors likewise in no way diminished Bright's evangelistic fervor.[19]

While Bright found himself ill-suited for Princeton's academic and theological climate, his business prospects unraveled during his time on the East Coast. When he uprooted for Princeton, Bright had left his candy business in the hands of two associates, both friends from Hollywood Presbyterian. "He would call up every few days to see how his candy store was doing," says Dan Fuller, whom Bright had met on his first night in Los Angeles and was now a classmate at Princeton, "and about November he found the graph was going downhill." Bright left Princeton and returned to Los Angeles, where he ended the business relationship with his two friends but failed to improve the business's sagging balance sheet. In order to restore his candy business to profitability, Bright looked for investors to provide the enterprise with a needed infusion of cash. Howard Taylor, a congregant at Hollywood Presbyterian, was impressed with Bright and invested $10,000 of his savings into the business. His son Jim Taylor, a friend of Bright's, began running many of the business's daily operations, while Bright continued to purchase inventory and market the products. Even with the elder Taylor's investment, the candy business continued to languish. Chocolate returned to the market quickly after the war and rendered Bright's brandied confections less desirable. As of mid-1947, Bright had not realized his dream of quick financial success in California. Moreover, after leaving Princeton, he was not certain he would continue his seminary education.[20]

Soon, however, an intense spiritual experience that again involved Henrietta Mears overshadowed Bright's business and vocational struggles. As of 1947, Mears could proudly point to a thriving College Department, well-attended college-age conferences at Forest Home, and numerous male protégés studying for the ministry. Yet she, like many evangelicals, wanted to do more than create a few beacons of Christianity in a secularizing culture. She wanted to train leaders who would restore America to its Christian heritage. That spring, Mears returned from a tour of Europe's war-torn capitals. In light of the devastation, she reflected on Europe's plunge into the abyss of totalitarianism. "Rationalism, secularism, the cult of the scientific, the worship of man, relativistic ethics," reasoned Mears, "all these led to the godless society of Adolph Hitler." Mears believed that the danger had not passed with the Allied victory. In Britain and France, she cautioned, millions had turned away from God, leaving a vacuum that communism threatened to fill. Mears did not confine her worries to distant shores. She told her teachers of her fear that "the same is taking place in America today." For Mears, warning signs included a rising divorce rate, crime, and especially a lack of Christian education in public schools and homes.[21]

Mears articulated themes that were standard fare for Christians of many stripes at midcentury. After World War II, Christians from Billy Graham to Fulton J. Sheen directed their followers' attention to the communist threat but insisted that an America restored to its Christian roots could triumph over secular and anti-Christian enemies. For many Protestants in particular, their fears centered not only on communism but also on a nagging sense that they were losing their rightful place as the leaders of American society. Protestants from Charles Clayton Morrison to Ockenga to Mears recognized that secularism and other competing philosophies had scored victories during past decades. "The naked truth," concluded Morrison, who edited the liberal *Christian Century*, "is that American society was once predominantly Protestant and is no longer." In fact, both mainline and more conservative Protestants worried that Catholics—and to some extent Jews—were weakening the unofficial establishment of American Protestantism. While mainline Protestant leaders could celebrate the influence of men like John Foster Dulles, fundamentalists and evangelicals felt this sense of loss more acutely. Mainline Protestants continued to try to block them from purchasing radio time, and evangelicals had no assurance that the brief glow of revivalism toward the end of the war would continue. Yet despite their persistent outcries over threats abroad and at home, American Protestants hoped that a golden age of American Christianity lay just beyond the postwar horizon. Although some mainline and evangelical leaders believed that renewed influence could come through a greater intellectual engagement with modern society, most evangelicals placed their overwhelming emphasis on evangelism. Evangelical leaders during and after the war skillfully interwove calls for conversion and Christian dedication into a defense of the nation against secularism and communism.[22]

"There must be a Christian answer to the growing menace of communism," Mears warned at a Forest Home training conference on 24 June 1947. The answer, Mears proclaimed, would be evangelism and missions, a full presentation of Christian truth without compromise. "God is looking for men and women of total commitment," she told her teachers. "We must be expendables for Christ," she proclaimed, summoning up wartime images of soldiers who plunged into dangerous situations without regard for their own safety or self-interest. If the youth of America would dedicate themselves to Christian discipleship, American Christians could reverse the ominous tides of secularism and communism. Mears perceived a particular need for young male Christian leaders—many of her own church's young men had perished during the war. Meditating on the challenge that Mordecai gave to Esther, Mears believed that she and her Hollywood collegians had "come to the kingdom for such a time as this." Reflecting the influence of Keswick spirituality, which emphasized "absolute surrender" and the subsequent empowerment of the Holy Spirit, Mears urged her listeners to fully commit themselves to Jesus Christ and to pray for divine wisdom to discern if God was calling them to mission work either overseas or at home.[23]

Mears's message galvanized her audience, which included many young men recently returned from the war. Louis H. Evans Jr., the son of Hollywood Presbyterian's pastor, had returned from the navy. Jack Franck, one of Mears's assistants, had been an army ranger. Bright had missed out on the experience of wartime service, but he also responded to Mears's call for total commitment. After absorbing Mears's call to arms, Bright, Evans, Franck, and several other young men—including Richard Halverson, a young minister at Hollywood Presbyterian and future chaplain of the U.S. Senate—went to her cabin. Those present recall a time of prayer and confession followed by an intense encounter with the Holy Spirit. "I was agitated in mind," recalls Evans. "A plow had gone into my soil and turned it over." "What could happen," he wondered, "if we, the [members of the] College Department, really gave our lives to Christ?" "We were overwhelmed with the presence of God," remembered Bright.[24]

Bright and the other young men formed the "Fellowship of the Burning Heart," a movement devoted to "evangelizing the youth of the world for Christ." They pledged to spend one hour each day in Scripture and prayer, to maintain "Christ-like . . . chastity and virtue," and "to seek every possible opportunity to witness." They formed small cell groups that sought to replicate themselves evangelistically. In conjunction with Mears, the group also decided to hold what they titled a "College Briefing Conference," to which they invited collegians from around the country. Bright, Evans, and others traveled to California churches witnessing to their mountaintop experience and inviting young people to both Christian commitment and the upcoming conference. Promotional literature for the August 1947 event warned that "we live in a militantly pagan world" and offered hope that a revival could "stave off" "the complete annihilation of civilization." At the conference, Mears repeated her concerns about world communism and encouraged a group of more than six hundred students to commit themselves as "expendables for Christ." Jim Halls, in attendance at the conference, remembers a persistent emphasis on the threat of communism. Halls also recalls the conference leaders' belief that without proper biblical instruction, college-age Christians would lack the spiritual armor to withstand the assaults presumed to follow their matriculation at secular institutions. The College Briefing Conferences—at which students received their marching orders before heading out to do battle with naturalism, secularism, and communism—became an annual Forest Home tradition.[25]

College-age meetings and conferences have long played a pivotal role in American evangelicalism, particularly in the evangelical foreign missions enterprise. An 1806 group of Williams College students meeting for prayer took shelter under a haystack during a thunderstorm, formed an intimate bond with each other, and a few years later founded the first American foreign missions agency. Several generations later, one hundred students pledged themselves to foreign missions at Dwight Moody's 1886 conference at Mount Hermon School in Northfield, Massachusetts. That outburst of collegiate missionary enthusiasm led to the formation of the Student Volunteer Movement (SVM) and its watchword, "the evangelization of the world in this generation." In the 1940s, evangelicals and fundamentalists embraced the SVM watchword with renewed fervor. Technological advances and American victory in World War II made global evangelization seem more feasible, and in the wake of the war conservative Protestants formed numerous foreign missions agencies, including World Vision and the Far Eastern Gospel Crusade. Once again, student conferences took center stage in the American missionary enterprise. In 1946, Inter-Varsity Christian Fellowship held its first foreign missions conference, at which three hundred students pledged themselves to serve overseas. The College Briefing Conferences also reflect this trend. Mears consciously hearkened back to earlier evangelical student movements and encouraged her young listeners to consider whether God was calling them to foreign missions. "In the nineteenth century," informed the brochure for the first College Briefing Conference, "God chose, through Dwight L. Moody, sixty Oxford University students as missionaries to carry the gospel of Jesus Christ to the whole world." "In this the twentieth century," the brochure continued, "He is calling for greater numbers." Mears asked those in attendance at the conference to pin their names to a country, and Bright attached his to the Soviet Union. "[I] made a commitment," Bright later wrote, "to pray for that nation and, if God so led, to go as His ambassador to reach others for Him."[26]

Through the College Department and at Forest Home, Bright absorbed Mears's understanding of Christianity and American culture. Mears saw evangelical Christians as under attack by the forces of secularism, which she believed had usurped their rightful place at the center of American society. Colleges and universities were the perfect example—Mears lamented the transformation of previously Christian institutions like Harvard and Yale into bastions of secularism. Yet Mears did not think the battle was lost—her followers at UCLA and USC could reverse the trend. Bright and his fellow Burning Heart members could mimic the communists, form Christian "cells," and slowly build a movement of committed Christian youth.

Moreover, although Bright initially focused his evangelistic energies on local universities and colleges, he, like Mears, viewed American students as potential recruits to take the evangelical message to the world.

Down from the Mountaintop

Shortly before he headed to Forest Home for the 1947 College Briefing Conference, Bright submitted an application to enroll as part of the inaugural class of students at Fuller Theological Seminary in Pasadena. Bright informed the seminary of his intention to become a "pastor and evangelist." Accepted as a student, Bright listened to Harold Ockenga, Fuller's president, convene the seminary with a speech addressing "The Challenge to the Christian Culture of the West." Ockenga, the most prominent symbol of New England evangelicalism at the time, recognized the growing strength of Southern California evangelicalism. "Why . . . should the west forever look to the east for its preachers?" asked Ockenga. He also repeated the theme of cultural loss and crisis voiced by Mears several weeks earlier at Forest Home. Despite serious challenges to Protestant hegemony over Western civilization, Ockenga also believed the battle was not yet lost. He anticipated the eventual return of Jesus but reminded his audience that "Jesus told us to 'occupy' till He comes." In particular, he hoped that the aspiring pastors in his audience would emerge from Fuller prepared to "in an intellectually respectable way present an apology for God" and for the classical doctrines of Christian belief. Against separatists like Carl McIntire, Ockenga repudiated "come-out-ism" and called for the "positive presentation of the Gospel in a critical world," signaling that Fuller Seminary would align itself with the emerging evangelical bloc within American fundamentalism. When Ockenga discussed "the spiritual program" of the seminary, however, he turned away from intellectual struggles and stressed the primacy of evangelism. "Though we'll stress the academic preparation of these young men," he maintained, "their first and primary task is to be missionaries to the world."[27]

Ockenga's emphasis on evangelism probably affirmed Bright's decision to attend the fledgling seminary. As he had done at Princeton, Bright plunged into evangelistic activities. Despite his lack of success with the method at Princeton, he rounded up a few dozen classmates, including Dan Fuller (who had left Princeton to attend the seminary funded by his radio evangelist father) and Gary Demarest, to "Gospel bomb" the campuses of Pasadena College and Caltech. The results duplicated those of his efforts at Princeton, and Demarest and Bright had to return to Caltech to pick up the refuse left by this environmentally unfriendly evangelistic tool. Other attempts at evangelism showed greater promise, however. Bright and Demarest made appointments with the student body presidents of USC, UCLA, and Occidental College. The young man from USC committed his life to Christ and invited the pair of seminarians to speak at his fraternity. Whether his efforts succeeded or failed, Bright's evangelistic fervor only grew. Bright complained to Dan Fuller that he had trouble persuading others from the Hollywood Presbyterian College Department to join him in local evangelistic efforts. "Nobody cares about winning souls," Bright lamented to Fuller. "What's the matter with this church?" Despite such complaints, Bright involved himself in numerous evangelistic efforts at the church, joining "deputation" teams to local jails, hospitals, and "skid row."[28]

Bright went to classes in the morning, lunched with local college students, participated in a heavy schedule of church activities, and tried to run his business either in the afternoon or at night. Perhaps due to his busy schedule, his academic performance suffered. During his first semester, he managed three Bs and four painful Ds, including one for his introductory Greek course. Since Fuller required a C-average for graduation, the faculty placed Bright on academic probation. They gave him a semester to raise his grades or face expulsion. Bright, however, was already thinking of leaving. On 15 December 1947, the faculty invited Bright and Demarest to lunch. According to Carl F. H. Henry, one of Fuller's original faculty members, the two seminarians were "having special success in dealing with student leaders on the big campuses" and had "led the president of the U.C.L.A. student body to Christ." Henry informed Ockenga that the two had been thinking of going into full-time student work after the first semester but reported "a happy alternative solution." Bright and Demarest would remain students for the time being.[29]

The "alternative solution" to which Henry alluded was evidently temporary, for the issue arose again in early 1948. Shortly after the establishment of Israel as a nation-state, Demarest and Bright were awaiting a lecture from Wilbur Smith, Bright's favorite professor at Fuller. Demarest recalls that Smith walked into the classroom, put his books down on the desk and exclaimed, "Gentlemen, the last of the prophecies have been fulfilled!" Smith excitedly interpreted the reestablishment of Israel as portending the imminent return of Christ. Perhaps remembering his trials with biblical languages, Bright resolved, "I'm not going to be sitting here studying Greek when Christ comes!" Once again, Bright and Demarest declared their intention to withdraw from the seminary and pursue full-time evangelism. According to Demarest, they told the faculty of their intention to leave "because Christ was coming." Once again, the two attended a faculty meeting, at which the professors produced essays the students had written upon their application to Fuller explaining their call to seminary. Bright no longer found his earlier rationale persuasive. "Bill really nailed his decision," says Demarest, "and he was not going to continue in seminary." Nevertheless, he did stay through the spring semester. Not surprisingly, his grades further deteriorated—he earned three Ds and two Cs. Although the faculty should have dismissed him for academic reasons, they decided to give Bright one final opportunity. Carl Henry, in a letter to Bright, explained that although "your grade point average was not adequate during the probation semester," the "faculty voted to extend the probation period" for an additional semester. Henry confided that the faculty regarded Bright "as one of the most promising men in the student body." Furthermore, they ventured "that it is not a lack of ability, but a lack of dedication to the primary demands of academic study, that has defeated you in this matter." In all likelihood, the Fuller faculty adopted a lenient approach toward Bright because of their own belief in the primacy of evangelism. Henry's efforts, however, were in vain. Either because of his prophecy-inspired resolution, his academic frustrations, or a lack of funds, Bright withdrew from Fuller Seminary.[30]

That summer, Bright resolved another long-standing internal debate. Since the spring of 1946, he had been engaged to marry Vonette Zachary. Zachary, five years younger than Bright, had also grown up in Coweta, and Bright—whom Zachary's friends dubbed the "Candy Man"—initiated a long-distance romance with her in the summer of 1945. Engaged after a weekend visit, the couple—with the prompting of Zachary's parents—agreed to delay their wedding until Zachary's 1948 graduation from Texas State College for Women. Over the next two years, the relationship endured the typical strain of a romance separated by nearly fifteen hundred miles. Moreover, Bright and Zachary found themselves divided spiritually as well as geographically. Like Bright, Zachary had joined the Methodist Church while in grade school, and she had walked forward to publicly "receive Christ" shortly after her high school graduation. These initial expressions of faith, however, did not translate into a serious commitment. "Christ was not real to me," she later wrote. She attended church

Bill Bright and Vonette Zachary (center of middle row) at the 1948 College Briefing Conference at Forest Home. Courtesy of Forest Home Ministries, Forest Falls, Calif.

and prayed on occasion, but she grew wary when Bright—following his encounter with the Holy Spirit in the summer of 1947—talked about Jesus Christ as the most significant aspect of his life and began mailing her Bible passages and prayer requests.[31]

Zachary graduated from Texas State in the spring of 1948. She began looking for employment as a home economics teacher and initially decided to take an offer in Colorado. Both she and Bright knew that they needed to make a final decision about their relationship. He encouraged her to attend the late-summer College Briefing Conference at Forest Home, and her parents reluctantly gave her the money for the trip. At the conference, she was impressed with the young Christians in attendance: doctors, lawyers, and actresses. All seemed eager to talk about their relationship with Jesus Christ and told her about divine answers to prayer. Zachary concluded that the attendees were "the sharpest bunch of kooks I've ever seen." She planned to return Bright's engagement ring at the conclusion of the conference if she could not cure him of his "fanaticism." Bright, meanwhile, persuaded Zachary to meet individually with Henrietta Mears. Mears told Zachary "that, just as a person going into a chemistry laboratory experiment follows the table of chemical valence, so it is necessary to enter God's laboratory and follow His formula in order to know Him." "Miss Mears explained," Vonette Bright later wrote, "that receiving Christ is simply a matter of turning my life—my will, emotions, and intellect—completely over to Him." At the end of the conversation, Zachary prayed, asking Christ to come into her life. Her decision healed the breach between the couple, and they married in Coweta on 30 December 1948. After returning to Los Angeles, Vonette Bright obtained a job teaching home economics at a junior high school.[32]

Other aspects of Bright's future, however, remained unsettled. Between his classes at Fuller and his attempts at evangelism, Bright had devoted little time to his business partnership with the Taylor family. The candy business never revived; instead, Bright and the Taylor family took on debt, and the Taylors grew upset at Bright's management of the business. "Jim [Taylor] felt like he was abandoned," comments Bright's friend Lou Scroggin. "[H]e really relied on having Bill present in the business." "He [Bright] walked away from a situation that from his standpoint was intolerable," adds Esther Brinkley. Bright and the Taylors sold "Bright's California Confections," with the proceeds from the sale paying off some of the debts incurred by Howard Taylor. Taylor insisted that Bright return his $10,000 investment and claimed that Bright had cosigned loans for which he was partly responsible, whereas Bright maintained that Taylor had simply lost his investment to the vagaries of business.[33]

The Taylors initiated a lawsuit against Bright, but Hollywood Presbyterian's Louis Evans Sr. intervened and encouraged the parties to settle. Evans invited both Bright and the Taylors to present their arguments to several leading elders and businessmen in the congregation. The unofficial arbitrators encouraged Bright to repay Taylor the $10,000 and designed a monthly installment plan. Bright never conceded that he either legally or ethically owed the Taylors any money, but he agreed to the settlement and slowly repaid the money. "If he was willing to settle for something," Esther Brinkley says of Bright, "that was just to be peaceful." Although both the Taylors and the Brights kept the details to themselves, the conflict became public knowledge at Hollywood Presbyterian when the church nominated Bright as a deacon. When the nominating committee presented its slate of candidates, Taylor's father-in-law stood up and denounced Bright as dishonest in front of the congregation. "It was a very uncomfortable meeting," remembers Candy Bayliss, then a member at Hollywood Presbyterian. Since Evans had participated in the arbitration settlement, he defended Bright before the nominating committee, and the congregation affirmed Bright's election as a deacon.[34]

Total Surrender

Fortunately for Bright, other experiences distracted him from the lingering conflict with the Taylor family. Despite the collapse of the candy business, Bright sought fresh entrepreneurial opportunities. He organized a new business connecting customers with local wholesalers, offering clothing, jewelry, furniture, and other products at only 10 percent above the wholesale price, with the markup forming Bright's profit. "It wasn't a success either," recollects Ted Franzle, who knew the Brights through Hollywood Presbyterian. Although several young men at Hollywood Presbyterian bought their engagement rings from "Bright's Purchasing Service," selling goods on commission did not provide a steady income. Vonette Bright's $2,400 annual income tided the couple through Bill's business struggles and enabled the couple to remain in their small, rented Hollywood home. Although Bright did not achieve the lasting wealth he envisioned upon his move to the Golden State, he always retained the persona of a successful businessman. He remained "impeccably dressed, even as a student," recalls seminary classmate Gary Demarest. "Every time I see Bill Bright he looks like a little man who just came off a wedding cake," Dan Fuller remembers his mother commenting. "He tended to want people to think that he was successful in business," shares Lou Scroggin.[35]

During his period of vocational uncertainty, Bright became even more heavily involved in evangelistic activities at Hollywood Presbyterian. In 1948, he and several friends (including his Fellowship of the Burning Heart comrades Dick Halverson and Louis Evans Jr.) formed a Friday night deputation team that targeted local college students. Bright, who chaired the group, organized his friends into small groups that visited local fraternities, sororities, and dormitories. While the group's efforts met with varying degrees of evangelistic success, members of the College Department remember many young people coming to Christ. Anna Kerr recalls "a lot of people coming to Christ in fair proximity of each other." Colleen Townsend, a rising Hollywood actress who made a Christian commitment at the 1947 College Briefing Conference, recalls "a real openness to the Gospel" among collegians.[36]

Then in late 1949 Billy Graham caught the nation's attention during an eight-week revival in Los Angeles. The 1949 College Briefing Conference, at which Graham spoke shortly before his crusade began, earned a particular place of note in the history of American Christianity for its impact on the young evangelist's ministry. Graham arrived at Forest Home

Bill Bright and Billy Graham at Forest Home, ca. 1950. Courtesy of the Billy Graham Center Archives, Wheaton, Ill.

worn out from several mediocre crusades and from an internal debate over the trustworthiness of the Bible. Through discussions with Mears and the evangelist and historian J. Edwin Orr, Graham surrendered his intellectual doubts and placed his faith in the Bible. According to Orr, Graham then felt himself "filled afresh with the Spirit of God" and empowered for the upcoming event. Graham's experience, accessibility, and preaching made an impression on the five hundred individuals at Forest Home. Bright described the conference as an "extraordinary student awakening." "I feel a communion of spirit with him," Bright wrote of Graham, "because it was here the Lord spoke to many of us, giving us a new challenge for service plus a greater sense of urgency for the lost." "The Lord was there in power," wrote Orr, "and not only was there repentance, private and public confession, restoration, and thorough revival, but conversions of the most unhopeful sinners occurred every day."[37]

Over the following weeks, Bright and the other members of the Hollywood Presbyterian College Department watched Graham gain local and national renown with a mixture of evangelistic preaching and alarmist statements about the threat of communism. Already acquainted with Graham for several years, Mears facilitated connections for him with local celebrities. Shortly after the Fellowship of the Burning Heart experience,

Mears had formed the Hollywood Christian Group. This elite gathering—open only to persons in the entertainment industry and a few invited guests—nurtured Christian stars such as Colleen Townsend, Roy Rogers, and Jane Russell and evangelized other entertainers, including Stuart Hamblen. Ronald Reagan attended one meeting. As an associate of Mears, Bright had the chance to visit the home of Christian entertainers Roy Rogers and Dale Evans and went on movie sets with several members of the Hollywood Christian Group. Hamblen's endorsement of Graham's crusade and his well-publicized conversion partway through the campaign provided a wave of publicity in large part responsible for Graham's success in Los Angeles. The newspaper publisher William Randolph Hearst told his reporters and editors to "Puff Graham," and Graham's crusade began to generate nationwide attention as well as local evangelistic success. Once again, Bright experienced evangelical Christianity as a vibrant, growing movement attracting the best and the brightest of the postwar generation.[38]

Perhaps rejuvenated by the 1949 Briefing Conference and Graham's Los Angeles campaign, Bright rededicated himself to a ministerial vocation. Despite his previous academic shortcomings, Fuller Seminary reinstated him as a student in the spring of 1950. His grades improved significantly during the following semester. But from the moment he returned, he was again contemplating leaving, telling classmates that he was thinking of starting a full-time ministry to college students across the nation. Moreover, it became evident that he would not obtain ordination as a Presbyterian minister. Bright's transfer to Fuller created a conflict with the local presbytery, the governing body that determined Bright's fitness for ordination. The Presbytery of Los Angeles, like several other California presbyteries, refused to support candidates who attended Fuller and pressured them to study at San Francisco Seminary, a denominational institution. Most evangelical Presbyterians in California, according to Louis Evans Jr., in turn considered San Francisco Seminary a theological "anathema." Eugene Carson Blake, pastor of Pasadena Presbyterian Church, was one of Fuller's most vociferous opponents, and he confronted Bright about his choice of seminaries at a presbytery committee meeting. When Bright refused to transfer, the presbytery ended his candidacy for ordination.[39]

As he continued juggling his academic, business, and evangelistic aspirations, Bright's academic performance took another nosedive. In the fall of 1950, he failed both Greek and Hebrew, two requirements for graduation. By the spring of 1951, Bright was struggling in all of his courses, and he was also studying for another attempt at the nettlesome languages. With greater dedication, he might have eventually succeeded, but in the spring of 1951, graduation was still a distant prospect. Grades aside, the entire nature of seminary education—at least at Princeton and Fuller—frustrated Bright. Bright found Fuller wanting because he saw little connection between the education he received and his ability to grow as an evangelist. In his opinion, effective ministry equaled effective evangelism, and biblical languages and theology had nothing to do with effective evangelism. "In all the years, five years, that I was sitting at their [his professors'] feet," Bright later complained, "there was only one occasion where I ever heard one of my professors talk about leading anyone to Christ." Bright ultimately rejected Fuller as largely irrelevant to ministry.[40]

Although Fuller Seminary has received considerable attention from scholars as an example of the new evangelicalism that emerged out of fundamentalism, the Fuller faculty's advocacy of intellectual engagement was rare in evangelical and fundamentalist circles. Bright's mind-set was not strictly anti-intellectual. Much as he had appreciated literature and poetry growing up, Bright had enjoyed sitting in lecture halls at Princeton soaking up information about the Old Testament. Yet to Bright, such pursuits, however pleasant, were luxuries that threatened to distract Christians from more immediate tasks. Two subsequent examples illustrate Bright's attitude toward academic study. Bright once visited Dale Bruner, another Hollywood Presbyterian College Department alumnus at Princeton Seminary. "Just two hundred yards away men and women are going straight to hell," Bright cautioned Bruner, "and you Dale are just sitting here studying all night." Similarly, Dan Fuller recalls that Bright questioned the utility of his doctoral education in Basel. In 1960, while visiting Fuller in the capital of Swiss evangelicalism, Bright looked at the books scattered around Fuller's room and exclaimed, "How on earth can you stay in this room and study theology when all Switzerland and Europe is going to Hell?" Bright's attitude was common among evangelicals. "When God gets ready to shake America," Billy Graham informed the audience during his Los Angeles crusade, "He may not take the Ph.D. and the D.D. . . . God may choose a country boy." Many evangelicals felt the sting of academic inferiority when they interacted with mainline ministers and theologians, and evangelicals eagerly embraced the academic titles conferred by honorary doctorates. Devotion to intellectual pursuits, however, seemed imprudent compared to the urgency of winning souls.[41]

While Bright struggled through another difficult semester at Fuller Seminary in the spring of 1951, he and Vonette endured a brief marital crisis.

Without informing his wife, Bill and several others at the church counseled an unwed mother following Sunday school. Bill did not return until hours after the morning worship service, and Vonette was displeased that he had not notified her of his whereabouts. An argument ensued, and the Brights settled the conflict by drawing up a contract with God and with each other, "sign[ing] our names as a formal act of commitment to Christ and his cause." It was another expression of Keswick spirituality, a crisis leading to absolute surrender. And surrender again led to empowerment. A few days later, Bright was studying for a Greek exam with his friend Hugh Brom. Abruptly, Bright put down his Greek language cards and asked Brom to go for a run. Brom recalls confusedly running up and down the streets near Bright's home as his classmate explained that he had finally received a vision from God about how to begin his ministry. "The experience of Forest Home was repeated," Bright later wrote. "I suddenly had the overwhelming impression that the Lord had unfolded a scroll of instructions of what I was to do with my life." After Brom left, Bright woke up Vonette and told her of his plan to recruit leaders from evangelical seminaries and begin a nationwide ministry to college students. After conferring with Wilbur Smith, Henrietta Mears, and Louis Evans Sr., Bright decided that he would sell his wholesale business and irrevocably withdraw from Fuller Seminary. Smith suggested the name "Campus Crusade for Christ."[42]

Since leaving Oklahoma in 1944, Bill Bright had enjoyed numerous moments of exhilaration: his conversion, his 1947 communion with the Holy Spirit, successful attempts at personal evangelism, and his marriage to Vonette Zachary. Still, until his 1951 vision, Bright had also endured a series of frustrations, from multiple failures at theological education to the messy collapse of his candy business. As an entrepreneur, however, Bright never lingered in self-doubt after such failures and always quickly switched his focus to a new enterprise. Given Bright's evangelistic focus, Campus Crusade would primarily be a mission for individual souls. However, Henrietta Mears and Billy Graham had illustrated for Bright that evangelicals were not only contending for the souls of individuals but for the soul of the American nation. Much as Mears outlined at the annual College Briefing Conference, Bright envisioned his ministry as part of a crusade against international communism and as a struggle to reverse the secularization of the college campus. Evangelical leaders believed that they had lost their rightful place of leadership in American society. Like Bright, they had endured embarrassments and setbacks. They were, however, a resilient and confident minority hopeful that evangelism would reconnect America with its Christian heritage. Through Campus Crusade for Christ, Bright would pursue that goal by targeting the rising generation of post-war American leaders.

Campus Ministry at America's "Trojan Horse"

After deciding to found Campus Crusade for Christ, Bright wrote potential supporters to outline his vision, which fused spiritual and political concerns and objectives. He asserted that "the average collegian is spiritually illiterate" and—probably not counting Catholic or Jewish students—"estimated that less than five percent of the college students of America are actively engaged in the church of today." After noting that virtually all American colleges and universities "were founded as Christian institutions," he lamented that "many of our state universities and colleges and other institutions deny the deity of Christ, the Bible as the Word of God, and offer not so much as one Christian course in their curriculum." Furthermore, Bright believed that the campus would resolve the question of "Christ or Communism—which shall it be?" "Communism has already made deep inroads into the American campus," he warned in a bulletin promoting his newly formed organization, "and unless we fill the spiritual vacuum of the collegiate world, the campus may well become America's 'Trojan Horse.'" While Bright's primary focus was evangelism, he viewed the work of Campus Crusade through the lens of Cold War geopolitics. "Win the campus today," Crusade's motto promised, "win the world tomorrow."[1]

When historians identify groups of Americans discontented with the status quo of the 1950s, they typically discuss beatniks, overburdened housewives, and people excluded from the material abundance of the American dream. Evangelical leaders, however, also sharply criticized the postwar status quo. Despite the heady publicity surrounding Billy Graham and other manifestations of religious revival, many evangelicals remained worried about the direction of American society and their place in it. Evangelical leaders applauded the material prosperity of the postwar boom but cautioned that it alone could not satisfy spiritual yearnings. Like many Americans, they were disconcerted by crime, juvenile delinquency, and real and perceived communist threats at home and abroad. Evangelicals in the 1950s were on the march, battling the domestic and international demons that threatened their vision of a Christian America. In keeping with the militaristic tone of American culture that affected everything from politics to literature to swimwear, some evangelical activists conceived of themselves as soldiers primed for spiritual combat. Henrietta Mears had established an annual "briefing" conference to prepare collegians for battle against campus secularism. Bright launched a "Crusade" that featured evangelical "invasions" of allegedly hostile university campuses. A number of men who joined the Campus Crusade staff in the 1950s recall thinking of themselves and their colleagues as the "shock troops" of a Christian army. Such militaristic imagery had, of course, long been standard fare for American Protestants, yet the intensity of militaristic rhetoric in the late 1940s and 1950s suggests evangelicals were not at peace in postwar America.

Religious conservatives focused a sizable portion of their postwar anxieties on the nation's university campuses. Although fundamentalists in the 1920s gained notoriety for their efforts to expunge evolution from public school curricula, conservative Protestants in the early 1900s also expressed horror at the evolution of American higher education. Fundamentalists alleged that modernist professors were importing dangerous German philosophies into American lecture halls, turning pious Christian students into what Bob Jones termed "campus shipwrecks" and state universities into—in the words of William B. Riley—"hot-beds of skepticism." Still, only a small percentage of Americans went to college in the early twentieth century, and most fundamentalists who pursued postsecondary education attended denominational colleges or Bible institutes. By midcentury, however, fundamentalist worries had advanced into more widespread evangelical alarm about the state of American colleges and universities. The number of Americans resident at institutions of higher education jumped by nearly one million between only 1946 and 1950. Over two million veterans utilized the higher-education benefits of the G.I. Bill. As public universities expanded rapidly, their enrollments began to outnumber those of private institutions. This tidal wave of students—many of whom were first-generation collegians—attended universities and colleges that had gradually divested themselves of the most pronounced aspects of their denominational heritage, such as required chapel attendance.[2]

As enrollments skyrocketed, evangelical concerns about campus secularism intensified. In *God and Man at Yale*, William F. Buckley—a Yale alumnus and a Catholic—portrayed his alma mater as an "institution that derives its moral and financial support from Christian individualists and then addresses itself to the task of persuading the sons of these supporters to be atheistic socialists." Evangelical leaders shared Buckley's fear that American universities were becoming breeding grounds for communism and other subversive ideologies. At the same time, the university campus became a target of anticommunist campaigns against suspected subversion. State legislatures alleged widespread communist infiltration of the campus and passed laws requiring university employees (and other state employees) to sign loyalty oaths. These anxieties about American higher education helped Bill Bright find staff and donors for his effort to evangelize and re-Christianize the nation's universities. In the early 1900s, fundamentalists had responded to concerns about the secularization of the academy by founding their own colleges, seminaries, and Bible institutes. Such efforts continued throughout the twentieth century, but by 1950 it was clear that most American students would attend institutions that did not subscribe to evangelical verities. Thus, it was a highly auspicious time for Bright to launch Campus Crusade, which combined evangelicalism and anticommunism to offer salvation from both sin and subversion.[3]

The Little Red School House

In the spring and summer of 1951, Bright spent six months planning the launch of his ministry, preparing a two-pronged offensive against "the present pagan condition of our campuses." Drawing on the evangelistic strategy employed by Hollywood Presbyterian deputation groups, he hoped to recruit one hundred seminary and Bible-college graduates to be "dispatched in teams of five" across the country to hold evangelistic meetings and meet student leaders. He also designed an evangelistic wrinkle to the basic deputation strategy. Appropriate for a budding evangelist converted in Tinseltown, Bright planned to produce an evangelistic film that his teams could show to campus groups. Set on "an ivy-league campus," "The Great Adventure" would have depicted a student body president who converts to Christianity and then debates a fellow student who is "radically anti-God, having embraced popular Marxist philosophies." The film would also have highlighted the "references to God" in the founding documents of the United States and portrayed "such men as Lincoln, Webster, Adams, and Jackson" giving "testimonies of their faith in God, Christ, and the Scriptures." "The Great Adventure" reflects several aspects of Bright's mind-set: an anxiety about campus radicalism, an interest in film and other media, an appeal to a golden age of Christianity in American history, and a focus on the conversion of student leaders as a means of reaching the broader campus population.[4]

Eliminating the need to establish permanent campus chapters, Bright expected other ministries and local congregations to "disciple" Campus Crusade's converts, much as Billy Graham partnered with local churches. Bright, however, neither developed a close relationship with existing campus ministries nor chose to work within the confines of Hollywood Presbyterian or the Presbyterian denomination. According to Donn Moomaw, an early Crusade convert at UCLA, Hollywood Presbyterian minister Louis H. Evans Sr. counseled Bright during a Forest Home retreat to operate from within the church. "God impressed me," Bright replied to Evans after a night of prayer. "I'm going to have to go it alone." Moomaw explains that "there was some of that separatist stuff in his gut." Louis Evans Jr. comments that Bright "did not have a whole lot of hope for the Presbyterian Church as an institution." Moreover, Bright believed few congregations— Presbyterian or otherwise—would actually nurture the evangelical faith of his converts. With the exception of Hollywood Presbyterian, comments Moomaw, "he wasn't real pleased with sending his converts back into the church [because he] felt they would freeze up." Bright's negative conception of most churches reflects evangelicalism's heritage of fundamentalist separatism. Although many evangelicals retained their membership in the mainline denominations, they were disenchanted with those institutions. Moreover, Bright's desire to start a new campus organization reflects the entrepreneurial and unstructured nature of parachurch evangelicalism. Despite pressure to work within established channels, he only needed donors and staff to start his own ministry.[5]

Bright wrote seminaries across the country seeking "100 men" for his budding organization, but he did not find anyone willing to join an unknown and unproven ministry. Moreover, he lacked the $24,000 deemed necessary to produce "The Great Adventure." Instead, he recruited several friends from Fuller Seminary and Hollywood Presbyterian to help him start his ministry locally. Bright began by taking his volunteers to UCLA, an obvious choice for the first battleground in his spiritual war for the American campus. As a member of Hollywood Presbyterian deputation teams, Bright had already spoken in fraternity and sorority houses on the campus. Moreover, Bright viewed UCLA, which he said many called "the little Red school house," as the fountainhead of faculty and student radicalism in California. Although investigative committees produced no evidence of actual communist infiltration, Bright later maintained that the "communists were making an impact on the campus" and that UCLA "in 1951 had a strong, radical minority which was exercising great influence and was causing unprecedented disturbances." Bright surmised that "this would be one of the most difficult campuses on which to begin."[6]

Campus Crusade's early years at UCLA coincided with a nationwide upsurge in campus religiosity parallel to the more general religious boom of the postwar years. Across the United States, university officials pointed to thriving denominational ministries, the establishment of academic courses in religion, and the success of "religious emphasis" weeks as evidence of Christian vitality. Periodicals like *Time* and *Newsweek* maintained that collegians in the 1950s were more religious than their 1920s counterparts. At UCLA, there was considerable evidence of religious activity. At least ten Christian groups—from the Presbyterian Westminster Club to the pacifist Fellowship of Reconciliation—advertised in the UCLA *Daily Bruin* during the 1951–52 academic year. Thousands of students listened to Billy Graham during the evangelist's visit to campus in October 1951. Louis H. Evans Sr. addressed the Westminster Club in December 1951, and Bright's Fellowship of the Burning Heart comrade Richard Halverson spoke to UCLA's Inter-Varsity Christian Fellowship chapter the following spring. Such activities, however, do not mean that UCLA was a Christian university, at least not as evangelicals would have defined the concept. R. G. Sproul, president of the entire University of California system, commented on the state of religion on campus in conjunction with UCLA's 1953 religious emphasis week. Sproul maintained that the university should encourage "a code of Christianlike behaviour" in its students and help them to understand that "there is significance to men's existence." However, Sproul insisted that faith "lives in the hearts of men of a thousand different creeds, and joyously dwells with men who know no creed at all." In short, UCLA retained the ethical and moral ideals of liberal Protestantism without promoting any particular faith. Yet the university had also created an open religious marketplace in which a wide range of groups—including evangelical parachurch organizations—could effectively promote their own brands of religion.[7]

Like Henrietta Mears, Campus Crusade targeted prominent student leaders, anticipating that high-profile converts would attract the attention of other students. Also like Mears, Crusade attached a special significance to cultivating male leaders: star athletes, fraternity presidents, and student body leaders. "Women are more responsive sometimes to the Gospel than men are," explains Roe Brooks, who joined Crusade's staff in 1952, "and the biggest problem you have in your work is to be sure that you always have enough men." "Once it becomes a 'girls' movement,'" Brooks continues, "men are going to depart . . . so we found that you've got to present a masculine image." Crusade went to great lengths during its early years to highlight robustly masculine leaders. Male students will "listen to a football player," explained Bob Davenport, a star fullback at UCLA and one of Crusade's most prominent early speakers, "because they don't figure you're a sissy." In addition to exhibiting long-standing Protestant concerns about inculcating a spirituality and atmosphere attractive to men, Crusade's strategy may also reflect the nature of postwar university enrollments. Throughout the 1950s, nearly twice as many men as women attended American universities.[8]

Given this focus on male leadership, Crusade ironically experienced its initial success in a UCLA sorority. Bright and his evangelistic team made an appointment to speak at the Kappa Alpha Theta house, which Bright referred to as the "house of the beautiful women." He commented that the sorority apparently selected its pledges "for their good looks and personalities." Members of the team gave their "testimonies"—they told the assembled sorority sisters how personally knowing Jesus Christ had changed their lives. Bright later wrote that when he finished giving his message, "many girls remained behind to talk to us" and expressed "their desire to become Christians." "We invited the girls to join us the next evening for a meeting in our home nearby," he recalled. Several of the interested women brought their boyfriends, including Marilyn Amende, who invited UCLA's All-American linebacker, Donn Moomaw. Bright, recognizing the potential influence that a converted Moomaw could exert on the campus, asked Moomaw and Amende to accompany him to Hollywood Presbyterian that weekend. Like Bright, Moomaw grew up in "a Christian home"—his family belonged to a Presbyterian church in Santa Ana—but had not attended church since coming to UCLA. Moomaw's recollection of his encounter with Bright that Sunday reveals the basic contours of Crusade's early message and approach:

We went back to Bill's house, and the girls [including Marilyn Amende and Vonette Bright] were preparing lunch, and Bill was talking to me in the living room, and he began sharing through the Scriptures what would later be called the Plan of Salvation. . . . He used Romans 3:23 — "all have sinned and come short of the glory of God." And then we talked about that a little bit. And I said, "Yeah, I admit that I have fallen short of the glory of God." . . . Then he read Romans 6:23 — "the gift of God is eternal life through Jesus Christ his son." And then he went back to John 1:12 — "to as many as receive him, to them gave he power to become the children of God, even to those who believe in his name." . . . and he said, "Is there any reason right now why you don't first of all confess your sin and secondly receive Christ as your savior?" And I said, "Well, there's probably a lot of reasons why I should not do it, but I'm open to doing it right now." He said, "Then let's kneel here on the floor." . . . So I knelt down with Bill, and he prayed with me and then he asked me to pray, and it wasn't a very eloquent prayer. I just prayed from my heart and opened my heart to Christ. When I finished praying, I knew that something had happened to me.

We went in and had lunch, and this is Bill's way of confirming that experience, [to] immediately have you share it with someone. So he asked me to share it with the girls, the ladies at the table. I did share. Bill's way of follow-up for young converts was as soon as you can, share it. And because I was high visibility through my athletics, he had me going out sharing my conversion experience everywhere.[9]

Moomaw's conversion, publicized in the *Los Angeles Times*, gave Campus Crusade considerable publicity. In 1953, Billy Graham invited Bright and Moomaw to appear on his popular *Hour of Decision* television program with moderator Cliff Barrows. It was a remarkable opportunity for Bright and his young organization. The segment began with highlights of Moomaw in the Rose Bowl. Moomaw then told Barrows about his conversion, and Barrows asked Bright about Campus Crusade. "Today we're endeavoring to bring Christ back to his rightful place on the university campus," Bright answered. "We're seeing a great heart hunger—scores, hundreds of these wonderful young men and women are coming to Christ." During the spring of 1953, Moomaw wrestled with the question of entering the NFL draft, which would have committed him to playing on Sundays. After consultation with Mears, Evans Sr., and Graham, he decided to forego NFL football in order to attend Princeton Seminary. When Moomaw informed Bright of his decision, Bright responded, "Let me set this up for you. I'll have a press conference and we'll have it in my house, and you can tell these reporters your decision." "Bill was using this to build Campus Crusade," Moomaw later reflected on the press conference, which attracted reporters asking about Bill Bright's role in Moomaw's conversion. "I'm not saying it was wrong," he comments. "I'm just saying he was . . . using every way possible to get that organization out before the public and before people who could support it monetarily. . . . He was an entrepreneur for Christ."[10]

It would be misleading, though, to highlight only the entrepreneurial aspects of Bright's leadership. In front of a group, Bright was an ordinary speaker. "I thought he was a very poor speaker by far," comments Earl Palmer, a Presbyterian seminarian who traveled from Berkeley to investigate Crusade's success at UCLA. "It seemed he always had the same message and he repeated it all the time." Others came away from Bright's talks impressed with his quiet focus and sincerity. Regardless, Bright overcame any oratorical shortcomings by meeting with students individually. "His popularity or his notoriety on campus was legend[ary]," comments Moomaw, "because he was the greatest one-on-one evangelist that I've ever known." Students involved with Crusade at UCLA emphasize Bright's spiritual leadership, displayed in long, patient counseling sessions with students. Dick Edic, who made a "decision for Christ" at a UCLA fraternity meeting in 1957, recalls regular two-hour sessions with Bright for months after his conversion.[11]

Although she received less public attention, Vonette Bright played a critical role in Crusade's early ministry at UCLA, as neither Bill Bright nor his male assistants were prepared to disciple the large numbers of interested women. Despite some initial misgivings about Bill's decision to sell his wholesale business and start Campus Crusade, she quickly began working with female students. "During the first semester," she later wrote, "I saw at least fifty young women receive Jesus Christ as their Savior." After a Crusade team visited a sorority, Vonette made appointments to meet with each interested student. "In almost every case," reported Crusade's *Communique*, "the girl receives Christ as Saviour." "Vonette has been used in a special way to bring many to the Lord Jesus," Bill praised his wife to Bob Jones Jr. "It seems that someone makes a decision almost every day with her." Vonette continued teaching for a year after her husband started Campus Crusade, but she then decided to devote herself fully to the ministry.[12]

For the Brights, the ministry at UCLA provided deliverance from years of indecision and false starts. Campus Crusade claimed two hundred fifty conversions within several months, "including the student body president, the editor of the newspaper, and a number of the top athletes." In 1953, Crusade rented a tiny office on Westwood Avenue in Los Angeles, which became the organization's headquarters through the early 1960s. Also in 1953, Henrietta Mears—following the death of her sister and longtime companion Margaret—invited the Brights to share a palatial Bel Air home adjacent to the UCLA campus. The arrangement solidified the success of the ministry at UCLA, as students and financial supporters alike flocked to hear Mears speak at Crusade functions. Most of the stars on UCLA's 1954 national-championship football team—nicknamed the "Eleven from Heaven"—were outspoken Christians, many of whom made "decisions for Christ" through Bright's influence. Bright later reminisced that "the chimes [on campus] began to play Christian hymns at noonday."[13]

How to Have Success at Selling Jesus

Buoyed by his initial success at UCLA, Bright quickly organized evangelistic teams that traveled to other campuses. In order to facilitate further expansion, he recruited several Fuller Seminary students and graduates, including Daniel Fuller, who believed that a crash course in evangelism under Bright would prepare him to inherit his father's mantle. Bright also made recruiting trips to a number of seminaries and Christian colleges but generated little interest at these schools, with the notable exception of Bob Jones University (BJU) in South Carolina. Glenn Zachary, Vonette Bright's brother, was a student at BJU. He told classmates about the success of Campus Crusade at UCLA and distributed the movement's promotional literature. Bill Bright had also met Bob Jones Jr. at the 1950 College Briefing Conference at Forest Home. BJU shared Crusade's intense focus on aggressive evangelism. "We fit into Crusade just like a glove," explains Bob Kendall, a 1954 BJU graduate. "Bob Jones was the best training ground for Crusade of any place in the world." According to Kendall, BJU students engaged in many hours of evangelism each week and regularly submitted reports documenting their experiences. Bright's account of the ministry at UCLA impressed Gordon Klenck, one of Bright's first BJU recruits. Like many conservative Protestants, Klenck considered "secular" campuses hostile territory for evangelists. "I had not heard or seen college students who had no interest in spiritual things responding the way Bill was describing," he recalls. BJU graduates like Kendall and Klenck brought an unabashed enthusiasm for evangelism and anticipated greater results with Campus Crusade than they had previously experienced.[14]

The relationship between Campus Crusade and BJU, discussed more fully in Chapter 3, illustrates the as yet incomplete and porous boundary between evangelicals and fundamentalists in the early 1950s. Bob Jones Sr. and his son were paradigmatic figures within American fundamentalism because of their strident defense of traditional Protestant doctrines—such as the virgin birth of Jesus, the inerrancy of the Bible, and the atoning death of Jesus on the cross—and their refusal to publicly cooperate with any Christians who did not share those doctrinal commitments. The Joneses also represented the stance of separatist fundamentalism toward American culture. Although BJU established excellent programs in theater, music, and cinema, the school punished students caught listening to "music considered 'jazz.'" BJU insisted that its students adhere to decorous behavior and clean living, and the school prohibited dancing, card playing, and dice throwing. Male and female couples could only spend time together in the presence of a chaperone or in designated public spaces on campus. An anonymous article in the *American Mercury* satirized BJU (then Bob Jones College) as "a college where your boy may be put in solitary confinement for a month for smoking one cigarette, where your daughter is restricted to the campus for refusing a date, where four hundred boys and girls do not dare speak to each other except when crowding into the dining room." Although Bill Bright would not have openly disagreed with BJU's approach, he and Vonette were not part of the same fundamentalist subculture. Young adults at Hollywood Presbyterian Church went to the cinema, enjoyed popular music, and attended dances. Vonette Bright had always enjoyed dancing, and Bill had at least consented to escort her. This greater openness to popular culture was an important characteristic that differentiated emerging evangelicals from their fundamentalist counterparts in postwar America. Yet in the early 1950s, shared theological beliefs and a mutual commitment to evangelism masked such potential areas of disagreement between different segments of conservative Protestantism.[15]

Bill and Vonette Bright took their initial six full-time recruits—all men —to Forest Home for the 1952 College Briefing Conference. After Henrietta Mears returned to Hollywood, the Brights used her cabin at Forest

Home—nicknamed the "Biltmore" after the luxurious Los Angeles hotel—as the center for several additional weeks of training in evangelism and other aspects of campus ministry. A major focus of the training was campus etiquette. Vonette taught staff recruits how to dress appropriately and use proper table manners, and she accompanied the BJU recruits to wholesalers in the Los Angeles area to select appropriate clothes for campus work. Bill and the new staff members also hammered out Crusade's basic theology and methodology during the early staff training sessions, held as annual retreats at Forest Home. They studied writings by R. A. Torrey, an associate of Dwight Moody in Chicago and later dean of the Bible Institute of Los Angeles. Reflecting the spirituality of the Keswick movement that had influenced Mears, Torrey promised his readers that if they completely surrendered themselves to God they would receive the power of the Holy Spirit and be empowered for service. The group also read Oswald Chamber's *My Utmost for His Highest*, a fundamentalist devotional favorite. Chambers, who like Torrey had attended the British Keswick conference, also stressed complete devotion to and dependence upon God as the means to holy and fruitful living.[16]

Bright, however, did not restrict the reading list to fundamentalist classics. He also asked his recruits to digest Frank Bettger's *How I Raised Myself from Failure to Success in Selling*. Bettger, a positive-thinking disciple of Dale Carnegie whose book sold half a million copies during the 1950s, emphasized personal attractiveness and unflagging enthusiasm. He stressed the importance of securing personal appointments with potential clients and discussed sales techniques, such as the use of an introductory questionnaire to establish rapport. Bettger found that most sales resulted from the first or second contact with a customer and recommended quickly moving on from unmotivated buyers. Bright was not alone among evangelical leaders in his appreciation of Bettger. One of Oral Roberts's early patrons gave the healing evangelist a copy of Bettger's book, and Roberts later claimed to have read it annually. The relationship between evangelism and other forms of salesmanship was obvious to many evangelists, including Billy Graham, who sold Fuller Brushes for a summer after his high school graduation. "I'm selling the greatest product [Christ] in the world," Graham once commented, "why shouldn't it be promoted as well as soap?" Bright wrote that he provided his staff recruits with "instruction in . . . Christian salesmanship (soulwinning)." Bright recognized that evangelists—"soulwinners" in fundamentalist and evangelical parlance—were spiritual salesmen. In this respect, he was the ideal leader for Campus Crusade. "He was terrific at selling whatever he believed in," affirms Colleen Townsend Evans, who participated in Hollywood Presbyterian deputations. "He knew he was a charmer," explains Bright's friend Esther Brinkley, "and he knew he could talk anybody into anything." "He is," Paul Little of Inter-Varsity Christian Fellowship described Bright in 1961, "essentially a salesman first, last, and always in his outlook and approach to evangelism."[17]

At the first Forest Home training session, Bright asked his new staff members to practice their sales pitch, an evangelistic talk appropriate for a fraternity meeting. "All of them [the talks] were so poor," confides early recruit Gordon Klenck, "[because] they weren't really geared to the mind-set of the average college student." The new staff members then asked Bright to model his presentation, which they refined into a standard talk for evangelistic meetings. The "clincher," as they termed the talk, began with a description of the Cold War "crisis hour" and cited prominent authority figures such as MacArthur and Eisenhower on the need for a spiritual awakening. Crusade staff cautioned students that religion, even Christianity, "becomes the opiate of the people, restricting, limiting, inhibiting man," whereas "Christ sets man free, bringing new life and new hope." Crusade staff explained that human sinfulness separates people from this new life and pointed to symptoms such as "worry, irritability, [and] lack of purpose in life" as "evidence that a man is cut off from the only One Who gives him the power to live life to the full." Staff members then discussed the deity of Jesus of Nazareth and emphasized that Jesus paid the penalty for human sin. "Are you ready to say 'Yes' to Christ tonight?" the "clincher" concluded. In either a follow-up meeting or in individual counseling sessions, Crusade staff encouraged individuals to ask Christ to "come into" their lives, maintaining that a short prayer—if genuine—provided the antidote to sin and produced peace, joy, and meaning. In constructing the "clincher," Bright followed the example of other postwar religious leaders—such as Rabbi Joshua Liebman, Norman Vincent Peale, Billy Graham, and Fulton Sheen—by presenting an easily accessible spiritual solution to anxiety and malaise. Like these other postwar religious popularizers, Bright presumed that Americans wanted more than the material goods that accompanied the postwar economic boom and were searching for deeper happiness and meaning. He believed that collegians—even star athletes and beauty queens—endured the same anxieties and yearnings as other Americans, and he offered them a simple, optimistic solution.[18]

Cleaning House for Jesus

Armed with this basic evangelistic message, Bright's early staff recruits attempted to replicate his success at UCLA as they "invaded" West Coast campuses. They sought opportunities to speak to fraternities, sororities, athletic teams, and other student groups. Staff also identified and contacted fraternity leaders, student government officials, and newspaper editors and spoke with them individually about Jesus Christ. "We know from experience," asserted a promotional newspaper, "that when these leaders accept Christ, they can help to influence a whole campus for the Lord Jesus Christ." In the early years of the ministry, Crusade developed an additional technique to facilitate contacts with students. Perhaps embracing Frank Bettger's suggestion, Crusade staff developed a questionnaire that posed a series of questions about religious beliefs and practices. The final question asked students if they were among a majority of collegians "looking for a faith." If the answer was affirmative, the staff member would transition into an evangelistic pitch along the lines of "the clincher." "By using the questionnaire," maintained Barbara Ringo, an early staff member, "a Crusader can easily meet any student and without loss of time, discern whether that one is open and ready to receive the Saviour." As Bettger identified likely buyers, Crusade staff efficiently recognized the most likely prospects for conversion and spent time with those students.[19]

As the movement spread to other campuses, Crusade experienced a mixture of setbacks and successes. Many staff simply could not replicate the results that Bright had achieved at UCLA. Dan Fuller found the few months he spent as a full-time Campus Crusade worker at USC to be among the more agonizing experiences of his life. "I had an awfully hard time," Fuller recollects. "I had doors slammed in my face." Especially difficult was explaining his lack of success to Bright, who informed Fuller that "the revival is still going on in some fraternity houses over here at UCLA" and responded incredulously when Fuller reported that "nothing happened" at USC. There was a high turnover rate, as some recruits found they were ill-suited for aggressive campus evangelism. Roger Aiken toiled for two years in Oregon with few converts and concluded that as someone without a fraternity or student government background, he was unable to effectively employ Crusade's evangelistic strategies. Fuller speculates that only staff with certain personality traits succeeded: "You had to be a Bill Bright. You had to be a student body president. You had to have been a fraternity president." Other staff, by contrast, enjoyed gratifying results. "We had no

Staff member Judy Kifer getting a response to Campus Crusade's questionnaire from a student at the University of Texas, 1963. Courtesy of Judy Kifer.

trouble making appointments and having converts," early recruit Bob Kendall recollects. "I could pray with people all day long to receive Christ. It was not hard." Crusade's success depended on dedicated, engaging, and attractive staff who boldly took the initiative on campus. "My first day on the UCLA campus," Kendall recalls, "he [Bill Bright] had a clipboard and a questionnaire . . . he took two or three surveys and then he just handed me the clipboard and said, 'Go to it!'" Bright knew that not all of his recruits would succeed. He considered campus evangelism a weeding out process that would confirm whether or not God had called individuals to the ministry. Aiken asserts that Bright "demanded that all of us on CCC staff 'prove' that we were called to work as evangelists on college campuses." Despite the organization's high rate of staff turnover, by 1955 Crusade had thirty staff members (some only part-time) scattered on campuses across the country.[20]

At first, Bright only recruited single men under thirty years of age with seminary or Bible school training, though he quickly revised his standards to accept college graduates and both older and married men. "In the past," he wrote in 1953, "it has been the policy not to recruit girls for the Crusade work." Jens Christy, one of Crusade's first student converts at Berkeley, remembers discussing with Bright the potential hazards of male staff members providing spiritual counsel to female students. Christy recalls that Bright initially remained adamant about only recruiting male staff but soon changed his mind. In 1953, Bright attributed the changed policy to the fact that "the spiritual hunger among the girls on the campuses has been so great." Moreover, female students and other women impressed with the organization expressed a desire to join staff. Crusade publications from the era refer to unmarried women on the staff as "staff girls" or "campus girls" and married women as "staff wives." By contrast, men on staff were usually referred to simply as "men." Female staff typically worked along the same lines as the men: witnessing to students on campus, speaking at sorority and other meetings, and leading Bible studies. Unlike men, women did not start new campus chapters on their own, and if there were multiple staff at a single campus, women did not serve in supervisory capacities over men. Also, Bright did not ask women to serve in the layers of regional management Crusade gradually added as the ministry grew. Women filled other organizational niches. Several women ran the tiny office in Los Angeles, including Dorothy Hauser, office manager and Bright's secretary in the mid-to-late 1950s. Dianne Ross and Shirley Milligan became traveling speakers and served as Crusade's first national "women's representatives," visiting campuses to deliver evangelistic talks to female students and guidance to female staff members.[21]

Married couples were in ministry together, and individuals from outside the organization who married a staff member were expected to join staff and were not allowed to pursue outside employment. Single staff had to consider the possibility of giving up their ministry with Campus Crusade should they choose to marry a non-staff member. Given that requirement, it is perhaps not surprising that "[m]arriage between staff members was encouraged," as Bright's biographer Michael Richardson states. Crusade encouraged married women on staff to remain as active as possible in evangelism while making domestic responsibilities their first priority. "The wife's first responsibility is to her husband," asserted a Crusade brochure targeting potential staff recruits. The brochure explained that Campus Crusade wives both experience "fruitful ministries working with women students"

Dianne Ross (left) and Shirley Milligan, 1962. Courtesy of J. Kent Hutcheson.

and concentrate "on making their homes attractive for students to visit for friendly counsel, prayer, and fellowship." In the same brochure, Crusade pictured a number of men as "Area Director" and their wives as "Wife of Area Director." Such language reflects a mind-set that married women served as assistants to their husbands instead of filling important positions in their own right. Dianne Ross and Shirley Milligan no longer filled formal leadership positions after they married fellow staff members. When a married couple was assigned to a campus, the wife worked with female students. If a couple had children, however, she drastically reduced the amount of time devoted to the ministry. Crusade sought to alleviate this difficulty by assigning single female staff to "each campus where a Crusade ministry is active."[22]

Although Crusade organized joint meetings for men and women on each campus and the entire staff met together each summer, the campus ministry often proceeded along largely homosocial lines. "In Campus Crusade," explained Vonette Bright in 1991, "we have always encouraged men to witness to and disciple men, and women to do the same with women."

Male staff members met with and gave questionnaires to college men, and female staff members interacted with female students. Bible studies, often held in dormitories, were usually also single-sex. "It has been proven more effective for women to counsel with women," claimed the ministry, "as they are likely to have a better understanding of another woman's problems and spiritual needs." To a substantial extent, the campus women's ministry was "a separate segment," although both men and women attended weekly College Life meetings and traveled to retreats and conferences.[23]

Vonette Bright struggled with her role in the organization during the 1950s. After the Brights moved into Henrietta Mears's new home in Bel Air and adopted two boys, she found herself consumed with entertaining guests and changing diapers and had much less time for the ministry. Wives of other staff members and female students took over the counseling and evangelistic duties that she had performed during the early years at UCLA. Especially given Mears's penchant for frequent and elegant entertaining, Vonette found that "keeping the house clean, organizing refreshments, and being a good hostess was a full-time job, as was being an attentive, available wife and mother." "She wondered if she could keep on," comments Vonette's friend Esther Brinkley, "because [she was] in the kitchen all the time for these social events that Teacher [Mears] would put on." "I found myself physically and emotionally drained," Vonette later reflected. "My daily routine emerged as a monotonous and exhaustingly laborious job." She wanted to move, but Bill saw the "castle" (Mears's home) as "an asset to the ministry," leaving Vonette to "wonder if I should seek professional counsel." The situation worsened as Bill's travel schedule expanded with the growth of the ministry. She later reflected that she fell into "boredom and frustration" not unlike that described in Betty Friedan's *The Feminine Mystique*. During those difficult days in the 1950s, she found that an attitude of thanksgiving and service created happiness despite her circumstances: "I cleaned house for Jesus—not for Campus Crusade, not for Bill Bright, not for Henrietta Mears, not for my family—but I was doing it for Jesus."[24]

Vonette Bright's earlier hesitancy to abandon her own career and her discontent with domestic drudgery shed light on the conservative Protestant conception of gender roles in the early postwar period. Fundamentalists and evangelicals, who had often described missionary work as the highest possible calling for women as well as men, began exalting the role of homemaker even above such forms of Christian service. "God," insisted Billy Graham during his 1949 Los Angeles crusade, "meant for women to be home and to rear children rather than to be running all over the coun-

Bill, Brad, Zachary, and Vonette Bright at Forest Home, 1962. Courtesy of Dorothy Graham.

try." This conservative Protestant mind-set reflects larger trends in postwar America, as secular periodicals also promoted women's return to home-making and domesticity. In this context, it is not surprising that Vonette Bright forewent her own career even before having children. She often discussed Campus Crusade as "Bill's ministry" rather than "our ministry." Her reluctance to stop teaching and her largely unpublicized involvement in the ministry at UCLA, however, suggest that evangelical women did not simply retreat into the domestic sphere after World War II. Vonette positioned herself as a "helpmeet" to "Bill's ministry," contributing to Campus Crusade in critical ways without any formal leadership position or recognition. Many women on staff came from fundamentalist backgrounds in which women played a very secondary role in ministry. Bob Jones University, for example, sent its male students out to conduct aggressive evangelism while sending its female students to teach children's classes. Thus, women may have found more opportunities for evangelism within Campus Crusade than in some other evangelical and fundamentalist ministries. Women—single and married—on staff with Campus Crusade provided leadership in important and often unnoticed ways, ways that sometimes contradicted evangelical rhetoric about the place of women. Crusade, however, restricted most formal positions of leadership to men and encouraged married women to concentrate first and foremost on home, husband, and children. Campus Crusade's staff manual encouraged staff women to efficiently perform household tasks, sow buttons and mend seams for single men, and to sort their husband's mail. Like many American women, Campus Crusade wives both worked outside the home and were reminded that the domestic sphere was their special responsibility.[25]

It is also important to note that in the 1950s and early 1960s, Crusade was an organization almost exclusively comprised of white students and staff. Crusade staff witnessed to students of all backgrounds on the campus—early Crusade newspapers occasionally pictured an African American student convert and more frequently profiled international students from a variety of countries. Rafer Johnson, a world-class decathlete and future Olympian, received considerable publicity as an African American member of Crusade's UCLA ministry in the late 1950s. Bill Bright, at least on one occasion in the 1950s, accepted an invitation to speak at a predominantly black college. In 1955, Bright addressed students at "Prairie View A and M College for Negroes" in Texas, encouraging them to become "Christian ambassadors to their own people and to the world." He reported that "390 responded to the invitation to receive Christ as Saviour and Lord."[26] The organization did not seek to expand its ministry to such institutions in the 1950s and, like most other evangelical institutions, had very little to say on the issue of race. Campus Crusade sought to target the "leaders of tomorrow" and recruit staff who could relate to those future leaders. In the 1950s, with the exception of international students, Crusade envisioned those leaders as white and as male.

Jesus as Quarterback

Although Bright had initially envisioned Campus Crusade as an almost exclusively evangelistic ministry, he soon developed methods of nurturing his converts. In some locations, such as Berkeley, Crusade could simply plug converts into local churches that were staffed by former protégés of Henrietta Mears. On many campuses, however, Crusade staff themselves took responsibility for "following up" converts. Crusade adopted materials and methods prepared by the Navigators, whose founder, Dawson Trotman, Bright had met on his first night in Los Angeles. The Navigators favored one-on-one discipleship of all converts, who learned methods of Scripture memorization, prayer, and evangelism. Crusade staff placed a particular emphasis on encouraging students, especially new converts, to begin practicing evangelism. Many early Crusade staff members recall feeling overwhelmed by the responsibility of "follow-up." "I think follow-up," laments Bob Kendall, "was the biggest challenge we had." As the movement spread, it was impossible for Crusade staff to provide one-on-one discipleship for their converts and simultaneously continue evangelistic efforts. The ministry soon organized group Bible studies instead. Even so, Kendall remembers the "response was so great" that he could not provide Bible studies for all who expressed interest.[27]

The organization's persistent worry about how to "follow up" new Christians suggests that Campus Crusade experienced considerable success in campus evangelism. The organization published hundreds of brief student testimonies in its *Campus Crusade Communique*, a periodical primarily used for promotional and fund-raising purposes. Although Crusade edited the testimonies and the students probably received guidance while composing their stories, these conversion narratives provide a window into the ways students interpreted what they experienced through Campus Crusade. Such testimonies speak to a variety of themes, with a few students commenting on issues of sin, salvation, and eternal life. The majority, however, testified to the way that their newfound relationship with Christ transformed their everyday lives. Students often emphasized that before they "accepted Christ," they had experienced "emptiness," "doubts and vague fears," boredom, and a lack of satisfaction. After their decision to "accept Christ," by contrast, they enjoyed peace, "purpose in life," "meaning," and "full joy." Nancy Offutt, a student at the University of Southern California, recalled that before her conversion she "had no purpose, no real answers to life." "After prayer," she testified, "He took my life and gave me the purpose for which I had been seeking." Students also frequently asserted that their relationship with Christ had improved their academic, athletic, and social lives. Donn Moomaw attributed an interception and touchdown against USC in 1951 to prayers prompted by attending his first Crusade meeting, and he later commented that Jesus was now "the 'quarterback' on our team." "Since I have had Christ," affirmed Don Shinnick, another UCLA football player, "my grades have risen, my life is much richer and my new Christian friends have been a great challenge and blessing to me." John Helsel reported the dramatic changes in his life that followed a Campus Crusade visit to his fraternity house: "I had a bad temper and cussed a lot. Now I am controlling my temper and have cut out swearing. My school work was boring; but I find it interesting now. I had a goal in mind, but didn't know how to reach it. I found the way. Recently I met a wonderful girl whom I hope to marry." "None of this would have been possible without my having accepted Christ," Helsel concluded.[28]

Crusade self-consciously crafted a message that was free from theological complexity or "undue extremes" and "presented in a sane, sensible, intelligent way that reaches the heart and mind of the collegian." "Students want to know," insisted staffer Roger Aiken, "how Christ meets everyday needs." Crusaders rarely sought to convince students of the rational truth of Christianity but instead brought students into contact with others like themselves who could witness to the eternal and practical consequences of the gospel. Bill Counts, who joined staff in 1960, believes that Crusade's campus ministry effectively reached students because the organization viewed the campus "as a social center" rather than "as an intellectual center." "If you look at where the average student was at a big state university," Counts continues, "they weren't there because they were interested in studying all these academics in depth and they were reading all these books on philosophy. They were there because they were in a fraternity and sorority. They were going to football games." Christianity may have moved from the core to the periphery of campus, but to many students fraternities, locker rooms, and dormitories were the core of college life, and Campus Crusade found ways to penetrate those campus spaces.[29]

Crusade also actively countered stereotypes of fundamentalism, showcasing star athletes, fraternity presidents, and "campus queens" in its publications. Crusaders reassured their fellow students that they were not joining a group of dour fundamentalists. "Before . . . ," Jim Humphreys of the University of California reflected on his involvement with Crusade, "I had pictured college age Christians as anemic." "I thought they were probably rather stuffy and fanatical," commented Mary Fay Mathes of the University of Southern California. "Was I surprised when the members got up to speak! Not only were the girls very cute, but they also belonged to some of the top sororities and were also leading a busy college life." Crusade's publications from the 1950s reveal the respective male and female role models to which they felt students would feel an attraction. Ideal male leaders were athletes, student body presidents, and fraternity leaders—athletic, intelligent, and popular. While Crusade put forward some women because of their success in campus politics or as sorority leaders, the organization also clearly perceived the benefits of publicizing "cute girls" and "beauty queens." Bright had suggested that the Theta House at UCLA selected women on the basis of their "good looks and personality"—it appears that Campus Crusade at times looked for the same qualities when selecting "girls" and "coeds" to promote. Along the same lines, in the 1960s Campus Crusade adopted a "weight policy" that encouraged staff members to remain physically healthy and attractive.[30]

The historian Doug Rossinow argues that student disenchantment with the fruits of postwar affluence and politics resulted in "a widespread yearning for authenticity" on campus. Students beset by anxiety and meaninglessness sought experiences that were "real," "natural," and "authentic." Rossinow describes how groups of Christian existentialists at the University of Texas eventually perceived the civil rights movement as a moment for decisive action that could produce both personal and political authenticity. As Rossinow recognizes, both students involved in evangelical movements and those involved in progressive politics appear to have discerned a lack of meaning in everyday campus life and in the material fruits of the postwar economic boom. Students involved with Campus Crusade articulated similar worries about emptiness and boredom and similar desires for purpose and meaning. Unlike theologically and politically progressive organizations, however, Crusade did not set up a dichotomy between campus life and material prosperity on the one hand and its prescribed solution on the other, nor did Crusade prescribe political activism as the path to authenticity. Instead, Crusade told students they could find true meaning only in Jesus Christ, who should become the highest priority in their lives. They could, however, continue on with their social lives, athletic endeavors, and future careers. Thus, Crusade offered a critique, but only a partial critique, of American society and the American campus in the 1950s. Crusade presented a message that at once affirmed the basic contours of campus life yet also challenged students to adhere to a radical focus on evangelism. Moreover, the organization promoted a fairly strict behavioral code and disapproved of smoking, drinking, and premarital sex, though Crusade rarely discussed such taboos. A fundamentalist institution such as Bob Jones University would at the very least have felt the need to more vocally condemn the drinking, dancing, and sexual activity prevalent on campuses like UCLA. Charles Dunn, a fundamentalist and professor at Clemson University in the 1970s, later complained that "Campus Crusaders are not taught that membership in a Greek fraternity or sorority is sin, even though these societies throw some of the wildest drinking and sex parties imaginable." If Crusade asked students to give up a few aspects of campus life, the organization suggested that students would receive abundant blessings in return. After all, the Brights had sacrificed their materialistic dreams in order to serve Christ but lived in a Bel Air mansion. Yet if students in many ways remained as they were, Crusaders testified that their newfound faith imbued their lives with meaning and purpose. Crusade students, even while they cheerfully related their athletic, academic, and dating successes, also insisted that their priorities had undergone an eternal change.[31]

They Seek to Infiltrate the Classrooms

Crusade succeeded on the campus because dedicated and charismatic workers brought an attractive and compelling message to a receptive audience. If Crusade were to attain its goal of reaching all American campuses with its message, however, it needed to excel at reaching not only students but also financial supporters. Bright's early fund-raising appeals relied upon two basic messages: the spectacle of students becoming evangelical Christians and the specter of communism on the campus. His message appealed to evangelicals who worried about what would happen to their children on secular campuses: "[T]oday thousands of students from Christian homes and churches are losing their faith in the Gospel of the Lord Jesus Christ and the Word of God because of the ridicule and antagonism which abounds on the majority of campuses." Bright claimed that most students had not heard the Christian gospel and responded in droves when they finally did. Trumpeting such results, he told potential donors that there "is no place where the investment of your prayers and money will pay such great dividends."[32]

Bright did not, however, limit his fund-raising appeal to highlighting evangelistic successes. In a 1953 issue of the *Campus Crusade Communique*—near the height of McCarthy-era hysteria in the United States—Bright outlined a dire scenario within American higher education. He warned of communist professors "advocating the violent overthrow of the American government." Noting the rapid growth of communism since 1917, Bright predicted that at "the present rate the world could become communistic almost overnight." He believed that communists—following the same line of reasoning as his own organization—shrewdly targeted college students, "the coming leaders of the nation." Moreover, he argued that those college students would be easy pickings for communist infiltration because "God has been booted out of the very system of higher education which was established to bring light to the world." Bright envisioned a monolithic communist movement ready to pounce on this spiritual vacuum: "*Communism knows this, and there they fight the battle for the mind of youth*" (emphasis in original). Campus Crusade intended to bring the "message of a living Christ and vital faith" to the campus as a means of inoculating the rising generation of college leaders against the allure of communism. "Either students will serve the true God," predicted Bright two years later, "or they will follow materialism and communism." If anything, Bright's anticommunist rhetoric intensified as the 1950s progressed. "Here in America . . . ," Bright reminded the readers of the conservative *American Mercury* in 1956, "we have suffered reverses to the Communists on the battleground of higher education." Bright lamented that the Supreme Court had ruled "that a teacher could not be discharged for hiding behind the Fifth Amendment" and criticized the "powerful Association of University Professors" for "holding that even actual membership in the Communist Party is not a valid reason for discharging a teacher." Roe Brooks, on Crusade staff since 1952, believes that Bright used anticommunist rhetoric to interpret Crusade's success to potential donors. "It gets supporters, it gets attention," Brooks comments. "You can begin to build a national board, and you can begin to get the type of church support you need as a Christian movement." Bright perceived that donors would more readily lend their financial backing to an effort that was both a crusade for Christ and a crusade against godless communism.[33]

Bright's anticommunism represented mainstream evangelical belief and rhetoric in the early 1950s, as vigorous anticommunism was by no means confined to extremists like Gerald B. Winrod, William Dudley Pelley, and Billy James Hargis. Harold J. Ockenga, minister at Boston's Park Street Congregational Church and president in absentia of Fuller Seminary, commented on a espionage case involving a Justice Department employee in 1949: "When situations such as have developed recently in the Judith Coplon [espionage] case reveal the intrigue and unusual anti-God feeling so prevalent around our country, it's time for a revival." In 1951, Billy Graham urged American Christians to remain vigilant against "over 1,100 social-sounding organizations that are communist or communist-operated in this country." Three years later, Graham wrote of the "mysterious pull of this satanic religion": "It has attracted some of our famous entertainers, some of our finest politicians, and some of our outstanding educators." Graham's hope was that evangelical faith would provide America with the resolve to challenge its internal and external enemies. "Only as millions of Americans turn to Jesus Christ at this hour and accept him as Savior," Graham pronounced, "can this nation possibly be spared the onslaught of demon-possessed communism." Like Ockenga and Graham, many evangelicals used evidence of alleged communist gains as added motivation for revival.[34]

By the time Bright founded Campus Crusade, there was very little communism to speak of in the United States, and what little there was had scant appeal to most college students, whether Christian or not. At a few universities immediately following the war, far-left student groups such as the John Reed Club or the Communist Club attracted a handful of students, but such groups dwindled away rapidly in light of the growing tensions between the United States and the Soviet Union, the collapse of the Communist Party, USA, and the anticommunism that pervaded American society during the early years of the Cold War. Despite the lack of an actual communist threat on the campus, Bright—like most evangelicals—interpreted the Cold War as an essentially spiritual conflict, and he viewed Crusade's evangelistic campaigns as a critical offensive in that Manichaean struggle.[35]

Campus Crusade's early expansion paralleled the apex of the postwar religious boom in the United States. In the early 1950s, Americans added "under God" to the Pledge of Allegiance, followed their friends to Billy Graham revivals, and flocked to watch religious epics in movie theaters. Many contemporary observers and historians have described this revival of religion as superficial, transitory, and banal. Americans, J. Ronald Oakley maintains, viewed God as a buddy, "the man upstairs," or, in the words of actress Jane Russell, "a livin' doll." Oakley, echoing a contemporary observation made by Will Herberg among others, concludes that many suburban Americans joined churches "seeking not only God and salvation but identity, companionship, and reassurance." Herberg observed that Protestants, Catholics, and Jews blended together religion and nationalism into a package that effaced religious particulars and appealed to the masses. Although church attendance and public displays of religiosity soared, surveys revealed that Americans knew very little about the faiths to which they ostensibly adhered. Furthermore, many historians have pointed to the anticommunist and militaristic rhetoric of Billy Graham as an indication that postwar revivalism merely rode the wave of Cold War hysteria and American triumphalism. Similarly, Martin Marty argued in 1958 that the postwar "revival of interest in religion" "lack[ed] depth" and was the first to go "not against the grain of the nation but with it." The proliferation of biblically based movies, the frequency of Christian songs on hit radio stations, and the popularity of Norman Vincent Peale and Fulton J. Sheen all faded as the 1950s drew to a close, leading observers to conclude that the religious revival had produced only ephemeral excitement and little of enduring significance.[36]

In some ways, the early history of Campus Crusade for Christ brings to mind such criticisms of the postwar religious boom. Students involved with Crusade offered some banal expressions of religiosity. Crusaders referred to Jesus Christ as their "best friend," their "quarterback," or their "Head Coach." Bob Davenport, an All-American fullback at UCLA involved with Crusade, termed Jesus Christ "the greatest Coach and Quarterback ever." "I'm playing on God's varsity now," commented Moomaw upon his decision to enter the ministry. Students ascribed better grades, friendships, and athletic success to their relationship with Jesus. Furthermore, Crusade staff sometimes recorded "decisions" from students who never expressed any subsequent interest in Jesus. Finally, Campus Crusade, like Billy Graham and other evangelicals, used rhetoric designed to appeal to Cold War anxieties. Thus, in several significant ways Crusade seemed to follow the "grain of the nation" in the 1950s.[37]

Yet the early success of Campus Crusade also represents much more than a temporary religious response to geopolitical fears and a revival of superficial "interest in religion." Rather than encouraging students to explore a vague religiosity, Crusade invited students to make a commitment to Jesus Christ and to join a local "Bible-believing" church. If there was some methodological overlap with the therapeutic ethos of popular religious self-help books, evangelicalism in this era was more than a dose of self-esteem and positive thinking. Crusade staff certainly did not prescribe a superficial religious life for their converts. Many of the above banalities represent not the entirety of Crusade's beliefs but rather a simple "hook" to get the attention of potential converts and gain a hearing for a more substantive presentation. Crusade was mostly uncritical of campus culture, but the organization placed other demands on those converts with whom it established enduring relationships. Crusade staff urged new converts to participate in evangelistic efforts as soon as possible, incorporated them into Bible studies, and urged them to memorize caches of Scripture verses. Bright expected his staff recruits to tirelessly practice evangelism in return for $150 per month.

Moreover, despite the revival of religion and the renewed public success of evangelicalism in the 1950s, Crusade did not understand itself as operating "with the grain of the nation." Instead, Bright and his organization viewed American Christianity as under siege. "History confirms America as a Christian nation!" trumpeted an editorial that Crusade paid to have run in UCLA's *Daily Bruin*. The editorial insisted that "religious freedom does not mean we ought to repudiate the Christian faith which gave birth to America!" Crusade complained that "whenever the historic Christian faith is talked about or promoted publicly there are those who set up the hue and cry of intolerance." After several students wrote letters of complaint to the *Daily Bruin*, the newspaper declined to run further paid religious editorials or testimonies. Upset at the *Bruin*'s decision, Bright complained to the UCLA administration that the newspaper allowed the publication of "anti-God" material and unfairly singled out Campus Crusade. The administration responded that because paid advertisements should not contain lengthy editorializing, the paper had erred in accepting the editorial and an earlier series of published testimonies by athletes involved with Crusade. Both the editorial and Bright's complaint imply that Bright wanted more than an opportunity to operate at the margins of the university. They also suggest an agenda beyond the simple attempt to introduce college students to "life with a purpose." Bright felt evangelical Christianity—both on the campus and in American society more broadly—deserved more than a place within a pluralistic framework. He, like many evangelicals, felt that Christianity deserved recognition as central to America's founding and necessary for the nation's continued freedom. Bright's rhetoric suggests that evangelicals in the 1950s still saw themselves as a beleaguered minority but remained determined to recover their custodial leadership of American society.[38]

The renewal of evangelicalism in the late 1940s and 1950s was both part of and yet far more than the transient fashionableness of religion. Alongside the more general religious boom of the era, this renewal laid the foundation for long-term evangelical growth and vitality. Evangelicals founded and supported a host of parachurch organizations—from the Billy Graham

Evangelistic Association to World Vision to Campus Crusade for Christ—that carved out enduring places on the American religious landscape. Once Stuart Hamblen was off the music charts and Billy Graham's crusades generated less frequent headlines, evangelical organizations were still growing and expanding their ministries.

3

Sibling Rivalries

At the 1943 convention of the National Association of Evangelicals, Harold Ockenga asserted that "the United States of America has been assigned a destiny comparable to that of ancient Israel." Evangelicals recognized that in order to fulfill that destiny, they needed to reassert their position of leadership in American society. "It is not boasting," William Ward Ayer had maintained at the NAE's 1942 organizing meeting, "to declare that evangelical Christianity has the America of our fathers to save." The founders of the NAE believed Bible-believing Christians could not "save" America unless they put aside theological and ecclesiastical infighting and united behind the cause of evangelism. By the 1950s, Billy Graham had achieved international fame, evangelistic success, and invitations to the White House. Moreover, evangelicals had founded a host of thriving parachurch organizations, including Youth for Christ, World Vision, and Campus Crusade for Christ. "The future . . . ," predicted Baptist theologian Vernon Grounds in 1956, "is bright for the evangelical cause if somehow it can counteract its fissiparous tendencies." In part because of those self-destructive tendencies, however, evangelicals did not achieve significant cultural or political influence until the mid-1970s. During the 1950s and early 1960s, Campus Crusade confronted several intra-evangelical fissures, including parachurch competition on the campus, the clash between fundamentalists and evangelicals, and the uneasy relationship of evangelicals with Pentecostal and charismatic Christians. Bill Bright's navigation of those controversies sheds light on the bitter divisions among conservative Protestants in America and also illuminates Crusade's early theology, methodology, and spirituality.[1]

Open Competitors

Campus Crusade's early years were successful enough that other university ministries, most notably Inter-Varsity Christian Fellowship (IVCF), observed Crusade's rapid growth with great interest. IVCF had expanded from its roots in Great Britain to Canada and the United States in the late 1920s and 1930s, as the precipitous decline of both the YMCA and the Student Volunteer Movement created an opening for a new evangelical campus ministry. IVCF reasserted evangelical verities, including the inspiration of Scripture, the deity of Christ, and his vicarious sacrifice. Given the movement's British background, however, IVCF was further removed than Crusade from the subculture of American fundamentalism and more interested in helping students approach Christianity from intellectual and academic perspectives. IVCF grew quickly during the 1940s and established chapters on many large American universities in the West, Midwest, and Northeast. Under the leadership of C. Stacey Woods, IVCF balanced a variety of objectives: evangelism, discipleship, apologetics, and leadership training. Evangelism and missions, however, were paramount among IVCF's early priorities. The organization declared the academic year 1950–51 "The Year of Evangelism" and brought evangelistic speakers—including Billy Graham—to campuses across the country. In 1951, Inter-Varsity attracted sixteen hundred collegians to its triennial foreign missions conference at the University of Illinois–Urbana.[2]

Since Inter-Varsity was active at both UCLA and USC, the established IVCF chapters took careful note of Crusade's well-publicized results. According to Bright's later recollection, some IVCF students "joined us on evangelistic team meetings in local fraternities, sororities, and dormitories, with the thought that they would make contacts and bring into their fellowship the students who responded to the gospel and help follow them up." Bright in turn was impressed by an evangelistic campaign that IVCF organized at USC, which included lectures as well as meetings in fraternity houses. However, a "terrific clash" occurred between Bright and Mel Friesen, the IVCF staff member at USC. Many years later, Bright wrote that "the students associated with Inter-Varsity were soon asked by their local director not to be involved with us" because he "felt that we were competitive." Moreover, he explained that this lack of cooperation "forced us into a totally different posture" and caused Crusade to begin its own "follow-up work." The clash between Friesen and Bright set the tone for subsequent interactions.[3]

In the spring of 1951, Stacey Woods and Bright tried to establish a more positive relationship. After Bright visited Woods's home in Geneva, Illinois, Woods reported that he found Bright a "smooth operator" but a "charming person." Furthermore, he optimistically suggested that "the difficulty between Mel [Friesen] and Bill Bright is not necessarily . . . a national difficulty or a difficulty that will apply to all Inter-Varsity staff, but may have something to do with Mel himself." Woods predicted that Bright "will make a big impression across the United States." Evidently both Bright and Woods believed IVCF and Crusade could collaborate, with Crusade spearheading evangelistic missions and IVCF incorporating converts into local chapters. "He suggested," wrote Woods, "that on quite a number of the campuses he believed that IVCF would be able to take care of this follow-up program and there would be no need for them to do anything of a permanent nature."

Despite these overtures, tensions mounted between the two evangelical campus ministries as Crusade expanded nationally. Crusade staff member Gordon Klenck remembers an encounter in which Woods encouraged him to cease Crusade work at the University of California at Berkeley. Bob Kendall recalls the IVCF faculty adviser at Michigan State informing him that he "had no business coming in there," complaining that he had not "checked with them first." These local encounters mirrored a budding conflict between Bright and Woods. "We do not have one instance," Woods complained in 1953, "where he [Bright] has ever kept to any agreement that he had either with Mel Friesen or with me." In particular, Woods asserted that Crusade "seemed very often to go to our students and try to win them away to his operation from Inter-Varsity." Furthermore, Woods claimed that Bright had agreed to keep Woods abreast of his expansion plans and to explore circumstances in which IVCF students could participate in Crusade's evangelistic teams. Woods also took umbrage when Bright talked of sending Crusade staff to "unreached campuses," some of which had established IVCF chapters. In Woods's opinion, Bright's stated willingness to cooperate "was nothing more than hot air." "He had no intention . . . of so doing," Woods concluded, "although one must refrain from judging motives." IVCF also criticized Crusade's methodology. In a 1958 IVCF manual, Charles Hummel insisted that an IVCF student leader "must not be a recent convert" and lamented that "how often today a Christian group chooses its leader primarily because of personality, prowess as an athlete, popularity, effectiveness in public speaking or genius for organization." As opposed to Crusade's willingness to send its staff on evangelistic blitzkriegs, Woods warned against "a sudden, brief evangelistic campaign for a month or two." IVCF's complaints and criticisms irritated Bright. IVCF regional director James Nyquist reported in 1960 that Bright "thought Stacey [Woods] was dishonest and critical of CCC and that he never had been [critical] of IVCF."[4]

Despite occasional attempts at reconciliation, the relationship between Crusade and Inter-Varsity remained stony into the 1960s. When Charles Troutman succeeded Woods as IVCF's national secretary in 1961, he sent a conciliatory letter to Bright: "I am anxious to do everything I can that our energies may be directed toward the enemy and not against one another." "Screwtape [C. S. Lewis's personification of the devil] must be delighted," he allowed, "at the way we pull strips off one another." Bright responded in kind. In a 1961 form letter to Crusade staff and supporters, Bright called IVCF "obviously a work of God" and emphasized that "there is no other honest attitude a Christian can take but to thank God for Inter-Varsity." He did, however, insist upon Crusade's right to expand to campuses with IVCF chapters and delineated some differences between the two organizations. "I.V.C.F.," Bright asserted, "is primarily a Christian fellowship with an evangelistic program," whereas "Campus Crusade for Christ is a Crusade, with a strong follow-up program." Such statements rankled IVCF because of the implication that IVCF was less than fully committed to evangelism. Nevertheless, better relations briefly seemed possible. Paul Little, a top IVCF official, attended a Crusade staff training conference in 1961, and Bright planned to participate in IVCF's triennial missions conference. Troutman, however, soon abandoned efforts at intra-evangelical détente. In 1962, he referred to Crusade as "an open competitor of Inter-Varsity in that they seek to establish another group on campus and generally begin their work through IVCF students." Troutman, who asserted that Crusade "represent[s] the attitude expressed in this country by the ultra-right-wing fundamentalist," alleged that Crusade staff workers "gain enthusiasm by distorted and inflated stories of campus activity." John Alexander, who succeeded Troutman as IVCF's president in 1965, concluded in an internal memorandum that it "is impossible for CCC and IVCF to cooperate on campus" and observed that whenever "CCC opens a work on a campus, attendance at IVCF functions drops."[5]

Ultimately, poor relations persisted between Crusade and Inter-Varsity because the two groups competed in the same religious marketplace. According to Troutman, denominational ministries perceived IVCF as a competitor when IVCF began expanding its work in the 1940s. Ironically, IVCF reacted similarly to Crusade's advent. Although only a small percentage of students became active in either IVCF or Crusade and the two organizations often targeted different groups of students, IVCF as the established group sensed a competitive threat. During the years when, according to IVCF long-term staff member and historian Keith Hunt, "fraternity and sorority life reached its heyday" on the campus, Crusade intelligently targeted the Greek system and athletic teams, and Crusade's reports of evangelistic success impressed supporters and helped Crusade recruit additional staff. Although IVCF also grew during the 1950s and achieved considerable success with its triennial foreign mission conventions in Urbana, Illinois, Stacey Woods's correspondence reveals an abiding concern that Crusade's publicity would reflect poorly on IVCF and thus hurt both student membership and financial support. Just as companies selling similar products to the same market view each other as rivals, Crusade and IVCF developed a relationship marred by rancor, suspicion, and jealousy.[6]

Campus Crusade's growth also sparked concern from mainline Protestant campus ministers, who sometimes communicated with each other about how to respond to the new ministry's presence. Jim Shields, the director of the Methodist Wesley Foundation at the University of Oklahoma, wrote an inquiring colleague that Crusade exhibited a "kind of 'self-righteousness' which considers everyone who has not had 'their kind of religious experience' to be 'unconverted.'" Many mainline campus ministers complained that Crusade did not work cooperatively with their organizations. At the University of Miami (Fla.), the directors of four Protestant ministries objected that Crusade recruited members of other religious groups and violated student privacy by witnessing in dormitories. Their report concluded that the "churches of this campus do not desire the services of Campus Crusade for Christ and feel that the university has the right and the responsibility to regulate the entrance of religious clubs to the campus." Crusade staff recall substantial animosity from Protestant campus ministers. "They were all very liberal," says Jim Craddock of the denominational ministries at the University of Oklahoma, "[and] very much opposed to Campus Crusade." Jan Lindsey encountered stiff opposition at Southern Methodist University. "I had to go and speak before a faculty committee to explain why I felt Campus Crusade was needed on the campus," recollects Lindsey, who remembers the hostile presence of "the school chaplain" and "several other bigwigs" at the meeting. Mainline ministries lobbied the administrations of several universities to block Crusade's access to campus.

In 1961, Bright reported that "[o]rganized opposition by Religious groups which deny the basic doctrines of the Christian faith is becoming more frequent."[7]

As Bright's comment suggests, substantive disagreements lay beneath the competition between Crusade and mainline Protestant ministries. Mainline campus groups varied widely in terms of their theology and approach to campus ministry, but on average, mainline Protestant campus ministers were far more theologically and socially liberal than the typical Campus Crusade staff worker. A 1963 survey found that only 8 percent of denominational campus ministers considered the Bible "an infallible revelation of God's will," and a majority believed their own denominations were too socially conservative. Jim Shields observed that Crusade's approach to biblical study "is pretty far off from what most 'main-stream' protestant groups hold to in biblical interpretation," and numerous mainline campus ministers criticized Crusade's lack of emphasis on social action. Similarly, the Presbyterian Synod of Arkansas issued a 1966 report describing the theological inadequacy of Crusade's methodology. "'Evangelization,' 'witness' and 'mission' are no longer adequate words," the report maintained, "for they suggest a Christian behavior of speaking before listening, of calling people away from their natural communities into a Christian grouping, and of a preoccupation with the soul at the expense of the whole of life." By contrast, evangelization, witness, and mission comprised Crusade's core principles.[8]

Both Crusade and IVCF represented the intrusion of a very different religiosity into a campus religious marketplace previously dominated by mainline denominational ministries. By the early 1960s, four evangelical parachurch organizations were active on many large campuses. The Navigators, originally a ministry to sailors, increasingly sent its staff members to campuses at which they primarily engaged in one-on-one discipleship with Christian students. The Fellowship of Christian Athletes (FCA), a campus organization founded in 1954 by Don McClanen with the assistance of Donn Moomaw and Louis Evans Sr., began witnessing to and forming Bible studies among college athletes. The unregulated world of parachurch evangelicalism spawned competition, between evangelical and mainline ministries, between IVCF and Crusade, and later between FCA and Crusade's own Athletes in Action ministry. At the same time, that sometimes rancorous competition caused evangelical ministries to fill different niches, and the combined efforts of Campus Crusade, IVCF, the Navigators, and FCA reintroduced an aggressive evangelical presence onto many American campuses.

The Divorce of Evangelicalism from Fundamentalism

Bright constantly sought to expand Campus Crusade's staff, impatiently striving throughout the 1950s to reach an initial goal of "100 consecrated young men." "We are asking God," Bright wrote Bob Jones Jr. in March 1953, "to increase our full-time number from 13 to 100 workers for next fall." "We have an urgent need," Bright wrote Jones four years later, "for at least additional fifty workers to join our staff." Bright frequently mentioned such concerns to officials at Bob Jones University because the school had become a reliable supplier of new staff for Campus Crusade. Bright made annual trips to the school, spoke on the BJU campus, met with students, and cultivated relationships with Bob Jones Sr., Bob Jones Jr., and Gilbert Stenholm, BJU's director of extension and later dean of BJU's School of Religion. Stenholm reported that twenty-six Crusade staff were BJU graduates as of 1957, and the majority of Crusade's area directors (who supervised geographical divisions of the campus ministry) had attended the fundamentalist school. "There is a place in Campus Crusade," wrote Bright to Bob Jones Sr., "for anyone from Bob Jones University who has your endorsement." For his part, Bright encouraged students planning on becoming ministers or full-time Christian workers to attend BJU, as he wrote Bob Jones Jr. in 1953: "I am thoroughly sold on B.J.U. and your wholesome Christ centered evangelistic emphasis."9

Until he developed Crusade's relationship with BJU, Bright—through Hollywood Presbyterian and Fuller Seminary—had mostly operated in the circles of what was becoming known as evangelicalism. By forming close ties with BJU, however, Bright introduced a dose of separatist fundamentalism into his young organization. Even so, until the mid-1950s conservative Protestants did not have to choose between fundamentalism and evangelicalism, especially since the latter term in particular remained only vaguely defined. Bob Jones Sr. had initially supported the NAE, calling on "orthodox Christians . . . [to] magnify the things about which they agree as much as they emphasize the things about which they disagree." The Joneses, though, became disenchanted when a rising generation of scholars associated with the NAE struck a more moderate theological tone—

Billy Graham receiving an honorary degree from Bob Jones Jr. at Bob Jones University, 1948.
Courtesy of the Billy Graham Center Archives, Wheaton, Ill.

particularly on the issue of biblical inerrancy—and when the NAE's leadership began emphasizing social action and education alongside evangelism. Also bristling at a series of perceived personal slights from the NAE, the Joneses severed their ties with the NAE in 1950.[10]

Despite the Joneses' withdrawal from the NAE, the unifying success of Billy Graham's crusades helped the conservative and moderate wings of fundamentalism maintain an uneasy peace. From the start, Carl McIntire of the American Council of Christian Churches was deeply suspicious of Graham because of his association with the NAE. Yet other fundamentalists, including Bob Jones Sr. and John R. Rice, editor of the popular weekly *Sword of the Lord*, were impressed with the results of Graham's evangelism. Moreover, Graham had briefly attended Bob Jones College in 1936 and later asked Bob Jones Sr. to think of him as "one of his boys." As McIntire hammered away at Graham, Jones and Rice publicly defended the young evangelist. However, as Graham evidenced a growing theological irenicism and associated with religious leaders outside the fundamentalist camp, Rice and Jones began to reconsider their support. Like the founders of the NAE, Graham was a self-avowed fundamentalist in the 1940s, but he explicitly distanced himself from that heritage in 1955 by telling a Scottish audience that he was "neither a fundamentalist nor a liberal." Graham also evidenced a growing willingness to cooperate with mainline Protestant ministers whom Rice and Jones considered theologically liberal. While such steps won Graham growing acceptance from many mainline church leaders eager for religious revival and higher church attendance, his evolution deeply distressed Jones. BJU's founder, nevertheless, continued to publicly endorse Graham.[11]

The issue that sundered the relationship between Graham and Jones was the sponsorship of Graham's crusades. Separatist fundamentalists believed that "orthodox" Christians could not and should not actively cooperate with "modernists" and "liberals" in spiritual or ecclesiastical matters. Graham himself had once espoused this position. In 1948, while president of Northwestern Schools in Minneapolis, Graham asserted that "[w]e do not condone nor have fellowship with any form of modernism." For several years after his 1949 Los Angeles campaign, Graham pledged to not have modernists sit on the platform with him and to not knowingly obtain sponsorship from groups that included modernists in their ranks. "We have never had a man on our committee," Graham wrote Jones Sr. in 1952, "that denied the virgin birth, the vicarious atonement, or the bodily resurrection." Then in 1957, Graham went to New York City under the sponsorship of the Protestant Council of the City of New York, a local affiliate of the National Council of Churches. To fundamentalists, the NCC symbolized ecumenism and apostasy. Jones and Rice were horrified at the possible outcome of the planned New York meetings. "They [the New York Council] invited Dr. Graham," warned John R. Rice. "They will get most of the results." Jones insisted that regardless of whether "cooperative sponsorship" would increase evangelistic success, it was a biblically forbidden method. "[I]t is not right to do wrong," he proclaimed regularly at BJU chapel services, "to get a chance to do right." When Graham accepted the Protestant Council's sponsorship of his New York crusade, Jones and Rice publicly broke with Graham, who showed no sign of reversing his new stance. "I intend," he proclaimed at the 1957 NAE convention, "to go anywhere, sponsored by anybody, to preach the Gospel of Christ." Jones and Rice responded with harsh, detailed critiques of Graham in Rice's *Sword of the Lord*.[12]

The wisdom of Graham's decision aside, the aging fundamentalists trenchantly identified a significant shift in policy. Moreover, they perceived Graham's evolution as a personal affront. In the writings of the two Joneses and other fundamentalists, it is easy to perceive their deep emotional hurt that mainline churches and ecumenical leaders were basking in the glow of Graham's revivals while the Graham organization ignored loyal "orthodox" supporters. Bob Jones Jr. complained to the Billy Graham organization that Graham's sponsorship was "unfair to the brethren who have stood for the Gospel and endured the attack of these . . . liberals and modernists." The rhetoric used by both sides quickly became vitriolic. "'Ichabod,'" wrote J. Elwin Wright, one of the chief architects of the NAE, to Jones Sr., "will most certainly be written over your doors unless you repent and confess your sin." "I do seriously think," Jones Jr. wrote to G. Archer Weniger, a BJU alumnus and San Francisco pastor, "he [Graham] may be the fore-runner— the John the Baptist of the anti-Christ, as he is the Judas of the brethren." With the split irrevocable, a conservative Protestant ground war ensued, as backers of Jones and Graham sought to rally support for their respective positions. Jones insisted on what came to be known as "double separation"—"orthodox" Christians, in his view, should separate themselves not only from modernists and liberals but from those who cooperated with modernists and liberals. If movements or individuals wanted the support of Jones after 1957, they had to take a firm stand against Graham and "cooperative evangelism." While Graham never insisted that his supporters denounce or distance themselves from BJU, his organization also worked hard to secure endorsements from conservative evangelicals.[13]

In this context, Bill Bright would eventually have to make a difficult decision, as both Graham and Jones Jr. served on Campus Crusade's advisory board. At first, it seemed Bright would position Crusade with BJU. In early 1957, Bright enjoyed another "pleasant and profitable" trip to BJU, only a few months before the start of Graham's New York crusade. There is no record of his discussions with BJU officials, but it is clear from the resulting correspondence that they insisted he clarify Crusade's doctrinal positions and methodology. Roe Brooks, who joined Crusade's staff in 1953, asked Bright at the time whether Crusade had a statement of faith. Brooks recalls that Bright informed him that "the Westminster Confession of Faith is basically our statement of faith." BJU evidently expected something more recent. When Bright returned to California in March 1957, he sent Jones Sr. a copy of a new statement of faith, which avowed Crusade's confidence "in the plenary inspiration of the Old and New Testaments, holding them to be the very Word of God." The creed also affirmed "the Virgin Birth and Deity of our Lord Jesus Christ, His substitutionary atonement for sin, His bodily resurrection and His personal visible return to earth." While Jones would have insisted on such fundamentals, he was probably most interested in Bright's intention to channel student converts into "those churches who are true to the orthodox Christian faith, who subscribe to the statement of faith in general as outlined above." Bright promised to ask his executive board to add the statement to Crusade's Articles of Incorporation. Bright sent Jones an approved, slightly revised statement later in 1957 and informed him that every "member of our staff is required to sign this creed each year." Furthermore, Bright continued to express his solidarity with BJU. Bright assured Gilbert Stenholm that "our message is the Gospel as revealed in the New Testament and taught at Bob Jones University."[14]

Jones Sr. clearly felt that Bright was on his side and worked to ensure his loyalty. "Bill," Jones explained in a March 1957 letter, "the line is being drawn now. . . . You are on record, and other organizations are getting on record." Jones promoted Campus Crusade to his network of fundamentalist friends. He encouraged John R. Rice to "give him a little boost" in the *Sword of the Lord*, praising Crusade as "a real, honest-to-goodness orthodox movement . . . not one of those wit-matching movements of the neo-orthodox crowd." "He [Bright] also tells all of his converts," Jones informed Rice, "to go into an orthodox, Bible-believing church and tries to help them make such a contact." "I rejoice in your uncompromising stand," Jones complimented Bright. He was somewhat puzzled about Bright's Presbyterian Church membership but "trust[ed] the Lord will guide you about your personal church affiliation." "There is so much compromise in this day and time," Jones lamented. "If there is anything we can do to co-operate with you, we will be glad to do it." He was eager to cultivate new allies after his break with Graham. "Billy Graham's campaigns," Gilbert Stenholm wrote Bright in May 1958, "are doing tremendous harm to the cause of evangelism." "We have to stick together and fight this battle," he encouraged Bright.[15]

When Stenholm wrote those words, Graham had already begun a two-month crusade at San Francisco's Cow Palace. Unlike the New York crusade, the local ecumenical councils of churches (in San Francisco and Oakland) did not officially sponsor the campaign, although they both endorsed it. Graham's support was broad, and a number of Bay Area fundamentalist pastors, including Archer Weniger, criticized Graham's ecumenical backing. Jerry Riffe, director of Campus Crusade's ministry at Berkeley, refused to support Graham's meetings. Following a "decision for Christ" at UCLA, Riffe had with Bright's encouragement studied for the ministry at BJU. In response to Riffe's stance against Graham, the Berkeley Campus Crusade committee—made up of businessmen and pastors who supported the local ministry—resigned en masse. Bright traveled to San Francisco to meet with Riffe, and he initially expressed agreement with Riffe's stand.

Bright, however, also found himself courted by Graham's organization. Shortly after Graham began his San Francisco crusade, Vonette and Bill Bright heard Graham deliver a "stirring challenge" at the renowned Ambassador Hotel in Hollywood. "We rejoice," Bill Bright wrote to Graham's father-in-law L. Nelson Bell, "to hear of the souls that are being won to Christ in the San Francisco Campaign." Shortly thereafter, Graham invited Bright to San Francisco. At stake, according to Bright, were "hundreds of friends and thousands of dollars." According to Dorothy Hauser, Crusade's office manager and a BJU alumna, some of Bright's most important financial supporters and members of his board urged him to support Graham. Beyond such pragmatic concerns, Bright had long admired Graham and, along with others at Hollywood Presbyterian, had supported his earlier Los Angeles crusades.[16]

Bright made the trip to San Francisco, where he observed Graham's Cow Palace meetings and admired Graham's preaching and the response it generated. Graham invited the Brights to sit on the platform with him. They hesitated. Bill decided to accept the invitation, but Vonette, still unsure about whether Graham or Jones was correct, sat in the crowd instead. Jones Sr., whom Weniger and Riffe kept well informed of events in San Francisco, quickly got wind of Bright's action and wrote him demanding an explanation. Bright answered by insisting that his "stand against liberalism and modernism in all their varied forms has not been altered one iota." He reaffirmed his opposition to ecumenical sponsorship but noted that the "sponsorship of Billy Graham by the Council of Churches in New York City to which so many of us have objected so strenuously does not exist in San Francisco." Bright maintained that "Billy's position has been changed since his New York campaign." Jones, of course, took issue with Bright's statement, which ultimately was not an accurate interpretation of Graham's trajectory. Furthermore, he saw it as a personal betrayal. "Bill," he lamented, "your letter has made me sick at heart." "You are the last man on earth," he explained, "that I would have thought would have betrayed the cause and betrayed Bob Jones University in this battle as you seem to have done." He threatened to write all of the BJU alumni on Crusade staff "and tell them how I feel about this situation." He insisted that Bright clarify his position and informed Bright that he had to choose between BJU and Billy Graham. "There are no two sides to this proposition," Jones threw down the gauntlet. "You have to be either on one side or the other, and you have taken the Billy Graham sponsorship side."[17]

In response, Bright exhibited elements of both fundamentalism and the

"new evangelicalism." "For several years," he began, "I have had a growing conviction of the evils of any theological position which denied the
fundamentals of our Faith in the Lord Jesus Christ and His inspired Word."
Bright insisted that he would oppose any Graham campaign sponsored by
a liberal-controlled Council of Churches but insisted again that Graham
had operated without ecumenical sponsorship in San Francisco. Bright explained that he had spent "several hours with members of the Billy Graham
team" and was "personally satisfied that the Lord is leading Billy back to his
original position of refusing the sponsorship of any group, be it the Council of Churches, or any other which denies the basic fundamentals of the
Christian faith." However, he expressed reluctance "to try to categorize"
Graham supporters "into various theological camps." Bright maintained
that he could endorse and support both Billy Graham and BJU: "I do not
believe it is necessary to be against you just because I have come to the
above conclusion, anymore than that I should be against Billy because of
my fondness for you and the school."[18]

Jones, of course, would not let Bright off the hook. "Bob Jones University and you had a deal," he wrote. "We entered into an agreement. You
stated your position. We boosted you to the sky." "I have never been as disappointed in a man in my life as I am in you," he concluded. Bright bristled
under such attacks. In particular, he rejected the accusation of betrayal:
"To what agreement do you refer? And what do you mean by betrayal?"
He insisted that his "position is based on definite facts and not a result of
soft-soaping palaver." Bright sought an appointment with Jones Jr. during
the latter's July trip to a BJU alumni event in Los Angeles. Jones Jr. decided
he was "too heartsick and disappointed" to meet with Bright, though he
discussed the matter with Vonette Bright and Dorothy Hauser. Vonette
Bright reminded Jones Jr. of Campus Crusade's vigorous support of BJU
and insisted that a "wait-and-see policy" would form the best approach to
the issue of Graham's sponsorship. Neither Jones Jr. nor his father, however,
would reconcile with Bill Bright unless he confessed error and repudiated
Billy Graham's sponsorship. Bright remained unwilling to do so.[19]

The dispute simmered over the summer. In August, Bob Jones Sr. wrote
all of the BJU graduates and students working with Crusade. Most received the letters while attending Crusade's staff training event on Lake
Minnetonka in Mound, Minnesota, where the organization had recently
moved its summer headquarters. Jones reminded them that "we did not
boost Campus Crusade until we had the assurance that Campus Crusade
stood exactly where Bob Jones University stands." He went on to "apolo-

gize for recommending that you become a part of the work of Campus Crusade" and insisted that "you cannot consistently go on with Campus Crusade until the head of Campus Crusade openly reverses the position which he has recently taken." BJU alumnae recall receiving threats that if they remained on Crusade staff their alma mater would cut them off from the university and not recommend them for pastorates. Jones warned Dave Coterill, a BJU student at the training event, "if you are planning to go ahead with Campus Crusade. . . . Do not come back to school, because we are not going to have any of that propaganda on Bob Jones University campus." "So you have lined up with the other side," Jones wrote Dorothy Hauser, "and by so doing *you have severed your relations* with the university I founded" (emphasis in original). Two weeks later, Jones alleged that Bright had called him a "liar and a blackmailer" at the Mound conference and threatened to sue him for slander. Jones Jr. demanded that Crusade immediately remove his name from its organizational letterhead.[20]

The conflict caused a deep rift within the young organization. According to Bill Greig of the Midwest Keswick Conference, which had sold Crusade the Lake Minnetonka property, with the arrival of the letters "a pall . . . fell over the [staff training] conference." It was an agonizing time for the organization's seventy staff members, particularly the BJU alumnae. The recent graduates in particular had heard Bob Jones Sr. regularly speak against Graham's "cooperative evangelism" in chapel addresses. "It was like being indoctrinated daily for years as a student there," recalls Lee Etta Dickerson, "and then suddenly being called a traitor, a compromiser." The emotions aroused by split loyalties were "destroying a family feeling that had been there since the inception," comments Coterill, who along with Riffe packed his bags and left during the conference. Stenholm later reported that fourteen BJU alumnae resigned from Campus Crusade. Other BJU graduates believed that the evangelistic fruit they were witnessing on the campus confirmed that God had called them to work with Campus Crusade. Moreover, although they remained appreciative of the training they had received at Bob Jones, they had become acquainted with a wider Christian world that pushed them beyond their fundamentalist schooling. Whereas BJU students shunned lipstick, movies, and fine clothes, those who joined Campus Crusade met Hollywood Christians who were much more comfortable with such manifestations of mainstream culture. "As each year rolled by," explains Ray Nethery, "I began to realize that God's a lot bigger and a lot more diverse than I had originally conceived of in terms of my background." Those who remained with Crusade did so at substantial personal cost—the decision cut them off from BJU and soured if not destroyed many personal friendships. "It was kind of like the kids in a family going through a divorce," reflects Dickerson.[21]

The conflict over Billy Graham and "cooperative evangelism" finalized the division of conservative, non-Pentecostal Protestantism into a larger "evangelical" wing and a smaller "fundamentalist" bloc. The fundamentalist bloc, however, remained consequential—with the addition of figures such as Jones and Rice, it was much larger than the ACCC of the 1940s. Tim LaHaye, a BJU alumnus and pastor of a rapidly growing church in Southern California, largely affirmed his alma mater's separatist stance. LaHaye, the future coauthor of the popular *Left Behind* series, at one point removed Campus Crusade's publications from his church's bookstore. John Walvoord, president of Dallas Theological Seminary, also initially distanced himself from the "new evangelicalism." Jerry Falwell, who first gained notice in the 1960s for his opposition to the civil rights movement, espoused fundamentalist separatism. The twin issues of cooperation and separation remained points of controversy through the 1970s. Given such contentious infighting among conservative Protestants, it was difficult to imagine a movement of "Bible-believing" Protestants gaining significant cultural influence.[22]

In early 1958, it would have been reasonable to describe Campus Crusade for Christ as a "fundamentalist," "evangelical," or "orthodox" ministry. By late 1958, Crusade had positioned itself as part of the "new evangelicalism." As with many "new evangelical" organizations, the heritage of fundamentalism left a deep imprint on Campus Crusade. Bright had not altered his approach to evangelism, Crusade's 1957 statement of faith defined the organization as theologically conservative, and Crusade avoided "liberal" sponsorship even after Bright's break with Jones. Moreover, although Crusade did not publicly condemn drinking and dancing on the campus, Bright found it necessary on occasion to allay concerns on such fronts. "With regard to this matter of dancing," he wrote one BJU alumna in 1962, "we absolutely do not allow our staff to appear on the dance floor." He later struggled in vain to convince European staff members to forswear alcohol. Like most evangelicals, Bright still believed in some sort of separation from the world, but such issues did not define Campus Crusade. If Bright had followed Jones's doctrine of double separation, he would have sharply limited Crusade's future prospects. Crusade sought financial support in the broad world of conservative Protestantism, including evangelical congregations within mainline denominations, a source of funds that after the 1950s would have been closed to an organization aligned with BJU. Moreover, Crusade's more open stance toward culture enabled the organization to creatively adapt to future changes on campus. For fundamentalists like Jones, evangelism was of central importance but subordinate to purity. Bright cared about doctrinal purity but made the evangelistic harvest his paramount objective.[23]

Rebound and Keep Moving

Crusade's relationship with Bob Jones University forced the organization to begin to define itself theologically. During the same years that Bright grappled with the issue of cooperative evangelism, he also articulated a teaching on the Holy Spirit that became central to the ministry's evangelistic outreaches and staff training. Crusade's dedication to aggressive evangelism and its penchant for new methods and technology have sometimes obscured the spirituality that undergirded the organization's growth. In addition to Bright's evangelistic vision, numerous staff members cite Bright's understanding of the Spirit-filled life as a primary reason for their decision to join Crusade's staff. Jim Craddock, on Crusade staff from the late 1950s to the early 1970s, comments that Crusade's emphasis on the Holy Spirit was the "glue that held" the ministry together.[24]

Moreover, this aspect of Crusade's theology and spirituality also highlights another significant point of contention among conservative Protestants. Given the recent political alignment of such figures as George W. Bush (Methodist), John Ashcroft (Assemblies of God), Bill Frist (Presbyterian), Pat Robertson (Southern Baptist), and James Dobson (Church of the Nazarene), it is easy to forget that only a few decades ago the different branches of American evangelicalism remained sharply divided over the doctrine of the Holy Spirit and the issue of speaking in tongues. Since the early twentieth century, most conservative Protestant denominations, organizations, and leaders had remained at best skeptical of Pentecostalism. The 1928 meeting of the World's Christian Fundamentals Association condemned glossolalia, and Carl McIntire denounced tongues as one of the chief signs of the great apostasy. As a sign of greater openness, the NAE welcomed several Pentecostal denominations, including the Assemblies of God, into its membership in the early 1940s. These signs of cooperation, however, did not end evangelical wariness of Pentecostalism. During the 1950s, Pentecostal denominations grew rapidly, and other Christians began to notice the healing revivals conducted by William Branham and Oral Roberts. Mainline and evangelical Protestants criticized what they perceived to be outrageous fund-raising practices, emotional excess, and spurious accounts of healing. Moreover, the emergence within mainline churches of "charismatic" Christians who spoke in tongues and claimed other "Pentecostal" gifts of the Spirit led to the reemergence of hostility against such practices. Both evangelicals and mainline Protestants seemed to dislike speaking in tongues more when it occurred within their own churches than when it occurred in urban storefronts and beneath Oklahoman tents. When Dennis Bennett, Episcopalian rector of St. Mark's parish in Van Nuys, California, spoke in tongues in 1959, he resigned under pressure, and Bennett's bishop forbade further tongues-speaking at St. Mark's. Although some mainline leaders gradually moved toward a more positive appraisal of Pentecostalism and the charismatic movement, evangelical and fundamentalist opposition hardened in the early 1960s.[25]

There is no record of Bright's early impressions of Pentecostalism, though he could hardly have been unaware of the movement's presence. Many of the most famous healing revivalists—including Oral Roberts, Jack Coe, and T. L. Osborn—haled from and preached in parts of Oklahoma not far removed from his hometown of Coweta. In his biography of Oral Roberts, David Harrell comments that by the 1930s "most people in polite [Oklahoma] religious circles were aware of the Pentecostal subculture" and disdained "the 'barbaric rhythm' of their music and the declaiming in 'unknown tongues.'" There was an Assemblies of God congregation in Coweta—Vonette Bright's sister Deanne Rice recalls the boisterous sounds of Pentecostal worship emanating from the church. Likewise, it would have been impossible for a ministry in Los Angeles to ignore either Pentecostalism or the charismatic renewal that began in local mainline churches. Los Angeles was home to the Asuza Street Mission, one of the birthplaces of twentieth-century Pentecostalism. Aimee Semple McPherson's Angelus Temple was only a short drive from Hollywood Presbyterian. In 1953, Demos Shakarian founded the Full Gospel Business Men's Fellowship, a lay Pentecostal movement headquartered in Los Angeles. Bennett's parish lay on the outskirts of the city. Closer to home, as many as six hundred people at Hollywood Presbyterian, including some in the College Department, experienced speaking in tongues in the early 1960s. Campus Crusade's location in Southern California likely encouraged Crusade's leadership to explore the doctrine of the Holy Spirit and take a stance vis-à-vis Pentecostalism and the charismatic movement.[26]

In the 1950s, however, Bright focused his attentions on the role of the Holy Spirit in his own spiritual life and that of his staff. Since his 1947 communion with the Holy Spirit at Forest Home, Bright often lamented that the intense power of that encounter dissipated over time and was only briefly revived during the experience that preceded Crusade's founding. Henrietta Mears had exposed Bright to Keswick-style spirituality that promised spiritual empowerment to individuals who completely surrendered themselves to Jesus Christ, which usually occurred in an act subsequent to conversion. Mears once told her protégé Dale Bruner that she had never known "'a man of God who had not had a crisis, a second experience'" that prompted complete surrender to God. J. Edwin Orr, an evangelist and historian of revivalism who spoke at Forest Home and for whom Bright edited a periodical in 1950, spoke at the 1949 College Briefing Conference on the need for "the Filling of the Holy Spirit" and insisted that to "be filled with the Spirit requires an experience of full surrender." Bright, however, had already experienced crises and complete surrender but nevertheless endured a personal "sense of spiritual defeat." He desired some sort of deeper and more consistent spiritual experience, which he sought through Scripture, prayer, evangelism, and even fasting. Bright and his staff recruits read several books and pamphlets on the Holy Spirit, including R. A. Torrey's *The Holy Spirit: Who He Is and What He Does*.[27]

Bright and others on Crusade's staff yearned to continually live in the power of the Spirit. "All of us on staff," recalls Ray Nethery, "were hungry and desirous to be more effective in our witness for Christ . . . the emphasis upon the theology of the Holy Spirit . . . came out of that hunger for more of God." In 1954, several Crusade staff went with Bright to Forest Home to counsel college students during the College Briefing Conference. Orr was one of the principal speakers. "His sermons there," remembers Bob Kendall, "caused many to go out into the night and seek an experience of some kind." Kendall himself aspired to "a deeper experience," and Orr encouraged him "to just go out there and pray . . . wait on God." After the conference ended, the Crusade staff remained at Forest Home for several weeks for the annual staff training event, which in those years included as much fellowship and strategic planning as actual training. Bright and the others longed to be filled with the Spirit. "We spent the weekend on our knees," recalls Kendall, "praying and begging God for something." Kendall himself was unsure of the expected result but shares that "most of us thought it was tongues." Over the weekend, however, "nothing happened," which left the group confused. Was there some sort of sin in the group that prevented the blessing of the Spirit? If Christians, following Orr's advice to pray and wait, did not receive the Spirit, what could be the explanation?[28]

According to Bright, the breakthrough came late at night while he and Vonette were vacationing at Charles Fuller's Newport Beach home. "That night," Bright later wrote, "God gave me the truths concerning the Person and work of the Holy Spirit that have been basic to the ministry of Campus Crusade." "Bill finally came," explains Kendall, "to his belief that we are filled with the Holy Spirit by faith." Bright's conclusion was an accepted evangelical belief. Torrey had provided a like explanation: "Whether you have felt it [the fullness of the Spirit] or not, you can claim it by simple faith in the inerrantly inspired Word of God." Billy Graham also stressed a similar understanding of the Spirit in the early 1950s. "When you are fully cleansed of every known sin," Graham wrote in *Peace with God*, "and completely yielded and surrendered to Christ, then you can accept by faith that you are filled with the Spirit of God."[29]

In light of these events and reflections, in 1956 Bright wrote "Ye Shall Receive Power." In this pamphlet, Bright observed that few Christians — perhaps only 10 percent — experienced consistent victory over sin and the fruitful ministry that followed such victory. Bright explained this problem by positing that such "defeated" Christians were not filled with the Holy Spirit. Bright drew on a rubric common to Keswick-oriented evangelists such as Torrey and Andrew Murray, one of Bright's favorite authors. Such thinkers divided humanity into three groups: natural, carnal, and spiritual. Non-Christians were "natural," living in a state of sin without Christ. Carnal Christians had accepted Jesus Christ but were not "filled with the Holy Spirit" and therefore experienced defeat in their Christian lives. In "Ye Shall Receive Power," Bright outlined stark divisions between the "carnal" and "spiritual" Christian. "Only a yielded and sensitive Spirit-filled Christian," he stated, "is able to converse with God." Moreover, Bright made effective evangelism a test of whether a person was Spirit-filled. In a subsequent revision of "Ye Shall Receive Power," he had pointed words for those Christians not actively seeking to share their faith: "If you have no desire to be Jesus Christ's witness or if you have no power in your witness, you may be sure that you are not filled with the Holy Spirit." Conversely, Bright expected Christians who received the power of the Spirit to immediately become enthusiastic and effective evangelists.[30]

Colonel Robert B. Thieme Jr. exerted a significant influence on Bright's application of this teaching in the late 1950s. Thieme, a graduate of Dallas

Theological Seminary (DTS) and pastor of Berachah Church in Houston, met a number of the students and staff involved in Crusade's ministry at Rice University and spoke regularly at Crusade events. Thieme injected an additional dose of militarism into the organization—he insisted on being called "Colonel" and enjoyed doing push-ups with male Crusade staff members. According to Dave Coterill, Thieme was like a "machine gun"— he "unloaded" his teaching when he took the stage or microphone. The presence of Thieme helped channel a substantial number of DTS graduates to Campus Crusade in late 1950s and early 1960s—by the mid-1960s, a number of Crusade's top leaders were DTS alumni. In his talks, Thieme exhorted Crusade staff and students to "rebound and keep moving"; that is, individuals should confess sin and resume victory in Christ without an extended period of contrition or sorrow. Drawing heavily on this concept, Bright explicated what he termed "spiritual breathing." Greg Barnett, on staff briefly in the 1950s, comments that "the spiritual breathing [concept] came straight from Thieme." Bright urged Christians who commit "a definite act of disobedience" to "breathe spiritually": "confess your sin" (exhale) and "surrender the control of your life to Christ, and appropriate (receive) the fullness of the Holy Spirit by faith" (inhale). Bright believed that spiritual breathing could smooth out the peaks and the valleys of Christian experience through a focus on God's promises in the Bible rather than on human emotions. Earlier Keswick speakers like Murray and Torrey prescribed long hours of Bible study and prayer each day as prerequisites for uninterrupted fillings of the Spirit. Bright endorsed such practices, but his concept of spiritual breathing also created a spiritual paradigm more appropriate for busy campus workers in modern America. According to Bright's model, Christians should simply confess their sins and then immediately continue on with victorious evangelism. He expected something very close to "sinless perfection." "You need never again be a carnal Christian," Bright encouraged his audiences, "more than a moment of time."[31]

The division of Christians into two classes provided the foundation for many of Campus Crusade's ministries. Bright and Crusade focused increasing attention on helping "defeated" Christians become witnessing, "Spirit-filled" Christians. "I am now convinced," wrote Bright, "that the luke-warm, carnal Christian can be changed into a vital, dynamic, witnessing Christian if he will surrender his will to Christ and be filled with the Holy Spirit." Crusade's evangelism was thus two-pronged, directed at both non-Christians and "lukewarm," "carnal" Christians. On the campus, Crusade staff asked students professing to already be Christians whether they had made the "discovery" of the Spirit-filled life and whether Christ was on the "throne" of their lives. A negative response indicated a "carnal" state, and Crusade instructed its staff to "simply invite the Christian with whom you're speaking to pray with you, to confess any known sins . . . and to thank God for filling him with the Holy Spirit." Since Bright estimated that 90 percent of American Christians lived "defeated lives" and were not filled with the Spirit, Crusade looked beyond the campus and also viewed America's churches as a potential mission field. In the spring of 1958, Bright spoke at an adult conference at Forest Home. He reported that "approximately 200 [at the conference] . . . expressed a desire to be filled with the Holy Spirit for a more victorious life and effective ministry as He empowers." Crusade's teaching on the Holy Spirit became a powerful evangelistic tool, especially when the ministry expanded beyond the college campus in the 1960s.[32]

Given the ministry's focus on the Holy Spirit and the growth of Pentecostalism and the charismatic movement in Southern California, it is not surprising that Bright and his staff grappled with the issue of speaking in tongues. In "Ye Shall Receive Power," Bright expressed a cautious but irenic attitude toward the issue. "It is possible for a Christian to speak in tongues when he is filled with the Holy Spirit," Bright wrote, "and it is also possible for a Christian to be filled with the Spirit and not speak in tongues." Bright did not consider tongues to be a standard manifestation of the Spirit but instead expected most persons to "experience a calm assurance" "that God is going to use them in a way they have never been used before to introduce others to Christ." Bright's open attitude toward tongues reflected that of Henrietta Mears, who developed a friendship with Oral Roberts in the mid-1950s and invited the Pentecostal evangelist to Forest Home. Through the 1950s Crusade resisted defining its position on tongues, considering it a nonessential issue and seeking to avoid offending Pentecostals. Crusade had a number of substantial financial supporters who had experienced "the gift of tongues" yet were attracted to Crusade's emphasis on evangelism and the ministry of the Holy Spirit. According to Ted Martin, a DTS graduate who joined staff in 1960, Crusade's policy at the time was that supporters and staff with "the tongues gift" "wouldn't push it publicly in the context of Crusade." "It was an issue that had to be treated so gingerly," comments former staff member Jan Lindsey, "because a lot of the supporters of Campus Crusade were people who did speak in tongues."[33]

In the 1960s, Bright and Campus Crusade gradually moved away from this irenic attitude. It is difficult to identify the precise reasons for the

hardening of the organization's policy, though several factors likely contributed. As mentioned above, a number of Dallas Seminary graduates
joined Crusade staff in the late 1950s and early 1960s, and DTS alumnus
Robert Thieme argued vigorously against speaking in tongues. DTS was a
bastion of dispensationalist theology. Dispensationalists insisted that certain gifts of the Spirit, including tongues, had ceased after the time of the
apostles. By the early 1960s Bright was personally skeptical of the validity
of tongues. He became annoyed when members of the charismatic movement sought to convince him of the need for tongues or would pray—in
his presence—for him to receive the gift. Bright later recalled that he was
"invited to meetings where I was encouraged to speak in tongues. Hands
were laid on me, and different people prayed that I would be 'baptized
with the Holy Spirit.' Still nothing happened." Peter Gillquist, who joined
Crusade staff in 1960, remembers Bright explicitly critiquing the charismatic movement at a staff training event in Minnesota: "One night . . .
he was warning us against the charismatic movement, and he broke out
into tongues. And he said, 'what you heard tonight was not tongues. It
was psychobabble.'" Bright worried that charismatic students, staff, or supporters would promote the experience of speaking in tongues rather than
devote themselves fully to Crusade's ministry of evangelism. "Bill was very
frightened of the charismatic movement," explains Donn Moomaw. "He
just didn't want someone to come in and make that the central thrust of
his ministry . . . so he would be very careful not to let anyone on the staff
who was going to sing that song too much."[34]

In light of these concerns, Crusade changed its policy on glossolalia
shortly after 1960. A policy statement explained that "Campus Crusade
does not wish to take an official theological stand on the issue of tongues"
but felt the need to take "a practical stand" because of the "divisive and
controversial nature of tongues." "No staff member," stated the revised
policy, "will be permitted to speak in tongues in public or in private or
to promote tongues either to groups or to individuals." The document
did, however, emphasize that the new policy did not represent "a condemnation of the tongues movement" and suggested that under changed
circumstances, Crusade might revisit its ban. In the mid-1960s, however,
Crusade further defined its position. In a cessationist framework typical
of DTS, Crusade now maintained that "[a]fter the completion of the New
Testament the need for apostles, prophets and certain other specially gifted
individuals apparently ceased and these gifts died out." The document cau-

tioned that an emphasis on tongues would threaten Crusade's "relentless" emphasis on "the necessity and privilege of every believer's appropriating the filling of the Holy Spirit on the sole basis of grace through faith." The evolution of Bright's thinking and Crusade's policies reveal that relations between evangelicals on the one hand and Pentecostals and charismatics on the other remained complex in the late 1950s and early 1960s. Evangelicals, Pentecostals, and charismatics all emphasized the need to appropriate the power of the Holy Spirit and live a supernatural life in the Spirit. Pentecostals and charismatics who longed for the baptism in the Spirit and sought to introduce others to that baptism were not all that different from Campus Crusaders who longed for the fullness of the Holy Spirit and sought to introduce others to the Spirit-filled life. Yet the issue of speaking in tongues prevented evangelical ministries such as Campus Crusade from forming close ties with Pentecostal and charismatic Christians.[35]

Campus Crusade's split with Bob Jones University and the response of Crusade to the charismatic movement both illustrate a basic pragmatism that has increasingly characterized American evangelicalism since 1945. Crusade has defined itself theologically when forced to do so by fissures within the conservative Protestant world. An internal document in the early 1960s cautioned that the ministry "should avoid becoming too highly defined in a doctrinal way." Although Crusade would "carefully guard the basic foundational issues, such as the verbal plenary inspiration of Scripture and those concerning the person and work of Christ," the organization intended to "stick to these basics and keep our cutting edge in evangelism." In its evangelistic and fund-raising efforts, moreover, Crusade always emphasized its basic mission of evangelism rather than any particular theological beliefs. Bright did not want to fall into any particular evangelical camp theologically, be it dispensationalist, charismatic, or Reformed. According to former staff member Ray Nethery, Bright was theologically "eclectic" and invited speakers to Crusade training events from a variety of theological backgrounds. Nethery comments that "the theology of Crusade was never set in cement."[36] Despite the influences of Bob Jones University and Dallas Theological Seminary, Bright wanted Campus Crusade to appeal to a broad cross-section of American evangelicals. Although he possessed a core of theological principles, he also modified his principles in ways that would optimize Crusade's growth. Bright made such decisions based on his own theological principles, trends within the broader evangelical world, and the pressure he received from Crusade's most prominent supporters. In the early 1960s, neither extreme separatism nor speaking in tongues represented mainstream evangelicalism.

In the early 1960s, it seemed that the mission of the NAE had failed. Were it not for the star power of Billy Graham that drew many wavering conservatives toward the evangelical camp, the split between fundamentalists and evangelicals would have been even more pronounced. The issue of speaking in tongues, especially when it arose within evangelical congregations and organizations, led to estrangement between many "mainstream" evangelicals and their charismatic and Pentecostal counterparts. This estrangement did not hamper the growth of either the charismatic or noncharismatic wing of the evangelical movement, as evangelical churches and ministries and their charismatic and Pentecostal counterparts grew rapidly during these decades. However, if intra-evangelical dissension did not retard evangelism and growth, it did hinder evangelicals from moving closer to their goal of "saving" America. Whether or not evangelicals could surmount these differences would in large measure determine the extent of their cultural and political influence in subsequent decades.

The Conservative Impulses
of the Early 1960s

Despite Campus Crusade's conflicts with Bob Jones University and the emerging charismatic movement, the organization grew quickly in the early 1960s, tripling in size to nearly three hundred staff on 108 campuses by 1963.[1] The ministry maintained its small office in Los Angeles and the summer training grounds on Lake Minnetonka in Mound, Minnesota. Bill Bright remained an evangelical entrepreneur, launching ministries in Asia and Latin America, beginning an evangelistic ministry to American laypeople, and experimenting with evangelism through various forms of media, including records and radio. As Crusade grew, Bright and his top assistants further standardized their evangelistic approach and adopted more formal means of staff training. The growth in staff and the organization's overseas expansion also caused Crusade to move away from an older evangelical tradition of "faith missions" toward the embrace of modern fund-raising and marketing tools.

Fund-raising needs precipitated Bright's entrance into circles of theologically and politically conservative businessmen in Texas, Arizona, and California. Bright's relationships with Sunbelt businessmen shed light on an important dynamic within the organization. Crusade's evangelistic mission at American universities pushed the ministry to adapt to campus culture. At the same time, Crusade secured funding for its evangelistic programs from businessmen who were mostly political, theological, and cultural conservatives. These relationships encouraged Crusade to maintain a much greater tension vis-à-vis mainstream American society and nudged Bright in particular toward political activism. Through connections with businessmen such as Nelson Bunker Hunt and Gerri von Frellick, Bright became even more alarmist in his anticommunist rhetoric and supported an early effort to involve Christians in precinct-level politics. As the decades passed, Bright and Crusade would find themselves caught between these countervailing pressures. Despite the early 1960s growth of politically conservative student groups like Young Americans for Freedom, the right-wing politics advocated by many donors had little broad appeal to collegians. The evangelistic impulse encouraged cultural adaptation and an apolitical stance, while the custodial impulse drew Bright into the world of partisan politics.

Win the World for Christ Tomorrow

As Henrietta Mears had done at Forest Home, Bright hung a world map in the Campus Crusade chapel at Lake Minnetonka to signal the global breadth of his evangelistic vision. At first, he merely hoped that international student converts would "carry His message of salvation back to their own people." Along those lines, in 1954 Crusade announced that Idowu Johnson had become "Campus Crusade's first overseas representative." Johnson had come to the Los Angeles area to pursue graduate studies and was converted after a Crusade staff member took him to meet with Bright. After he returned to his native Nigeria, Johnson spoke with his students about Christ, preached sermons, and distributed Bible verses for memorization. Bright saw Johnson's work as an opportunity to remind supporters that American treatment of international students was an important aspect of the global struggle against communism. Crusade's promotional newspaper warned that "Communists invite leaders from other lands to study in Russia where they are wined, dined and propagandized until many of them return home to be ambassadors for Karl Marx and Communism." On the other hand, Crusade warned, many foreign students who come to the United States "lose not only their faith in God but in the American way of life because of the prejudiced treatment they receive." Johnson periodically sent reports to Crusade headquarters, though the ministry eventually lost contact with him.[2]

Bright established Crusade's international work on a more permanent basis by recruiting Joon Gon Kim of South Korea, who met Bright shortly after enrolling at Fuller Seminary in 1957. In several ways, Kim was ideally suited to import Crusade to his homeland. He was already a successful pastor and possessed contacts with a large number of young ministers and students in Korea. Moreover, he was a committed anticommunist who appreciated Crusade's strong opposition to communism. During the Korean War, communist troops had murdered Kim's wife and father, and Kim himself had suffered grave wounds. Bright and Kim perceived Korea as a strategic country from which Christian evangelists would contain and perhaps even roll back the spread of communism in Asia. Noting that many Korean students "speak Russian, Japanese, and Chinese fluently," Bright predicted that once Korean students "are captured for Christ," they would "help to win other countries of Asia to Him." Bright began fund-raising for the movement in Korea, and Kim assembled a staff of fifteen by 1965. Shortly after Bright hired Kim, he met a Pakistani student at Fuller, Kundan Massey, and invited him to a Crusade summer conference. Attracted to Crusade's teaching on the Holy Spirit and to "Bill Bright's vision to reach the world for Christ," Massey founded Campus Crusade in Pakistan.[3]

Bright's interest in overseas expansion accelerated in the early 1960s. In 1961, he directed an outreach to students during a Tokyo crusade sponsored by World Vision, an evangelical ministry founded by Youth for Christ evangelist Bob Pierce in 1950. Vonette accompanied Bill on the venture, which was their first trip out of the country. Bright was apprehensive that his evangelistic methods would prove ineffective in reaching Japanese students, but he reported that the results far exceeded his expectations. Following the time in Tokyo, Vonette returned to the United States while Bill visited Kim and Massey and proceeded to other Asian countries to explore the possibilities of launching additional ministries. As a reflection of Bright's expanding vision, he began signing his letters "yours for fulfilling the Great Commission in this generation." Evangelicals have long referred to Jesus's instructions in Matthew 28:18–20 ("Go therefore and make disciples of all nations") as the "Great Commission," which functions in evangelical circles as an imperative for evangelism and for foreign missions in particular. Bright's phrase hearkened back to the "evangelization of the world in this generation" watchword of the Student Volunteer Movement, which had persuaded thousands of young Americans to pledge themselves to foreign missions in the late nineteenth and early twentieth centuries. In keeping with such language, Bright quickly formed lofty goals for overseas expansion. He hoped to "recruit, train, and send 1,000 qualified workers to the leading universities of the world" and to help Bible translation organizations recruit "an additional 6,000 workers."[4]

Over the next ten years, Crusade's international work expanded, though

Bill Bright outlining his strategy for "fulfilling the Great Commission in this generation" at Campus Crusade's Lake Minnetonka headquarters, ca. 1961. Courtesy of Joanne McClurkin.

not at the pace Bright initially foresaw. Bright appointed two top campus ministry leaders, Ray Nethery and Bob Kendall, as the directors for Crusade's work in Asia and Latin America, respectively. Nethery and Kendall traveled across their regions in order to find suitable directors for each national ministry. Crusade did not have sufficient funds to send American missionaries overseas, and Bright added that the world had entered "a day of Nationalism when traditional missionary methods are suspect in many countries" and "the American . . . is less and less popular in many countries of the world." Nethery and Kendall hoped international staff members would raise their own support and expenses but soon realized that Crusade needed to provide funds on a continuing basis. They formed boards of American supporters, each of which gave money to support the ministry in one country. Nethery even took a year off from active Crusade work to launch a series of franchised Svedenhouse restaurants—the profits from each of the five restaurants paid the expenses for one overseas ministry. Although Crusade encouraged indigenous leadership, it did not promote national autonomy, as the organization required national ministries to strictly adhere to Crusade's methodology. However, despite the considerable amounts of travel by Nethery and Kendall, there was relatively little supervision and coordination during the earliest years of Crusade's international work. Some ministries, such as those in South Korea and Pakistan, flourished because of capable national leaders and their dedication to Campus Crusade's vision and methodology. In other locations, national leaders proved less enthusiastic about Crusade's evangelistic approach or simply tended to develop their own methods and priorities.[5]

In addition to fund-raising, Crusade encountered other obstacles as it expanded internationally. The domestic clash with Inter-Varsity Christian Fellowship continued overseas. In 1947, IVCF had organized a worldwide alliance of evangelical student organizations, known as the International Federation of Evangelical Students (IFES). When member organizations heard about Campus Crusade, they sometimes wrote the American IVCF office for advice and counsel. The advice received was often harsh and rehearsed the earlier conflicts between the two organizations. "I can't think of anything at the moment that will so damage the evangelical cause in Australia as Campus Crusade coming in competition," IVCF president Charles Troutman counseled Ian Burnard, an Australian colleague. The British IVCF tried in vain to persuade Crusade to abandon its plans to begin a ministry in Great Britain, and Crusade faced similar pressures in other countries. From Crusade's perspective, IFES groups jealously sought to prevent the legitimate operations of a new ministry. Kendall remembers a five-hour meeting with "the international IV" in Peru. "They wanted to crucify me for bringing Crusade in there," explains Kendall. "They said, 'What right do you have to come in here?'"[6]

Crusade's expansion overseas reflects the general burst in American evangelical foreign missions in the years following World War II. Given the wartime devastation of Europe and the stagnation of mainline Protestant missions, American evangelicals became the dominant force in Protestant foreign missions. The Cold War also injected an added dose of urgency to evangelical missions. The 1949 Communist victory in the Chinese civil war shut the door on one of the largest Western missionary endeavors, and supporters of the Protestant missionary enterprise comprised a major portion of the China lobby that badgered the Truman administration following the "loss" of China. A Cold War mentality colored Bright's view of postwar missions, as he outlined a spiritual version of the domino theory. Bright worried that student-led communist demonstrations in Japan threatened all of Asia, and he identified World Vision's Tokyo Crusade as a crucial moment in the war against communism. "The battle for control of the Orient will be decided in Tokyo," he asserted. Bright warned his supporters that if the communists triumphed in Japan, "the rest of the Orient will soon be enslaved also," and he cautioned that "America may

Bill Bright and Bob Kendall, Mexico City airport, ca. 1965. Courtesy of Bob Kendall.

well be next." For Bright, the Cold War was as much about spiritual warfare as military strategy and weaponry, and in his mind, the domino theory
could also operate in reverse. He believed the evangelization of Japan and
South Korea would inoculate other Asian countries against the contagion
of communism. Evangelicals long motivated by the goal of evangelizing
the world would have supported foreign missions in any event, but the
backdrop of the Cold War created an additional marketing tool for evangelical leaders boosting their overseas ventures.[7]

God Loves You and Has a Wonderful Plan for Your Life

While Crusade's international initiatives remained inchoate, the ministry
aggressively expanded to additional American campuses in the early 1960s.
Bob Horner, who joined staff in 1964, recollects that Crusade "virtually
every year moved all of its staff." "You open a new campus," Horner explains Crusade's strategy for expansion, "you move to another one. You
leave somebody there and move on."[8] By the mid-1960s, Crusade had active ministries on most large campuses in the Midwest, the old South-
west (especially Oklahoma and Texas), and the West. Crusade made little
headway in the Northeast, where evangelicalism as a whole constituted a

more marginal presence. Crusade also expanded more slowly in the Southeast, perhaps due to the relatively vitality of Baptist and Methodist campus ministries.

As the ministry expanded, Crusade refined its evangelistic techniques. In 1957, Bob Ringer, a salesman and member at Hollywood Presbyterian, spoke at Crusade's annual staff conference. Ringer lectured the group on the danger of "presentation fatigue" and noted that effective salesmen—and effective ministers—stick to one pitch. Given Bright's background in sales and his earlier recommendation of Frank Bettger's sales manual, it is not surprising that Bright took Ringer's advice to heart. In response to Ringer's insight, Bright wrote "God's Plan for Your Life," a twenty-minute presentation of Crusade's basic message. Previously, Crusade had encouraged its staff to use a set "clincher" talk at evangelistic meetings but had also given them some latitude to develop their own approaches. Now, the entire staff became a more standardized evangelistic sales force, as they memorized "God's Plan" and employed it both in meetings and when counseling individuals. "God's Plan" began with a question: "Has it ever occurred to you . . . that God has a wonderful plan for your life?" The talk, much like the "clincher," discussed the problem of sin and presented "Jesus of Nazareth" as "the one person who could bridge this chasm between man and God." In counseling sessions, Crusade staff ended by asking students, "Wouldn't you like to know Him today as your very own Saviour and Lord?" "Because of this one presentation alone," Bright asserted, "our ministry was multiplied a hundredfold during the next year."[9]

Some staff members disliked having to memorize "God's Plan," mostly because of its length. "It was difficult to memorize that much material and be able to present it," comments Joanne McClurkin. Bill Counts felt "God's Plan" was "too long and cumbersome." Bright recognized that "we needed a much shorter version of the gospel," and he tightened up "God's Plan" over the next several years. By 1959, Bright had condensed the talk to highlight four basic points:

I. God loves you and has a wonderful plan for your life.
II. Man is sinful and separated from God, thus he cannot know and explain God's plan for his life.
III. Jesus Christ is God's provision for man's sin through whom man can know God's love and plan for his life.
IV. We must receive Jesus Christ as Saviour and Lord by personal invitation.

Bright termed these principles the "Four Spiritual Laws" and introduced them by contending that "as there are laws in the physical realm which are inviolate, so there are laws in the spiritual realm which are definite and true." Bright initially had planned to have the statement on "man's sin" comprise his first law. The Brights spent an evening working with several female staff members on a draft of "God's Plan" for the staff manual. As he had recently returned from a trip, Bright "left Vonette and the girls to finish the typing." "I was in bed," Bright later chronicled, "just at the point of going to sleep, when suddenly there came clear as a bell to my conscious mind the fact that there was something wrong about starting the Four Laws on the negative note of man's sinfulness." The revision was very much in keeping with the positive evangelistic approach employed by Crusade since its inception. "The love of God," Bright explained, "had been the basis of my presentation of the gospel ever since I had become a Christian."[10]

When approaching an individual on campus or elsewhere, Campus Crusade staff members would typically begin by asking "Have you ever heard of the Four Spiritual Laws?" When sharing the longer "God's Plan," Crusade staff members would write out the "four laws" and draw accompanying diagrams. "When we would meet students," remembers Lois Mackey, "we'd write them on napkins." In 1965, Gus Yeager, a Toledo businessman friendly with Crusade, took the initiative to compile the new material into a booklet. Gordon Walker, a local staff member, showed the booklet to Bright, who loved the new format. "Within a month or so," recounts Walker, "Bill had had it printed up in large quantities and was distributing it." Bright soon recommended that staff read the booklet to prospective converts rather than deliver the longer "God's Plan" talk. The new format contained the four laws themselves, a few supporting scripture verses, a small amount of commentary, and several supporting diagrams. The only substantive change made from the four laws contained in "God's Plan" was an emphasis on the exclusive power of Christ to solve the problem of sin—the pamphlet now referred to Jesus as "God's *only* provision for man's sin." In conclusion, the booklet encouraged the reader or listener to pray the following prayer: "Lord Jesus, I need You . . . I open the door of my life and receive You as my Savior and Lord. Thank You for forgiving my sins. Take control of the throne of my life. Make me the kind of person You want me to be." Campus Crusade believed that when individuals prayed those words in faith, Jesus Christ entered their hearts, gave them eternal life, and began to direct their earthly lives.

Witnessing with the Four Spiritual Laws *at a Campus Crusade Christmas Conference in Dallas, 1970. Courtesy of Sharyn Regier.*

Have You Heard of the Four Spiritual Laws? became Crusade's most famous evangelistic tool. David Harrington Watt, the most perceptive scholarly critic of the pamphlet, surmises that "[n]ext to the Bible it is the work that contemporary evangelicals are most likely to have encountered." Indeed, by 1970 Crusade had already printed twenty-five million copies in a number of different languages. Watt observes that the booklet presents a positive message with no mention of hell, rejects religious pluralism while seeking to avoid offending non-Christians, and places "less emphasis on what the gospel can do for human beings in the afterlife than on what it can do for them here and now."[11]

Perhaps the most significant aspect of the *Four Spiritual Laws*, however, was not the booklet's message or presentation, as evangelicals had long used tracts, and many evangelicals by the 1960s were talking more about love and less about hell. Bright considered the *Four Spiritual Laws* an excellent distillation of theological truth but praised the booklet primarily because it worked. He verified it as an effective spiritual pitch by engaging in extensive market-testing. He himself found it much easier to lead people to pray to receive Christ by using the booklet than by any other method. Given that some of Crusade's staff members resisted "canned" approaches, such as the "clincher" and "God's Plan," Bright recognized that his staff might resist simply reading a booklet during witnessing encounters. Returning from a 1965 tour of Crusade's international ministries, Bright composed a letter to his staff informing them of his results with the new booklet. "The effectiveness of the Four Spiritual Laws was demonstrated over and over again with dramatic results," Bright wrote. "Whereas I used to write out the Four Laws and draw the diagrams as well as write out the prayer," Bright continued, "I now limit my remarks generally to what is contained on the pages of the booklet. *Though it's hard on the ego, the results are greater*" (emphasis in original). Perhaps in the era of television, a brief advertisement for Jesus closed an evangelistic sale better than a wordy discourse. Evangelistic pragmatism—as old as evangelism itself—did not begin with Bill Bright and Campus Crusade, but Bright embraced such pragmatism with unusual enthusiasm.[12]

Crusade did not suggest that Christian instruction ended with the *Four Spiritual Laws*, and the organization encouraged new converts to join Bible studies and proceed through a set of study materials about various Christian doctrines. At staff training events, all new staff members took basic courses covering the Bible, theology, and church history, but Bright felt his staff would benefit most from the continual study and practical application of Crusade's teachings on evangelism and the Holy Spirit. On at least one day during training events, students and others in attendance would go out into the community and, armed with questionnaires and the *Four Spiritual Laws*, witness to strangers. Frequently, students and staff who came to the Arrowhead Springs headquarters would journey to Southern California beaches for a day of evangelism among their vacationing peers. These lessons in practical evangelism helped interested students discern whether they should join Crusade.

Against critics who objected that the *Four Spiritual Laws* and other Crusade tools were too simplistic, Bright had a ready defense. "The longer I worked with the intelligentsia," Bright responded wryly, "the more I realized the necessity of developing simple how-to's for the Christian life." At training events, Bright told his staff members that they needed to choose between the "simple" and the "scholarly," and he still discerned little positive connection between advanced theological education and effectiveness in ministry. "Some of the most decadent, fruitless people I know," he lamented, "have several degrees." "It's hard [to witness effectively]," he cautioned, "after four years of exegesis, learning the original languages, Hebrew and Greek." "The average person," he warned potential staff recruits, "to whom you speak, even on the college campus, is not interested in the theology of Barth and Brunner, and Tillich and Niebuhr and the rest." "You must be prepared to communicate in the most simple terms," he challenged them, "and I do not know a more simple way than the Four Spiritual Laws." When Bright explained his *Four Spiritual Laws* to a group of Berkeley faculty in 1967, a professor asked him how he would present his message to "a genuine intellectual." "Bill said," recollects Howard Ball, "'I would probably read it more slowly.'" Bright's comments on seminary education and disdain for the excessive intellectualizing of the Christian life closely resemble what Richard Hofstadter in 1962 identified as a deep well of anti-intellectualism in American evangelicalism. Hofstadter correctly suggested that in the minds of American evangelicals and fundamentalists, "learning and cultivation appear to be handicaps in the propagation of faith." What Hofstadter perceived was not necessarily Philistinism or a lack of interest in theological and intellectual debates. Bright's oldest son Zachary explains that his father's "pragmatic and entrepreneurial side" often overshadowed an "artistic literary side" that included a love for literature and classical music. What might be personally pleasurable was not necessarily helpful for Crusade's mission, however. At least during Crusade's early years, Bright did not perceive any beneficial connection between the life of the mind and the mission of evangelism, even when the primary target of that mission was the university population. Bright taught his staff that the urgency of the hour would not permit the luxury—and possible risks—of intellectual pursuits.[13]

Faith and Money

Campus Crusade's success depended on people as well as methods. Most staff workers were highly dedicated and industrious. They had to be, because those recruited by Crusade did not merely take on a job assignment—they adopted a way of life. A staff worker on an individual campus kept up a rigorous schedule of witnessing, evangelistic meetings, Bible studies, and promotional work. Many staff workers traveled regularly to visit nearby campuses, attend conferences, and meet with financial supporters. Every summer, the entire staff uprooted for several weeks and traveled to an annual training conference. Salaries for staff members increased significantly but remained modest. Single staff in the early 1950s received $100 per month. By 1965, a single staff worker received a monthly stipend of $250—U.S. per capita income in 1965 was $3,705—and married couples received $350, with an additional allowance for up to four children. Staff advancing to administrative positions or top leadership posts did not receive higher stipends.[14]

In the early years of the organization, Campus Crusade placed very little emphasis on fund-raising. Bright initially hoped to earn enough money in business to fund his ministry and avoid the necessity of asking for donations. Even after he sold his wholesale business and launched Crusade, Bright maintained a penchant for coming up with money-making propositions and investment schemes. He purchased a few "well-drilling rigs" and formed Bright's Oil Company, seeking to exploit wells in Oklahoma. He "envisioned making millions of dollars" to "invest in the cause of Christ," but Bright's Oil Company never became profitable. "It wasn't a paying deal," explains his nephew, Charley Bright. "We just didn't get the oil." Maud Wetzel, a member at Hollywood Presbyterian and on Campus Crusade's advisory board, invested in the company and lost money. Bright's financial supporters believed in his evangelistic vision and ministerial integrity but lost confidence in his skill as an entrepreneur. Louis Scroggin, on Crusade's board in the 1950s, remembers an occasion when Bright had a discussion with Bill Jones, Crusade's biggest donor in the early years of the ministry: "Bill [Jones] said to him . . . 'Bill if you ever go into any kind of a business again you'll never see me again.'"[15]

Fortunately for all involved, Bright never formed another business, but he did continue to hatch plans to provide income for the ministry. Dale Smith, on staff briefly in the mid-1950s, remembers that Bright asked her and her husband to sell vitamins door-to-door as a means of raising money. Then in the early 1960s, Bright adopted a fund-raising initiative pioneered by World Vision. Crusade encouraged supporters to donate funds to "The Cattle Project" for the purchase of calves. The ministry then paid ranchers to raise the calves and later sold them for a profit. Crusade utilized the plan effectively for a short time and then decided to expand the venture, which had special appeal for Bright because of his childhood on an Oklahoma ranch. According to former staff member Jim Craddock, the ministry "bought hundreds and hundreds of head of cattle on notes from businessmen that signed." However, the "cattle rustler" Crusade hired made off with the livestock and began to sell them. Bright assigned Craddock, who was also from Oklahoma, to recover and fatten up the remainder of the cattle, which the ministry sold to cover its losses. Crusade purchased a ranch in Oklahoma and continued "to raise cattle for support of staff" through the mid-1960s.[16]

During the early 1950s, Bright and the rest of the staff debated whether they should actively solicit funds or whether they should rely primarily on prayer and faith. "I think the biggest question we had," remembers Dorothy Hauser Graham, Crusade's office manager throughout most of the 1950s, "was should we trust the Lord for the financial input or shall we let people know we need it?" According to Graham, the organization went back and forth between "letting people know" and "trust[ing] the Lord." Money was always scarce, and a donation from a supporter at an opportune time often answered prayers and relieved anxiety. Bright's initial reluctance to engage in aggressive fund-raising reflects the evangelical tradition of "faith missions," which eschewed direct fund-raising and saw the arrival of needed funds as answers to prayer and proof of God's blessing. Fundamentalists and evangelicals had debated the issue for many decades. A number of prominent late-nineteenth- and early-twentieth-century mission organizations had articulated the faith mission ideal, while Dwight Moody and William B. Riley had embraced fund-raising. Some postwar evangelicals, such as Dallas Theological Seminary's John Walvoord, remained skeptical of fund-raising and modern advertising methods, but most evangelicals eventually adopted aggressive fund-raising and marketing. The use of modern fund-raising tools, however, does not appear to have supplanted older theological interpretations, as evangelicals continued to see the arrival of donations as evidence of God's blessing. In evangelical ministries, the older motifs of faith missions often blended seamlessly into the modern world of advertising, direct mail, and big-donor support.[17]

By the mid-1950s, Bright was disappointed because he was not receiving as much financial support from Hollywood Presbyterian congregants as he expected, and he could not raise enough funds to enable a rapid expansion of Campus Crusade's staff. Bright discussed his frustrations with Louis Scroggin, who suggested that Bright "make each [staff] person responsible for raising his own support . . . plus a certain percentage for office overhead." Scroggin predicted that staff members would be able to cultivate supporters impressed with Crusade's ministries in their own communities. In light of financial realities and Scroggin's suggestion, Bright asked his area directors to raise money for the staff in their areas and eventually asked individual staff members to raise their own salaries. In addition to relying on friends, family, and home churches, staff on each campus made contacts with local businessmen and churches and asked them for assistance. Staff fund-raising produced a much steadier income and allowed Bright to concentrate on raising funds for new projects. As he traveled around the country on campus visits and recruiting tours, he met potential donors and broadened Crusade's base of financial supporters beyond his initial contacts within Hollywood Presbyterian. The success of Crusade's staff members in raising their own support led other evangelical parachurch organizations such as Inter-Varsity and Young Life to follow suit.[18]

As the decision to have all staff become fund-raisers suggests, Crusade largely shed its early inhibitions about asking for money. The organization developed fund-raising literature and a slideshow that staff presented to potential donors, and Bright mailed regular appeals to donors and a growing list of contacts. In 1957, Bright outlined "an urgent need for $6952.50 for living allowances and bills due and payable." Similarly, Bright in 1960 asked his supporters to provide $28,000 to cover living allowances, bills, and "notes due and payable." He noted that Crusade's annual budget was only $180,000 and that the staff received a "subsistence wage." He evidenced some concern that the shortfall would alarm his supporters but reassured them that after "this deficit is raised, we are not likely to find ourselves in this financial condition in the future." "The greatest hindrance to the fulfillment of the Great Commission is not manpower," Bright informed supporters, "but money."[19]

In addition to placing a greater emphasis on raising money, Crusade slowly developed an administrative structure. As the campus ministry expanded, Bright appointed men as campus, area, and regional directors. Bright had also formed a board of directors and an advisory board soon after launching Crusade. As of 1957, his board of directors included Henrietta Mears and Richard Halverson from Hollywood Presbyterian, a few California businessmen, and Mark Hatfield, then Oregon's secretary of state and a future U.S. senator. While on the faculty of Willamette University, Hatfield had taken an interest in Crusade's campus ministry. The board met a few times a year at the residence the Brights shared with Mears, usually over a breakfast prepared by Vonette Bright. Despite the formation of the board, decision making took place in a very informal manner. During a board meeting in the late 1950s, Bright discussed "a new phase of the ministry." Scroggin asked him how he had arrived at the plan. Bright replied that he had talked with Vonette and Dorothy Hauser and then had "phoned Gordon Klenck up in Berkeley and Roe Brooks, and we all decided that was the thing to do." "What board members usually do at board meetings is to make decisions for the organization," Scroggin responded to Bright, "but they seem to be made in other ways." Scroggin recommended that Bright form an internal board reflecting the actual locus of decision-making authority. The rest of the board nodded in agreement, and as a final item of business, Crusade's board of directors resigned. The issue did not sour the board members on the organization, as Scroggin and the others remained on Crusade's advisory board.[20]

Bright took Scroggin's advice and formed an internal board that provided him with information and counsel. At first, he selected a few top campus staff and office manager Dorothy Hauser. Within a few years, Bright organized the board to include his area directors for the campus ministry, new office manager Breta Bate, and Vonette Bright. According to Bob Kendall, the internal board had no formal authority and very little actual influence. "He [Bill Bright] would receive suggestions from us," Kendall recalls, "but plans were pretty well formed and expected to be adopted by us." "Bill ran the Crusade," Kendall explains. "I can't think of a time when his ideas or plan was rejected." "It was generally understood," concludes Kendall, "that those of us on staff had very little influence with Bill." In fact, according to John Goodwin, who was briefly on Crusade's staff in the late 1950s, staff members rarely gave back negative reports or questioned his ideas. "He didn't want to hear anything negative," explains Goodwin, "so we didn't tell him anything negative, so he didn't always get a complete picture of what was happening." Goodwin told Charles Hummel of IVCF that he considered Bright "an example par excellence of positive thinking" who was unable to "seriously accommodate the existence or presence of a problem." Given these internal dynamics, Crusade closely reflected Bill Bright's vision, authority, and will.[21]

It Is Happening Here

As Crusade grew and expanded in different directions, Bright looked to new sources of guidance and advice. In the early 1950s, he had turned primarily to Mears, Halverson, and Dawson Trotman. By the late 1950s and early 1960s, Bright spent considerable amounts of time with politically conservative businessmen and, according to Kendall, "looked to his closest business friends for advice." "Bright tended to surround himself with guys who were wealthy," observes Jon Braun, who joined Crusade in 1960, "[and] most of them tended to be Republican conservatives." Bright found that his strongest base of financial support was located in Texas—ranchers and oilmen were major contributors—and the Sunbelt, particularly Arizona and Southern California. Partly through his friendships with politically conservative businessmen, Bright's political interests became more evident.[22]

Bright's foremost political concern remained the threat of communism, and his anticommunist warnings became more frequent and more dire. In 1960, Bright sent copies of an anticommunist tract—*It Can Happen Here*—to supporters. The author, C. Calvin Herriott, had briefly been on Crusade's staff in the early 1950s. Herriott warned that "Communism fully intends to conquer the world by or before 1973, and the Reds consider their program to be as much as five years ahead of schedule." Bright felt Herriott was not alarmist enough in his warning. "A careful examination," wrote Bright, "of the Communist strategy to capture the college campuses of America reveals that it *is* happening here." As evidence, Bright claimed that "[h]undreds of professors are known to be Communists while thousands of their colleagues are known sympathizers." Bright believed that little time remained to contain the communist threat and continued to portray Campus Crusade as an antidote for student radicalism and communist infiltration. "Through this ministry," he asserted, "radical groups have lost their influence in student government and with campus newspapers." Bright argued that the answer to communism was not social action, but evangelism. "If America is to remain free or if America is to regain her strength, morally and spiritually," he explained at a prayer breakfast hosted by the governor of Arizona, "it will be because individually we have become awakened to our dependence upon Christ." At the same time that Bright saw America under siege from communist forces abroad and domestically, he still believed that God's special blessing remained upon the United States. After he returned from his 1961 trip to Asia, Bright instructed his supporters to "thank God for our Country." Bright commented that his trip had helped him "to realize as never before how God has blessed our country above all others." Like many other evangelicals, Bright believed that God had blessed the United States in order to use American Christians to "fulfill the Great Commission." America alone had "the necessary manpower and finances."[23]

Despite Bright's articulation of this evangelical manifest destiny, he was not optimistic about the direction of the country. The election of John F. Kennedy in 1960 seemed a particularly ominous sign. Dale Bruner, who knew Bright through Hollywood Presbyterian, recalls Bright's fear that "the pope was going to have a hotline to the White House." Jon Braun remembers Bright's fear that Kennedy's election would be "'the last time we'll see a free election in America.'" Bright's fears were common in evangelical circles. Citing official Catholic rejection of the separation of church and state, many evangelicals and some mainline Protestants worried that a Catholic president would be beholden to Vatican directives. Bright, moreover, was just as alarmed over Kennedy's party affiliation as over his religion. "I remember him complaining highly about the politics of JFK," recollects Bill Counts. Bright's political views had evolved little since leaving Oklahoma. "Bill, coming from rural [Oklahoma] outside of Tulsa . . . ," explains fellow Oklahoman Jim Craddock, "that is extremely conservative territory up there, and so Bill was very, very conservative politically."[24]

Shortly after Kennedy's election, Bright endorsed Christian Citizen, a fledgling political movement organized by Gerri von Frellick, a Denver real estate developer active in Republican politics and a Crusade donor. Bright wrote an endorsement of the movement and contacted figures such as Congressman Walter H. Judd and L. Nelson Bell (Billy Graham's father-in-law) to encourage them to support Christian Citizen. Although "evangelism is my major concern," Bright wrote Bell, "I am becoming increasingly aware of the need for strong Christian leadership in government from the local precinct to the White House." As civilization faced "its darkest hour," he tendered hope that "Christian Citizens can help to bring Christ and Christian principles back into our government more than any movement of its kind." According to newspaper accounts of Christian Citizen, Bright planned to write a study guide for the movement.[25]

Von Frellick, with the encouragement of political conservatives from Herbert Hoover to J. Howard Pew, launched Christian Citizen to encourage Christians to become politically active in precinct-level groups. Although until recently scholars have paid little attention to evangelical political activism prior to the 1970s, Christian Citizen illustrates that some evangelical leaders were looking for political vehicles much earlier.[26] Christian Citizen—the organization's logo was an American flag overlaid with a cross—was a blend of evangelical faith, anticommunism, and economic individualism. An organizational manual chided "evangelical Christians [who have] abdicated citizenship responsibility" and reminded readers that the foundations of the United States "were laid in the Christian faith." A "precinct primer" added that "America, and the Constitution, is primarily a story of Christians . . . carrying out their convictions." Christian Citizen warned of the dangers of government centralization and socialism and encouraged American Christians to defend their religious, political, and economic freedoms. Von Frellick won the backing of Howard Kerschner's

Christian Freedom Foundation, a conservative economic think tank and advocacy group that offered to make its journal *Christian Economics* the official organ of Christian Citizen. With the assistance of Texas youth evangelist Gene Edwards and Arizona lawyer and aspiring politician John Conlan, von Frellick sought to establish state chapters across the country, making the most headway in Texas, Arizona, and California.[27]

Von Frellick made some effort to differentiate his organization from groups such as Billy James Hargis's Christian Crusade, Fred Schwarz's Christian Anti-Communist Crusade, and Robert Welch's John Birch Society. He termed Schwarz's organization "terrific" and lauded the Birch Society for "making a tremendous contribution to alerting the American people [to the danger of communism]." However, he criticized both groups for a "sense of despair" and promised instead to "offer a positive program to combat communism." Moreover, he maintained that unlike the Birch Society, Christian Citizen was "solely an educational program" and "not a political action group." Bright assured Bell that Christian Citizen was a "not an extreme, fanatical movement . . . or I would not want anything to do with it myself." Reflecting the low esteem in which groups such as the Birch Society were held in the media and in the mainstream population, von Frellick responded to negative media coverage of his fledgling organization by further distancing himself from the reputations of these other anticommunist organizations. After a brief splash, Christian Citizen quickly faded from the American political scene. Gene Edwards lost interest, and von Frellick soon transferred his attention to an ultimately unsuccessful campaign for the Colorado governorship.[28]

Conservative anticommunist networks exerted influence on Campus Crusade in the early 1960s, as the organization grew alongside other anticommunist organizations in the Sunbelt and tapped wealthy anticommunists for needed funds. "He had," affirms Peter Gillquist, "a lot of John Birchers supporting Crusade, a lot of men that were very politically conservative, like the [Nelson Bunker and William Herbert] Hunt brothers and others that really saw Crusade as the answer to the spreading threat of communism on the campus." Bunker Hunt, one of four sons of the Texas oil magnate H. L. Hunt, began supporting Crusade in the early 1960s and also gave generously to the Birch Society. "Many of the early people attracted to support Crusade financially were of the John Birch Society," comments staff member Frank Kifer, who says that some Texas ranchers distributed "John Birch tapes" and tapes of Schwarz and Edgar C. Bundy—another fiery anticommunist lecturer—to Campus Crusade staff. It is difficult to know exactly where to place Bright on the anticommunist spectrum of the early 1960s. "I would say [his anticommunism was] somewhere between Nixon and John Birch," comments Jon Braun. "I would have never called Bright a John Bircher, but I think he was sympathetic." The line between respectable and extremist anticommunism was ill-defined in the early 1960s. Bright's alarmist warnings about international and domestic communism resembled the rhetoric of anticommunists like Fred Schwarz, but he never engaged in red-baiting along the lines of Birch founder Robert Welch. Welch believed Franklin Roosevelt, George Marshall, and Dwight Eisenhower to be communist sympathizers, if not communist agents. Bright—like most conservative anticommunists—admired figures such as Douglas MacArthur and J. Edgar Hoover but did not attempt to smear individual moderates and liberals with the taint of communism.[29]

Campus Crusade remained first and foremost an evangelistic ministry, but the pull of political anticommunism exerted a decided and sometimes divisive impact on the organization in the early 1960s. Bright remained anxious about the political trajectory of the United States as the 1960s progressed. "He said to our staff leaders in 1964," recalls Gillquist, "that if we don't elect Goldwater, the Communist flag will be hoisted over the White House." According to Braun, during the "Goldwater era" "there were many Campus Crusaders actively campaigning . . . down on the streets of San Bernardino." Despite the broad sympathy for anticommunism and conservative politics in evangelical circles, many evangelicals were wary of political activism, and most Crusade staff members remained focused on evangelizing students. Crusade's anticommunism "did not necessarily flow down beyond Bill," interprets Jim Craddock, "because [contrary to Bright's thinking] on the campus itself communism wasn't a problem." According to Gordon Klenck, Bright's anticommunism was so pronounced that it may have turned off some potential contributors. "I think because Bill was so strong on that [anticommunism]," he reflects, that "for some moderate evangelicals who didn't feel quite as strongly it caused a slight pulling back." Furthermore, Bright's involvement in the Christian Citizen bothered some staff members. "One or two of them," comments Gene Edwards, who was von Frellick's assistant in 1962, "said to him [Bright] in my presence, 'I didn't join Crusade to get into a political movement.'" While anticommunism formed a salient part of his worldview, Bright retained his primary dedication to spiritual causes. "You could never separate Bill from personal evangelism," asserts Craddock.[30]

The unease of some staff and supporters with political activism and his own desire to keep Crusade focused primarily on evangelism led Bright to mostly avoid public involvement in politics. "He did not take big public political stands," says Bill Counts, "because he wanted the movement to be focused on evangelism." Similar reasoning also led Bright to discourage staff members from involving themselves in the civil rights movement of the early 1960s. "Bill made me get out of the NAACP," says Frank Kifer, on Crusade staff since the mid-1950s. "I wanted to go to Selma when I was the Crusade director at Texas." "He [Bright] said," Kifer continues, "'I totally sympathize with what they're doing, but we don't take political stands or we'll get our focus off evangelism.'" Bright's restriction on Kifer's activism was ironic given his support for Christian Citizen, but his cautious attitude toward the civil rights movement was typical of other evangelical leaders outside the South. "Bill was deaf in the left ear," comments Kifer, "and he was deaf in his left ear politically too." Crusade was still a small organization in the early 1960s, and Bright's political rhetoric and activism attracted very little attention. As Crusade became a more prominent organization on the evangelical landscape, Bright would find it more difficult to keep his political interests from attracting public notice.[31]

What Kind of a Movement Is This?

Although Bill Bright and Campus Crusade had already accepted the necessity of fund-raising, Crusade took a step in 1962 that forced the ministry to focus more intently on cultivating major donors. In 1961, Bright sent Gordon Klenck to investigate the potential purchase of the Arrowhead Springs hotel and resort, nestled in the mountains above San Bernardino. Attracted by the natural hot mineral springs, the explorer David Noble Smith built a sanitarium at the future site of Arrowhead Springs in 1854. Subsequent owners operated a casino at the spa. In 1940, a hotel and resort opened on the property that initially attracted A-list Hollywood stars like Rita Hayworth. By the 1950s, celebrities and other affluent vacationers were traveling to new locations, and the resort became "something of a white elephant" for several subsequent owners. By 1961, it had been virtually unused for several years when Bright learned that it was available for $2 million. Klenck returned from his scouting mission gushing that the acquisition of Arrowhead Springs would transform the ministries of Crusade "a hundredfold." It had only been three years since Crusade had acquired the Lake Minnetonka grounds, but the organization had already outgrown that facility. The number of staff had more than tripled, and the organization lacked the space to host large student conferences. Moreover, the Minnesota location made little sense for an organization whose founders still lived in Southern California.[32]

Bright himself drove up to see the 1,735-acre resort and envisioned the ministry being able to host a thousand students at a time, many of whom would be much more eager to visit Southern California than Minnesota. On the downside, he reflected, "from the time our work had begun we had had only enough money for our daily needs"—Crusade's annual budget was around $200,000. Bright later wrote that he fell to his knees and asked God whether or not Crusade was meant to purchase the property. "Then," Bright chronicled, "though not in an audible voice, God spoke to me as clearly as if there had been a public address system in the room." "Unmistakably," Bright continued, "I heard Him say, 'I have been saving this for Campus Crusade for Christ. I want you to have it, and I will supply the funds to pay for it.'" Bright cried tears of joy and responded to the divine message: "I claim this property in your name." In order to get further advice and begin laying the fund-raising plans, Bright invited a number of prominent supporters to Arrowhead Springs early in 1962. At first, they were skeptical. Arlis Priest, an Arizona real estate broker and Crusade supporter, remembers that many of the men were somewhat taken aback by Bright's audacious idea, particularly when Bright informed them that Crusade had no financial resources to commit to the purchase. "I'm a real estate man," comments Priest, "and I'm asking myself at that time, 'How do you buy a two-million-dollar property with no money?'" Priest's recollection helps explain how these evangelical businessmen became enamored with Bright's vision. "The first day we didn't think he could possibly buy it," continues Priest, "but then listening to his dreams . . . he really felt God wanted Crusade to have that as a headquarters."[33]

A number of Bright's top staff balked at the thought of committing the thriving ministry to such a risky proposition. "That decision was made over a lot of opposition from some of us on the inside," states Bob Kendall. "But the big hitters money-wise encouraged Bill, and it happened." In November 1962, Crusade borrowed the money to make a $15,000 deposit and then raised enough funds to make a $130,000 payment within a month. On 1 December, the ministry moved into its new home. Priest offered to donate a year of service to help Bright organize the transition to Arrowhead Springs and oversee the process of updating the hotel's infrastructure. He quickly sold his home in Arizona and along with Bright, Ray Nethery, and Crusade's office staff, moved into the organization's new headquarters. Priest's memory of his first days at Arrowhead Springs provides a window into the ethos of the organization at the time. The morning after they moved into the new headquarters, Priest found himself up at five o'clock to unload office furniture that Crusade's secretaries had driven to Arrowhead Springs. "I thought," comments Priest, who was used to hiring people to perform such work, "what kind of a movement is this?" Arrowhead Springs was, in fact, something of a white elephant. The facilities needed to be painted, the toilets leaked, and the sewage system needed overhauling. Priest asked Bright about the remodeling budget. "Arlis," replied Bright, "we don't have any money. We'll have to raise it.'"[34]

Crusade's first months at Arrowhead Springs were both exciting and harrowing. The ministry quickly reaped benefits by hosting much larger student conferences, and it was easy for the staff to foresee years of rapid growth ahead. The financial deadlines, however, were a constant shadow over the ministry. "The monthly payment schedule," wrote Bright eight years later, "was a very stiff one and there followed a series of financial cliff-hanging experiences that forced us to depend wholly upon the Lord." Many of the Brights' friends avoided them because they knew of the organization's mounting financial pressure and expected the Arrowhead Springs acquisition to fail. Also, tension between Campus Crusade and charismatic Christians flared up. A number of charismatic businessmen from San Bernardino expressed an interest in donating toward the new headquarters. According to Christian Citizen's Gene Edwards, the businessmen began to claim that "Bill Bright had been in a hot Pentecostal meeting and had spoken in tongues." Edwards confirms that the businessmen prayed for Bright to speak in tongues at the meeting. "Bill Bright," he explains, "didn't do anything in the world but smile graciously." Once Crusade hardened its policy against speaking in tongues, the ministry lost the financial support of some Pentecostal and charismatic donors. In light of such difficulties, Crusade staff remember the anxiety caused by constant fund-raising deadlines. "We'd all be praying," recollects Kendall, "and if we didn't get this payment made, we'd lose it [the Arrowhead Springs headquarters]. All of a sudden Bill would come out and say, 'Praise the Lord, the payment will be made.'"[35]

In light of the monthly payments and the need to make the facilities operational, Crusade began to develop the fund-raising skills for which the ministry would become famous. Guy Atkinson, a construction mogul, pledged $300,000—more than the entire ministry's annual budget as of

Campus Crusade's new Arrowhead Springs headquarters, ca. 1967. Courtesy of J. Kent Hutcheson.

1960—if Crusade could raise the remaining $1.57 million within a year. Crusade secured Atkinson's donation through frantic fund-raising and a $1 million dollar loan backed by a number of businessmen. Bright proved much more effective at asking for money than making it, as the connections that he had slowly built up over the prior decade paid off. "Bill," says Klenck, "contacted lots of entrepreneurs and any people that he knew that had funds who were committed believers and challenged and invited them to help purchase the property." Bright attributed the acquisition to God's favor and answered prayer, but it is also clear that by this point Bright had shed any lingering inhibitions about asking donors for money. Although he had no prior experience, Arlis Priest also became a consummate fund-raiser. Priest called companies all across Southern California and found businessmen willing to contribute moving trucks, sandblasters, tractors, and plumbers. Although evangelical businessmen were especially eager to help, Priest found that he could also persuade non-Christians to support the ministry. "I made it sound like we were really reaching young college students," explains Priest, "getting them off drugs and crime and stuff to make it [Crusade's ministry] attractive." Even after the $1 million loan was secured, Crusade still needed to raise $135,000 annually to make the payments. Priest found it to be an easy task. He was assisted in fund-raising efforts by Howard Ball, who joined Crusade's staff in 1964 to organize church-based "Lay Institutes of Evangelism," which targeted church members rather than students. Priest and Ball prayed that they would receive $10,000 from each person they called so that it would only take them a few days to raise the money. If a donor offered a lesser amount, they diplomatically asked the donor to pray about giving the full amount requested. "We raised the annual payment in a half a day," says Priest.[36]

Crusade did not rely only on donations. Bright and the organization continued to develop schemes to provide the ministry with income. One plan, proposed by former staff member Paul Allen, involved the management of apartment buildings purchased at rock-bottom prices from the Federal Housing Administration (FHA). Crusade formed a subsidiary, Campus Associates, to handle these transactions. A third-party group of investors purchased the properties and gave them to Campus Associates—which, as a nonprofit, could receive rental income tax-free—with the expectation that some of the properties would be returned several years later. Ray Nethery, Crusade's vice president at the time, opposed the plan and questioned its legality. According to Bright biographer Michael Richardson, the FHA investigated Campus Associates' $727,000 purchase of a Fort Worth apartment complex in 1965 and concluded that the acquisition was "regular in every way." In any event, such investments were risky. The FHA foreclosed on the Fort Worth property when Campus Associates failed to develop an adequate rental income flow to cover the mortgage and pay its taxes. Because Campus Associates had also failed to pay some of its employees' withholding and social security taxes, the IRS filed a tax lien against Campus Associates and Campus Crusade, and the U.S. Justice Department planned a lawsuit. The foreclosure generated negative publicity for the ministry—"Crusade Richer, U.S. Holds Bag" read the *Fort Worth Press* headline. Given Bright's history in business and investments and the increasing success of Bright and Priest in simply asking for money, Crusade probably should have simply relied on prayer and fund-raising to meet its debt obligations. Nethery, despite his vigorous dissent from the plan, does not believe that any gross improprieties were committed. "On the one hand you kind of groan over some of the details," he explains, "but on the other hand . . . I think almost any ministry has some areas where there are feet of clay." Nethery decided to stay on staff, but Bright promoted Bob Kendall, Crusade's director of affairs for Latin America, to vice president in his place.[37]

In early 1963, Campus Crusade prepared to formally dedicate its new headquarters at Arrowhead Springs. Bill and Vonette left the Bel Air residence they had shared for nearly ten years with Henrietta Mears. It had been the only home their two sons had known. Although Mears had considerable help from her assistants at the church, she had also relied extensively on Vonette Bright to help with the housekeeping and entertaining. Increasingly, however, the demands of the ministry were taking the Brights away from Los Angeles. Although Bill often traveled alone because of the inconvenience of taking small children on trips, the entire family had on occasion spent several months at the Lake Minnetonka facility. Still, the idea of leaving Mears behind in Los Angeles detracted from the joy of moving into the new headquarters in the San Bernardino Mountains. They brought Mears up to the resort for an early conference, and they "had even talked and prayed about the possibility of her coming to make her home with us here at Arrowhead Springs." It would probably have been inconceivable for their spiritual mentor to move so far away from Hollywood Presbyterian. Mears, however, died on 20 March 1963. Bill Bright was one of the pallbearers at her celebratory and crowded funeral. Nearly two months later, Crusade officially dedicated its new headquarters.[38]

It was the beginning of a new era for the ministry. Before the purchase of Arrowhead Springs, Campus Crusade was a fledgling evangelical ministry with a shoestring budget and a tiny, cramped office in Los Angeles. The acquisition of a large headquarters and conference grounds gained the attention of the evangelical world and accelerated the ministry's growth. When Crusade dedicated its new headquarters at Arrowhead Springs on 17 May 1963, it symbolized the ministry's success. "I think it put Crusade on the map," comments Curt Mackey, on Crusade's staff since 1957. The hotel helped the ministry attract participants for "executive seminars" that both presented the gospel to businessmen and their families and showcased the ministry to potential donors. Crusade constructed a series of dormitories on the property that enabled the ministry to invite thousands of students to conferences at which they received evangelistic training, traveled to Southern California beaches to practice evangelism, and were asked to consider joining staff. Many of them did.[39]

5

The Jesus Revolution
from Berkeley to Dallas

On Monday, 23 January 1967, the campus of the University
of California at Berkeley appeared poised to explode into another round of student protest and turmoil. The preceding
Friday, the California Board of Regents—prodded by newly
inaugurated Governor Ronald Reagan—fired Clark Kerr,
president of the University of California system since 1958.
During his gubernatorial campaign, Reagan had spoken dis-
paragingly of the "mess at Berkeley" and "sexual orgies so vile
I cannot describe them," and he lambasted Kerr for failing to
impose order on disruptive students. A scant two years before
his firing, Kerr had struggled with mixed success to navigate
the university through the Free Speech Movement and subsequent protests. Student radicals were suspicious of Kerr as an
establishment figure who had helped cement the connections
of the "knowledge industry" with government and business,
particularly the defense sector. Nevertheless, although radical students dissented from Kerr's establishmentarian liberalism, they more passionately loathed Reagan's anticommunist
conservatism.[1]

That Monday, a large crowd gathered around the steps of
Sproul Hall, the locus of campus activism at Berkeley. Most
of the students came to protest Kerr's dismissal and expected
to hear student leaders denounce Reagan's action. Instead,
they found themselves listening to Christian folk songs performed by the New Folk, a Campus Crusade traveling musi-
cal ensemble. Crusade had reserved the area several weeks in
advance and refused to allow other student groups to make
a statement on the Kerr firing. According to Jo Anne Butts,
a local Inter-Varsity staffer, the "mocking in the crowd was

almost unbearable as a result." Butts reported that Crusade interpreted the large audience produced by Kerr's dismissal as a divine blessing. Protests aside, most Berkeley students had already moved from folk music into edgier forms of rock and roll. After the New Folk finished their performance, the crowd—at a university where campus life no longer revolved around athletics and the Greek system—heard a football player from a large Southern university speak about how Jesus Christ had changed his life. Finally, Jon Braun, Crusade's top university speaker, took the platform. Braun estimates that around five thousand students were in attendance and that "about two-thirds of them were probably there because of Clark Kerr." A charismatic and adroit speaker, Braun managed to proclaim his message despite the crowd's discontent. According to Peter Gillquist, Braun went after one heckler and "shut him down." Braun talked about God's love as the only solution for the world's problems. Following the talk, hundreds of Crusade staff and students approached those in the audience and sought to evangelize them using the *Four Spiritual Laws*. It was a rather bizarre encounter between two very different American subcultures: late-1960s Berkeley and evangelical Christianity.[2]

Contemporary and later accounts of student culture in the late 1960s have mostly focused on two phenomena: the New Left and the counterculture. The New Left, which briefly became a mass movement through its strident opposition to the Vietnam War, grew out of a mixture of Old Left labor advocacy, radical pacifism, and white civil rights activism. The counterculture, a generational mood rather than a coherent movement, was a cultural rebellion centered on sex, drugs, and rock music that broadly permeated youth culture in the late 1960s and early 1970s.[3] Recently, scholars have begun to explore conservative forms of 1960s student activism, such as Young Americans for Freedom (YAF).[4] Yet despite the recent burst of interest in the conservative movements of the 1960s, historians have paid relatively little attention to the cultural and political significance of conservative evangelical activism—student and otherwise—in the late 1960s.[5] When they discuss the religious activism of the era, historians more commonly focus on left-leaning activists like Daniel and Philip Berrigan, William Sloane Coffin, and Martin Luther King Jr.[6] Moreover, many scholars are more fascinated by the "new religions" that made modest inroads among some segments of the American population than they are by the more widespread and influential evangelical movements that played a central role in American culture and politics for the remainder of the twentieth century.[7] Evangelicals, however, contributed in significant ways to American activism in the late 1960s and early 1970s. For example, on 4 July 1970, Billy Graham presided over an "Honor America" event in Washington at which he urged Americans to "wave the flag again!"[8] One key locus of evangelical activism was the university, where Campus Crusade responded vigorously to the New Left, antiwar protests, and the counterculture.

The late 1960s and early 1970s were a tumultuous, creative, and fruitful time for American evangelicals and for Campus Crusade. In an era known for student experimentation with leftist politics, hallucinogens, sex, and Asian religions, Crusade grew rapidly as it responded adroitly to a changing campus culture. Crusaders learned about grassroots organizing and protesting from the New Left and the antiwar movement, haltingly adopted some elements of the counterculture through the Jesus Movement, and began to become more socially aware, especially on the issue of race. Precisely as Crusade was capturing the attention of a new generation of students, the ministry found itself staggered by internal strife, much like other activist organizations such as YAF and Students for a Democratic Society (SDS). Bill Bright's firm grip on the ministry helped Crusade transcend internal discord, and the organization entered the 1970s in a position to achieve cultural influence far beyond the university campus. In 1972, Crusade hosted Explo '72, an evangelistic youth conference and festival in Dallas. Explo '72, which featured rock music, racial diversity, and an inchoate theological ecumenism, would have been an unrecognizable anathema to an evangelical audience a decade earlier and showed the extent of the evangelical commitment to remain close to the mainstream of American culture. Richard Nixon's interest in utilizing Explo '72 for his own political purposes also foreshadowed the courtship between evangelicals and conservative politicians that accelerated in the mid-1970s.

Why Not Try Christ?

When Campus Crusade brought hundreds of staff, students, and supporters — including Billy Graham — to Berkeley in January 1967, the ministry's stated objective, as usual, was evangelism. If the organization had intended to maximize evangelistic results, however, Crusade would have chosen a school at which the Greek system and athletics still dominated campus life, as the ministry had always experienced its greatest success in fraternities and sororities and among athletes. Crusade chose to go to Berkeley because the campus was, in Bright's words, "the fountainhead of the radi-

Campus Crusaders telephone students during the "Berkeley Blitz," January 1967.
Courtesy of J. Kent Hutcheson.

cal movement." "Many kinds of radical groups had been bidding for the minds and lives of students," wrote Bright shortly after the event. "Part of it [the Berkeley convention] was to ding the noses of the free speech people," explains Gillquist. "The other part was to do some bona fide evangelism." Crusade undoubtedly perceived that a high-profile evangelistic campaign at Berkeley would create media attention useful for building organizational momentum, attracting financial supporters, and recruiting additional staff. When Crusade initially planned its "Berkeley Blitz," it did not know how prescient its timing would be. The week before the blitz, a confluence of New Left organizers, "acid devotees," and old beatniks— Gary Snyder, Timothy Leary, and Jerry Rubin all made appearances—held a "Human Be-In" in Golden Gate Park in an unsuccessful attempt to establish unity. Kerr's dismissal then added to the chaotic atmosphere in the city and on the campus itself. Such developments heightened media interest in Crusade's campaign.[9]

The approximately six hundred Crusaders who "invaded" Berkeley used student directories and a phone bank assembled at a local sorority to telephone each of Berkeley's twenty-seven thousand students. Several Crusade events—including concerts, dinners for international students, and a performance by André Kole, an illusionist on staff with Crusade—were well attended. Billy Graham keynoted a closing event at the campus's

Greek Theatre, which drew eight thousand people, many of them students. Crusaders made a concerted effort to contact students individually, both through the telephone bank and on the campus itself. James Berney, an Inter-Varsity staff member, claimed to "know students who were talked to some fifteen times on campus." At Berkeley, Crusade augmented its standard evangelistic presentation with rhetoric tailored for a more activist student generation. "Jesus Christ was history's greatest revolutionist," trumpeted Bright repeatedly. "Right revolution—spiritual revolution," he insisted, "comes through the spirit of the living Christ." Graham sought to establish common ground with student activists. He conceded he could not "defend the church for the many things it has done in the name of Christianity" but maintained that spiritual renewal at Berkeley "could change a generation" and produce needed social reforms. Graham proclaimed Jesus Christ the solution—a source of joy, victory, fulfillment, and love—to a young generation's headaches, illusions, and emptiness. Underneath the updated rhetoric, Crusade relied on its basic approach. Following lectures and other events and through telephone calls and campus witnessing, Crusaders approached students and asked to share the *Four Spiritual Laws* with them, telling them that Jesus is "God's only provision for man's sin."[10]

Crusade also articulated conservative positions on premarital sex and drug use in response to changing campus mores. Although only a minority of college students joined in the counterculture's demand for "free love," students on many campuses challenged parietal rules and spoke openly about premarital sex. Crusade had worried about changing sexual mores for some time. In particular, Crusade's leadership was concerned that women who wore suggestive clothing might lead male staff and students astray. Bright addressed this issue in a mid-1960s message to staff and students:

[S]ome young men have come to me to say that during the course of the summer that they could no longer go to the cabana [at Crusade's Arrowhead Springs headquarters]. Why? "Well, I can't keep my mind pure for God around lovely girls who are dressed in suggestive two-piece bathing suits." Now, you girls don't know what's wrong because you say, "Well, that's silly. It doesn't affect me that way!" But, you're not a man, and women somehow just can't understand why a man would respond as he does. But a man will lust. Godly men will get back on that throne [of self] and Satan will have a heyday with them.

Jon Braun delivering his "Sex, Love, and Marriage" lecture at Illinois State University, 1966. Courtesy of Peter Gillquist.

Bright encouraged the women to "go back to your homes, learn how to dress as Godly women so that you will not cause your brother to stumble." He insisted that he did not mean for them "to dress dowdy" but encouraged them "to read the Scriptures and see how best to dress."[11]

Such concerns were more pronounced by 1967. When Jon Braun visited campuses, including Berkeley, he gave talks on "Sex, Love, and Marriage." Braun counseled students not to "settle for sex instead of love" and warned that "multiple experiences in intercourse before marriage" drastically reduce the likelihood of a successful marriage. "'Free sex,'" Braun cautioned, "isn't free at all." When he spoke at UCLA in a similar "Blitz," Graham explained that collegians experiencing loneliness and emptiness have turned to "sex, dope, LSD, alcohol or anything that will give them a new kick." "When the kick is over," Graham warned, "all they have to show for it is a headache . . . and a greater sense of emptiness than they had before." "You've tried everything else," Graham appealed to the experimentation of the age, "why not try Christ?"[12]

Crusade's campaign made a splash on the Berkeley campus, as evidenced by the lively discussion on the pages of the *Daily Californian*. The paper editorialized against Crusade's tactics: "[T]here are limits to these activities which should not be overstepped; this group of zealots has managed to transgress those boundaries with gay abandon." The paper contended that

Crusade's "methodology . . . is seemingly inappropriate to the product, for it is hard to believe that anyone will buy the offerings when the sales pitch is so commercially produced." Student letters in the *Californian* remonstrated that Crusade representatives telephoned them early in the morning, and a Berkeley professor complained that advertisements for André Kole's magic show "did not mention the sermon or the sponsoring organization." Christians at Berkeley had mixed reactions to Crusade's blitz. "I don't like Christ to be 'sold' the way you would sell encyclopedias," responded Jeff Porro, an avowed Christian and member of Cal–Berkeley's Young Democrats. "CCC approached people as customers not as people," Porro alleged. A number of IVCF staff voiced similar complaints. "The overwhelming impression," wrote Paul Griffith, president of the Berkeley IVCF chapter, "is that CCC behaves much as a salesman who has a product to sell regardless of the disposition of the prospective buyer." Some Christians critical of Crusade's effort, however, offered grudging admiration. Griffith allowed that the blitz "stimulated many worthwhile discussions between members of other Christian groups and people normally disinterested." "Crusade has an enthusiasm about the Lord's work that is contagious," commented Jo Anne Butts. "It makes the rest of us take inventory and get busy."[13]

Crusade declared an evangelistic triumph at Berkeley, and Bright brushed off criticisms of his ministry's methodology. "We don't try to sell Christ on the telephone," he responded, and he stated that he had not encountered "one single person who has not responded in a friendly way." Crusade's official account of the blitz stated that "over half the students in most of the fraternity, sorority, and dormitory meetings indicated they would like to know how to become Christians when Bill Bright . . . spoke in their houses." Bright maintained that approximately forty "radicals"—"street people" and "hippies"—"prayed to receive Christ during that week." In total, Crusade reported seven hundred "commitments to Christ." IVCF staff at Berkeley were skeptical of Crusade's claims. "They exaggerate statistics in order to impress the Christian public," alleged Butts. The accuracy of the reports is impossible to verify. Given the hundreds of participating Crusade staff and students, each Crusader would only have had to obtain a positive response from one or two students for the organization to have recorded seven hundred "decisions." Gillquist, however, later conceded that "we know of only two [students] who really followed through" with their commitments. "Dollar for dollar," Braun stated, "I think it was one of the weakest things we ever did."[14]

In addition to reporting hundreds of conversions, Crusade claimed to have scored a blow against student radicalism. During the week at Berkeley, Bright struck a conciliatory tone toward campus protests. "We need dissent in society," he was quoted in the *Los Angeles Herald-Examiner*. "The radicals have probably done more than anybody to loosen up the campus for what we're doing." Despite the display of sensitivity, Crusade presented itself as having won a battle against an enemy of its cause. "Billy Graham Quiets Berkeley Radicals," shouted a headline in a Crusade newspaper published shortly after the blitz. Bright claimed that Crusade's initial rally outside Sproul Hall defused a potential crisis. "Had it not been for our presence there," Bright wrote several years later, "few doubt that the Berkeley campus would have been the scene of the most radical of all the demonstrations in the state." Crusade claimed to have out-organized the "radicals, [who were] accustomed to being hailed as the best student organizers." Such brash statements vastly overstated the political impact of the Berkeley Blitz. Crusade's efforts failed to curtail student radicalism on the campus, as evidenced by the "People's Park" protests that produced considerable turmoil and violence during 1968 and 1969. Crusade exerted no significant influence on the trajectory of campus culture at Berkeley. "As has been true following other disturbances," concluded IVCF's Paul Griffith, "the campus lives on, remarkably unperturbed by all the activity of the past week."[15]

Students Denouncing Sin

If the impact of Campus Crusade on Berkeley was transient and uncertain, the impact of Berkeley on Crusade was pronounced and more enduring. By the beginning of 1967, a few Crusade staff members worked on campuses that possessed significant New Left movements or manifestations of the counterculture. More staff, however, came from places like Rice University, Michigan State University, or Oklahoma University where the campus culture had not evolved as quickly. "Everything in Houston was still as it always had been," explains Beverly Counts, whose husband traveled to the Berkeley Blitz. Jimmy Williams, a staff member from Texas, was shocked to find himself kept up all night in Berkeley by "loud acid music" from the adjacent hotel room and even more shocked to see Timothy Leary coming out of the room the next morning. Looking back, longtime staff member Jim Green views the blitz as a "mixed" success but adds that the week changed the direction of the movement. "It was a little shock to the system," he comments, "to run into radical students who were openly expressing themselves in those ways that you weren't used to." Green maintains that the Berkeley experience "radicalized a lot of our staff and students . . . made them more bold in learning how to communicate and express themselves." Up through the mid-1960s, Crusade had grown primarily through its formula of evangelistic outreach to campus Greek houses and athletes. The ministry had already made some accommodations to changes in youth culture. For instance, Crusade replaced its gospel quartet with a folk-singing group—the short skirts and the swaying hips of the young women in the group raised the ire of some culturally more conservative Christians. Rather than rely on quotes from Toynbee and Eisenhower about the need for spiritual awakening, Crusade speakers talked about the revolutionary impact of Jesus Christ. If some of Crusade's top leaders had already perceived the drift of campus culture, the week at Berkeley went far to create a movement-wide recognition that Crusade had entered a new era of campus ministry.[16]

Given its presence on geographically and politically diverse campuses, Campus Crusade responded in several ways to the cultural changes slowly spreading across the nation's colleges and universities. On any campus with significant New Left or antiwar activity, Crusade counterprotested at demonstrations. For example, in 1969, when SDS planned a major fall gathering at the University of Texas in Austin, Crusade sent several hundred staff and students to stage a counterdemonstration. Like members of other conservative groups, Crusaders borrowed tactics from the New Left in an effort to expose what they perceived to be the futility of the New Left agenda and to publicize their own beliefs about Jesus Christ. At such events, Crusade students and staff carried a variety of informative and sometimes clever signs: "Spiritual Reality in Jesus Christ," "Students Denouncing Sin," and "Boycott Hell! Accept Jesus." "We'd get right up there with the students," remembers Jim Green, "and carry signs and banners, [saying] 'Jesus is a Revolutionary.'" "[The] sloganeering and things that they were doing, the radicals were doing," continues Green, "you could just do the same thing."[17]

Crusade staff utilized free speech platforms to answer the New Left, to oppose communism, and to talk about Jesus Christ. Crusade sometimes reserved platforms at key times; on other campuses, Crusaders prepared in advance to seize microphones and engage crowds. After some initial attempts by Jon Braun, Josh McDowell played the key role in this effort. McDowell was a young seminary graduate who became Crusade's most prominent campus speaker in the 1970s and 1980s. Assigned to Crusade's

Campus Crusade event featuring Josh McDowell at the University of Texas, fall 1970.
Courtesy of Sharyn Regier.

ministry in Argentina, McDowell engaged Marxist students at Latin American universities and returned to the United States in 1968 prepared to verbally combat the New Left. "He would get up with a bullhorn," says Alan Scholes, a student involved with Crusade in the late 1960s who later joined staff, "and say, 'I challenge anybody to come and debate me on Marxism.'" After a crowd appeared, McDowell would discuss his encounters with communists in Latin America and then talk about his relationship with Jesus Christ. "Students would be trained . . . to divide and conquer when he was done," explains Scholes. Crusade staff and students imitated McDowell's bold tactics. "I remember certain days," states Glenn Plate, on staff at the University of Minnesota, "that every other student [on the platform] was a Campus Crusade student."[18]

Most Campus Crusade staff members from the late 1960s recount opportunities to confront, debate, and occasionally convert student radicals. "We gathered at the Crusade house in Minneapolis and made signs," Plate recalls, "because we knew everybody was marching on the federal building the next day." "I was carrying a sign that said SDS . . . and then it said Students Denouncing Sin," continues Plate. "[I] literally had people with the Weathermen run by and knock me down and try to take my sign." Conrad Koch, then on Crusade staff at the University of Iowa, also relished being at the center of the maelstrom. In 1968, he went to Chicago during the 1968 Democratic National Convention. "Some of the CCC guys and I were down in Grant Park when the tear gas was coming through the park," Koch remembers. "We were down there talking about Jesus Christ . . . you want peace in Vietnam, well no peace in Vietnam without the prince of peace [Jesus]." "We would have the whole evangelical lingo addressed to the protest movement," explains Koch. In December 1969, Crusade representatives handed out literature during a antiwar rally attended by a quarter of a million at the Washington Monument.[19]

Crusade made some attempts to develop an acculturated outreach to countercultural and radical students. Crusade sent a few staff members to Berkeley to quietly attempt an outreach to student radicals and hippies. The men involved grew beards and wore bib overalls; women grew long straight hair and wore blue jeans. The group, headed by Jack Sparks, evolved into a separate movement called the Christian World Liberation Front (CWLF), whose name played off that of the radical Third World Liberation Front. CWLF received some funding and support from Campus Crusade, but Crusade kept its involvement very low-profile out of fear of offending both its more conservative donors and potential CWLF converts. Within a few months, explains Sparks, "the work I was doing was quickly 'too hot' for him [Bright] to handle." The ties with Crusade largely dissolved. CWLF engaged the New Left more aggressively than most other Crusade staff members, establishing safe houses and "crash pads" for drug addicts, infiltrating SDS meetings, and seeking to persuade student radicals to forego violence. In 1970, antiwar protesters set the Berkeley ROTC building afire in part because of CWLF's refusal to yield the steps of Sproul Hall.[20]

Campus Crusade as a whole did not decide to "go native" during the late 1960s. While confronting the student left, Crusade sought to maximize its opportunities to witness to the broader student population. Many antiwar protests attracted a mixed multitude of true believers, thrill seekers, and curious or uncommitted onlookers, and only a small minority of students across the country associated themselves with radical politics. While Crusaders may have converted a few student radicals, they chiefly found opportunities to engage conservative and moderate students who were unconvinced by the agenda of the New Left. Campuses with strong New Left movements, such as the universities at Austin and Madison, also contained large populations of students receptive to Crusade's anti–New Left, evangelical message. "I think our target was not so much the radicals," comments Bob Horner on the Berkeley Blitz. "The people we reached at Berkeley were the average kids, and the radicals just gave us a platform."[21]

Indeed, although Crusade made some adaptations to changes in campus culture, many of those changes were superficial. As Mark Oppenheimer has observed, at some point in the late 1960s "even the conservatives began to dress down, talk more informally, and listen to different music." Most Crusade staff members grew out their crew cuts and dressed more casually but still remained at arm's length from the counterculture. For example, Bright forbade his male staff members from growing long hair. "The Apostle Paul," he asserted, "was against long hair [for men] and I don't think you would find any Bible scholar who would say Christ had long hair." Bright added that "[w]e make an emphasis on cleanliness for our staff." Also, Bright agonized about the use of Christian rock music. "The New Folk drifted into hard rock for a while," Bright explained, "but we felt that wasn't for us" because of the complaints of "ex-addicts." Moreover, Crusade's bread-and-butter evangelistic approaches remained central to the movement despite the tumult of the late 1960s. If the Greek system and athletics had lost prestige and influence on some campuses, they still controlled the social scene at other schools, and Crusade still found such groups ripe for its evangelistic harvest. In 1966, Crusade formed an "Athletes in Action" division whose staff members—many of whom were recent college graduates—formed basketball and wrestling teams that competitively challenged collegiate teams in exhibitions. Newer strategies supplemented rather than supplanted the older approaches, and Crusade altered its style more than its substance.[22]

At least in terms of organizational growth and visibility, Crusade's multifaceted strategy worked. Almost uniformly, Crusaders look back on the late 1960s and early 1970s as the organization's golden age of campus ministry. Crusade attracted thousands of new staff members, most of whom were recent graduates who had been recruited on the campus. Crusade found it easy to gain an audience for its message and developed large evangelical student movements on scores of campuses, particularly at the large universities of the South and Midwest. "It was a wonderful [time] for Christianity," reflects Jan Lindsey, "because the students were looking for something, and they were open to all kinds of crazy ideas." "If you went out with a loud speaker on the free speech platforms . . . ," she continues, "you could draw a crowd of hundreds of people no matter what kind of crazy philosophy you had." Crusade grew from an organization with a staff of several hundred into an influential evangelical ministry of several thousand. Crusade's growth illustrates the broader success of evangelical youth movements in the Age of Aquarius. The Navigators and Inter-Varsity also used new evangelistic strategies on the campus in the 1960s and early 1970s;

in some instances, the three organizations teamed up to bring speakers like Josh McDowell to free speech platforms. In a much more radically counter-cultural brand of evangelicalism, Chuck Smith baptized hundreds of young "radical Christians" in the Pacific Ocean and incorporated many of them into his rapidly growing Calvary Chapel. A variety of ministries similar to the CWLF also adopted countercultural forms of evangelicalism and became known as the "Jesus People" or "Jesus freaks."[23]

In the late 1960s, conservative organizations such as Campus Crusade and YAF flourished alongside New Left movements, even though conservative and radical groups articulated very different objectives and values. Campus Crusade and SDS, for example, undergirded their respective missions with diametrically opposed philosophies. The Port Huron Statement, the SDS manifesto, proclaimed that "[m]en have unrealized potential for self-cultivation, self-direction, self-understanding, and creativity" and that "[t]he goal of man and society should be human independence." By contrast, Crusade's *Four Spiritual Laws* condemned "self-will" and insisted that true meaning and joy came through the subjection of the self to Jesus Christ. SDS sought radical political change and envisioned a "participatory democracy" establishing a socialist economy. Crusade mobilized students to practice a lifestyle of evangelism and consider overseas missions.[24]

Underneath the surface, however, there were similarities between these two campus groups. "We are people of this generation," explained Tom Hayden in the Port Huron Statement, "bred in at least modest comfort, housed in the universities, looking uncomfortably to the world we inherit." The same description could be applied to most Campus Crusade staff members, who, if perhaps bred in somewhat less comfort, were at least as uncomfortable about their inherited world. Indeed, students on the right and the left shared an alienation from mainstream American society and expressed similar yearnings for authenticity and meaning. Furthermore, many persons involved in the New Left as well as their evangelical counterparts vacillated between a sense of present calamity and a utopian vision of the future. Bright was not given to colorful apocalypticism — he was skeptical of the eschatological emphasis of his staff member Hal Lindsey, who shortly after leaving Crusade published the best-selling *Late Great Planet Earth*. Nevertheless, Bright shared Lindsey's conviction of a world on the brink of collapse. He frequently alluded to "the riots, the plunderings, the burnings, the bloodshed and even the murders that have left many of the nation's campuses in shambles." A 1969 Crusade newspaper warned that because of "militant organizations," "this could well be the last year of the college and university as they stand today." Yet Bright and his staff suggested college students could overcome these problems through an intense commitment to evangelism. He believed that all individuals, if they obtained a proper understanding of Christianity, would accept Jesus Christ. Such hopes were wildly optimistic, but Bright's utopian vision for Campus Crusade coalesced with the activist and optimistic ethos of the late 1960s college campus. Evangelical and radical students shared in some of the key characteristics of the era: idealism, alarmism, and a belief in the possibility of radical change.[25]

In the late 1960s, vocal evangelicals like the students and staff of Crusade comprised a decided minority on the campus. Like YAF, Crusade was more of a thorn in the side of SDS in the late 1960s than a viable competitor. Conservatives of all sorts faced an uphill battle on American campuses. Only a small fraction of students—perhaps one-sixth or one-fifth of the overall student population—labeled themselves as "conservative" or "Far Right" in a 1971 survey. Moreover, only 42 percent of American students told Gallup pollsters in 1970 that "organized religion" was a "relevant" part of their lives, far below the response of the general population. Despite their move toward popular culture, popular culture hardly embraced evangelical organizations like Campus Crusade. In a 1970 issue on "190 things to avoid" in order to achieve happiness, *Esquire* placed Crusade at the head of "ten movements to have no part of," ahead of the Weathermen and the Communist Party, USA. Despite such trends and attitudes, however, religion was not disappearing from campus life. Instead, the locus of campus religiosity was shifting. Mainline campus ministries found themselves less able to attract students to their events than they had been in the 1950s and early 1960s. Some mainline campus ministries, which sometimes still enjoyed tacit support from university administrations, endorsed student protest and sought to align their theologies with current campus politics. Jim Wallis, now publisher of the progressive evangelical periodical *Sojourners*, recalls that when he became active in antiwar demonstrations and radical politics, leaders of the Wesley Foundation (a Methodist campus ministry) at Michigan State University told him that he belonged to the "real church." Crusade, by contrast, embraced the activism of the student left but sharply dissented from its political agenda. As Robert Ellwood noted in an early appraisal of the Jesus Movement, the anti-institutionalism of the late 1960s and early 1970s campus ironically worked to the advantage of theologically conservative evangelical organizations rather than the comparatively liberal denominational ministries. Although campuses appeared less hospitable to Christianity in the late 1960s than they had been in the 1950s, Campus Crusade rapidly expanded and maintained a vigorous ministry at many universities and colleges long after the decline of left-leaning campus activism.[26]

Law and Grace

Shortly after reaching the peak of its influence, SDS dissolved amidst internecine warfare in 1969. Internal dissent also crippled YAF. Similarly, Crusade faced its own crisis of authority. Dissatisfied with Bright's leadership and the direction of the organization, the majority of Crusade's top campus directors (each overseeing a geographic division of the campus ministry) resigned in 1968. By the late 1960s, the organization had developed a generation of talented and experienced campus leaders who desired to move Crusade in directions contrary to Bright's focus on evangelism. Specifically, staff discontent emerged around several clusters of issues. Many staff, including some who chose to remain with Crusade, disliked what they perceived to be the rigid and performance-oriented nature of the ministry and desired greater latitude to explore new ways of evangelizing and discipling students. "Everything in Campus Crusade," comments Jan Lindsey, "was regimented and done by the manual which we had set up in the early years . . . there wasn't much room for creativity." Staff also resented having to fill out weekly performance reports. Jim Craddock, the only top campus director who did not resign during the crisis, remembers that all staff members had to document "fifteen follow-up appointments and fifteen evangelistic appointments each week, with a hundred decisions a year, or else you were put on probation." Crusade rarely dismissed staff members who failed to meet expectations, but according to Peter Gillquist, the organization moved those with less evangelistic fruit to "assignments that weren't 'strategic.'" "It was almost like a sales organization comparing figures," remarks Bill Counts. The directors of the campus ministry became the most disgruntled about the requirements, because Bright expected them to maintain the same level of personal evangelism despite their additional responsibilities. "I can remember Friday afternoons," recalls Gillquist, "I'd have thirteen people [listed on the report], and I'd just go out and crank out the last two in the energy of the flesh."[27]

A second area of discontent focused on the effectiveness of Crusade's strategy for campus evangelism and discipleship. Braun states that Crusade's "greatest struggle" was its failure to motivate students to become involved in local churches. It was relatively easy for Crusade's charismatic speakers to persuade a group of students to pray to "receive Christ," but it was more difficult to get even those who had made serious commitments to look beyond the local Campus Crusade chapter to the wider Christian world. "I would literally go around," remembers Gillquist, "and try to pick kids up Sunday morning to go with us . . . they just didn't want to go." Students sometimes asked staff members to baptize them or to give them communion. In order to avoid giving the appearance that the organization was usurping the functions of local churches, Crusade did not allow its staff members to perform such sacraments. Hal Lindsey, against Crusade policy and to Bright's chagrin, baptized several students near Arrowhead Springs. Braun also baptized students on occasion. Part of the frustration for Braun and his followers was their increasing doubt that Crusade's program of evangelism could achieve social change without incorporating student converts into churches that would encourage them to persevere in their Christian commitments. "What we're doing isn't changing the world," Gillquist concluded, playing on Crusade's *Come Help Change the World* slogan. "The world's getting less Christian, not more Christian. . . . Just getting decisions out of people and giving them no place in which to follow him [Christ] does not produce long-lasting results." Braun was quite skeptical of most of the churches in the San Bernardino area and around many of the universities he visited. He longed for a purified, New Testament church, and he befriended some individuals loosely connected to the local church movement of Witness Lee, which formed a number of small "house churches" in California during the 1960s. Given these impulses, the logical solution, as far as Braun and Gillquist were concerned, was for Crusade to form its own churches.[28]

Finally, a host of Crusade's top leaders questioned Bright's leadership. Their chief complaint was that Bright micromanaged Crusade and hesitated to delegate substantial power to his top assistants. Crusade's directors would often have to wait for hours in order to see him. Especially as the ministry grew rapidly during the mid-1960s and Crusade created an overseas ministry, a lay ministry, and an athletic ministry, a bottleneck tended to grow outside of Bright's office. "There's something wrong," comments Gordon Walker, campus director in Ohio at the time, "when every single decision, whether it be a life-threatening decision or just a decision about what kind of flowers we put in the flowerbed, has to go through one man." Also, when Bright felt strongly about an issue, he was willing to decide counter to the consensus of his top assistants. "There was a top leadership council," recounts Walker. "At first I think there were seven of us on that, and I think it was later expanded to eleven men, and literally I've seen Bill overrule all eleven of us." "If he wanted to go a different way," Walker comments, "that's the way he went." Bright "ran Crusade like a benevolent dictator," says Bill Counts. "I think if he'd been willing to have more feedback and listen . . . he might have been able to handle it [the crisis with Braun and Gillquist] better." Part of the problem was that many of Crusade's top leaders were seminary graduates who desired greater autonomy. "They were all chiefs," interprets Jan Lindsey, "and very few braves."[29]

In 1966, Jon Braun assumed the position of U.S. field coordinator, in essence national director of the campus ministry. "He was just phenomenal," says Bailey Marks, who sided with Bright during the crisis. "He had more charisma than you could possibly imagine. He was sharp. He was good looking. He was articulate. We've never had a speaker equal to him." Braun and a number of his assistants were among those who chafed under the weekly reports. In part because of his frustrations with what he termed the organization's "legalism," Braun began more strongly emphasizing a message of grace in his campus lectures, stressing that "our standing with God is not based on a performance but is based on the grace of God." It was hardly a new message for an evangelical to employ, but perhaps Braun's talks on grace were especially well suited to a student generation yearning for authenticity and liberation. "I'd be preaching on this stuff," claims Braun, "and you'd see these kids out there in the audience [with] tears streaming down their face because they realized that God loved them in spite of their failure to be perfect." At the same time, some staff members close to Braun began to think about grace as greater freedom from Crusade's staff manual and an ability to experiment with different ideas and approaches to ministry. "Somebody made the statement," shares Gillquist, "'the law came by Bill Bright, but grace and truth came by Jon Braun.'" "Bill got word of this," continues Gillquist, "and was furious . . . that was kind of the beginning of the end." Other staff imitated Braun's message, which, although it did not contradict Crusade's basic evangelistic presentation or the *Four Spiritual Laws*, created a new emphasis and a locus of charismatic authority around Braun.[30]

While Braun developed a noteworthy following among the campus ministry staff, others within the ministry accused him of fomenting division, confusion, and discontent. "They weren't talking about grace in any sense that we didn't already understand," maintains Swede Anderson.

"It was clearly bringing division . . . it was creating a group who were in a sense a spiritual elite who felt they'd had an experience that the rest of us hadn't." Braun and his followers began questioning the need for Christians to regularly confess their sins, emphasizing that Jesus's sacrifice made such confession unnecessary. Bright vetted Braun's ideas with evangelical leaders such as Dan Fuller and Harold Lindsell, who warned him against a slippery slope into antinomianism. Josh McDowell considered Braun and his followers "more committed to strange dogmas and ideas than to Bright's original vision [of evangelism]." Staff loyal to Bright worried that the conflict could tear the ministry apart and felt that Braun, Gillquist, and others who were discontented should simply have left Crusade. "Rather than resigning from the team," comments Kent Hutcheson, "they sought to change the organizational and philosophical culture of the team in a conspiratorial manner." "I think the heart of the conflict was the problem these men had with authority," Hutcheson concludes.[31]

Beginning in 1966, Braun and Gillquist spoke several times with Bright about their concerns. Despite his reputation for authoritarian leadership, Bright did not hinder their preaching about grace and initially defended their teachings to concerned evangelicals like Lindsell. In October 1967, however, the disaffected leaders decided to make a more concerted effort to address their grievances. While Braun was on a speaking tour in Kansas, he asked sympathetic colleagues to meet him in Lawrence. They drew up a list of their concerns—focusing on administrative problems, Bright's leadership, and their desire to function more like a church—which they planned to present to Bright. For instance, they wanted a council rather than Bright alone to make decisions about the campus ministry. Crusade's founder and president learned of the meeting and was incensed by the time the group arrived back at Arrowhead Springs. The following Saturday, Bright organized a meeting designed to mediate between the two sides. He invited Henry Brandt, a psychologist and author popular in evangelical circles, to facilitate the session. Bright also brought his board of directors—by that time, he had formed a board made up primarily of businessmen who supported Crusade. Brandt tried to foster a conciliatory tone. He gave the complaints about Bright's leadership a sympathetic hearing, and Bright agreed to address some of the administrative concerns. According to *Christianity Today*, in early 1968 the organization eliminated the requirement that each staff member make fifteen appointments a week with non-Christians. Bright, however, disagreed vigorously with the suggestion that Crusade needed to operate more like a church, which would have pushed the ministry in a sectarian direction and imperiled its broad base of donors. Braun, Gillquist, and the others were satisfied enough with the results of the meeting to remain on staff temporarily, but they and like-minded staff gradually left over the course of 1968. Crusade lost its U.S. field coordinator, five of its six regional directors for the campus ministry, and its director for ministries in Asia. Estimates of the number who left range from several dozen to nearly three hundred, a sizable departure for an organization with approximately one thousand staff members. Braun, Gillquist, and several others eventually became convinced that the Orthodox branch of Christianity represented the continuation of the New Testament church, formed the Evangelical Orthodox Church, and became priests in the Antiochian Orthodox Christian Archdiocese.[32]

The rupture devastated Bright; he felt betrayed by leaders he had recruited and trained. Publicly, he said very little. He wrote a book entitled *How to Love by Faith*, which functioned partly as a description of how he felt he had treated those who had wronged him. Bright at times responded to his critics with displays of charity and grace. Shortly after Gordon Walker submitted his resignation, his wife suffered serious injuries in an automobile accident. According to Walker, "Bill allowed us to stay on staff long enough to get hospitalization for my wife [paid for by the organization]." At the same time, the lingering hurt from the episode continued to simmer and affect his administrative decisions. A second, smaller clash developed between Bright and another group of staff. Several staff centered on the UCLA campus—Hal Lindsey, Bill Counts, and Linus Morris—shared many of Braun's concerns about organizational rigidity but did not believe that Crusade should become a church. They wanted greater latitude to spend more time teaching and training students. Lindsey made apocalyptic prophecy the centerpiece of his campus messages, focusing on what he termed "seven signs" that the end of the world and Christ's return were near. Morris, who was campus director at UCLA, had invited Braun to speak on campus before the latter's resignation and did not rescind the invitation after Braun left staff. Morris also likened the Crusade manual to the "Mosaic law" during a staff meeting. "He [Bright] didn't want anybody to be critical of the organization from within," emphasizes Bill Counts. Bright summoned Morris to Arrowhead Springs for an explanation. When Morris explained that he was following the emphases of Lindsey and Counts, Bright believed he had identified another cluster of rebels. He asked Morris to resign or face dismissal and met with Counts and Lindsey. The three left.[33]

Remarkably, the intraorganizational maelstrom did not retard Crusade's accelerating expansion. Hundreds of recruits joined the organization and gathered at Arrowhead Springs that summer. Bright interpreted the growth as a sign of God's approval. He wrote a letter to all of the staff exulting in the fact that the "dissidents have left us," allowing the ministry to concentrate on its mission.[34] Although some staff rejected Bright's leadership, more saw his vision as a vehicle for the change that all campus activists desired. Moreover, many young evangelicals also admired Bright for his forthright and transparent personal faith. Gene Edwards, who knew Bright through the Christian Citizen initiative of the early 1960s, comments that he "was more Christ-centered than evangelism-centered." Edwards, who later became associated with the "house church" movement, considers Bright one of the few people he has met who was actually "comfortable talking about the Lord Jesus Christ." In the early 1970s, Ron Jenson, who would eventually become involved in Bright's attempt to found a university in San Diego, traveled around the country interviewing Christian leaders as part of a graduate school research project. Jenson recalls that most of the leaders he interviewed expressed passion for their ministries and programs but had relatively little to say about their own spiritual lives. "When we talked with Bill about the ministry," Jenson explains, "he dismissed it, and he talked about Jesus and wept for about an hour."[35]

In some ways, Campus Crusade for Christ appeared similar to other late-1960s campus organizations, sharing with some New Left groups an intense dissatisfaction with the status quo on campus, a utopian vision, grassroots organizing and protesting, and stark internal divisions. Crusade, though, was a very different kind of movement. Already a multinational organization with a variety of ministries, Crusade revolved around the visionary leadership of a single individual who relentlessly pursued his twin goals of building his organization and remaining focused on the task of evangelism. If it was perhaps inevitable that staff members would chafe against Crusade's methodological rigidity and Bright's authoritarianism, Crusade's centralized power structure also enabled it to weather the storms of the late 1960s on a steadier course.

A Christian Woodstock

At the Berkeley Blitz, Peter Gillquist noticed that "Bill [Bright] stayed in the background, which was unusual for him." "I sensed he almost felt out of his element," Gillquist explains. "This is a white-shirt [man] who wears a suit every day and a necktie, by now all passé on the campus . . . I think in the midst of the rabble-rousers he just felt out of place." A *Los Angeles Times* reporter once commented that Bright looked "less like a revolutionist than anyone since Mahatma Gandhi." The Jesus Movement—typified by countercultural evangelicals who sported long hair and blue jeans—gained the attention of the nation's media in the late 1960s and early 1970s. Through its connection with the CWLF and its engagement with the New Left and the counterculture, Crusade often grew side-by-side with the Jesus Movement yet remained a more straitlaced, culturally and politically conservative organization. Bright wryly informed the *Cincinnati Enquirer*, "I like to say that I've been in the Jesus movement for 20 years."[36]

In 1972, Crusade became associated with the tail-end of the Jesus Movement when the ministry hosted a weeklong International Student Congress on Evangelism in Dallas, Texas. Calling the gathering Explo '72 (short for "spiritual explosion"), Crusade aimed to fill the Cotton Bowl with collegians for training in evangelism. It was the sort of mass event Bright had long envisioned. Back in the late 1940s at Hollywood Presbyterian Church, he had hatched an unsuccessful scheme to hold an Easter outreach service at the Los Angeles Coliseum. The more immediate impetus for Explo '72 came at a 1969 Billy Graham Congress on Evangelism in Minneapolis, where Bright arrived at the idea to bring one hundred thousand students to an evangelistic training event.[37]

Bright's most common way of communicating key decisions to his staff and supporters was to inform them that God was directly leading him to do something. "I use the word 'vision' lightly," explains Swede Anderson, who after Braun's departure became the campus ministry's national coordinator. "I think in Bill's walk with the Lord," continues Anderson, "he would say, 'The Lord said to me. Not an audible voice, but just I have this strong impression from the Lord.'" Bright later wrote of a 1968 "vision" that he should "believe God" for the fulfillment of the Great Commission in the United States by 1976 and the world by 1980. In other words, Bright expected American Christians to evangelize their entire country in the next eight years and to participate in the evangelization of the world shortly thereafter. He conceived of Explo '72 as a means of moving toward the fulfillment of this broader vision. Bright frequently attached specific numbers or targets to his visions: one hundred thousand to Explo '72, the United States by 1976, the world by 1980. On the attendance goal for Explo, Anderson comments that one hundred thousand is "an easy figure to remember." "It's possible," he adds, "that what the Lord said was one hundred thousand."[38]

Bright announced his vision for a hundred-thousand-student training event to his directors in January 1970. By that point, Steve Douglass and Bruce Cook, two Harvard Business School graduates who joined staff in the wake of the 1967–68 crisis, had organized a "President's Cabinet" consisting of the six regional directors of the campus ministry and several other ministry heads. The cabinet at first responded incredulously to Bright's idea. "It was an old trick that had been tried many times," explains Jimmy Williams. "He'd have a vision, and then we'd have to put arms and legs to it." "Bill's style wasn't to get consensus," comments Bruce Cook, "it was to come in and to tell you what God had told him." Given Bright's leadership style and tendency to regard skepticism as disloyalty, they agreed to the plan, if with little enthusiasm. None of the established top leaders took charge of the project. Jim Green, Crusade's Big Ten regional director, recommended his protégé, Paul Eshleman, at the time a twenty-seven-year-old campus director in Wisconsin. Cook recalls that Crusade's top leadership purposefully refrained from sending the organization's most talented individuals to Dallas to assist Eshleman. The cabinet, Cook observes, "put in a horrible staff so he [Eshleman] couldn't succeed."[39]

Despite his staff's lack of enthusiasm, Bright and Eshleman began laying the groundwork for the event. In late 1970 Bright persuaded Billy Graham to serve as honorary chairman of the event and make several addresses during the congress. Graham's endorsement and presence gave the undertaking instant credibility in the evangelical world and beyond, and Graham's organization provided invaluable advice and promotional services. Also, Bright and Eshleman made a wise decision to bill the event as an "Explo" with a "Jesus Music Festival" featuring Johnny Cash and Kris Kristofferson rather than as a somber "International Student Congress on Evangelism." At the grassroots level within the organization, on the other hand, progress was far slower. Bright and Eshleman were depending on the campus and lay staff to recruit students to attend the congress and mail in advance registrations. In early 1972, less than six months before Explo, registrations lagged far behind expectations. Knowing that many of his staff were only lukewarmly supporting the congress, Bright brought his leadership team to Dallas in early February. He told the men—at the time, Crusade's formal leadership did not include any women—he would not proceed with the congress without their support. They were free to voice their objections, but he insisted that they pray about the matter together. "People started confessing sin . . . ," recalls Bruce Cook, "it was a spiritual watershed." Alan Scholes, a campus director on the West Coast, received an audiotape of this unusual meeting. The tape included the leaders "confessing through tears their bad attitude and their sin in resisting Bill." "I'm sure the reason that it was sent out to all the campus directors," comments Scholes, "was that they were pretty sure the disgruntlement was more widespread." Swede Anderson fired one regional director who did not cease his criticism. Whether out of genuine repentance or grudging duty, the organization successfully marshaled its troops to promote Explo's success.[40]

In February, Crusade's leadership team also faced the decision of whether to invite President Richard Nixon to Explo '72. At Graham's urging, Nixon aides Charles Colson and H. R. Haldeman discussed ways to foster a relationship between Nixon and Bright. Graham and Nixon feared that Democratic nominee George McGovern—an ordained minister—might compete effectively for the moderate and conservative Protestant vote. Graham, out of a mixture of personal friendship and partisanship, arranged appearances for Nixon before evangelical audiences and encouraged Nixon to forge ties with other conservative religious figures such as Oral Roberts. Haldeman and Colson hoped that Graham could persuade Bright to take an active role in mobilizing evangelical youth to vote Nixon in the fall election. Colson, according to his assistant W. Richard Howard, felt that a presidential meeting with Bright "would be much safer at this time than trying to tie into the 'Jesus Freaks.'" On 1 February, an assistant informed Haldeman that "the President definitely wants to try to attend" Graham's "big youth deal that he's putting on in Dallas in June." Bright wanted to invite Nixon to Explo, but his assistants voiced opposition, asserting that Nixon's presence would hinder Explo's evangelistic goals. On 2 February, Graham relayed the results of Crusade's "stormy session" to Haldeman. On this occasion, Bright acquiesced to his staff's reasoning.[41]

Approximately eighty-five thousand young people joined Crusade staff members in Dallas for Explo '72.[42] Over the previous few months, the staff had rallied to the cause. Although Bright envisioned a training event for collegians, the majority of young delegates were high schoolers. Explo was also more diverse than many evangelical gatherings. E. V. Hill, an African American pastor from Los Angeles friendly with many white evangelicals, received a prominent role in the festivities. There were between two and three thousand African American delegates, a sizable number of international students, many Pentecostal and charismatic Christians, and a variety of "fringe" groups, from left-leaning evangelical protesters, to the "Chil-

Paul Eshleman, Billy Graham, and Bill Bright at Explo '72 in Dallas, June 1972. Courtesy of J. Kent Hutcheson.

dren of God" movement, to conservative fundamentalist reporters ready to expose any scandalous dress or music. The delegates spent the mornings in various seminars, scattered across Dallas on two afternoons to practice "winning souls for Christ," and attended a mixture of concerts and lectures in the evenings. Explo's message was very similar to that proclaimed at the 1967 Berkeley Blitz. "Changed people in sufficient numbers," Bright promised his youthful audience, "make a changed world." "Hearts must be changed," Graham affirmed, "before problems can be solved." Speakers delivered messages on "how to be filled with the Holy Spirit," and delegates learned how to approach individuals and share the *Four Spiritual Laws*. The evangelists challenged the delegates to commit themselves to Crusade's goal of changing the world through evangelism. Crusade drew a positive contrast between its evangelistic prescription and left-leaning campus activism. "Explo '72," Bright avowed, "can do more to bring peace to the world than all of the antiwar activity combined."[43]

In early June, Billy Graham caused something of a stir in Dallas-area churches when he described the upcoming event as a "Christian Woodstock." According to the *Dallas Times Herald*, Explo officials hastened to reject the notion that the congress would "bring a contingent of sub-culture or counter-culture followers—hippies." The influence of the Jesus Movement, however, was palpable at Explo. The *New York Times* reported that

Johnny Cash performs at the Explo '72 Jesus Music Festival. Courtesy of J. Kent Hutcheson.

Explo delegates raised "their arms with clenched fists and the index finger pointed upward as a sign that Jesus is the 'one way'" to heaven. Young people shouted out, "Jesus yells" in unison. Every night, Christian rock music had the delegates in the Cotton Bowl swaying and singing before Bright or Graham took the stage. The *New York Times* termed Explo "the largest and most conspicuous public outpouring thus far of the Jesus Movement." In many ways, however, Explo '72 symbolized a conservative evangelical appropriation of the Jesus Movement: carefully planned, toned down, and commercialized. By 1972, the Jesus Movement was well enough established for street vendors and peddlers to travel to Dallas hawking pins, bumper stickers, and other "Jesus" kitsch. "These aren't religious nuts," the *Dallas Times Herald* editorialized, "or 'Jesus Freaks.'" "The Campus Crusade for Christ is behind it all," the *Times Herald* noted, "and that gives earnest of the orderly, if zealous, manner in which Explo will be conducted." Of Crusade staff, the *Dallas Morning News* wrote, "[t]heir dress is conservative—suits, ties, dresses and pantsuits. They don't smoke, they are soft-spoken, smile a lot and they carry a Bible." Edward Fiske, the religion editor of the *New York Times*, portrayed Crusade's leadership at Explo as "bright, enthusiastic, and aggressive executives, who pride themselves on their ability to bring modern communications and marketing procedures to the ancient task of spreading the Christian message."[44]

The local and national media were fascinated by this gathering of young people, which diverged from contemporary stereotypes of youth culture. "What the press is going to find out at Explo," predicted Billy Graham, "is that there is another group of young people—not the silent majority—but the 'silenced' majority—comprised of great, wonderful young people." The *Dallas Morning News* conducted a survey of 470 Explo delegates, 61 percent of whom were under eighteen years of age. By a margin of more than five to one, they favored Nixon for president over McGovern. They also favored stronger penalties for marijuana possession and overwhelmingly believed that American attitudes toward sex were "too permissive." The delegates, with the exception of a few dissenters, vigorously applauded military representatives on a patriotic Flag Day celebration. An official military chaplain periodical had encouraged the participation of military personnel in a special Explo gathering entitled "5,000 Military for the Master." According to a Crusade publication, the Explo crowd "participated in a salute to the Stars and Stripes and the customary pledge of allegiance." In a procession of international flags, the banner of South Vietnam produced a "sustained ovation" from the crowd. The crowd listened to a telegram from Nixon, who echoed the congress's theme by reminding delegates, "the way to change the world for the better is to change ourselves for the better." During the week of the Watergate break-in, which occurred on the night of Explo's Jesus Music Festival, Nixon called for a "deep and abiding commitment to spiritual values." More liberal Protestants and left-leaning evangelicals noticed such manifestations of cultural and political conservatism and criticized Bright, Graham, and Explo accordingly. The People's Christian Coalition, led by Jim Wallis and other evangelical seminarians from the Chicago area, unfurled a banner that read, "300 GIs killed this week in Vietnam won't be reached in this generation." "I've got no problem with Flag Day . . . ," commented African American evangelist Tom Skinner. "But to associate God with that is bad news." Crusade's staff, for the most part, were conservative Republicans, and the young delegates were more culturally and politically conservative than their average peers. As did Crusade's engagement with the student left at Berkeley, Explo '72 provides evidence of conservative evangelical activism typically overlooked in historical accounts of the 1960s and early 1970s.[45]

Explo '72 was a milestone for Campus Crusade for Christ. If Bright fell somewhat short of his target of one hundred thousand students, he came close. Crusade accomplished its goal of training thousands of teenagers and young adults how to become Christians, how to be filled with the Holy Spirit, and how to practice evangelism. Explo '72 garnered the ministry significant exposure in the national media for the first time, and the press coverage was overwhelmingly positive.

Despite the signs of political conservatism on display on Explo '72, the event illustrated the extent to which evangelicalism had evolved over the previous half-decade. Campus Crusade by 1972 had not become socially activist or liberal, but like many evangelicals, Crusaders were becoming more socially aware. For instance, although Crusade only possessed a handful of African American staff, the organization made a painstaking effort to highlight African American speakers and recruit black delegates. Crusade—an organization that had forbidden staff members from participating in the civil rights movement of the early 1960s—pointed to the transcendence of racial barriers as a tangible proof of Explo's success. Crusade obviously privileged evangelism over social activism and social reform, but Graham talked about the need for converted Christians to save the environment, to tear down interracial walls, and to ameliorate poverty. A second trend evident at Explo was a budding evangelical ecumenism, demonstrated by the smattering of Catholics and the large number of charismatic Christians present. Thomas Zimmerman, general superintendent of the Assemblies of God, spoke at Explo, though Bright asked Pentecostals and charismatics not to promote speaking in tongues. Finally, Crusade, like many evangelical groups, was adapting rapidly to changes in American popular culture. While rejecting what the ministry saw as its permissive values, Crusade embraced, or at least tolerated, some of the counterculture's style. Whereas most fundamentalists continued to decry rock music as satanic, Crusade now embraced the new genre despite Bright's earlier hesitation.

Explo '72 was less a reflection of rigid evangelical conservatism than an example of the dynamic and adaptive evangelicalism that was beginning to attract the attention of secular America. As the *Dallas Morning News* editorialized, these "modern conservatives" were hardly the stereotypical conservatives clinging to the status quo, as "they propose to do nothing less than change the world by the end of the decade." The *Morning News* probably overstated the innovativeness of Explo's goal, as evangelicals had long dreamed of evangelizing the world within a short span of time. But the newspaper was correct to dub the Explo delegates "modern conservatives," as evangelicals had changed dramatically over the past five years. The counterculture and the Jesus Movement impacted Campus Crusade in the late 1960s and early 1970s, as the rhetoric and music of the organization changed dramatically, and the ministry evidenced much greater social awareness than it had in the early 1960s. These proved to be enduring changes for Campus Crusade, even though its embrace of the Jesus Movement was only partial and temporary. Crusade appropriated the spirit of the Jesus revolution and maximized its ability to engage, convert, and recruit young people for its evangelistic vision. The Jesus Movement faded from the American religious consciousness within several years, but the success of Explo enabled Campus Crusade to switch its focus from the campus to its broader evangelistic goals. "It's only the beginning," Bright repeatedly emphasized in Dallas. Given that Bright had outlined the goal of evangelizing the entire Untied States by 1976, Crusade staff members should have expected to hear about even more audacious schemes after Explo '72.[46]

The Evangelical Bicentennial

The mid-1970s were heady times for American evangelicals. Dramatic conversions were front-page news. Shortly after going to prison for his role in the Watergate scandal, Charles Colson announced his Christian faith in the best-selling book *Born Again*. Arthur DeMoss, a Philadelphia-based insurance mogul and a major Campus Crusade donor, posted half of the $100,000 bail for Eldridge Cleaver upon his return to the United States. The former Black Panther, who had spent years abroad as a fugitive from the U.S. criminal justice system, was baptized in the Arrowhead Springs swimming pool in October 1976 while Crusade celebrated its twenty-fifth anniversary. In addition to showcasing born-again celebrities, evangelicals staked their claim to the nation's airwaves, bookstores, and suburbs. By 1975, Pat Robertson's *700 Club* reached audiences in America's largest cities, such as New York, Chicago, and Los Angeles. Two former Campus Crusade staff members wrote books that ranked among the top ten best-selling books of the decade. Hal Lindsey's *The Late Great Planet Earth* predicted an imminent apocalypse, whereas Marabel Morgan's *The Total Woman* encouraged evangelicals to enjoy and explore sexual intimacy within marriage. While mainline Protestant denominations hemorrhaged members during the 1970s—the largest Presbyterian, Episcopal, and Methodist denominations all lost at least 10 percent of their members between 1965 and 1975—many suburban evangelical churches began the rapid growth that would make them the megachurches of subsequent decades.[1]

In addition to these signs of increased visibility and institutional growth, during the 1976 presidential campaign all of the major candidates spoke about their faith in ways tailored to evangelical audiences. Jimmy Carter, who became the Democratic nominee, was a Southern Baptist who had supported a Billy Graham film crusade in the 1960s and comfortably talked about his faith in Jesus. "Christ guarantees you, God guarantees you," Carter told his Sunday school class in front of a group of reporters, "that you will be forgiven." The *New York Times*, in an effort to explain such peculiar utterances, attributed Carter's religiosity to his roots in a small Georgia town, a "little rural village" in which the church formed "the sole center of community life" and hosted periodic springtime revivals. Carter's faith garnered the most headlines, but other candidates also told voters about their personal knowledge of Jesus. Alabama governor George Wallace, running briefly for the Democratic nomination, stated clearly that he knew "from experience that God is alive and that Jesus saves." "Because I've trusted Christ to be my Savior," wrote President Gerald Ford in a published letter, "my life is His." Ford's Republican challenger, Ronald Reagan, who attended Crusade convert Donn Moomaw's Bel Air Presbyterian Church, told an interviewer that "I have had an experience that could be described as 'born again.'" Like Ford, Reagan remained hesitant and uncomfortable with evangelical jargon, but he gained evangelical followers by passionately talking about his belief in prayer, his opposition to abortion, and his condemnation of homosexuality as "immoral." In light of high-profile conversions, the popularity of evangelical broadcasters, and the overtly Christian talk from all of the major presidential candidates, *Newsweek* proclaimed 1976 to be the "Year of the Evangelicals."[2]

Bill Bright's support of Christian Citizen provides an early example of evangelical political activism, but evangelical political efforts in the mid-1970s became far more influential and noteworthy. One simple yet often overlooked reason for evangelicals' newfound political significance was the dramatic growth of evangelical institutions. In the 1960s, few evangelical leaders—with the exception of Billy Graham and possibly Oral Roberts—commanded large and visible institutions that held the potential for political influence. By the mid-1970s, the evangelical universe seemed crowded with a new generation of stars: Robertson, Rex Humbard, and Jim Bakker were all notable television personalities with large audiences. Campus Crusade evolved into a ministry of several thousand staff members by the early 1970s. Politicians took note of these personalities and institutions and identified them as vehicles through which they could court an emerging constituency. Whereas Bright in the 1960s had assiduously cultivated relationships with Congressman Walter Judd and FBI director J. Edgar Hoover, in the 1970s Senators Strom Thurmond and Jesse Helms showered attention on Crusade's ministries in Washington.

Evangelicals also both participated in and benefited from a shift in the terrain of American politics. In the 1950s and 1960s, anticommunism dominated evangelical political discourse, particularly outside the South. Politicians appealed to evangelicals by stridently establishing their anticommunist credentials, a tactic that appealed to all political conservatives—along with many other Americans—without requiring any special effort to establish relationships with evangelical constituencies. While evangelicals retained their anxieties about global communism in the 1970s, a whole cluster of new issues emerged. Amidst what seemed an unending string of moral crises, evangelical leaders began to focus their attention on perceived threats to the American family, symbolized most prominently by abortion, the Equal Rights Amendment (ERA), feminism, restrictions on school prayer, and homosexuality.[3] In response, conservative politicians began addressing these issues in terms that resonated with evangelicals. This shift also narrowed the place of evangelicals on the political spectrum. In the 1950s and 1960s, Senators Frank Carlson of Kansas and Mark Hatfield of Oregon attended evangelical prayer breakfasts and openly discussed their faith.[4] While Carlson and Hatfield belonged to the liberal wing of the GOP and while Carter sought evangelical votes in 1976, by the end of the 1970s most of the prominent politicians close to evangelical leaders were conservative Republicans.

Many evangelical leaders, long frustrated by their exclusion from national influence and power, were grateful for the new respect bestowed upon them by politicians. Yet amidst all of the publicity given to Graham's relationship with Nixon and to Jimmy Carter's outspoken faith, it is easy to overlook how controversial partisan politics remained within the evangelical world. Graham and Bright both felt it necessary to publicly refute accusations that they wielded political influence or engaged in political efforts. Although Bright espoused a conservative political agenda and supported conservative politicians, Campus Crusade staff based in the nation's capital urged Bright to avoid partisanship. Only a small minority of Crusade staff wanted to make conservative politics their primary calling, and those who did typically left staff and entered the political world. Still, the fact that a ministry comprised primarily of individuals dedicated to evangelism became associated with right-wing politics in the mid-1970s testifies to the growing politicization of American evangelicalism.

Perhaps as a result of the uneasiness with which many evangelicals approached the realm of partisan politics, it was sometimes unclear whether evangelical leaders and organizations were working toward spiritual or political ends. Understanding evangelical political engagement, particularly in the years before the Moral Majority or the Christian Coalition, requires a broad conception of politics and attention to a diverse range of activities. Evangelicals drew no clear boundaries between the religious and political spheres. For example, evangelicals responded to the rise of modern feminism both by organizing in opposition to the ERA and by attending marriage and family conferences. Evangelicals reacted to Watergate and the myriad other political issues of the mid-1970s both by supporting politicians with evangelical stripes and by promoting evangelistic campaigns to restore the country to its Christian past. Most evangelicals were attracted primarily to activities that were not explicitly political, but evangelistic campaigns and FamilyLife conferences stimulated political awareness and laid the groundwork for more open political activism. The line between evangelical religion and evangelical politics—never entirely separate—became even more blurred.

Freedom to Preach the Gospel

Campus Crusade for Christ exemplified the growth and increased visibility of evangelical institutions in the 1970s, as Bright busily promoted Crusade's ever-expanding ministries—the campus ministry, a high school ministry, the Lay Institutes for Evangelism, and a ministry to the armed forces. The success of Explo '72 helped the ministry double its staff from roughly fifteen hundred in 1971 to three thousand in 1974, and Bright groomed a new generation of leaders to fill the void created by the 1968 crisis. Swede Anderson assumed the directorship of the U.S. campus ministry and later took charge of Crusade's Latin American ministries. Paul Eshleman succeeded Anderson as director of the campus ministry in 1972 and the next year assumed oversight of Crusade's entire American operations.[5] Bright invited Josh McDowell to become the ministry's new traveling speaker. Steve Douglass and Bruce Cook, the Harvard Business School graduates, gradually assumed administrative leadership at Arrowhead Springs. Douglass and Cook streamlined Crusade's organizational structure, reduced the number of people reporting to Bright, and taught management training classes to all staff members serving in positions of leadership. Bright also found it easier to trust this new cadre of top leaders, although the earlier staff revolt remained a sore that healed slowly. Eshleman earned considerable respect from Bright when he wholeheartedly sought to implement Bright's vision for Explo '72 at a time when others considered the task impossible. Bright admired the willingness of Douglass and Cook to forego lucrative business careers and instead raise money to join Crusade's staff.

The ministry also continued to evolve and grow overseas. Through the 1960s, the international ministries—incorporated in individual countries and staffed by nationals—developed unevenly because of a lack of funding and coordination from Crusade's headquarters. After Ray Nethery, Crusade's director for Asia, resigned in 1968, Bright asked Bailey Marks to bring more organizational unity to Crusade's Asian ministries. Marks immediately visited all nine Asian countries in which Crusade had an active presence. Marks explains that local translations of the *Four Spiritual Laws* were all that he could find that were "indicative of the fact that these men belonged to an organization called Campus Crusade for Christ." "I found our ministry there going in many different directions," he later wrote. According to Marks, Crusade had recruited a group of pastors in each country, given them minimal training, left them dependent on finances from Crusade's American donors, and unrealistically expected them to duplicate Crusade's campus ministry in their own countries. With Bright's approval, Marks moved to Asia, built a training center in Manila, and brought all of the Asian staff to the Philippines for basic training in Crusade's philosophy and techniques. Crusade did not abandon its principle of indigenous leadership, but the ministry made clear that indigenous leaders were required to follow the policies emanating from Arrowhead Springs. The international staff members resisted Marks's attempt to standardize their ministries, and one-third of the ninety Asian staff members resigned. After these initial difficulties, however, Crusade recruited new Asian leaders who more enthusiastically implemented the organization's evangelistic models.[6]

In 1974, the South Korean ministry took center stage, when Joon Gon Kim organized an "Explo '74" in Seoul. Since 1971, Kim had envisioned a large-scale training event that would motivate Korea's rapidly growing Protestant population to convert the entire nation by the end of 1975. Billy Graham hosted a successful 1973 crusade in Seoul, and Explo '74 built on Graham's momentum. The ministry constructed some of the world's largest rice cookers and produced six hundred tons of rice to feed the anticipated throngs. Mass rallies during the evenings—Crusade claimed that on two occasions the crowds topped a million people—featured Bright (through a translator), Kim, and other evangelists. Even conservative crowd estimates indicated that upwards of 1 percent of the entire South Korean population attended Explo '74 events. Much as Explo '72 had done in the United States, Explo '74 provided Crusade with international legitimacy.[7]

Upon his return home, however, Bright faced a small avalanche of skepticism and criticism. Harold Lindsell and Edward Plowman of *Christianity Today*, an evangelical publication normally sympathetic to Crusade, suggested that Bright had overestimated the number of people in attendance at Explo '74. Plowman reported that roughly three hundred thousand attended the nightly rallies on Yoido Plaza, rather than the over one million reported by Crusade. "The best way to count crowds," comments Plowman, "is to count them—as I did—and not pull gee-whiz estimates out of the air." "I am not a head counter," Bright responded to Plowman. Bright, however, pronounced himself "happy to let the matter drop and to continue to praise God for the many lives that were transformed during the unbelievable experience of Explo '74."[8]

More seriously, Bright's comments on the political and religious atmosphere in South Korea generated a brief media firestorm. In 1972, Korea's president Park Chung Hee declared martial law and imposed a new constitution that expanded his powers and allowed him to remain in office indefinitely. Since the unveiling of this "Restoration Constitution," a number of Park's Catholic and Protestant critics, including Catholic Bishop Daniel Chi, had been arrested and jailed. By contrast, most evangelicals—including Crusade's Kim—supported the Park regime, in large measure because of a mutual commitment to anticommunism. When Bright and a group of Crusade's major donors visited South Korea in 1965, Park met with Kim and a portion of the American delegation and expressed his admiration for the ministry. In a 1971 letter to Billy Graham, Bright noted that Kim had "personally introduced to Christ the present Prime Minister some six years ago" and "meets frequently with President Park for spiritual counsel and prayer." According to historian Chung-Shin Park, Kim preached in support of President Park's Restoration Constitution. Political and religious tensions in South Korea reached a fever pitch during Explo '74 itself, as several dissident church leaders received stiff prison sentences and an assassin murdered Park's wife.[9]

During Explo '74, members of the international press asked Bright to comment on reports of religious persecution in South Korea. "There is no religious repression here," Bright stated unequivocally. "It is only political, and I believe it is for good cause." "If there is allowed any division or any

Bill Bright and Joon Gon Kim at Explo '74 in Seoul, South Korea, August 1974. Courtesy of J. Kent Hutcheson.

dissension," he continued, reflecting an argument commonly employed by the Park regime, "instantly North Korea would pounce upon it." Bright, like many evangelical leaders, still interpreted world events through the lens of early Cold War anticommunism, a consensus to which the nation's media no longer subscribed. "Those who oppose the (South Korean) regime," the *Washington Post* quoted him, "are militant in their attack on anything that speaks of God, and if they had their way every Christian in South Korea today would be slaughtered." Probably with the *Post* in mind, Bright complained that "one large U.S. metropolitan daily" had distorted his views, and he insisted he had never endorsed Park's policies and did not "question" the "motives" of imprisoned individuals. However, in a press release he pointed to the hundreds of thousands in attendance at Explo '74 and argued "that there is more freedom to preach the gospel of Jesus Christ in Korea than there is here in the United States." He noted that the government encouraged evangelical efforts to spread the gospel and that "Explo '74 could never have occurred without the approval of government officials." Furthermore, he clarified that those "church leaders who are in prison are there because they were accused of being involved in politics—not because they were preaching the gospel of Jesus Christ." Bright's comments equated religious freedom with the freedom to evangelize—he dismissed the prisoners' freedom to follow political implications of the gospel when those implications contradicted his own geopolitical views.[10]

The American Home

Although Bright and most other evangelical leaders remained outspoken opponents of communism, new enemies were gathering on the horizon. Evangelical leaders organized a number of high-profile campaigns over alleged threats to "the American family,"[11] including crusades against the ERA and gay-rights ordinances. Beneath the surface, evangelical uneasiness over modern feminism and changes in traditional gender roles had been simmering for a number of years, and the late 1960s birthed a new wave of leaders who spoke, wrote, and held conferences about the family. Henry Brandt, Bruce Narramore, James Dobson, and J. Allan Peterson became influential authors and speakers in the evangelical world by placing modern psychological teachings on marriage and parenthood within an evangelical framework. In October 1975, Campus Crusade sent several staff members to the Continental Congress on the Family, an event organized by Peterson. The congress, which featured evangelical luminaries such as Narramore, Mark Hatfield, and Edith Schaeffer, helped signify the arrival of the "family" as one of the central spiritual and political concerns of evangelicals.

The congress was also the catalytic event in Crusade's formation of a "Family Ministry." The initial impetus for the initiative came less from political or cultural concerns than from the personal struggles of staff members. Don and Sally Meredith, campus leaders at the University of Arkansas in the early 1970s, found that students repeatedly asked them questions about marriage for which they were unprepared to give clear answers. Don Meredith asked Bright for permission to launch a "marriage ministry" within Crusade, but Bright declined, perhaps because the idea deviated from Crusade's standard emphasis on evangelism. According to Howard Hendricks, a professor at Dallas Theological Seminary and a good friend of Crusade's president, Bright "for a period of time was starting things like it was going out of style." By the time Meredith offered his suggestion, Bright had grasped the need to restrain his entrepreneurial tendencies. However, Ney Bailey, a traveling women's representative for Crusade, grew increasingly uneasy watching Crusade staff couples gain promotions within the organization while enduring marital disharmony. Most Crusade staff worked long hours, and married men typically traveled frequently, especially as they moved into positions of leadership. "I thought," reflects Bailey, "how long are we going to be reaching the world for Christ and have it not be good on the inside?" Bailey tearfully presented her concerns at a national staff meeting chaired by Paul Eshleman, who sent her and several colleagues to Peterson's congress.[12]

Held in St. Louis and attended by more than two thousand evangelicals, the congress featured lectures, discussion, and resolutions on a wide range of topics, including abortion, education, and sexuality. The conference gave voice to a surprisingly diverse range of opinions on controversial topics, including the role of women in the family and church. In fact, compared to the positions of later organizations such as Focus on the Family, the Continental Congress on the Family carried a cautiously progressive tone. In a lecture at the congress, Letha Scanzoni argued that "genuine equality [between men and women] plainly means that there is no 'fixed' or ultimate head; power is shared equally." The gathering issued a statement on homosexuality declaring that "while we acknowledge the Bible teaches homosexuality to be sinful, we recognize that a homosexual orientation can be the result of having been sinned against." The Congress denounced "unjust and unkind treatment given to homosexuals" and urged Christians "to help them to change their life style in a manner which brings glory to God." Other speakers discussed the various ways that modern society threatened the health of family life and prescribed a mixture of biblical and psychological solutions. Peterson challenged conferees to adopt a personal strategy to address family issues within the American church.[13]

Responding to Peterson's challenge, Ney Bailey resolved to create a premarital conference program for Crusade staff members. Bright remained skeptical of the initiative but gave permission for the creation of a "Marriage Preparation and Family Emphasis." Don Meredith organized the initial series of conferences, attended by several hundred staff. After single and married staff members also expressed an interest in attending the conferences, Crusade expanded the program and began inviting the general public to conferences several years later. Meredith left Crusade soon after the launch of the new ministry and was replaced by Dennis Rainey. "FamilyLife," as Crusade renamed the ministry, maintained that the Bible provided a blueprint for family dynamics, including gender roles and relationships between children and parents. In particular, FamilyLife emphasized the husband's role as the spiritual leader of the family.[14]

FamilyLife's teachings on distinctive, or complementary, roles for men and women flowed out of the staff manual that Campus Crusade had developed since the 1950s. Like other conservative evangelicals, Crusade maintained that God endows men and women with different biological and nonbiological characteristics. For instance, Crusade taught that women tend to respond to situations emotionally while men respond rationally. "In matters of disagreement," Crusade instructed its staff, "a staff girl should realize that girls get emotionally involved in decisions to be made." "She should usually," the manual recommended, "defer to the man's decision." Partly because of such characteristics, Crusade expected men to assume positions of leadership within the family and within the organization. "He [the husband]," read the manual, "must 'rule' with love and kindness and delegate responsibilities to the wife and others in the home to see that all runs smoothly." "A woman in a place of leadership should not try to compete with the men," Crusade told its female staff, warning them that women who threaten male leadership "tend to become dictatorial and irritating." By the mid-1970s, the organization's official teachings on the respective roles of men and women had evolved little. If anything, they had become more rigidly patriarchal.[15]

Crusade's leadership was leery of the feminist movement, which Vonette Bright termed "not very feminine." Simultaneously, however, the ministry engaged the rise of modern feminism by promoting women's leadership in ways that did not overtly threaten traditional gender roles. Several women, including Ney Bailey, made an effort to organize conferences for female staff members and held student "feminars" on campus. At the "feminars," Crusade challenged those in attendance to think about what they as women could do to "reach the world for Christ." Despite its emphasis on male leadership, Crusade did not expect women to only work as homemakers or discourage women from becoming leaders within the confines of overall male headship. Vonette Bright discussed the possibility of a woman holding a position of spiritual authority in the church. "I think that as long as she acts under the authority of her husband and under the authority of her minister," she maintained, "then this would be perfectly fine, if she is capable." Bright herself assumed a much more prominent role in the 1970s. When the Brights' sons left Arrowhead Springs for college, she undertook speaking tours and directed Crusade's prayer ministry, which organized groups of Christians in local prayer groups and at public prayer rallies. Many Crusade women, especially single women, continued to find significant opportunities for leadership. For example, Judy Downs edited

Crusade's periodicals in the early 1970s, and Ney Bailey served as Crusade's personnel director in the 1960s before becoming a traveling speaker.[16]

Although the hesitant promotion of women's leadership indicated a cautious openness to changing cultural values, Crusade simultaneously positioned itself in opposition to other aspects of modern society. "The American home," wrote Bill Bright, "even the Christian home, is in a state of chaos, disarray and disintegration." Like many evangelicals, some Crusaders came to see the American family as besieged by feminists, secular humanists, and homosexuals, and they targeted abortion and divorce as signs of moral decay. "To this point, Protestant evangelicals have generally played the sleeping giant on abortion," lamented Crusade staff member Bill Horlacher in the ministry's *Worldwide Challenge* magazine, "while Roman Catholics have fought the fight." Crusade speaker Linda Raney Wright warned supporters that the "homosexual movement" "seeks to remove restrictions from job opportunities so that homosexuals can continue unabridged in their sin, while forcing public and private schools to lose their freedom of choice as they try to protect children from unrighteous models." Articles trumpeted Anita Bryant's campaign against a gay-rights statute in Dade County, Florida, and praised organizations seeking to provide counseling for homosexuals wishing to pursue a heterosexual lifestyle. Crusade's focus on this new cluster of issues marked a departure for an organization that with the exception of the fight against global communism had focused almost exclusively on evangelism and basic discipleship. The "family" became central to evangelicalism in the 1970s, reflected both in politicized rhetoric about abortion and homosexuality and also in the conferences organized by FamilyLife and other evangelicals, including Peterson, Bill Gothard, and Tim LaHaye. Most of the conferences were not explicitly political, but the subject matter sensitized attendees to the political implications of contemporary debates over abortion, the ERA, and homosexuality.[17]

The Evangelical Bicentennial

While he grew increasingly concerned about the American family, Bright remained committed to his goal of evangelizing the entire United States by 1976. Seeking to carry out this vision, Crusade's top leaders planned citywide evangelistic campaigns in order to reach the vast majority of Americans living in urban areas. They identified 265 metropolitan areas representing 75 percent of the U.S. population and proposed that Crusade partner with local churches to evangelize those cities. One assistant approached Bright with a plan to evangelize the 16 largest cities by 1976 — Bright told him that if he could not devise a strategy for reaching all 265, he would "get somebody who will." Once again, some of Bright's top assistants rejected his strategy. Howard Ball, head of Crusade's lay ministry since 1964, had organized evangelistic conferences in churches for nine years and felt that too few local churches would be adequately prepared for the proposed campaign. "I think you need to be aware," Ball told Bright, "that how you sense God leading you is just the opposite of what I think he's saying to me about what churches need." Ball resigned rather than remain at odds with Bright over the strategy, though he later rejoined the ministry. Glenn Plate, who helped organize the national effort, maintains that the "biggest difficulty was getting the staff on board and getting them sold on it." Plate asked for the resignations of several Crusade directors who "literally were leading a rebellion . . . against it."[18]

To develop a nationwide strategy, Bright sent Bruce Cook to Atlanta to experiment with citywide evangelistic methods. After a year's planning, Cook launched an unsuccessful door-to-door witnessing campaign. Crusade had only a limited number of staff and contacts and needed to bring together a broader coalition of Atlanta-area Christians. Most pastors, however, hesitated to throw their weight behind Crusade's untested aspirations. Cook had a series of meetings with Charles Stanley, pastor of the city's prominent First Baptist Church. After "the fifth or sixth meeting," recalls Cook, Stanley agreed to co-chair a second trial campaign. Sam Coker, an influential Methodist minister, also came on board. Since Baptists and Methodists comprised most of Atlanta's evangelical community, the endorsements of Stanley and Coker provided enough credibility and momentum for Cook to quickly recruit ninety churches, including a number of African American churches. An endorsement from Governor Jimmy Carter lent Cook's efforts even greater legitimacy. Crusade staff went to the churches and trained their members to witness using the *Four Spiritual Laws*. Cook consulted with Jeb Magruder, a former Nixon aide who, like Charles Colson, had undergone a post-Watergate conversion. Magruder provided advice on how to conduct neighborhood campaigns according to successful Republican election strategies.[19]

Even with a larger number of churches participating, Crusade lacked the human resources to organize a door-to-door campaign that would reach the entire city. Therefore, the linchpin of the effort became a media blitz designed by Bob Screen of the Russ Reid Agency, a Christian advertising firm based in Southern California. In the spring of 1975, billboards, bumper stickers, and television and radio advertisements announced the slogan, "I found it!" with no accompanying explanation. A few weeks later, Crusade changed the message to "I found it! You can too!" and provided a telephone number. Volunteers staffed phone banks at local churches and asked callers if they would like to be "closer to God," sharing the *Four Spiritual Laws* with those interested. Much as Crusade's campus staff had done for years, the volunteers tried to schedule appointments so that they could continue the conversation in person and invite the prospective converts to local churches. Simultaneous to Cook's Atlanta-area campaign, which Crusade titled "Agape Atlanta," two other Crusade staff members experimented with different strategies in Dallas and Nashville. Agape Atlanta produced the greatest results—Cook reported that the initial effort had contacted one hundred forty thousand households, received twenty-five thousand phone calls, and recorded ten thousand "decisions for Jesus Christ." Bolstered by those figures, Bright asked his staff to replicate the Atlanta campaign across the country by the end of 1976.[20]

When Cook flew back to Arrowhead Springs, however, he told Bright that Crusade could not move from the pilot campaign to all 265 cities within the next eighteen months. The ministry had not yet formed solid church coalitions in many cities, and Cook observed that many churches used to working with Billy Graham remained unfamiliar with Crusade. "He [Bright] turned on me," remembers Cook, "questioning my call." "Where's your faith, your loyalty?" Bright asked Cook. Cook knew that Bright had been scarred by the staff conflict of 1968 but felt that he—like Steve Douglass and Paul Eshleman—had proven his loyalty. Instead, Bright interpreted Cook's questioning of the 1976 deadline as disloyalty and a lack of faith rather than as constructive criticism. "The reaction was so intense," concludes Cook, "that you would not have guessed it was Bill Bright." Cook also provoked Crusade's founder at a staff meeting by presenting materials that Bright had not previously approved. "If you try to get too visible in areas that he hadn't seen," explains Cook, "it's like it throws a switch."[21]

Bright had no intention of backing away from the totality of his vision. "What happened," comments Cook, "is he got locked in [on] the '76 impact of our bicentennial." "The next 16 months . . . ," Bright maintained in a memo to staff and supporters in September 1975, "will very likely determine the destiny of our nation and the future course of history." At a time when even some evangelicals moderated their anticommunist rhetoric, Bright still feared a Russian invasion. "Unless there is a great turning to God," he warned in early 1976, "God will use a great atheistic power like Russia to chasten us." Moving from impending apocalypticism to hopeful utopianism, Bright anticipated that "Here's Life, America"—as Crusade titled the nationwide campaign—would stem the rising tide of atheism and immorality, stave off divine wrath, and restore America to its divinely appointed role. "The goal [of Here's Life]," he wrote, "is to introduce at least 25,000,000 people to Christ before the end of our bicentennial celebration."[22]

Many other evangelical leaders shared Bright's focus on 1976 and argued in bicentennial jeremiads that unless the United States quickly returned to its Christian roots, the nation would lose God's divine favor. In September 1975, Bright joined Jack Hayford (a popular Pentecostal pastor in Los Angeles), Pat Robertson, Pat Boone, and Billy James Hargis at a "Summit Conference of Church Leaders for Prayer for the Nation" in Chicago. "The hour is late," Bright cautioned at the summit. "We have fourteen months before the November 1976 elections to turn the tide." Otherwise, he warned, "we will experience another thousand years of dark ages." Evangelicals in 1976 blended jeremiads with more cheery expressions of patriotism. Evangelical singers produced patriotic albums, evangelical publishing houses promoted bicentennial books, and churches gave out "God Bless America" bumper stickers. Such phenomena were to a large degree standard fare for American evangelicals, but displays of patriotic fervor intensified in the mid-1970s. Regretting that a "considerable portion of the younger generation has been brainwashed into feeling guilty and apologetic about America," Bright explained his patriotism to Crusade supporters in an essay titled "Why I Am Glad I Am an American." "My spine still tingles," Bright wrote, "when I hear the thrilling strains of the Star Spangled Banner." Although he cautioned that "Christian faith does not depend on a particular ideology or form of government," Bright celebrated American freedom, material abundance, and social mobility.[23]

Bright's comment that "we have fourteen months before the November 1976 elections" suggested that he was thinking about American politics in addition to Here's Life, America. As 1976 approached, Bright encouraged Christians to become active in politics and elect fellow Christians to office. "Part of the great spiritual awakening," he revealed in late 1975, "is a plan to help bring Christ back into the government." "There are 435 congressional districts," Bright continued, "and I think Christians can capture many of them by next November." Bright offered a ready defense of Christian involvement in politics and government: "Every group except the Christians is organized, and I'm unashamedly saying to Christians, 'Let's get involved.'" At a time when many evangelicals remained worried that political activism would distract Christians from their primary duty of evangelism, Bright displayed no such inhibitions. In 1976, Bright published a pamphlet entitled *Your Five Duties as a Christian Citizen*, in which he encouraged his readers to pray for a spiritual and political awakening and organize precinct committees to "elect godly people." In the pamphlet, Bright cautioned prospective Christian voters to evaluate candidates "on the basis of the Word of God" and "remember that a candidate's principles are far more important than his party." When asked by *Christianity Today* whether "400 people of God in Congress" would make American politics any different, he replied "1,000 per cent different."[24]

Through new Campus Crusade ministries, Bright sought to exert a spiritual and potentially political influence on the federal government. At first, Crusade's plans were very modest. In 1974, one staff woman, Eleanor Page, began a Bible study for military and congressional wives in the home of

Irene Conlan, wife of John Conlan. Now a conservative Republican congressman from Arizona, Conlan knew Bright through the Christian Citizen movement. In 1975, wealthy donors provided the initial funds for the organization to establish a permanent ministry to Washington's political elite. With Bright overriding the financial objections of his board members, Crusade purchased the Chase-Devore Mansion from Washington's Catholic Archdiocese for $550,000 and sent twelve staff members to befriend congressmen, diplomats, and other officials, introduce them to Jesus, and involve them in Bible studies and evangelism. Bright termed the new outreach the "Christian Embassy."[25]

Although not a political front, the Christian Embassy blended evangelistic and political aspirations. "We want a more Christian government," asserted Rolfe McCollister, a financial supporter who became the embassy's first president. "We plan to do that by evangelizing official Washington." "Crusade was not doing political activism," states Swede Anderson, who became the embassy's director in 1976. Instead, Anderson explains, Crusade founded the embassy "to carry the same message [of evangelism and discipleship] that we were carrying other places to the top leadership of the country." Yet according to Anderson, Bright hoped that evangelism in Washington would produce political and social changes. "At his heart was always to lead these people to Christ," explains Anderson, but Bright felt that a relationship with Christ "would also affect how they would think politically." For instance, according to Anderson, Bright believed that with a Christian worldview, "you come down real clear on issues like abortion." Officially, the Christian Embassy was nonpartisan, and embassy staff evangelized both Republicans and Democrats in Washington, albeit with more success among the GOP. Tension developed, however, over Bright's perceived partisanship. When Anderson agreed to become the director, Bright assured him that the embassy would not become involved in partisan politics. Anderson discovered, however, that Bright periodically adopted a partisan tone and offered unofficial endorsements of conservative politicians during frequent trips to Washington.[26]

Bright cultivated relationships with a series of conservative politicians in the 1970s. He regularly invited J. Edgar Hoover to speak at Arrowhead Springs. "I have long admired you," Bright informed Hoover, "and the outstanding direction which you have given to the Federal Bureau of Investigation." In 1975, he wrote former congressman Walter Judd, "I only wish that you were the occupant of the Oval Room in the White House." Judd, a former medical missionary to China, a staunch anticommunist, and an economic conservative, was one of Crusade's most visible supporters in the 1960s and 1970s. John Conlan made several appearances at Arrowhead Springs, and Crusade's *Worldwide Challenge* ran several prominent articles on the Arizona representative. Conlan campaigned on a mixture of evangelical Christianity and social and fiscal conservatism, inveighing against "income-redistributing policies" and "warped concepts of compassion and justice." During a senatorial campaign in 1976, Conlan told voters that "a vote for Conlan is a vote for Christianity." At a time when Conlan hoped to use evangelical allies to propel himself toward a future presidential candidacy, Bright used his contacts in the worlds of business and evangelicalism to introduce Conlan to potential political and financial supporters. For Bright, the promotion of evangelical politicians, Here's Life, America, and the Christian Embassy were all prongs in an evangelical offensive against the disintegration of the United States. "What happens in this country this year," he said a few months before the 1976 elections, "will in my opinion determine whether or not we remain free."[27]

Walking in the Light

Given his sense of urgency, Bright had a busy start to 1976. In February, Crusade dedicated its Christian Embassy in Washington with Conlan and Strom Thurmond as prominent guests. Shortly thereafter, Crusade brought Here's Life, America to approximately twenty cities. The media, neighborhood visitation, and telephone campaigns functioned along the lines Bruce Cook had pioneered in Atlanta. For instance, according to *Moody Monthly*, five thousand Crusade-trained volunteers "attempted to call every home in the Dallas area" and share the *Four Spiritual Laws*. If the volunteers learned that an individual was Jewish, they used a "Jewish Telephone Presentation," a version of the *Four Spiritual Laws* modified to include only Old Testament passages and to present Jesus as the Jewish messiah. Bright sought to purchase network television airtime to accompany the campaigns. Robert Pittenger, Bright's personal assistant at the time, remembers an unsuccessful visit to CBS. "We walked into CBS offices," Pittenger recalls, "and he [Bright] said, 'We're going into Satan's kingdom.'" None of the networks would sell time to Crusade, so the organization bought time in local markets wherever possible.[28]

Bright devoted nearly all of his time to Here's Life throughout 1976, but media coverage of Crusade focused not on the evangelistic campaign but on speculation about his political activities. In April, Jim Wallis and Wes Michaelson, editors of the left-leaning evangelical periodical *Sojourners*, published allegations that Bright was involved in a clandestine effort to elect right-wing conservative Christians to political office. Wallis had been a thorn in Crusade's side for a number of years. He was among those who protested against the Vietnam War and Christian patriotism at Explo '72, and his magazine criticized Bright's comments about religious freedom in South Korea. In "A Plan to Save America," Wallis and Michaelson reported that Bright and Conlan had participated in a June 1974 meeting convened to further the activities of Third Century Publishers, an organization that in conjunction with Howard Kershner's Christian Freedom Foundation (CFF) intended to mobilize "born-again" Christians in precinct-level political activism. The CFF's efforts closely resembled those of Christian Citizen and involved many of the same individuals. Also present at the meeting were several board members of Campus Crusade—all wealthy and politically conservative businessmen. Furthermore, Wallis and Michaelson noted that Bright had endorsed *In the Spirit of '76*, a handbook for political organizing that was part of a literature package distributed by the CFF. Finally, they discussed the Here's Life campaigns that were springing up around the country as the article went to press. They conceded that Here's Life was not explicitly political but contended that "much of its motivation, clear from Bright's statements, flows from a larger political vision for 'saving America.'" Wallis and Michaelson, in a preface to their article, mentioned that they tried unsuccessfully to meet with Bright to discuss their allegations. "He [Bright] said," claims Wallis, "'If you write this article, I have some power in the churches . . . I will destroy you.'"[29]

One goal of the CFF, according to Richard DeVos, president of Amway, was to "get rid of those so-called liberal Christians like [Oregon Senator] Mark Hatfield." Bright and CFF president Jerry Hagee believed that Hatfield had orchestrated the *Sojourners* article in an attempt to destroy the CFF, whose supporters were creating an alternative Christian base in Oregon. Only two months before the article appeared, Michaelson had left a position as Hatfield's legislative assistant. In the 1950s and early 1960s, Hatfield had served on Crusade's board of directors, but as his opposition to the Vietnam War escalated, he found himself estranged from his former evangelical friends. The day that *Sojourners* published its allegations, Bright invited Hagee to dinner at the Christian Embassy. "Vonette and I are going to have dinner with you," Hagee remembers Bright saying on the telephone. "It's going to be the three of us, and we're going to pray the wrath of God on Mark Hatfield." Hagee recalls Bright as a significant adviser to the CFF. "Bill knew what we were doing," explains Hagee, "and he was always an adviser to members of the [CFF] board." Aware of the damage that the article could cause for both the CFF and Campus Crusade, Hagee and the Brights partook of a somber meal together. "We finished," says Hagee, "and he [Bright] said, 'I'm going to call the wrath of God [on Hatfield] . . . and we prayed.'" "He [Bright] knew Hatfield was behind it," explains Hagee, who adds that Bright later regretted his intemperate prayer. "We all knew Hatfield was behind it." Charles Colson, rapidly becoming an evangelical icon in Washington, arranged a meeting between Bright and Hatfield at which the former insisted that his efforts were "not political in any partisan sense." According to Garry Wills, who wrote an account of the meeting in the *New York Times*, Hatfield found the "distinctions elusive." The two men were not reconciled. The Christian Freedom Foundation lost momentum by the end of the year when Hagee resigned as president.[30]

By the fall, major publications were repeating *Sojourners'* allegations. Kenneth Woodward of *Newsweek* alleged that Bright and Conlan were "using local prayer groups, Bible-study meetings and the Sunday-school lecture circuit to create a grass-roots constituency for what could become a third political party of 'real Christians' only." Woodward primarily drew on the *Sojourners* article, but he also reported that Bright had castigated "political liberals" for their lack of "interest in spiritual matters" at a Portland, Oregon, prayer breakfast. Woodward noted that Bright conceded his presence at the 1974 CFF meeting detailed in *Sojourners* but only as a "silent observer." "John Conlan," Bright affirmed his support for the Arizona representative to *Newsweek*, "is the only man I know who has a plan for bringing Christians into politics." Woodward also interviewed Billy Graham about Crusade's alleged involvement in politics. "Bright has been using me and my name for twenty years," Graham told the reporter. "But now I'm concerned about the political direction he seems to be taking." Bright could afford criticism from Wallis and Michaelson, as *Sojourners* represented a small progressive evangelical fringe, but Graham's support had been critical to Crusade's growth and success over the past quarter century. Brad Bright charges that Woodward unfairly sought to create a rift. "He wanted that one statement ["I'm concerned"]," he comments, "so that he could use it as . . . a sledgehammer to drive a wedge between Bill Bright and Billy Graham." Most likely, Graham responded sharply to Woodward's questions in part because he himself had been deeply embarrassed by his very public support of Nixon in the 1968 and 1972 elections. Perhaps that sense of his own past missteps and his long friendship with Bright led Graham to quickly reconcile himself with Crusade's president, which he did on a televised broadcast shortly after the *Newsweek* article appeared.[31]

Bright remained adamant that he had not become involved in politics. In response to the *Sojourners* allegations, he sent out a circular to supporters with the heading "Campus Crusade for Christ Is Not Involved in Politics." In the letter, Bright maintained that "Campus Crusade for Christ has not spent one dollar for political purposes in the twenty-five years of its existence." "Satan is very unhappy about what God is doing today," Bright added, "and there are many attempts to thwart the movement of God's Spirit." In an interview with *Christianity Today*, he insisted that *Sojourners* and *Newsweek* "have added up two and two and come up with one hundred." Bright repeated his insistence that "Christians should be aggressively involved in politics," though he carefully pointed out that he wanted "men and women of God," including Jews, to hold office. Behind the scenes, Bright took steps to avoid future embarrassment. According to Brad Bright, his father—now convinced that John Conlan was using him to further his own political career—"created some distance" between himself and Conlan, whose bid for the Senate faltered.[32]

"I have no resentment [against Wallis and Michaelson]," Bright cheerfully maintained in a 1977 interview with the evangelical *Wittenburg Door*, "I'm too busy to be worried about what people say." In his interactions with the press, Bright remained unflinchingly positive. "[I]f I'm walking in the light as God is in the light," he insisted, "then I don't have any problems." It seems, however, that the swirl of allegations troubled him deeply. He revealed to the *Door* that when Wallis and Michaelson contacted him before their article's publication, he had told them, "You know you have lied." Richard Quebedeaux referred to the *Sojourners* article as "one of the two most devastating things that ever happened to Bill in his life." Indeed, the dispute between Bright and Wallis lingered into 1977. Early in the year, Bright and Wallis both attended an evangelical event preceding the annual presidential prayer breakfast. The organizers seated the two estranged evangelicals at the same table. According to Wallis, the group went around the table introducing themselves. "I'm the founder and president of Campus Crusade for Christ," Wallis recollects Bright introducing himself, "and I love everybody." "I even love Jim Wallis," Bright continued, "even though he's a liar." After several awkward moments, "[Tom] Skinner jumped up." "I am so damned tired of white, right-wing evangelicals," Wallis remembers Skinner saying. "A fist-fight almost broke out between Skinner and Bright," concludes Wallis. "It was that contentious."[33]

Some of Crusade's own staff worried that Crusade had become associated with a conservative political agenda. Spencer and Sherman Brand, staff members in Washington, D.C., informed Bright that "having Campus Crusade for Christ *implicitly* linked to a political preference is equally harmful to 'Here's Life, America' and the fulfillment of the Great Commission as the taking of an *explicit* political stand" (emphasis in the original). The Brands noted that Bright frequently appeared with Strom Thurmond and Jesse Helms "without a balanced public view of associations with individuals from other political viewpoints." "Do you realize, Bill," they continued, "that Strom Thurmond and Jesse Helms have voted against *every* major civil rights bill that has come before them in the Senate?" (emphasis in the original). "You cannot claim to be politically non-partisan," they objected, "and yet be publicly linked only with conservative people." They also expressed unease about Christians Concerned for More Responsible Citizenship, a Bright organization that had published his *Your Five Duties as a Christian Citizen*. The Brand brothers warned that "if the press were to discover that it is staffed only by political conservatives, you and Campus Crusade for Christ would be indelibly stamped as promoting a conservative political viewpoint." Bruce Cook alleges that Bright's linkage of Here's Life to anticommunism and an implied "political agenda" proved divisive and caused some potential supporters to back away from the campaign. Although many Crusade staff members shared Bright's political outlook, they worried that partisanship would impede Crusade's evangelistic mission.[34]

Less than two years after Crusade's founder emphasized that South Korea's jailed Christian dissidents were in prison "because they were accused of being involved in politics," Bright ironically found himself accused of the same thing by left-wing evangelicals, the media, and even members of his own staff. Others on his staff defended him. "The *Sojourners* attack on him was dishonest," asserts Swede Anderson, one-time director of the Christian Embassy. Bright's defenses were narrowly correct. Campus Crusade had not become a political organization, nor did it spend money for partisan causes. Furthermore, *Sojourners* probably exaggerated the extent of Bright's own political activities. At the same time, according to Jerry Hagee, Bright was more than a "silent observer" to the Christian Freedom Foundation. Moreover, Bright furthered connections between evangelicals and conservative politicians, and he dearly hoped that the fruits of evangelism would impact American politics. Bright denied that his intentions were partisan, but to outside observers—and to members of his own staff in Washington—the partisan ramifications were obvious. Bright's repeated protestations that he was not involved in partisan politics suggest that he knew a portion of Crusade's constituency would not approve if he became more overtly involved in conservative political efforts. Evangelicals expected their leaders to articulate moral stands on contemporary issues, but many evangelicals remained wary of the messy nature of political activism and wanted to concentrate on preaching the gospel. Should he become more openly involved politically, Bright did not know whether Crusade's thousands of staff and tens of thousands of financial contributors would follow his lead.[35]

Decisions and Commitments

In the fall of 1976, Crusade brought Here's Life, America to approximately one hundred fifty cities and planned another fifty campaigns in the spring of 1977—shortly after the original 1976 deadline. Here's Life, America ended with a final campaign in New York City. With donations from Mobil, Pepsico, and Coca-Cola as well as contributions from the city's evangelical community, 801 churches in New York participated in the effort. The nationwide evangelistic blitz generated both passionate support and biting criticism. J. Randolph Taylor, a Presbyterian minister in Atlanta writing in the liberal *Christian Century*, complained that through Here's Life the "glorious gospel becomes a commodity sold and delivered to the doorstep like a brush or a bar of soap." Taylor, who alleged that Here's Life "depends upon gimmicks," condemned the campaign as "fairly superficial, largely irrelevant, and unusually expensive." William White, president of the Chicago Church Federation, criticized the media campaign in Chicago as "manipulative," though he conceded that the Crusade-led effort possessed a "certain winsomeness, warmth, bounce, and spontaneity." Bright dismissed most criticisms of Crusade's evangelistic marketing campaign. "I reject the accusation that we use gimmicks," he bristled. "We're simply using our minds with our approach."[36]

More ominously, Flo Conway and Jim Siegelman observed that many "I Found It people"—like cult members, they implied—"become completely absorbed in their newfound faith." In an early December interview with *People*, Conway and Siegelman asserted that "members in the Campus Crusade for Christ . . . displayed the characteristics of the cult members we had interviewed . . . glazed eyes, a change in voice and posture, dropping all social activities to focus on one group and inability to carry on a normal conversation." Bright winced at the implication of the comparison made by Conway and Siegelman, particularly since the interview appeared just two weeks after the Jonestown massacre in Guyana, in which nearly one thousand people died in a combination mass suicide and murder. Conway and Siegelman's uncharitable depiction of Here's Life troubled a ministry that wished to avoid any association with the Children of God, "Moonies," and Jonestown. Crusade mailed a statement to its staff and supporters, defending the ministry while observing that "the New Testament apostles," Francis of Assisi, and Albert Schweitzer all reoriented their lives after encountering God.[37]

After Here's Life wound down, Crusade made its final assessment of the strategy. In addition to Crusade's recorded 535,000 "decisions" for Christ, Bright believed many more lives had been changed. "I am sure it would not be an exaggeration," he opined, "to say that through that [Here's Life] TV special alone, millions of people opened their hearts' door to Christ and God worked in the hearts of millions in answer to specific believing prayers." "I see no reason for the Here's Life movement ever to stop," Bright proclaimed. He expected to "repeat the media campaigns in every metropolitan area of the nation not more than two years from now." Furthermore, Bright suggested that recent Gallup polls illustrated the effect of Here's Life and other evangelistic efforts. In those surveys, 34 percent of Americans described themselves as being "born again," and even larger numbers indicated that they had at least once encouraged another person "to believe in Jesus Christ or accept Him as their personal Savior." Bright concluded that "a spiritual movement . . . is sweeping across America as millions of Americans are turning to God." Bright predicted that "out of the present great spiritual awakening will come major reforms that will affect the lives of everyone in America and much of the world." Specifically, he predicted "a considerable decrease in the divorce rate," a drop in crime, a decline in drug and alcohol addiction, solutions to "racial inequities," and a rejection of "secular humanism in the classrooms of America." A few years later, Bright labeled a drop in crime in 1976 and 1977 an "interesting by-product of the Here's Life, America movement" and asserted that the divorce rate had stabilized during the years of the campaign.[38]

Crusade invited Peter Wagner of the Fuller Evangelistic Association's Department of Church Growth to measure the growth of churches that participated in the campaign. Wagner reported that only 3 percent of those who indicated "decisions" became new church members, and churches on average gained only one new member per twenty-two campaign volunteers. Billy Graham's crusades had long been plagued by similar statistics, and, like Graham, Bright pointed out that many individuals who were previously church members could still have made life-changing decisions of faith. Campus Crusade staff members involved in the campaign express diverse opinions about its results. The architect of the campaign, Bruce Cook, believes that it succeeded in training thousands of Christians in evangelism and in transmitting its message to millions of non-Christians. Cook also contends that Here's Life changed the image of Campus Crusade in the evangelical community. "It moved Crusade up," he explains, ". . . because we were no longer a campus ministry à la Young Life [or] Youth for Christ." However, Cook concedes that the lack of church growth "came back to bite us in the leg," in large part because Crusade planned the campaign too quickly. Conrad Koch maintains that by relying on the media campaigns, Crusade lowered the bar in order to meet its 1976 target. "That was Bill Bright at his worst," Koch concludes, "the 'I found it!' campaign." Perhaps most indicative of the disappointment was the fact that Here's Life quickly lost momentum, and, contrary to Bright's expectation, Crusade did not repeat the media campaigns in the United States.[39]

Here's Life, America was Bill Bright at his best and his worst: the adamant pursuit of lofty goals and a refusal to critically examine the effectiveness of his methods. Bright was still a salesman, and in 1975 he had faced the difficult task of persuading thousands of local pastors and congregations to embrace Here's Life. In response, Bright had oversold Here's Life with the suggestion that the campaign would change the course of the nation and lead to rapid church growth, and such bold promises naturally led to disappointments. To his credit, Bright asked Wagner to candidly assess Here's Life, but at least in his public statements he refused to admit to anything less than a total success, which left observers with the impression that Crusade claimed more than it had actually delivered. "[I]t just so happens," he responded to one set of critics, "that a few million people have found the Lord through this." Peter Wagner's analysis suggests that Crusade often overstated its effect because it only reported on "decisions" instead of long-term commitments. Bright himself had often cautioned that "[o]nly God knows what really happens" when a person indicates a "decision," but in his defense of Here's Life he sometimes lost sight of such careful distinctions.[40]

Bright's bicentennial vision for the United States was, at best, only partly fulfilled. Yet through the efforts of high-profile campaigns like Here's Life, America, evangelicals gained considerable visibility in American society during the nation's bicentennial year. In particular, the presidential election suggested the growing clout of a potential evangelical voting bloc. For all of the publicity that evangelicals received in relation to the 1976 election, however, the direction of evangelical politics remained uncertain. Evangelicals split their votes in 1976 between Carter and Ford, though Carter won a majority of the Southern evangelical vote. Jerry Regier, a Crusade staff member who began working with the Christian Embassy in 1977, comments that some Crusaders "were very excited about Jimmy Carter" because "he had talked about being 'born-again.'" Carter appeared on Pat Robertson's *700 Club*, and Robertson claimed to have helped Carter win the Democratic primary in Pennsylvania. Although he almost certainly voted for the Republican candidate in the 1976 election, Bright was optimistic about having a president in the White House who had supported Agape Atlanta. In 1977, Bright wrote Carter to express his "deep gratitude for your faithful witness for our Lord and for your help in launching this miracle in Atlanta." "I believe," he affirmed to Carter, "that God has raised you up for this dramatic moment in history to help give spiritual leadership to our world in crisis." As of the mid-1970s, the relationship between evangelicalism and conservative politics was not yet a marriage but had become a lively, if still awkward and incomplete, courtship.[41]

Bright, and through him Campus Crusade, played a noteworthy role in advancing this courtship. From the earliest days of Crusade, Bright's evangelistic vision fused spiritual and political objectives, from combating communism to influencing the direction of Congress. It was only after Explo '72, however, that Crusade was a ministry large and influential enough for Bright to more actively seek to impact the trajectory of American politics. Organizations like Campus Crusade became attractive entry points for politicians looking to establish ties with a suddenly important evangelical constituency. As Bruce Cook observed, Crusade was "no longer [just] a campus ministry." Indeed, Crusade had expanded its sights far beyond American colleges and universities. In 1976, Crusade pulled many of its staff off the campus to participate in Here's Life, America. Through Family-Life, a growing number of Crusade staff focused on issues not directly related to evangelism, and Crusade's publications evidenced anxiety over abortion, feminism, and homosexuality. After 1976, Crusade concentrated on the second half of the vision that Bright had announced in 1969: the task of evangelizing the world by 1980. Yet even as he planned Crusade's most ambitious evangelistic campaign yet, Bright never abandoned his dream of redeeming American politics.

7

America and the World for Jesus

Despite the mixed success of Here's Life, America, Bill Bright foresaw a massive acceleration of Campus Crusade's ministries. Bright's entrepreneurial style had always been to charge ahead and tackle new challenges rather than linger over setbacks. Howard Hendricks, a professor at Dallas Theological Seminary, describes his attempts to give counsel to Crusade's president. When Hendricks and Bright met periodically, Bright asked his friend to "tell me what's wrong with Crusade." "He'd get out a piece of paper," recollects Hendricks, "[and I would] give him three, four, five things." Bright would express his appreciation, but "next year I'd come back [and] go through the same procedure," says Hendricks. "Finally, I said to him, 'Bill, you don't hear what's wrong with Crusade. I've already told you and you've done nothing about it!'" "He could not spell the word 'problem' as far as Crusade was concerned," comments Hendricks. Looking beyond 1976, Bright remained committed to the fulfillment of the Great Commission throughout the entire world by 1980, and he envisioned a wide array of Crusade ministries within the United States. "I have a lot of other plans that I believe are from God," Bright shared in a 1976 interview. "Plans that can change government, can change education, can change the media, can change the entertainment world."[1]

In the late 1970s and early 1980s, Bright remained a significant figure in what was becoming known in journalistic and political circles as the Religious Right, as Jerry Falwell, James Robison, Tim LaHaye and others openly mobilized evangelicals to support a conservative Republican presidential candidate in 1980. Worries about the "American family" continued to spur evangelical political concern, and Crusade's FamilyLife division occupied a place of increasing distinction within the ministry. Despite the tug of politics, however, evangelism always remained the raison d'être of Campus Crusade. In 1980, LaHaye, an evangelical pastor in Southern California, published *The Battle for the Mind*, in which he outlined a struggle between secular humanism and political liberalism, on the one hand, and Christianity and political conservatism, on the other. "Bill liked it so much," remembers LaHaye, "that he endorsed it, and it became a running fad among the Campus Crusade workers. He said the bookstore [at Arrowhead Springs] sold three thousand copies." A few months later, however, Bright called his friend and "apologetically said, 'Tim, I'm sorry to say this. We're going to have to quit recommending your book." Bright explained that "our workers get so into . . . *The Battle for the Mind* and the issues of liberalism versus conservatism that they aren't as keyed in on evangelism."[2] During the 1970s, Bright's staff had complained at several points when he departed from Crusade's standard emphasis on evangelism and discipleship. In this instance, the roles were reversed, and Bright worried his staff was drifting from the organization's mission.

That mission, in the early 1970s and 1980s, was the fulfillment of Bright's vision to evangelize the entire world. Although American mainline Protestant denominations had retreated from international missions by the middle of the twentieth century, evangelical ministries remained committed to the global spread of their gospel. Bill and Vonette Bright attended the 1974 Lausanne Congress in Switzerland, at which evangelicals from around the world reaffirmed their commitment to world evangelization. Much as American evangelicals formed the NAE as a counterweight to the Federal Council of Churches, evangelicals at Lausanne implicitly responded to the theologically and socially more liberal World Council of Churches (WCC), headquartered only thirty miles away in Geneva. The Lausanne Covenant defined and endorsed evangelism as "the proclamation of the historical, biblical Christ as Saviour and Lord, with a view to persuading people to come to him personally and so be reconciled to God." Furthermore, the Congress upheld the necessity of cross-cultural missions (for example, American missionaries traveling to Thailand), which the WCC and some mainline American church officials increasingly found repugnant. Delegates at Lausanne emphasized the need to concentrate evangelistic efforts on "unreached peoples," countries or regions with little exposure to Christian teachings. As the close of the twentieth century approached, Bright and other evangelical leaders expressed fervent hope that the evangelization of the world—aided by American wealth and modern technologies—could soon be completed.[3]

The Adventure of Giving

Even before Here's Life, America drew to a close, Bright laid the groundwork for Here's Life, World, an adaptation and exportation of the American campaigns. Crusade intended to bring Here's Life, World to over one hundred countries by the end of 1977, and the ministry launched a few international pilot Here's Life campaigns in 1976. The first attempt, in the Indian province of Kerala, relied upon door-to-door evangelism and large urban assemblies. Crusade asserted that the Kerala campaign produced 1.85 million "decisions for Christ" out of a population of 22 million. Bolstered by such statistics, Bright insisted that his staff and supporters "trust and obey" God for the global fulfillment of the Great Commission by 1980. Bright criticized the "pessimism" of those who dismissed his 1980 goal, and he maintained that the target could be reached "if enough Christians were completely committed to our resurrected and returning Lord and were controlled and empowered by His Spirit." He anticipated a great evangelistic harvest, claiming that internal surveys "suggest to us that one out of two who are not already Christians are ready to receive Christ when properly approached."[4]

Here's Life, World permanently changed the nature of Campus Crusade by transferring the ministry's primary focus to the developing world. Bright maintained that the redeployment of Crusade's resources overseas would produce more cost-effective evangelism. "On the basis of our surveys in Asia, Africa and Latin America," Bright explained, "[we] are convinced that, for every dollar we raise, we can expect at least one person to receive Christ." "We began to have a huge exodus of top campus ministry leadership," remembers Alan Scholes. "There was a great sense within the movement . . . that we've completed the biggest challenge we're ever going to have in the United States." The American campus ministry began to resemble a foreign missions agency, as its goal shifted from university evangelism to encouraging students to serve as missionaries with Crusade upon graduation. Between 1977 and 1981, the number of Crusade staff in the United States remained stagnant for the first time since the ministry's 1958 break with Bob Jones University. However, the number of American staff serving overseas more than doubled to 660.[5]

Through the mid-1970s, the vast majority of Crusade's revenues had come through the grassroots efforts of its staff members, who asked families, friends, and churches to pledge funds toward their individual salaries. "[T]here are no rich, right-wing millionaires supporting us," Bright commented in a 1971 interview. By the late 1970s at least, that was no longer the case. In November 1977, Bright and three key backers held a Washington press conference to announce a $1 billion fund-raising drive to support Here's Life, World. Wallace E. Johnson, founder of Holiday Inn, chaired the fund-raising effort, joined by the music and film star Roy Rogers and the Texas oil and silver mogul Nelson Bunker Hunt. Along with his brother William Herbert Hunt, Bunker Hunt had increased his wealth dramatically by speculating in the silver market in the early 1970s, though the pair later lost millions when the price of silver collapsed. Hunt was a significant financial backer of several conservative political causes, including the John Birch Society, the *Manion Forum* radio program, and the Christian Freedom Foundation. He had also donated a considerable sum to George Wallace's 1968 bid for the White House. Hunt, who once described Bill Bright as "the closest thing to Jesus on earth," became Crusade's most reliable donor during the 1970s and early 1980s.[6]

Shortly before the November 1977 announcement, Crusade hired Mayes International, a Dallas-based consulting group, to develop a strategy for raising the $1 billion. The consultants observed that neither Crusade's board of directors nor ordinary staff members demonstrated much enthusiasm for the drive. Crusade needed to convince its staff members to view fund-raising as an integral component of their ministries rather than as an occasional "nuisance." Mayes counseled Crusade to utilize the "new concept" of a "giving ministry," "which treats asking for money as something you are doing for a person instead of something you are doing to him." The consultants recommended that Crusade "accumulate, list, analyze, eliminate, and properly research the required data and facts on all the most able and concerned potential helpers and supporters. . . . No one who has come under the influence of Campus Crusade in any way should be overlooked in this listing." Although Crusade initially implied that Here's Life, World would fulfill the Great Commission by 1980, the organization soon talked of raising its $1 billion target over a period of ten years. With $30 million from major donors such as Johnson, Rogers, and Hunt, Crusade hoped to raise $100 million to spend on Here's Life, World during 1978 and 1979. Given this massive goal, Crusade made an even more concerted effort to identify and court major donors. Since the 1960s, the organization had invited businessmen to "executive seminars" at Arrowhead Springs for evangelistic weekends that also built relationships with potential supporters. As a major component of its attempt to raise $1 billion, Crusade organized a series of Here's Life, World conferences—several hosted by Bunker Hunt—to which it invited leading businessmen and other wealthy prospects. In the early 1980s, Crusade formed "History's Handful," an initiative that sought to persuade one thousand affluent donors to each pledge $1 million. The executive seminars, History's Handful conferences, and Bright's careful networking resulted in a sharp increase in large donations.[7]

Perhaps the least admirable aspect of evangelical fund-raising in recent decades has been the gambit of evangelists to promise their supporters supernatural benefits in return for their earthly wealth. For instance, in the 1950s Oral Roberts offered to form "blessing pacts" with his donors, promising his supporters that God would return "seven times" their donations to them—he even briefly offered a money-back guarantee to donors. In the early 1980s, Roberts mailed his supporters "prayer cloths" and vials of oil, implying that their financial support of his ministries would bring them the gift of healing. Rex Humbard, a popular televangelist in the 1970s and early 1980s, promised supporters that he would go before God in his "private study" with their individualized requests, implying that his intercession would produce the benefits they desired. In addition to promising financial blessings, many evangelists in recent decades have regularly bombarded their listeners with dire scenarios, begging for donations to stave off the end of their ministries. Again, Roberts serves as an extreme example of this tendency. In 1987, he told his followers that without $8 million in needed contributions, God planned to hasten his entrance into heaven.[8]

As Crusade's financial needs grew, Bright promised that God would reward Christians for their generosity, encouraged supporters to take on debt to give to his ministry, and warned Christians against hoarding their wealth. In the late 1980s, Bright published a book on Christian finances and stewardship entitled *As You Sow*. Although he cautioned his readers against giving in order to receive, Bright wrote a letter asking supporters to send him stories about Christians who received considerable financial rewards after giving money to worthy ministries. "Did God not only return the amount you invested in a kingdom enterprise but much more?" he asked. "Whatever you give up to follow Jesus," Bright promised in another book, "will be returned to you a hundredfold—plus eternal life," Furthermore, he called on potential donors to "consider 'borrowing for the kingdom.'" "We should prayerfully seek God's wisdom," he suggested, "concerning the giving of, or borrowing against, property, stocks and bonds to help win and disciple others for Christ in other countries." Bright, who continued to predict communist aggression against the United States, importuned his fellow Christians not to simply accumulate wealth. He recounted a conversation with "one of the most outstanding financial figures in America" who predicted "the almost-certain collapse of the U.S. economy and the possible loss of our freedoms to a foreign power unless there is a supernatural moving of God's Spirit throughout the world." In light of such predictions, Bright recommended "that individuals whom God has blessed in a material way should not hoard what He has given, but lay up treasures in heaven."[9]

Crusade's more aggressive solicitation of funds rankled some staff members. The Washington, D.C., Here's Life leadership team complained to Bright about "offensive and excessive fund raising," including telephone solicitation of persons supporting individual staff members. "Staff have expressed to us," complained the group, "the view that dollars are now wagging the ministry." "[Many] supporters and friends of the ministry," they continued, "see Campus Crusade as interested *only* in money." Although Crusade's fund-raising tactics reflected some of the less savory aspects of evangelical sales pitches, Bright never employed the histrionics and hysteria of Oral Roberts, Jim Bakker, or Jimmy Swaggart. Moreover, there is no evidence to suggest that the Brights ever used Crusade's revenues to aggrandize themselves financially. Compared to most successful evangelical entrepreneurs, they lived modestly. Ron Blue, a Christian financial planner who counseled "History's Handful" donors, concluded from a personal examination of Bright's finances that Crusade's increasing income "didn't benefit him personally in any way unless there's an ego satisfaction from having built the organization." In his writings, Bright encouraged his supporters to "live modest lifestyles" and "to wear the cloak of materialism loosely." Bright was one of evangelicalism's most effective fund-raisers, but he was no Elmer Gantry.[10]

The rapidly rising budgets of evangelical enterprises from Campus Crusade to the Christian Broadcasting Network reflect the massive increase in evangelical wealth during the post–World War II era. Although the patronage of evangelists by the business world long predated Bill Bright, few have equaled his ability to cultivate support from businessmen. "Whenever I go and meet a wealthy person," complained David Hubbard, longtime president of Fuller Theological Seminary, "I find that Bill Bright has been there first." In June 1981, Bright and Bunker Hunt hosted a "Financial Success Seminar" in Anaheim. At the event, speakers promoted various investment strategies (from jojoba bean farms to racehorses), speculated about the rise of the anti-Christ in the form of a computerized international banking system, and extolled the virtues of private enterprise. "The Lord is the all-time capitalist," proclaimed John W. O'Donnell, an evangelical tax-planner. Tim LaHaye, by then a key figure in the Moral Majority, observed that the result of the 1980 election was "almost as if God Almighty had given us a breath of freedom." Bright's old friend John Conlan encouraged affluent Christians to seek ways to protect their assets from taxes and other threats. Bright described what sounded like a fifth spiritual law: "There is a law of sowing and reaping . . . the great adventure of giving and, in the process, receiving." More than a quarter of the individuals who attended the Financial Success Seminar proceeded directly to a Here's Life, World conference also chaired by Bright and Hunt. The *Los Angeles Times* reported that ten individuals made commitments to donate at least $1 million to Campus Crusade's program of worldwide evangelization. The success of the twin conferences suggests that a potent mixture of evangelism, capitalism, and conservative politics helped persuade evangelical businessmen to support Crusade.[11]

Bright excelled at fund-raising because of his ability to form personal relationships with evangelical businessmen, his experimentation with fund-raising strategies, and his incorporation of anticommunist and politically conservative themes. Yet those characteristics were only partly responsible for his success. At the core of Bright's ability to recruit staff members and connect with affluent donors was his personal practice of evangelism. Even as his executive responsibilities expanded, Bright lived out his insistence that Christians regularly talk about their faith in Jesus Christ. Robbie Gowdey, Bright's personal assistant in the late 1970s, remembers trying to hurry Bright to a conference call with major donors to the Here's Life, World campaign, including Hunt and Rogers. On his way to his hotel room, Bright ran into "a young man in the parking lot" who had "been exposed to some hypocrisy in his upbringing in the church." "Bill was so burdened," remembers Gowdey. "We would leave and then he would . . . come back and approach this gentleman from another angle." While Gowdey fretted about being late for the call, "this was the most important person in the world right then and there with Bill." When Bright finally reached his room, he delayed further. "[H]e was on his knees by his bed weeping over this young man in prayer, crying out to God for this boy's salvation." For all of his pragmatism and concentration on fund-raising, Bright retained the respect of both his staff and his donors because of his transparent commitment to Crusade's evangelistic vision.[12]

In terms of both fund-raising and claimed converts, Here's Life, World was a major step forward for Campus Crusade. By 1981, the fund-raising drive had amassed $225 million. Even if the ministry fell short of its $1 billion goal, Crusade's annual revenues nearly doubled to $78 million between 1977 and 1981. Bright, in characteristic fashion, portrayed Here's Life, World—relying on advertising blitzes, door-to-door evangelism, and large evangelistic events—as an unparalleled success in the history of global evangelism. "It is no exaggeration to say," he opined, "that never before in the history of the church . . . has such a dramatic demonstration of the power of God resulted in such an unprecedented harvest." Crusade claimed a staggering rate of conversion and discipleship: 2.6 million "decisions to accept Christ as Savior and Lord" during a 1978–79 effort in Colombia, 89 percent of Tijuana converts enrolled in Bible studies, and 3 million "decisions" across Latin America in 1980 alone. Crusade's various Asian ministries counted an even more astounding 11 million "decisions" for Jesus Christ in 1980. In August 1980, Campus Crusade for Christ in South Korea organized a massive World Evangelization Crusade as the climax to the Korean Here's Life campaign. According to Crusade, three evening events drew more than 2 million people, 1 million people made first-time "decisions" for Christ, and 1 million pledged a commitment to some sort of involvement in world missions. Crusade officials asserted that the Here's Life campaigns were much more successful overseas than they had been in the United States, where the media blitzes had amounted to minor distractions on the American cultural landscape.[13]

Campus Crusade's emergence as a major foreign-missions entity reflects broader trends in foreign missions over the last half-century. According to Robert Coote, as the number of mainline Protestant missionaries continued to dwindle, evangelical and fundamentalist agencies accounted for more than 90 percent of North American foreign missionaries by 1980. Major missionary-sending churches and organizations included the Southern Baptist Convention (more than 3,000 missionaries), the Assemblies of God (1,214), the Africa Inland Mission (590), and the Missionary Aviation Fellowship (252). Crusade—with over 600 Americans overseas by 1981—formed a significant part of this development. Certainly, as the Lausanne discussions affirmed, American evangelicals believed in the appropriateness of Western evangelicals sharing their faith in other cultures. On the other hand, Crusade maintained a commitment to training international leadership, and as the twentieth century drew to a close, indigenous Christians filled the positions of leadership in most of Crusade's worldwide ministries. Moreover, Crusade helped inaugurate a post-Western missionary era in which missionaries from countries like Korea took their faith around the world. Observing the World Evangelization Crusade, *Christianity Today* concluded that the South Korean church "has deliberately moved from being a missionary receiving church to a missionary sending one." Bright believed that God had blessed America with its tremendous affluence precisely so that American evangelicals could spread the Christian gospel across the globe. In the late 1970s and early 1980s, Bright became the American evangelical leader most skilled at harnessing that affluence for the cause of worldwide evangelism. Bright primarily attracted donors through his fervent expression of his evangelistic vision, but he also courted wealthy businessmen by emphasizing the communist threat and extolling the virtues of traditional morality and free-market capitalism.[14]

The Gospel on Celluloid

Campus Crusade's most successful tool for global evangelism—and one of the most significant developments in the organization's history—came from an unexpected source. In 1976, John Heyman—a British film producer and financier of German Jewish background—contacted Bright. Heyman had helped to finance a number of major movies, including *Chinatown* and *The Rocky Horror Picture Show*, hardly evangelical favorites. Then in 1974, Heyman founded the Genesis Project with the intention of creating film versions of both the Hebrew Scriptures and the New Testament. He enlisted more than two hundred biblical scholars to provide counsel on the script and historical setting for his films. When Heyman completed his first films on the books of Genesis and Luke, he sought to market them through Jewish and Christian leaders. Heyman brought his films to the faculty of Yeshiva University, and he contacted Billy Graham, Jerry Falwell, and Pat Robertson. The early Bible films generated meager sales and lost money, but Heyman hoped to produce a feature-length film on Jesus that would attract larger audiences and fund the Genesis Project's more scholarly endeavors.[15]

While looking to market his films and obtain financing for his Jesus movie, Heyman traveled to Arrowhead Springs. After his move to California, Bright had asked Cecil B. DeMille to produce a talking version of his 1927 epic *King of Kings*, and he had long believed that a film about Jesus could become a valuable evangelistic tool. After meeting Heyman, Bright asked Paul Eshleman to consult with the filmmaker. Heyman's short film on the first two chapters of the Gospel of Luke sold Eshleman on the concept. Heyman and Eshleman futilely canvassed studios to obtain financing for the feature-length film, but Bunker Hunt guaranteed $3 million for the movie's production against its future theater revenue. According to Bright's biographer Michael Richardson, Crusade's leadership was initially uneasy with "a nonbeliever trying to put the Bible on film" and was disappointed that Crusade's other U.S. ministries would lose Eshleman's leadership. Bright approved the project over those objections and assigned Eshleman to work full-time on the film.[16]

The collaboration with Heyman would have been inconceivable in earlier decades. According to Bright's seminary friend Dan Fuller, Bright "had some very bad experiences dealing with Jews" during his years as a businessman in California. Furthermore, he had not enjoyed a trip to Israel in the early 1960s. "'All my old problems with Jews welled up again,'" Fuller remembers Bright saying. "'I was so glad when that airplane flew out of Tel Aviv to Zurich.'" "I was so offended," Bright later wrote, "by the vendors, the peddlers, the people hawking their wares, the commercialism that I determined that I would never return to Jerusalem." Given the virulent anti-Semitism of early twentieth-century fundamentalists such as William B. Riley, Bright's early attitudes are not remarkable. Jewish groups occasionally criticized Crusade for evangelizing Jewish students. During the 1960s, Hal Lindsey made a special effort to reach Jewish fraternity students at UCLA. Crusade officials denied that the organization as a whole singled out Jews for proselytization, but the ministry defended its mission to evangelize all individuals regardless of their religious heritage. "We make no special effort to convert Jews," Bright clarified, "but we don't avoid talking with them either." He added that some Jews "have a violent emotional reaction when you mention Jesus to them."[17]

After the establishment of the modern state of Israel in 1948—the event that helped induce Bright to temporarily leave Fuller Theological Seminary—many fundamentalists and evangelicals evidenced a positive stance toward Israel, if not necessarily toward the Jewish faith. The 1967 Six-Day War and Israel's occupation of the Old City of Jerusalem further excited prophetic speculation, and in 1971 Carl Henry organized the Jerusalem Conference on Biblical Prophecy, attended by many high-profile American evangelicals. By the 1970s, Bright's feelings toward Judaism and Jews had softened considerably. While under fire for his support of the Christian Freedom Foundation, Bright mentioned his admiration for David Lawrence, the politically conservative Jewish founder of *U.S. News and World Report*. Bright invited Heyman to talk about his own faith at the Arrowhead Springs event at which Bunker Hunt pledged to provide financing for his film. Bright's more tolerant views and actions reflect the gradual pilgrimage toward philo-Semitism undertaken by a portion of the American evangelical community over the past several decades. As evangelicals accumulated wealth and became more influential in the arenas of politics, entertainment, and education, they developed personal contacts with Jews, contacts that partly eroded earlier prejudices.[18]

Of course, Campus Crusade still sought to introduce anyone—Jew or Gentile—to its understanding of Jesus Christ. As work began on Heyman's Jesus film, Eshleman and Heyman discussed their respective faiths, and Eshleman shared the *Four Spiritual Laws* with his Jewish colleague. According to Eshleman, Heyman "received the Lord [Jesus] into his life" in March 1977. Heyman explains that although "it would be unfair to say it [Eshleman's claim] isn't true," any faith response he made to Eshleman and Bright comprised a portion of a longer spiritual journey and did not result in a lasting Christian commitment. "My major criticism of Campus [Crusade]," Heyman explains, "is that they accept commitments but do nothing to nurture the commitments and people are left out there dangling and still looking." "I am a Jew, born and bred," Heyman told *Christian Century* in 2001.[19]

Heyman's entire production of Luke's Gospel ran more than four hours. In consultation with Bright and Eshleman, he edited a shorter version for Campus Crusade. Eshleman and Heyman persuaded Warner Brothers to coordinate the film's release, and *Jesus* opened in American theaters in late 1979. The *Washington Post*'s Gary Arnold penned a withering review, describing Heyman's *Jesus* as "an uninspired trudge through selected pages of Luke," "monotonous," "amateurish," and "an audio-visual monstrosity that threatens to dull the senses of generations of Sunday School kids." Arnold labeled Brian Deacon—a British actor in the lead role—"an insipid Jesus," and he even criticized Heyman for using modern Bible translations and for taking "more license with scripture than he lets on." *Christianity Today* was kinder to Heyman, Deacon, and *Jesus*. Its review questioned the wisdom and practicality of putting the life of Christ on film—"we may all in the end conclude that we may as well have tried to reproduce Chartres in papier-mâché"—but conceded that Heyman's film "steers as true a course as one might ever hope to see in a film on Jesus."[20]

Utilizing a strategy Mel Gibson would perfect in 2004, Eshleman worked with churches (both evangelical and Catholic) to arrange group trips and discounts. Eshleman reported that "Warner Brothers was thrilled" with the early results, as "[c]rowds were being turned away in twenty cities." According to Eshleman, four million people saw *Jesus* over the next year. The final numbers, however, were less encouraging. Ticket sales left the project $4 million in debt. Heyman himself had been more interested in preparing scholarly translations of the Bible onto film rather than producing commercially appealing feature films. "I think it was a muddled attempt," he says of *Jesus*, "to turn something into a commercial success that was as bland as watching paint dry." Fortunately, Bunker Hunt converted his guarantee to a donation, but Heyman's vision of utilizing the movie's profits to subsidize his Genesis Project crumbled when the movie failed to attract mainstream audiences.[21]

After the movie's completion, the relationship between Campus Crusade and John Heyman deteriorated. Heyman complains that Crusade "never mentioned the source [of the film]" and "made a dozen different versions of the film to which they added or subtracted as they wanted." When in the late 1990s Campus Crusade released a shorter version, *The Story of Jesus for Children*, which included new footage, Heyman sued Crusade, alleging that the new version damaged his reputation. The parties settled out of court, but Heyman remains embittered by his collaboration with Crusade. "In my opinion they behaved in bad faith from the day I delivered the film onwards," he asserts. Despite his displeasure with Crusade as a whole, Heyman remains respectful of Eshleman. "I really do think that Paul Eshleman is a good man," Heyman comments, "[and] a true believer."[22]

Despite the deteriorating relationship with Heyman, Bright was more than pleased with the film. Steve Douglass later recalled that the first time they watched *Jesus* together, Bright wept during the crucifixion scene. "All of us had tears in our eyes," Douglass revealed, "but he almost couldn't control himself." Several years later the two watched the movie together again. "We got to the crucifixion scene," remembered Douglass, "and once again he wept compulsively." Even before *Jesus* left American theaters, Crusade proceeded with plans to turn the film into a global evangelistic tool. The ministry dubbed the film into other languages, and the film became part of the Here's Life, World campaigns. Crusade included an introduction on how Hindus or Muslims could understand the claims of Christ, and the ministry appended an evangelistic presentation to the end of the movie. Crusade arranged for urban theaters to show the translated films, and the ministry also formed small teams to take projection equipment to rural villages across Asia. Often a member of the film team would speak following a showing of *Jesus* and invite the members of the audience to "pray to receive Christ."[23]

In 1987, Bright announced what he termed New Life 2000, an attempt to evangelize the entire world by 2000—perhaps a tacit admission that Crusade had not fulfilled its 1980 goal—and record one billion "decisions for Christ." Crusade's plan called for dividing the world into five thousand "Million People Target Areas" and creating in each area a "New Life Training Center" at which Christians would receive training in evangelism and church planting. Back in the 1880s, the evangelist Arthur T. Pierson suggested that a proposed missionary council divide the world into manageable sections for cooperative evangelization by the year 1900. "Let the whole world-field be mapped out," Pierson wrote in 1885, "and divided and distributed among the evangelical denominations of Christendom, so that every province and district shall be under competent and responsible care." Like Pierson a century before, Bright preferred strategies to rapidly disseminate the gospel, and the *Jesus* film became the highest profile segment of New Life 2000. In 1987, Bright predicted that Crusade would assemble five thousand film teams to show the movie to five to ten million people each day by 1995.[24]

Largely through showings of *Jesus*, Bright hoped that Crusade would help form millions of churches in the developing world. During Here's Life, World, Crusade had established "home Bible fellowships" to nurture its converts, and those fellowships naturally evolved into churches. "In Asia and several places," explains Bailey Marks, "it just became very apparent [that] if we didn't start churches, nobody was going to start them." Without planting churches, he asks, "what were we going to do with our converts?" However, Bright still did not want Crusade to start its own churches or become a denomination. Therefore, Crusade formed church-planting partnerships with a wide variety of churches, organizations, and denominations. In Thailand, Crusade helped establish several thousand churches through an indigenous Christian organization. In 1997, Crusade formed a church-planting partnership with the Southern Baptist International Mission Board that used the *Jesus* film to evangelize remote areas.[25]

In addition to working with noncharismatic evangelicals like the Southern Baptists, Crusade also partnered with charismatic and Pentecostal denominations and churches. The church-planting partnerships completed the reversal of Crusade's earlier stance toward the charismatic and Pentecostal movements. Through the 1970s, Crusade held firm to its policy prohibiting staff members from speaking in tongues, even in private. Thomas Zimmerman, general superintendent of the Assemblies of God, talked with Bright about the issue in 1974. When Bright sent him a copy of the organization's policy, including a detailed theological refutation of the Pentecostal/charismatic understanding of tongues, Zimmerman complained to a colleague about a "new sense of resistance to the Pentecostal position" "in evangelical circles."[26]

Zimmerman did not know that the issue of speaking in tongues had become extremely personal for Bill Bright and his family. In the early 1970s, Bright's son Zachary spoke in tongues partly through the influence of Greg Laurie, then a young, long-haired pastor of a small charismatic church in Riverside. "I came home one night claiming to have been baptized in the Spirit at Calvary Chapel Costa Mesa," recalls Zachary Bright. Given Crusade's policy against tongues, he says, "everyone took it [his exuberance about the experience] personally." "My mom especially was so afraid that he'd gotten involved in a cult," remembers the Brights' younger son, Brad. "Although Dad had tried very hard to build bridges," Brad continues, "it was hard when all of a sudden it was in his own home." Zachary, who had recently graduated from high school, was working for Crusade at Arrowhead Springs. According to him, his father wavered when confronted with his experience, but Vonette Bright encouraged her husband to firmly enforce Crusade's prohibition. Bill asked Zachary to read the policy and expected his son to comply with the directive. Instead, Zachary moved out of the family home. A partial reconciliation took place within a year. Thus, it was against this backdrop that Bill Bright confirmed Crusade's policy against speaking in tongues to Zimmerman.[27]

In 1983, Campus Crusade altered its policy to allow staff members to speak in tongues, though at first only in private. A shared commitment to evangelism and conservative moral and political issues, Zachary Bright's charismatic experience, and Bright's personal relationships with charismatic and Pentecostal Christians all led Crusade to soften its stance toward churches and organizations that endorsed speaking in tongues. "We're growing up," Bright allowed during a 1982 visit to Oral Roberts University. "Some of us who . . . don't speak in tongues, are beginning to realize that that's not the issue." In addition to the developments in the United States, the rapid growth of Spirit-filled charismatic and Pentecostal churches in the developing world also encouraged Crusade to adopt a more ecumenical attitude. "Of the people involved in evangelism worldwide," commented Paul Eshleman, "the most aggressive come out of Pentecostal backgrounds, and we often find ourselves in partnership with them." As Pentecostal churches spread like wildfire in Latin America and Africa, Crusade partnered with what Harvey Cox termed the "fire from heaven." Old inhibitions about cooperating with charismatics and Pentecostals had completely disappeared by the late 1980s, and the Assemblies of God became one of Crusade's most significant international partners.[28]

The *Jesus* film also helped Campus Crusade overcome early obstacles the ministry faced in predominantly Catholic countries. "I think the *Jesus* film has probably done more than anything to bring us closer to the Catholic Church," explains Bailey Marks. The Catholic Church collaborated with Crusade to produce a version of the film more attuned to Catholic sensibilities and theology. In 2000, the Vatican showed the *Jesus* film in Rome as part of its Year of Jubilee celebration. Following a message by Pope John Paul II on 19 August, a crowd of an estimated one million watched *Jesus* in multiple languages, and volunteers throughout the city distributed nearly seven hundred thousand *Jesus* videos. By 2003, Crusade claimed to have shown its *Jesus* film to more than five billion people since 1980 — only three billion excepting repeat viewers, Eshleman estimated — and the organization recorded roughly twenty million annual "decisions for Christ" worldwide. Bill Bright, who had showered cellophane "Gospel bombs" on Southern California campuses in the 1940s, spread the "gospel on celluloid" around the world.[29]

A Thousand Days of Freedom

Even as he pursued his organization's mission of global evangelism, Bright continued to participate in attempts to influence America's spiritual and political future. After the negative publicity about his involvement with the Christian Freedom Foundation, Bright kept a much lower political profile. Jim Wallis believes that his *Sojourners* article was a "chastening experience" for Bright; Wallis's coauthor Wes Michaelson speculates that Bright "began to be more careful and to curtail some of his involvements." Crusade's board of directors cautioned Bright that partisanship would not only create unwanted publicity for the ministry but could also imperil its financial viability. "Everybody kept warning Bill," remembers Arlis Priest, on Crusade's board, "that we could lose our tax benefits if they [the IRS] decided he was in politics." According to Pat Robertson, Bright "wasn't quite as vocal [about political issues] because he didn't want to in any way jeopardize the tax-exempt status of Campus Crusade." Nevertheless, a series of events in 1980 drew Bright back toward the political arena.[30]

Although Jimmy Carter garnered noteworthy evangelical support in 1976 by openly sharing his "born-again" faith, evangelical leaders quickly became disenchanted with his administration. The problem was both one of policy and personal relationships. Carter and his evangelical critics, such as Jerry Falwell, Tim LaHaye, and James Robison, disagreed over issues of increasing salience to evangelicals: the Equal Rights Amendment, school prayer, and abortion. Moreover, a 1978 proposal by the IRS to revoke the tax exemption of private schools that failed to meet federal standards of racial integration caused considerable anger in evangelical circles, particularly in the South. To a certain extent, such disagreements made the evangelical abandonment of Carter inevitable. Yet a second and often overlooked part of the problem stemmed from the Carter administration's inconsistent—sometimes nonexistent—attempts to maintain his relationships with evangelical leaders. During Carter's first three years in office, he did not accept invitations to speak at the annual National Religious Broadcasters (NRB) conventions in the nation's capital, missing valuable opportunities to appear before the evangelical pantheon. Robert Maddox, who in 1979 became Carter's liaison to religious groups, considers Carter's failure to cultivate relationships with evangelicals through the NRB a "serious tactical mistake."[31] Even after evangelicals began to criticize the Carter administration over the ERA and other cultural issues, Carter and his aides did not initiate any sustained effort to repair the damaged relationships. Evangelical leaders, beginning to function as the representatives of a new special interest group, transferred their attention to finding an alternative candidate in 1980.

Abortion, the ERA, and the potential action of the IRS against Christian schools galvanized many conservative evangelicals into greater political awareness and activism. The older framework of anticommunism, however, remained salient to the political worldview of many evangelical leaders. Pat Robertson remembers a dinner with Bright in the late 1970s at which Crusade's president kept Robertson entranced until the early morning with his explication of the dangers of global communism. "He began telling me about the perils of the Soviet threat," recalls Robertson, ". . . how they were ringing our seacoast with nuclear submarines, and [how] they were subverting our government, and it went on and on." The two became so animated in their discussion of the red peril that Robertson forgot that it was his wife's birthday. "The obvious spread of communism throughout the world," Bright wrote in 1979, "is beginning to alarm even those who have pooh-poohed the idea that the communists have any plan for world conquest." For many conservative evangelicals, the global struggle between communism and the Christian, democratic West still defined the course of contemporary history.[32]

In 1979, Bright convened a meeting of the evangelical elite at a Dallas airport hotel. After Bright persuaded Billy Graham to attend the meeting, other conservative leaders agreed to come, including Robison, Robertson, and Adrian Rogers. The group discussed moral degeneration in the United States and the communist threat. "They [Graham and Bright] believed," Robison recalls, "that unless we had a philosophical change of principle . . . we had 'a thousand days of freedom' [remaining in the United States]." According to Robbie Gowdey, Bright's personal assistant at the time, Bright and the others expressed their unhappiness with the Carter administration's failure to address issues of concern to evangelicals, and they also worried that Carter's foreign policy had weakened the position of the United States. According to Robison's recollection, with the exceptions of Graham and Rex Humbard, all of the leaders agreed on the need to become more involved politically. The group discussed the upcoming presidential election and agreed to interview potential Republican candidates in order to select a potential political savior. Gowdey states that the group hoped to "mobilize the churches to get people out to register to vote." Bright told the gathering that he intended to organize a pastor's conference the following year in Washington to pray for the nation.[33]

During the summer of 1979, evangelical delegations vetted Ronald Reagan and John Connally, the former governor of Texas. At Connally's Texas ranch, Florida pastor D. James Kennedy asked the prospective nominee, "what reason would you give God for letting you [into heaven]?" According to John Conlan, a member of the delegation, Connally replied, "my mother was a Methodist, my pappy was a Methodist, my grandmother was a Methodist, and I'd just tell him [God] I ain't any worse than any of the other people that want to get into heaven." Connally's answer did not resonate with born-again sensibilities that linked passage to heaven with personal faith in Jesus Christ. Shortly thereafter, as part of his effort to evangelize key political leaders, Bright visited Connally while the latter was teaching at Harvard. Former Bright aide Robert Pittenger remembers that Bright asked Connally about his "relationship with Christ," whereupon Connally responded that his faith was "a personal matter." "Dr. Bright said," according to Pittenger, "'Governor Connally, with all due respect, Jesus Christ died on the cross in a very public way for you.'" Connally apologized for his initial statement, and Bright proceeded to share the *Four Spiritual Laws*. Several months later, Connally joined Bunker Hunt at a Here's Life, World fund-raising event. Connally learned how to speak the language of the evangelical constituency, although his encounter with Bright took place too late to improve his chances for the Republican nomination.[34]

Given his California roots, some occasional contacts with Reagan during the latter's gubernatorial years, and his relationship with Reagan's pastor and early Crusade convert Donn Moomaw, Bright almost certainly favored Reagan's candidacy. Indeed, Reagan rather easily won the support of most evangelical leaders. When the same group of evangelicals that had met with Connally met with the former California governor, Kennedy asked Reagan the same question about his qualifications for heaven. "I wouldn't give God any reason for letting me in," Reagan said, according to Conlan. "I'd just ask for mercy, because of what Jesus Christ did for me at Calvary." Reagan assured James Robison that Jesus was more real to him than his own mother. Although he could not match Carter's record of church attendance and Sunday school teaching, Reagan did not need remedial spiritual sessions with Bill Bright.[35]

Early in 1980, Carter made a brief attempt to win back the support of evangelical leaders. On 21 January, he spoke at the National Religious Broadcasters convention, reminding the audience that he was a "born-again Christian" and speaking about the need for presidents and televangelists to practice humility. Robert Maddox, Carter's religious liaison, comments that Carter's speech received a warm reception but that he had waited too long to begin courting evangelical votes for his reelection campaign. The morning after his speech, Carter invited a dozen evangelical leaders to an awkward breakfast at the White House. Carter equivocated on abortion and reiterated his support for the ERA, though he did say that he did not believe a homosexual couple comprised a family. Some of those in attendance were impressed by Carter's outreach. "It's easier to take potshots at the image on the screen," confessed Jim Bakker, "than it is when you're in the same room with a warm, decent man confessing his faith in Jesus." Others were not swayed. "We went outside, and we had prayer," recalls Tim LaHaye. "I remember I was hanging onto the black iron gates at the

White House, and we prayed that God would help us to do everything we could to keep him from being reelected." Perhaps policy differences alone would have prevented Carter from retaining his evangelical constituency. Still, Bakker's response demonstrates that Carter could have blunted evangelicals' opposition to him if he had carefully cultivated their support throughout his administration.[36]

In April 1980, Bright and Robertson co-chaired a Christian rally in Washington that focused attention on the widening chasm between evangelicals and the Carter administration. The event, entitled "Washington for Jesus" (WFJ), was the brainchild of John Gimenez, a charismatic Virginia pastor friendly with Robertson. Gimenez and Robertson turned to Bright in order to facilitate the participation of noncharismatic evangelicals at WFJ. Gimenez's assistant, John Gilman, flew to Arrowhead Springs to meet with Bright, who was still somewhat hesitant about collaborating with charismatics and Pentecostals. Bright said that if Gilman could "guarantee this won't be a charismatic meeting per se but will be truly a day of national repentance," he would shelve his own plans for a Washington prayer meeting and support WFJ. After accepting Gimenez's offer, Bright made phone calls to key evangelicals, including Southern Baptist Convention president Adrian Rogers. "I might have been the visionary," explains Gimenez, "but he [Bright] brought a whole wing of the body of Christ that would otherwise not have come." According to Gimenez, Bright was uniquely placed to bring conservative Protestants together, because he was not a "tribal leader." Bright's location outside a denomination or even a local church empire gave him the ability to reach out to a broad cross-section of the evangelical world.[37]

WFJ began with the goal of bringing one million Christians to the Washington Mall for a twelve-hour prayer rally, focusing on the need to restore God's favor to the United States through repentance. Gimenez chose 29 April to commemorate the 1607 planting of a cross by the Jamestown settlers at Cape Henry. The planned activities included showings of Crusade's *Jesus* film, a lobbying effort by a group titled "Intercessors for Congress," and a day of prayers and mini-sermons. In January, the rally's steering committee drafted a "Christian Declaration" outlining a list of legislative priorities, including restrictions on abortion rights and a reduction in government social spending. "Our poor have become per-petual wards of the state, and our armed forces weakened," read the position paper, which Bright and the other leaders signed. One WFJ official told invited members of Congress they would learn the Christian perspective on contemporary issues at the event. Senator Mark Hatfield complained that he had received a threatening letter from a WFJ coordinator warning that he would report on the senator's voting record. In the face of such criticism, WFJ withdrew the declaration and avoided overtly mixing religion and partisanship at the rally. For instance, WFJ organizers invited senators and representatives to the rally but did not invite them to speak. Although the *Washington Post* reported that Christian enthusiasm for WFJ was "drifting away," most evangelical leaders lined up behind the rally: Robison, Bakker, Rogers, Kennedy, and Charles Stanley. Jerry Falwell stayed away, evidently because he was hesitant to cooperate with charismatics and Pentecostals. Billy Graham, at a crusade in Indianapolis, did not attend the event but sent a message of support.[38]

The twenty-ninth of April 1980 began with a steady rain, but the clouds broke up as the rally began, a development that WFJ leaders linked to an eloquent prayer by the African American preacher E. V. Hill. From the platform, Bright offered his interpretation of the source of the country's problems, asserting that "[w]e've turned from God and God is chastening us." "You go back to 1962 and [196]3 [when the Supreme Court banned school-sponsored prayer and Bible-reading]," Bright argued, "and you'll discover a series of plagues that came upon America." Bright cited the Vietnam War, increased drug use, racial conflict, Watergate, and a rise in divorce, teenage pregnancy, and alcoholism as the result of those decisions. "God is saying to us," he concluded, "'Wake up! Wake up! Wake up!'" Many of the speakers predicted that abortion, homosexuality, and the repression of school prayer would bring God's wrath upon the country, most likely in the form of a Soviet attack. "Unless we repent and turn from our sin," warned Bright, "we can expect to be destroyed." "The scream of the great American eagle," lamented Adrian Rogers, "has turned into the twitter of a frightened sparrow." Just four days after a disastrous rescue attempt resulted in a downed helicopter and eight American deaths, Pat Boone sang a "song of intercession for the hostages" held in Tehran.[39]

"We have not come to Washington with a political agenda or to lobby for certain legislation," Bright clarified at WFJ. Like any large Washington gathering during an election year, however, WFJ inevitably carried political overtones and implications. Indeed, the rally's constant warnings about God's impending judgment on America and calls for repentance implied dissatisfaction with the Carter administration's stewardship of the nation. Moreover, WFJ leaders organized those in attendance by congressional district in order to encourage them to become involved in local politics. As might be expected, unsympathetic observers of WFJ noted the political implications. The National Council of Churches alleged that the rally was political, and James L. Farmer of the Congress of Racial Equality stated that "if the Jesus I knew were looking down on the Mall today he would probably feel compelled to say, 'Thank God I am not a Christian.'" Phil Shenk of *Sojourners*—the magazine remained a left-wing critic of Crusade and other conservative evangelical organizations—took pleasure in recognizing the irony and hypocrisy behind these more liberal Protestant pronouncements. Shenk noted that mainline churches also engaged in "lobbying efforts on Capitol Hill." Similarly, Edward Plowman of *Christianity Today* wryly observed that on the same day as WFJ, a Methodist delegation traveled to the White House to urge "the President's restraint in dealing with Iran." The argument was not about whether and how Christians should be involved in politics but about the substance of politics. Mainline Protestant groups and a few evangelical liberals like Hatfield pressed for disarmament and social justice, whereas conservative evangelicals called for a stronger defense against communism and restrictions on abortion. Leaders on both ends of the American Protestant spectrum claimed to be living out their faith, drew on passages in the Hebrew Scriptures calling for justice and repentance, and hypocritically criticized their theological rivals for confusing the religious and political spheres.[40]

Both the speeches at WFJ and discussions behind the scenes illustrated the estrangement of conservative evangelicals from the Carter administration. According to Gimenez, WFJ organizers invited only one politician to pray at the rally, Jimmy Carter. Carter demurred, probably not wanting to lend credence to jeremiads about the state of the country under his watch. "Carter refused to even acknowledge [us]," complains Gimenez. By contrast, Reagan—who missed few opportunities to solidify his evangelical support—asked to speak or pray at WFJ but did not receive permission to do so. Gimenez recalls that when Carter left town during WFJ, his plane flew over the rally, which to Gimenez symbolized how far apart Carter and conservative evangelicals had grown in only four years.[41]

In addition to Washington for Jesus, "family issues"—especially abortion, homosexuality, the ERA, and school prayer—focused evangelical attention on the nation's capital in 1980. That summer, the Carter administration organized a White House Conference on Families (WHCF), scheduled for three separate meetings in Baltimore, Minneapolis, and Los Angeles. Jerry Regier, a staff member at Crusade's Christian Embassy invited John Carr, the conference's executive director, to lunch to discuss why evangelicals were opposing the WHCF. Regier asked to see the invitation lists for the conference, and he recognized that the names did not include prominent evangelicals such as James Dobson and Clyde Narramore. Carr expressed a willingness to include a number of evangelical leaders, and eventually nine evangelical delegates—including Dobson and Vonette Bright—were added to the list.[42]

Despite the efforts of Regier and Carr, the WHCF highlighted the split between the Carter administration and its evangelical critics. Even before the meetings began, evangelical activists were alarmed at a change in the conference name from "Family" to "Families," which symbolized a decision to recognize nontraditional family structures. A delegation of conservative activists—headlined by Connie Marshner, an inveterate opponent of the ERA and head of the National Profamily Coalition on the WHCF—staged a public walkout from the Baltimore conference. Ironically, after the walkout the conference adopted by a single vote a resolution calling for an end to discrimination against homosexuals. Vonette Bright, after the Los Angeles conference endorsed abortion rights and the ERA, complained that years of evangelical complacency had allowed others to seize the initiative. "Because of our lack of involvement," she decried, "a handful of humanists have gained control of major decision-making opportunities." Simultaneous to the WHCF conference in Los Angeles, conservatives organized what they called "America's Pro-Family Conference" in Long Beach, California. Bill Bright spoke at the event, which attracted seven thousand sympathizers and passed resolutions in opposition to abortion rights and the ERA. Disappointed with the outcome of the WHCF, Regier soon left Crusade to form the Family Research Council, an evangelical advocacy group that sought to shape political opinion on family issues.[43]

A few weeks after the last WHCF session, Bright and several other evangelical luminaries traveled to Capitol Hill. At issue was a bill that would have removed state laws addressing "voluntary prayers in public schools" from federal jurisdiction (i.e., allow them to stand without review by federal courts). The Justice Department cast doubt on the bill's constitutionality, but Jesse Helms and Philip Crane promoted it in the Senate and House, respectively. After Crane and Helms appeared at the January convention of the National Religious Broadcasters, prominent evangelicals—including Bright—formed a Coalition for the First Amendment in support of the bill. After the Senate approved the measure, its sponsors hoped that the House would vote on the bill before the November elections. Since polls showed a majority of Americans favored voluntary prayer in public school classrooms, the bill stood a good chance of winning passage. Then the Carter administration, which had consistently opposed the measure, would either have had to embarrassingly reverse course or deliver a politically risky veto. Reagan publicly supported the legislation, and school prayer was one of the Moral Majority's signature issues in 1980. Given these dynamics, the Democratic leadership scheduled the subcommittee hearings in order to keep the bill away from the full House. Nevertheless, evangelical leaders made the most of their appearance. Bright, as he had maintained at Washington for Jesus, claimed that most of the country's recent ills had their roots in the 1962 and 1963 Supreme Court decisions that banned school-sponsored prayer and other devotional exercises from public school classrooms. "Our real problem is the humans who deny God altogether," Bright told the subcommittee. "They're the ones who control our educational system . . . preparing our students for no God."[44]

Following Washington for Jesus, the White House Conference on Families, and the school prayer debate, a final election-year event cemented the allegiance of evangelical leaders to Ronald Reagan. Robert Pittenger, who had helped Bright open the Christian Embassy and more recently had teamed with Bunker Hunt on the $1 billion fund-raising campaign, invited both Reagan and Carter to a "National Affairs Briefing" in Dallas in August 1980. The Religious Roundtable, a Washington-based organization dedicated to the political mobilization of evangelicals, funded the gathering. Ed McAteer, president of the Roundtable and the former national field director of the Christian Freedom Foundation, asked Pittenger to promote the event. In July, the *Washington Post* reported that Bright, along with Falwell, Gimenez, Robertson, and Bailey Smith, would speak at the meeting. Reagan accepted Pittenger's invitation, but Carter turned down another opportunity to confront his evangelical critics. Roughly fifteen thousand individuals, including many evangelical luminaries and a host of Republican politicians, traveled to Dallas for the briefing. Reagan, who had disappointed Falwell and other evangelical leaders by choosing George H. W. Bush as his running mate, solidified his relationship with the evangelical establishment in Dallas by vigorously defending the right of persons with "traditional religious values" "to contribute to public policy." He also highlighted the importance of the Bible by affirming "that all the complex and horrendous questions confronting us at home and worldwide have their answer in that single book." The gathering was officially nonpartisan, so Reagan did not receive a formal endorsement. Reagan mentioned this situation and then delivered the equivalent of a Campus Crusade "clincher":

"I want you to know I endorse you and what you are doing." Pittenger terms Reagan's appearance the "catalyzing moment" of the marriage between conservative evangelicals and the Republican Party. When Bright gathered evangelical leaders in Dallas in 1979, they wanted to identify a presidential candidate who would strengthen the American military and take a harder line against global communism. Reagan met those qualifications and would have won the support of most evangelical leaders without specifically reaching out to them, but he won their affection by meeting with key evangelicals and speaking at their events.[45]

Shortly after Washington for Jesus, Bright described 29 April 1980 as "the most important day in the history of our nation since the signing of the Declaration of Independence." Later on, Bright would assign the rally a similarly hyperbolic temporal significance. John Gimenez recalls a conversation that took place between Bright and Reagan following the 1980 election. "Mr. President, you were elected April 29, 1980, not in November," Bright told the newly elected Republican, ". . . because the people of God prayed, 'Lord give us righteousness.'" Although many factors helped determine the outcome of the 1980 election, Reagan's capture of a large majority of evangelical votes—a much higher percentage than that garnered by Gerald Ford in 1976—contributed to his margin of victory. Evangelicals still perceived themselves as neglected political outsiders, a feeling confirmed by the Carter administration's unresponsiveness to Washington for Jesus and its handling of the White House Conference on Families. Reagan, by contrast, made sure evangelicals knew he was one of them. He talked openly about his faith in God and Jesus, and the Republican platform reflected the growing strength of conservative Christians—opposition to Roe v. Wade, opposition to the ERA (which the GOP had backed in 1976), and support for school prayer. Moreover, perhaps learning a lesson from Carter's 1976 campaign, Reagan grasped the need to cultivate relationships with evangelicals. In 1976, evangelicals unexpectedly attracted media attention as an emerging political constituency. Only four years later, evangelicals had organized, flexed their political muscle, and announced their presence as a potentially decisive voting bloc.[46]

Although Tim LaHaye recalls that "Bill was very supportive of the Moral Majority," Bright neither commented publicly on the 1980 election nor openly endorsed Falwell's movement.[47] In fact, perhaps because events like Washington for Jesus and the National Affairs Briefing were officially non-partisan, Bright claimed to not be involved in politics. Yet as the 1979 Dallas airport hotel meeting and Bright's interpretation of Washington for Jesus illustrate, he hoped that his efforts would have political as well as spiritual ramifications. Behind the scenes, Bright and several of his assistants played significant roles in the mutual courtship between evangelicals and political conservatives. Bright developed contacts with influential politicians, publicly supported conservative issues like the school prayer amendment, and was instrumental to the success of Washington for Jesus. Campus Crusade staff members Jerry Regier and Robert Pittenger played major roles in two significant election-year events, the White House Conference on Families and the National Affairs Briefing. Although Bright did not seek the political limelight or focus on politics to the extent of Jerry Falwell, Tim LaHaye, or James Robison, he built many of the bridges that led members of the evangelical and political right together.

By 1980, many evangelicals had shed their inhibitions about political involvement, either by opposing the ERA, petitioning to stop the IRS from regulating Christian schools, or campaigning for Ronald Reagan. In the case of Campus Crusade, such concerns threatened to, but did not, displace the organization's emphasis on evangelism. If anything, Crusade's evangelistic aspirations accelerated in the late 1970s and early 1980s through the *Jesus* film and an expansion of the organization's activities overseas. On the other hand, many evangelicals—especially leaders like Bright, Robison, Falwell, and Robertson—sensed both a need and an opportunity to influence the course of American politics. They wanted to save both individuals and society, and though they had often spoken about saving society by saving individuals, events since the mid-1960s had made them too impatient to rely on that approach alone. Jerry Regier both witnessed to individual politicians in Washington and sought a voice for evangelicals at the White House Conference on Families. Robert Pittenger raised money for Here's Life, World and planned the National Affairs Briefing. Bright devoted the bulk of his time to world evangelization but still recruited evangelical leaders for Washington for Jesus and supported an evangelical alternative to the WHCF. Bright, Regier, and Pittenger viewed all of these diverse activities as part of a unified struggle for the soul of the United States. For evangelicals, evangelism and conservative politics were two strategies to arrive at the same end: a Christian America and a Christian world.

8

Kingdoms at War

Whether it was Josh McDowell speaking to university students, Senator Bill Armstrong speaking to a group of executives, or a staff member conducting a Bible study at a high school, Campus Crusade staff and associates regularly encouraged individuals to make a commitment to believe in and follow Jesus Christ. Yet Bill Bright dearly wanted to do more than evangelize individuals while watching the larger culture become less reflective of evangelical values. As Crusade continued to grow in size and stature, Bright and several others within the organization also focused their attention on evangelical solutions to the nation's ills. Bright never resolved the tension between his evangelistic and custodial impulses. "I've never been involved in politics," he told the *Los Angeles Times* in the mid-1990s, though he conceded that "some moral issues may look like politics." "At various times," comments former Senator Bill Armstrong, who was converted through the efforts of Crusade's Christian Embassy, "he [Bright] was tempted to take a . . . public political profile." According to Ron Jenson, who coauthored a book with Bright in 1986, "he always loved the foundation roots of the ministry . . . the win, build, send [philosophy of evangelism], but he knew that the ultimate battle was for the minds of men and women." "We are at war!" Bright and Jenson announced in *Kingdoms at War*. "The battle lines are drawn—God's kingdom of light, life and righteousness versus Satan's kingdom of darkness, death and wickedness." Although evangelical leaders concerned themselves with many aspects of this Manichaean conflict, such as the entertainment industry, their major concerns revolved around the institutions of government, education, and the family.[1]

Many Sleepless Nights

Bright was hopeful about the direction of the country during the Reagan administration. "I have no question," he commented years later, "he [Reagan] knows Jesus." In several ways, he participated in a minor revival of civil religion during the Reagan years. In 1982, Reagan signed legislation declaring 1983 the "Year of the Bible" in America, an initiative Bright suggested to the president shortly after his inauguration and that Bill Armstrong guided through the Senate. Bright recruited Catholic Cardinal John Krol, chancellor of the Jewish Theological Seminary of America Gerson Cohen, and the Pentecostal Thomas Zimmerman to serve as honorary vice presidents of the promotional activities surrounding the Year of the Bible. As part of the campaign, volunteer workers distributed a portion of the New Testament to Christian households and a portion of the Hebrew Scriptures to Jewish households. The proclamation, although congruent with Reagan's religious sensibilities, was one of a myriad of largely symbolic measures that Reagan used to curry favor with the evangelical community.[2]

Bright, who had interpreted Reagan's election as a sign of God's answer to the Washington for Jesus rally, believed the Year of the Bible proclamation led to a restoration of God's blessing on the United States. "Could God be hearing us and healing our land?" he asked, noting that shortly after the proclamation "our economy made a dramatic turnaround, employment rose, and inflation rates, crime rates and even divorce rates began to fall." A few years later, Reagan responded to a campaign organized by Vonette Bright, chair of the National Day of Prayer taskforce, and designated the first Thursday in May an annual day of prayer. Furthermore, Bill Bright respected Reagan's opposition to communism and commitment to a strong military defense. When a variety of left-leaning Christian leaders, from the antiwar veteran William Sloane Coffin to Jim Wallis, publicly opposed Reagan's Strategic Defense Initiative (SDI, commonly known as Star Wars), Bright joined the Religious Coalition for a Moral Defense Policy. The coalition, which included Jerry Falwell, Tim LaHaye, Jimmy Swaggart, and Jim Bakker, endorsed SDI as a "morally and perhaps militarily superior policy."[3]

Despite his support and admiration for Reagan, Bright remained troubled by the moral direction of American society. Like many religious conservatives, Bright blamed the entertainment industry for many of the nation's ills, complaining of "a growing tide of antagonism toward Christianity

. . . in the movies, on television, in the press, in magazines, and in newspaper articles." In 1988, many conservative Christians grew alarmed when Universal Pictures prepared to release Martin Scorsese's *The Last Temptation of Christ*, an adaptation of a 1955 novel. The film's opponents, including Los Angeles Archbishop Roger Mahony, denounced the film's portrayal of Jesus as battling sexual temptation before proceeding to the cross. The evangelical American Society for the Defense of Tradition, Family and Property pronounced the film "blasphemy." Bright stated that he endured "many sleepless nights after reading the script," and he offered to pay Universal the cost of the film's production if the studio would turn all copies of the film over to him for destruction. Universal dismissed Bright's offer as censorship and publicly lectured him on the "importance of standing up for freedom of conscience even when the view being expressed may be unpopular." *The Last Temptation of Christ*, despite all of the free publicity, fared little better in the theaters than Crusade's *Jesus*.[4]

Bright also grew increasingly forceful in his opposition to abortion. "I have not felt that fighting abortion is my number one priority," he stated in 1990, "for I try to evaluate everything I do each day in light of the Great Commission." However, Bright revealed, "God has been impressing upon me increasingly the urgency of using whatever influence He has given me to help put an end to this modern-day holocaust, far worse than the tragedy of Germany or any other similar persecution in history." Bright wrote a variety of religious and political leaders, asking them to sign a "Call to Compassion" outlining their opposition to abortion. The statement called for an end to "abortion-on-demand," abstinence counseling for teenagers, and support programs for women facing "the decision whether or not to abort a pregnancy." "With few exceptions," Bright asserted in a 1998 book coauthored with John Damoose, "abortions are a direct result of lust, greed, and selfishness—the same root as materialism." Bright at times contemplated more radical action. "I have several times proposed," he later shared, "to have myself lashed to the pillars of the Supreme Court until that horrendous ruling is rescinded." In addition to becoming more vocal in his antiabortion statements, Bright also supported efforts to defend the role of religious belief in American public life, particularly on the university campus. Along with James Dobson, D. James Kennedy, and other conservative evangelicals, Bright in 1994 helped found the Alliance Defense Fund (ADF), which often serves as a legal foil to the American Civil Liberties Union. The ADF has fought for the equal treatment of religious organizations on campus, for passage of state laws restricting abortion, and for the ability of communities, libraries, and cable television companies to limit access to pornography. The ADF has also contended against efforts to legalize gay marriage and to overturn the ban on homosexuals serving in the military.[5]

During the 1980s and 1990s, Bright remained a quiet influence in conservative political circles. He regularly attended the meetings of the Council for National Policy (CNP), an elite and secretive conservative club founded in 1981 primarily through the efforts of Tim LaHaye, Bunker Hunt, Paul Weyrich, and Richard Viguerie. Other evangelical members of the CNP have included Jerry Falwell, Pat Robertson, and James Robison. Since the early 1980s, conservative hopefuls have visited CNP meetings before election cycles. In the 1990s, Bright also lent his support to both the Christian Coalition and James Kennedy's "Reclaiming America for Christ" conferences. At the Christian Coalition's "Road to Victory" conference in September 1998, Bright described American politics as a struggle between "those who follow the ways of God and those who are anti-God." He also spoke at the 1999 "Reclaiming America for Christ" conference, where conservative Protestant leaders gathered to motivate each other for the 2000 election. "You have already been instructed in how to take precincts for Christ," Bright stated at a closing banquet. "The Supreme Court has led a great revolution to turn our country away from God," he continued, "and they need to be replaced. That won't happen unless we elect godly people from the precinct to the White House."[6]

Bright's insistence that he had "never been involved in politics" coexists uneasily with his attendance at Christian Coalition, Reclaiming America for Christ, and CNP conferences, his Reagan-era efforts at government promotion of American civil religion, his support for Star Wars, and his attempts to bolster evangelical opposition to *Roe v. Wade*. "Moral issues" did more than "look like politics," as Bright allowed. Over the last three decades of the twentieth century and into the twenty-first, such issues—abortion, homosexuality, and stem cell research—became hotly contested political terrain in the United States. Evangelical leaders often protested that they merely responded to liberal advocacy and judicial fiats (such as 1962's *Engel v. Vitale* ruling on school prayer), but at the very least, evangelicals eagerly fought political battles on this terrain. Politicians and religious leaders used "moral issues" to recruit countless evangelical voters into an unwieldy Republican coalition, and at times—as in 2004—they exerted a clear influence on presidential elections. Bright never focused on politics to the extent of Jerry Falwell, Pat Robertson, or James Dobson, and, because he never achieved the fame of a mass evangelist or televange-list, Bright's political statements and activities never attracted much public notice. Yet his dalliances with partisan politics and engagement on "moral" issues reflect the pervasive politicization of evangelicalism that now de-fines the movement for many secular and nonevangelical Americans. To most other Americans, evangelicals were no longer outsiders in America by the end of the twentieth century, yet evangelical leaders continued to portray themselves as a beleaguered remnant battling forces of seculariza-tion and liberalism. Through his advocacy of "moral issues," Bright occa-sionally stepped into the arena of government policy and partisan politics, but Campus Crusade fought this cultural war primarily on the battlefronts of education and the family.

God's Project

In the late 1970s, Bill Bright's top assistants received a startling visit from their boss. Bright informed his top administrators that he had realized how Campus Crusade could establish a graduate university, including schools of theology, communications, medicine, and law. "One day," Bright later wrote, "as I was praying in my office, the Lord gave me a specific plan of action. We were to find 5,000 acres of land, set aside 1,000 acres for the university campus and permit the rest to be used for industrial, commer-cial and residential use on an endowment basis to provide both short- and long-term financing." In response to his incredulous staff, who wondered how Crusade could purchase five thousand acres of land, he insisted that "[t]he Lord will provide the funds to pay for them since this project is His idea, not mine." Bright foresaw an evangelical counterweight to secular academia. "[T]here is not," he lamented, "a single international graduate university for Christians on the level of Oxford, Harvard, or Stanford." Even before acquiring any new land, Crusade opened a School of The-ology at Arrowhead Springs, intending for it to become the centerpiece of the projected university. "Bill was convinced," comments Ted Martin, who became the dean of Crusade's School of Theology, "that people went to seminary and they were trained in biblical and theological subjects but they really didn't come out as win, build, sending people" committed to Crusade's program of evangelism.[7]

Since the days of Jonathan Edwards, American evangelical leaders have founded countless educational ventures designed to further their Christian principles. In 1977, Pat Robertson decided to "build a whole university of graduate schools," a concept very similar to what Bright envisioned at about the same time. Evangelical colleges and universities have proliferated in part because, as Mark Noll has suggested, popular evangelical leaders "all assume that no previously existing educational enterprise is capable of meeting the demands of the hour." In addition to their penchant for large-scale projects, evangelical leaders establish Christian institutions of higher education because colleges and universities remain closely connected to cultural prestige and influence. The modern academy, Christopher Lucas has observed, remains "an object of mingled respect and ridicule." As Bright's sometimes derisive attitude toward intellectuals demonstrates, evangelical Christians have contributed to the ridicule of academia, but the founders of evangelical institutions have also envied the cultural respect enjoyed by Harvard, Yale, and other elite universities. Moreover, Bright by the late 1970s and early 1980s more readily recognized the potential influence that evangelicals with advanced degrees could wield in society. When staff member Kathryn Long informed Bright of her decision to leave staff and attend seminary in 1984, Crusade's president affirmed her decision and encouraged her to consider pursuing doctoral studies as well.[8]

Bright's intention to build his own university signified an implicit recognition that after twenty-five years of ministry, Campus Crusade had failed to "win the campus for Christ." In fact, Bright's rhetoric suggested an increasing dissatisfaction with the state of American higher education. "It is very sobering to think," he observed in 1977, "that many great universities are supported by Christians who send their children to schools where they are literally attacked philosophically and theologically by atheistic or agnostic professors." Bright alleged that the secularization of American higher education "has stricken our nation with a moral cancer." Along with other American evangelical leaders influenced by the theologian Francis Schaeffer, Bright by the late 1970s expressed fears about the rising influence of "secular humanism." "Today's believers," Bright appraised the situation, "have a negligible impact upon education which now embraces the 'religion' of secular humanism." Bright blamed secular humanism for the legalization and acceptance of abortion, the teaching of evolution in public schools, and an intellectual climate on the university campus hostile to Christianity. Crusade's inability to broadly impact the direction of American higher education through its campus ministry likely encouraged Bright to consider an alternative strategy.[9]

Although they probably agreed with his assessment of the state of academia, Bright struggled to convince his board of directors and financial backers to support his university vision. The board worried that debt and development expenses would imperil the ministry's financial health. The university "is an instance," explains former staff member Pat MacMillan, "where he was told 'no' by everybody, and he went ahead and did it." "He felt God called him to do this," comments Bright's friend Howard Hendricks. "It's a lot like what you will get in the Pentecostal movement or the charismatic movement." Despite the board's wariness, in 1979 Crusade formed a subsidiary company and in conjunction with a land developer purchased five thousand acres in the La Jolla Valley near San Diego for $27.5 million. Projected costs for the university climbed rapidly, with Crusade pegging the expenses at $65 million by 1983. Borrowing a tool used successfully by Oral Roberts and Pat Robertson, Crusade sought five thousand "founders" who would give $13,000 each and in return have their names inscribed on a tower on the proposed campus. Altogether, Crusade intended to raise $500 million for the university, but the ministry's donors were unenthusiastic about the project. "It [the university] was going to be a long time coming," comments Robbie Gowdey, Bright's personal assistant in the late 1970s, "and he had been presenting the urgency of the hour for so long for evangelism and fulfilling the Great Commission."[10]

Another type of urgency soon developed. Crusade had undertaken short-term loans, expecting to quickly raise funds to pay them off, but the sluggish fund-raising in conjunction with the high interest rates of the early 1980s created the most acute financial crisis in Crusade's thirty-year history. In the fall of 1982, a financial pinch forced the organization to delay paying staff members their stipends. The development was particularly troubling since all staff raised their own salaries. Donors mailed contributions for staff support to the Arrowhead Springs headquarters, which then deducted a portion for administrative expenses and reimbursed the remaining portion to individual staff members. Given this arrangement, organizational needs should theoretically never interrupt staff reimbursements. The university plans had overextended Crusade financially, however, and Crusade used all available funds to meet payments on the land debt. To address the crisis, Bright flew his top staff to Arrowhead Springs for an emergency meeting in September 1982, which became known as "Black Tuesday" among the staff. Like the board of directors, the staff had not been enthusiastic about the university, and some felt Bright's divine mandates precluded discussion and rational decision making. "I think the attitude in the movement was, 'stay away from this thing as far as you can,'" explains longtime staff member Bob Horner. "'Let the people at the top mess with it.'" The meeting sent shockwaves throughout the organization, and many staff members worried that Crusade would face bankruptcy. By official policy, Campus Crusade forbade its staff members from engaging in criticism. "A critical attitude," read the organization's *Campus Ministry Manual*, "of fellow staff, of the Campus Crusade ministry or of other individuals or groups shall be considered as evidence of disloyalty to Christ, and shall be accepted as an act of resignation." In a memorandum to his staff, Bright responded to disgruntlement and criticism related to the financial pinch: "Under no circumstances, allow yourself to be involved . . . in a gossiping campaign or a kind of carnal, critical spirit." "God will not bless you," Bright warned. "In fact, he will spank you, and the ministry will suffer . . . God hates those who sow discord among the brothers."[11]

The immediate financial crisis passed, and Crusade continued with its plans to develop the La Jolla Valley land into what the ministry christened the International Christian Graduate University. Crusade proposed a "life estate" residential development, under which individual plots would revert to the university upon the death of the owners. "We were convinced," Bright wrote, "that thousands of couples would move to our La Jolla Valley property on a lease or life-estate arrangement to help us build and endow this great University for the glory of God." In order to proceed with the development, Crusade needed to persuade the San Diego City Council to reclassify the valley from "future urbanizing status" to "present urbanizing status." Pete Wilson, the Republican mayor of San Diego when Crusade purchased the property, privately voiced his support to Bright, but Wilson's GOP successor, Roger Hedgecock, won the 1983 mayoral election on a "controlled growth platform." Supported by local environmental groups, Hedgecock publicly denounced Crusade's proposed developments as "planned urban sprawl" and urged city officials and the city council to reject the rezoning request. When Bright met with Hedgecock in March 1984, the new mayor maintained that Wilson's pledges were not binding on his administration. Brad Bright attended the meeting and remembers his father issuing Hedgecock a stern warning: "I want you to know you're not fighting against me, against man. You're fighting against God on this thing." "I'd never heard Dad tell anybody anything like this," observes Brad. "I was just dumbfounded in all honesty." Bright reiterated the same message to Hedgecock at a second meeting in April. Hedgecock later complained that Bright told him, "'You're opposing God's project.'"[12]

During the summer of 1984, both the San Diego Planning Commission and the city council agreed to a modified version of Crusade's development plan over Hedgecock's opposition. After the city council's approval, however, a coalition of environmental groups, including the Sierra Club, collected signatures for a November 1985 referendum. The measure, on the ballot as Proposition A, required the city's voters to approve any development projects in San Diego's northern land reserve. Furthermore, it applied to any projects proposed after 1 August 1984; thus, if passed, it would revoke the council's approval of Crusade's La Jolla Valley project. The campaign over Proposition A turned into a struggle between environmentalists and free-market evangelicals. Hedgecock and the Sierra Club rallied support for the measure, while the San Diego Evangelical Association and several other land developers mobilized opposition. "We continue," Bright wrote his supporters on 13 September 1985, "to encounter strong opposition from Mayor Hedgecock, the Sierra Club, San Diego's homosexual community and others." Hedgecock responded by terming Bright's letter "un-Christian."[13]

In November, San Diegans voted for Proposition A by a solid majority, thus scuttling Campus Crusade's plans to build a major university in Southern California. Hedgecock briefly basked in the glow of the referendum's success, but within weeks he resigned his office in disgrace following a felony conviction on charges connected with the financing of his 1983 campaign. Brad Bright connects Hedgecock's legal troubles to his opposition to Crusade's plans. "Either this is an incredible coincidence," he speculates, "or Dad really was communicating what was true and Roger paid an incredible price for stonewalling." Crusade, however, also paid a heavy price because of the university project's rejection. Claiming that Proposition A's retroactivity unfairly targeted the La Jolla project, Crusade filed a suit against the city for $70 million plus interest in March 1986. The lawsuit failed, and University Development, Crusade's subsidiary, filed for bankruptcy when a lender foreclosed on the property in late 1986. Glenn Terrell, a Texas land developer friendly with Crusade, spared the ministry more serious financial woes when he purchased the property. Bailey Marks comments that the "budgetary cutback" that followed the referendum provided a needed "financial pruning." For the remainder of the century, Crusade slowly paid off the project's debt.[14]

Bright found the university debacle painful and confusing. Initially, he refused to recognize that the referendum made the realization of his university vision impossible. "[W]e are in an expansion mode," he insisted in a December 1986 letter to his staff outlining alternative strategies for the university, ". . . the possibility of the original vision being fulfilled has never been brighter." However, Bright eventually conceded that Crusade would not found a series of graduate schools and struggled to understand why he had so strongly believed God was leading him in that direction. He frequently told those around him that he preferred to be wrong rather than disobedient, meaning that he had followed God's will as he had understood it at the time. Although many staff questioned Bright's handling of the university project, most still readily accepted his leadership. Staff member Conrad Koch explains that for most staff members, Bright's spiritual leadership trumped any unease stemming from poor entrepreneurial decisions. "The most significant trait about him is his love for God," comments Koch. "It's not his business acumen . . . when he talked about his savior, it wasn't phony." "Bill had made a bad decision," observes Koch. "The potential existed for us to go belly-up, but . . . Bill had this reservoir of goodwill."[15]

Although Bright never resuscitated his graduate university vision, Campus Crusade continues to operate schools of theology in several countries, and in 1998 the ministry began running The King's College, a Christian school based in New York City. Under the leadership of J. Stanley Oakes, the college leased ten thousand square feet in the Empire State Building and achieved accreditation from the New York Board of Regents after a lengthy and contentious struggle. With an enrollment of roughly two hundred fifty students as of 2005, the curriculum focuses primarily on training students for the worlds of business and government, and many students participate in short-term evangelistic mission trips overseas under Crusade's auspices.[16]

Men Are Not to Be Dictators

After the International Christian Graduate University setback, most staff members were relieved when Bright's full attention returned to Crusade's other ministries. As the *Jesus* film fueled Crusade's overseas expansion during the last two decades of the twentieth century, the ministry's Family-Life division became increasingly instrumental to the organization's activities in the United States. FamilyLife grew rapidly during the 1980s and 1990s, decades in which evangelical political discourse centered on "family values." During these years there was a proliferation of evangelical conferences, radio shows, and literature devoted to family issues, such as marriage and child-rearing. On some topics, such as the morality of homosexuality, evangelicals expressed broad agreement. At the same time, however, sharp disagreements emerged within the evangelical movement about the respective characteristics and roles of men and women.

Evangelical leaders have divided into two main camps, known as *complementarians* and *egalitarians*, over issues of respective male and female roles. In the 1970s and 1980s, as ideals emanating from the modern feminist movement found acceptance even in some evangelical circles, conservatives articulated a forceful traditionalist response. Formed in 1987, the Council on Biblical Manhood and Womanhood (CBMW) has been a leading promoter of what became known as the complementarian position. Complementarians emphasize biblical distinctions between men and women and male leadership within the family and church, rejecting the ordination of women as pastors. Egalitarians, by contrast, seek to widen opportunities for female leadership within churches and Christian organizations and are uneasy with attempts to delineate roles and nonbiological characteristics of men and women. The organization Christians for Biblical Equality (CBE) represents the egalitarian position, and in recent years a growing number of evangelical leaders—particularly faculty at Christian institutions such as Wheaton College, Gordon College, and Bethel University—have embraced egalitarianism.

Campus Crusade positioned itself within the complementarian camp. Bill and Vonette Bright became board members of CBMW and signed what became known as the Danvers Statement—so titled because it emerged from the inaugural CBMW meeting in Danvers, Massachusetts. The Danvers Statement decried the "widespread uncertainty and confusion in our culture regarding the complementary differences between masculinity and femininity" and endorsed the "principle of male headship in the family and in the covenant community." In recent years, FamilyLife director Dennis Rainey has pushed the rest of Campus Crusade's leadership to more visibly promote the complementarian position. In 1993, FamilyLife published a *Family Manifesto*, written by Rainey and his staff. Dedicated to protecting "the biblical institutions of marriage and family," the *Family Manifesto* distances itself from "the notion that a husband is to dominate his wife," but the document clearly assigns the respective roles of "head" to the husband and "helper" to the wife. While the manifesto concedes that "there are cases where a mother will find it necessary to work outside the home," Family-Life worries that "some couples have made career and lifestyle choices that result in de-emphasizing the mother's role as nurturer."[17]

Rainey explains that one reason FamilyLife adopted its manifesto was his concern that evangelicals were drifting into the egalitarian camp on family and church issues. He laments that "the Christian community has bent amidst the cultural winds of feminism at a time when it should have stood strong and called husbands to be the sacrificial servant lovers and leaders of their wives." "When you homogenize the sexes and you eliminate the distinctions [between men and women]," he contends, ". . . we fall into the enemy's [Satan's] camp." When FamilyLife finalized its manifesto, the ministry invited the Brights to a ceremony at FamilyLife's headquarters in Little Rock. Dennis and Barbara Rainey presented the Brights with a check for $100,000, "thanking them for allowing this ministry to be birthed within Campus Crusade for Christ," and the Raineys invited the Brights to be the first signers of the manifesto. "I think Bill was really pleased with that," recollects Rainey, "especially when it came with a check of $100,000, which interestingly enough Vonette scooped up and used for a women's ministry."[18]

Five years after FamilyLife wrote its manifesto, the Southern Baptist Convention (SBC) adopted a doctrinal statement on the family, the first revision of its Baptist Faith and Message in thirty-five years. The sentences on the respective roles of men and women generated considerable controversy in evangelical circles and the secular media. "The marriage relationship models the way God relates to His people," proclaimed the convention, and the statement affirmed the husband's "God-given responsibility . . . to lead his family." "A wife," the statement continued, "is to submit herself graciously to the servant leadership of her husband." Focus on the Family's James Dobson applauded the resolution during a keynote address at the convention, while a number of prominent Southern Baptists, including President Bill Clinton and Vice President Al Gore, criticized the doctrine. When few evangelical leaders initially spoke out in favor of the SBC resolution, Rainey mobilized evangelical support for the affirmation. He held a press conference to announce that fifty evangelical leaders — including Chuck Colson and Promise Keepers founder Bill McCartney — had signed a document supporting the SBC position. In August, Rainey took out a full-page ad in USA Today in which 131 evangelical leaders told the SBC "you are right!" At its summer 1999 staff conference at Colorado State University, Campus Crusade announced its adoption of the SBC stance. Given Crusade's pragmatic desire to cooperate with and raise funds from a broad spectrum of evangelicals, much of the ministry's leadership would have preferred not to take a public stand on the issue. Rainey, however, strongly urged the Brights to support the SBC position and to formally align Crusade with the complementarian camp. "Bill and Vonette," Rainey informs, "embraced that [the SBC statement] on behalf of Campus Crusade for Christ at my recommendation." For Rainey, the complementarian position is an article of faith. "If they hadn't [adopted the statement]," Rainey explains, "FamilyLife would no longer be a part of Campus Crusade."[19]

Rainey maintains that FamilyLife's manifesto and the SBC statement flow directly out of biblical principles—he considers the SBC statement "all so clearly taught in Scripture." As several scholars have suggested, however, evangelical arguments over gender frequently involve more than a simple defense of the Bible. By the 1980s and 1990s, complementarian positions were starkly at odds with mainstream culture, as large majorities of Americans supported a more egalitarian understanding of gender roles. Therefore, when evangelicals advocate complementarian positions, they often accompany scriptural arguments with critiques of mainstream culture. For instance, both Bright and Rainey supported ratifying the SBC statement in part as a rejection of modern feminism and modern culture. At Crusade's 1999 staff conference, Bright observed that the "marriage covenant" has been "shredded by an anti-God culture, resulting in every kind of sin, including abortion and divorce." Rainey worries that the principles of modern feminism have influenced the rising generation of evangelicals, including younger Campus Crusade staff members. "The college campus," he contends, "has been the number one place where feminists have been teaching and brainwashing our students for the past two or three decades." One reason Rainey so vehemently opposes the egalitarian position is because it echoes some feminist teachings. "I'm very suspicious," he confides, "of any doctrine that smells, looks, acts, and behaves like a doctrine of the world." Thus, Crusade's support of the complementarian understanding of family roles defines the organization in opposition to modern feminism, "culture," and the "world." After World War II, evangelicals repudiated much of the cultural separatism that had defined American fundamentalism, but the stance of conservative evangelicals on issues of gender partly belies this culture-affirming tendency.[20]

Even on the issue of gender roles, however, broader cultural trends have deeply impacted American evangelicalism. Contemporary evangelical rhetoric about gender roles does not necessarily reflect the actual dynamics of evangelical families. Bradford Wilcox contends that evangelical men are only "soft patriarchs," who receive "symbolic authority in the home in return for their exercise of greater responsibility for the well-being of their families." Similarly, David Harrington Watt suggests that although most evangelicals believe that, as a last resort, the husband should be the decision maker when a couple faces an impasse, male headship means very little in everyday life. Beyond the family, even complementarian evangelicals have embraced elements of women's leadership in certain ways. On the surface, the formal levers of power within Campus Crusade remain nearly exclusively in the hands of men. Vonette Bright serves as the only woman on Crusade's eleven-member board of directors. Crusade's eleven vice presidents are all men, and the organization's directors of affairs—who each oversee a geographical division of Crusade's ministries—are also exclusively male. At the same time, the organization has accommodated itself to changing cultural standards in ways that have attracted little public notice. "Staff girls" eventually became "associate campus directors" who speak, lead worship, and offer group prayers in coeducational meetings. Crusade still usually restricts the role of campus director to men, although there have been several exceptions. Gwen Martin explains that Crusade currently permits ministry directors in different segments of the organization and different countries to set their own policies on women's leadership. According to Steve Sellers, Crusade makes a conscious effort to invite women as speakers to its conferences, including its biannual staff training conference. Campus Crusade has slowly encouraged women to view themselves as leaders. "More and more women," explains Sellers, "have more and more opportunities to lead." In recent years, Vonette Bright and Judy Douglass have organized conferences to nurture and promote female leaders within the organization.[21]

In another example of rapprochement with mainstream culture, the organization distanced itself from an endorsement of heavy-handed patriarchy when it ratified the SBC statement in 1999. Seeking to avoid misunderstandings about male headship, the ministry included its own proviso. "The love between husband and wife," read the addendum, "will show itself in listening to each other's viewpoints, valuing each other's gifts, wisdom, and desires." "We felt we needed to explain," Bill Bright commented, "that men are not to be dictators." Although Crusade's statement did not employ the standard egalitarian phrase of "mutual submission," the addendum describes a marriage relationship of mutual respect. The addendum suggests that although Campus Crusade remains opposed to the egalitarian principles of modern feminism, the organization also has accommodated itself—more than the rhetoric of its *Family Manifesto* would suggest—to changing cultural standards of gender. Evangelicals want to be distinct from and in some key ways in opposition to modern society, but they do not want to be caricatured as patriarchal despots or allow "submission" to serve as a cover for sexual, physical, or verbal abuse.[22]

Moreover, the Brights' signing of the Danvers Statement and Crusade's endorsement of the SBC doctrine obscure the fact that a diversity of opinion on gender issues exists within the organization. "We are trying to work from a big tent mentality," explains Crusade's vice president for global campus ministry, Steve Sellers. "Whether you're conservative or liberal . . . in terms of your view of women," he continues, "we want to be a place where you can minister because our mission is very clear; that is, to help fulfill the Great Commission, not to take theological stands." The SBC statement only addressed the role of men and women within the family, and Campus Crusade has not adopted a position on the role of women within the church or a uniform policy on the role of women in leadership positions within the organization. According to Gwen Martin, a longtime Crusade staff member, the organization has considered and then tabled formal statements on women in leadership for at least twenty years. "We are not saying [women] can't do anything, and we aren't saying that they can do everything," Sellers told *Christianity Today* in 1992. "We felt like trying to address the issue, and coming out with something totally definitive . . . [would be] a limitation." Although Rainey is grateful that Crusade adopted the statement on gender roles within the family, he is disappointed that the organization has not adopted a complementarian position on gender roles within the context of ministry. "I had thought by now," he laments, "the organization would have taken at least a definitive stand of where its nondefinitive stand has been." Bill Bright's public affirmation of the Danvers Statement and the SBC stance belies his own basic pragmatism on the issue of women's leadership. In the 1950s and 1960s, Bright had mirrored Henrietta Mears's belief—common within evangelical circles—that prominent male leaders would attract both men and women to the organization. Toward the end of the century, as American culture moved away from the gender standards of Mears's day, Bright supported the growing prominence of female leaders within Crusade. For example, he encouraged Vonette Bright to assume a more active role within the ministry in the 1970s and spoke of her as the "co-founder" of Campus Crusade. The broader trend within American evangelicalism, even within officially complementarian organizations, has been toward greater recognition of women's capabilities as spiritual and organizational leaders.[23]

Although evangelicals are divided on the role of women within family and church life, they remain largely united in opposition to the acceptance of homosexuality and gay marriage. Bright feared that the questioning of the traditional heterosexual family was undermining America's social order, and his vocal denunciations of homosexuality gradually became more strident. "Militant homosexuals," he wrote in 1995, "parade half-naked down the streets of our nation's capital demanding approval and special rights as a minority." "Although homosexuals are small in number," he continued, "their far-reaching influence upon society is cause for alarm." "The homosexual agenda," Bright opined in an interview, "is being promoted and anti-God doctrines are permeating the classroom today." After several private institutions, including Tufts University and Middlebury College, threatened to ban evangelical organizations that refused to welcome homosexual students as officers, Bright complained that "Christians are ousted wherever possible on campus." "The homosexual agenda controls everything," he maintained. At a February 2000 Republican prayer breakfast in California, Bright endorsed Proposition 22, a ballot initiative passed later that year that amended the state's marriage law by stating that "only marriage between a man and a woman is valid or recognized in California."[24]

As the 2004 election approached, the issue of gay marriage prompted Dennis Rainey and FamilyLife to assume a more overtly political stance. FamilyLife does not have as high a public profile as Focus on the Family or the Family Research Council, two other evangelical organizations that have also encouraged Christians to participate in the political process to oppose abortion, pornography, and gay marriage. FamilyLife, however, is not an apolitical organization, as Rainey explains. Although he states that he has "never endorsed a candidate," Rainey has "attempted to speak to individual Christians about their civic duty and responsibility not merely to register and to vote but to vote their Christian worldview." Like Bright, he has encouraged Christians to support pro-life candidates and politicians opposed to gay marriage. For instance, Rainey articulated a very strident stance against same-sex marriage following the Massachusetts Supreme Judicial Court decision legalizing such unions in November 2003. Alluding to the terrorist attacks of 11 September 2001, Rainey proclaimed that the "four judges just flew their 'plane' into the twin towers of marriage and family." He urged the Massachusetts legislature to pass a "Defense of Marriage Act" and warned that "a [federal] Constitutional Amendment is America's last line of defense to preserve and protect the centuries-old marriage tradition from extinction by a radical judicial oligarchy."[25]

FamilyLife helped rally evangelical opposition to gay marriage in the months following the Massachusetts decision. Rainey and other Family-Life authors expressed contrition for past "gay-bashing" by Christians and urged evangelicals to adopt a more sensitive and loving approach to homosexuals. Nevertheless, FamilyLife concentrated on the need for Christians to oppose the moral acceptance of homosexuality and gay marriage. Rainey and his colleague Bob Lepine informed the readers of FamilyLife's *Family Room* magazine that homosexuals "are maintaining a lifestyle built around a sexual rebellion against God" and suggested that even homosexuals ostensibly committed to a single partner regularly engage in promiscuous sex. Several other articles urged Christians to contact their elected officials and voice their support for a constitutional amendment outlawing gay marriage. Rainey and Lepine warned readers that should the United States legalize gay marriage, their children might learn to tolerate homosexuality in public school classrooms and companies might face bankruptcy when forced to provide benefits for "domestic partners." "And may I put my arm around you," Rainey asked his readers, "and encourage you to vote for those candidates who are most consistent with what the Bible teaches and values about children and family?" Rainey spoke at a 15 October 2004 "Mayday for Marriage" rally in Washington that attracted tens of thousands of Christian opponents of gay marriage. Rainey criticized American Christians for their implicit toleration of divorce, called for a "family reformation," and asked the federal government to "[g]ive us some fortifications to protect our families."[26]

Many factors decided the outcome of the 2004 election, but the vigorous efforts of evangelical leaders to mobilize opposition to same-sex marriage —accompanied by GOP attempts to woo evangelical voters—contributed to George W. Bush's victory in battleground states. In Ohio, for instance, a proposed amendment to the state constitution banning gay marriage helped bring evangelical voters to the polls. Until the Massachusetts Supreme Court decision, few politicians and pundits predicted that gay marriage would become a significant "wedge issue" in the 2004 election. When the issue emerged, numerous organizations were ready for battle, as Focus on the Family, the Family Research Council, and FamilyLife had all built large constituencies in recent decades by articulating conservative positions in cultural conflicts over gender.[27]

Despite its political advocacy on moral issues, FamilyLife's primary activities remain its conferences, radio programs, and publications. In 2005, FamilyLife attracted more than seventy-five thousand attendees to its

FamilyLife's Dennis Rainey speaking at the 2004 "Mayday for Marriage" rally in Washington, D.C. Courtesy of FamilyLife and photographer Teresa Roorback.

"Weekend to Remember" conferences, accelerated its military marriage seminars, and expanded its listening audience for *FamilyLife Today*, the ministry's flagship radio program. The ministry, which already has an annual budget of roughly $40 million, is partway through a $100 million fundraising campaign and recently constructed a new headquarters in Little Rock. Moreover, Rainey observes that FamilyLife gains access to more than two hundred countries through Crusade's international ministries. A number of Crusade staff members who previously worked on foreign campuses have switched their focus to adapting FamilyLife conferences and materials for different cultural settings. Given the already large numbers of evangelical ministries in the United States that focus on the family and conduct marriage conferences, FamilyLife will continue to explore largely untapped markets for its services overseas.[28]

Winning or Losing the Campus for Christ?

Bill Bright often fielded questions and complaints about his organization's name. "Crusade" conjures up images of medieval violence and persecution that few contemporary individuals, evangelicals included, defend. Moreover, as Crusade evolved into a global missionary movement in the 1980s, the "campus" became only one of a plethora of ministries under the larger heading of "Campus Crusade." Crusade became an umbrella of ministries headquartered in various locations across the United States: FamilyLife in Little Rock, Josh McDowell's speaking and humanitarian ministry in Dallas, the *Jesus* film in San Clemente, and the remainder of Crusade's ministries at the organization's new headquarters in Orlando. This loose geographic structure allowed leaders with entrepreneurial tendencies akin to Bright's own to build their own ministries while operating with substantial autonomy. As Crusade's ministries continued to diversify, Bright recognized that his organization's name had become anachronistic. In 2000, he informed an interviewer that "we still call it Campus Crusade for Christ because we're so well known by that name" but added that Crusade had "launched what we call New Life as a possible alternative name."[29] Still, even as Crusade's ministries proliferated into many sectors of American society and expanded overseas, the American campus ministry remained Crusade's most significant single endeavor in terms of staff and funds.

Between the mid-1970s and 1990, the campus ministry stagnated, as Crusade struggled to attract students and recruit staff. Steve Sellers, who directed the U.S. campus ministry in the 1990s, explains that by the late 1970s "the cause orientation" on campus had disappeared and "we were moving into a more apathetic period of time." Crusade could no longer utilize free speech platforms and antiwar rallies to effectively promote Jesus as history's greatest revolutionary. "Christian students are still cause-oriented," commented a regional campus ministry director in 1984. "They just aren't riding a huge cultural wave anymore." Moreover, Crusade staff members found their standard talks on "God's Plan" less welcome at Greek houses. The Greek system and athletics no longer molded a relatively unified campus culture; instead, students at large universities formed many diverse subcultures that required a more flexible approach. Precisely as "Campus Crusade was broadening its focus to more than students," comments Sellers, "we weren't changing with where the students were." The result of such trends imperiled the future of the campus ministry and the entire organization. In the early 1970s, seven to eight hundred American students decided to join Campus Crusade's staff each year. That number gradually declined until only two hundred fifty students joined staff in 1990. Other campus ministries encountered similar obstacles in the 1980s. For example, InterVarsity eliminated its operations on scores of campuses during the 1980s. "Traditionally, parachurch ministry has been able to respond to changes almost immediately," stated Gordon MacDonald, the president of InterVarsity. "Perhaps the changes are coming too fast now." *Christianity Today* speculated that "high school and college ministries" had "outlived their purposes."[30]

Growing racial and ethnic diversity on campus also posed new challenges, as Campus Crusade struggled to expand its appeal beyond white students. As of 1981, only sixty of the organization's four thousand staff members were black. In the early 1970s, the organization's leadership had recognized the need to recruit African American staff, but such efforts were impeded by long-standing divisions between white evangelicals and theologically like-minded African American Christians. Crawford Lorritts, who began directing Crusade's ministries to African Americans in the late 1970s, recalls the discomfort of black staff members during a staff training presentation of "America, You're Too Young to Die," a 1986 video produced by the Arthur DeMoss Foundation. Crusade's black staff members, if equally concerned about the moral direction of the United States, dissented from the video's depiction of a past golden era of Christianity in America. According to Lorritts, the presentation implied "that all of American history was godly . . . and there was a blatant absence of that nasty part of our history called slavery." "A number of black staff got very upset," he recalls, although he adds that when they confronted Bright with their concerns, Crusade's president quickly apologized. Furthermore, the organization struggled to attract nonwhite students to its campus meetings. "Often white students come up from backgrounds that isolate them from other cultures," explained Tom Fritz, an African American on staff with Crusade since 1973. "Blacks and other minority groups see this as oppressive." Crusade struggled to adapt to the new reality of campuses that were more racially and ethnically diverse, less residential, and whose social life no longer revolved so tightly around athletics and the Greek system. As the organization grew in size and bureaucracy, it was more difficult for Crusade to adroitly respond to cultural change.[31]

After the period of stagnation in the late 1970s and 1980s, however, Crusade's campus ministry revived in the 1990s. According to Sellers, whom several others in the organization credit for the renewed success, Crusade recommitted itself "to the scope of reaching every student." Local campus directors received greater freedom to design creative evangelistic campaigns, and Crusade speakers no longer relied on the 1960s version of "God's Plan for Your Life." Crusade also embraced a different philosophy of reaching minority students. Beginning in the early 1990s, Crusade launched separate student movements for African American, Latino, and

Asian American students. The Impact movement, founded by Tom Fritz in 1991, holds its own meetings on campuses and invites African American students to regional conferences. At Impact conferences, students sing contemporary gospel music rather than the "contemporary Christian" rock music favored by white evangelicals, listen to a distinctively African American style of preaching, and focus more intently on community involvement and service. According to Sellers, rather than having one hundred fifty African American students at a typical Crusade "Christmas conference," an Impact conference draws two to three thousand black students. More recently, the organization has launched the Epic and Destino movements to focus on Asian American and Latino students, respectively. Dennis Chen states that Epic reaches some students who "would not set foot in your [predominantly white] meetings." Particularly at a time when some evangelical campus ministries have become predominantly Asian American, the racial and ethnic segmentation of campus ministries may also avoid "white flight" from groups that become too Asian or multicultural. Some within the organization remain uneasy about racially and ethnically segmented ministries, but the Impact movement has increased the number of black students involved with Crusade.[32]

On the campus in the early twenty-first century, Crusaders evangelize students through familiar and innovative means. Staff and involved students approach prospective converts and ask them to take a survey, ending with the question, "If you were to die tonight, can you be assured your soul will go to heaven?" Staff members cultivate relationships with athletic teams, Greek houses, and other campus groups and invite interested students to Bible studies. At the start of each academic year, Crusaders give incoming students "Freshman Survival Kits," containing Christian books, DVDs, and CDs, all designed to grab students' attention and lead into an opportunity to witness about Jesus. Students who become deeply involved in campus activities often attend a Spring Break or summer project organized by Crusade in popular student destinations, such as Virginia Beach, Daytona Beach, and Mission Beach in San Diego. On summer projects, Crusade students work day jobs, meet for training and Bible studies at night, and spend Saturdays witnessing to vacationers and beachgoers. Typically, Crusaders begin with the religious survey and seek to initiate a conversation that leads to the *Four Spiritual Laws*. However, Crusade today places somewhat less emphasis on Bright's booklet, instead encouraging its staff and students to adopt a more conversational approach to evangelism. "Students 'witness' to others," wrote the *Virginian-Pilot* of Crusade's summer project in Virginia Beach, "by sharing their stories of how they came to accept Jesus and how it has affected their lives." Bright, though hardly a proponent of abandoning the *Four Spiritual Laws*, commented in 2000 that "this generation is more open to an emotional approach, whereas another generation was open to a logical approach." Crusade published a revised version of the *Four Spiritual Laws* entitled *Would You Like to Know God Personally?*, which presents "principles" rather than "laws." Although Crusade still engages in aggressive verbal evangelism, the ministry also encourages its staff to patiently form friendships with students and to model Christian love as a means of evangelism. "The most powerful thing we can do," stated Bright in 2000, "is to reach out in love to our neighbors, our friends and our fellow students on the campus, because love never fails."[33]

In addition to personal evangelism and campus meetings, Crusade has used advertising and websites in attempts to interest students in its message. During the 1990s, a campus media blitz by Crusade illustrated the organization's positions on issues such as sex and drinking. One poster showed a pair of wedding rings with the message "For the best sex, slip on one of these." Another advertisement pictured a pile of condoms and the banner "Too bad they don't make one of these for your heart." Posters promoting abstinence from alcohol suggested to students that Jesus Christ can "Quench Your Real Thirst." Some media campaigns generated considerable controversy. In 1996, during National Coming Out Week, Crusade placed advertisements in university newspapers with testimonies from "former homosexuals"—some newspapers refused to publish the ads and others ran editorial rebuttals. Other campaigns demonstrated a new social awareness. One prominent series of posters highlighted biblical arguments against racism, and another campaign sought to convince African Americans of the African roots of Christianity and the relevance of Jesus to contemporary African American life.[34]

Crusade's recommitment to and diversification of its campus ministry has increased the ministry's visibility at many colleges and universities. By the early twenty-first century, Crusade maintained a presence on more than a thousand campuses and counted more than forty thousand involved students annually. Crusade—alongside the Catholic Newman Club—is the largest religious organization at many public universities, particularly in the West, South, and Midwest. At Ohio State, for instance, the six to eight hundred students who participate weekly make Campus Crusade the largest student organization of any kind. Crusade's presence at the private universities of the Northeast, although small, has also grown in recent years.

Several hundred students flock to Harvard's Science Center on Friday nights to sing "praise songs" and hear testimonies about Jesus at Campus Crusade's RealLife Boston, the organization's citywide student ministry. On some campuses, there are as many as six organizations operating under the umbrella of Campus Crusade: the standard campus ministry, the three ministries geared to minorities, Athletes in Action, and, particularly on the West Coast, Korea Campus Crusade for Christ.[35] Another measure of Crusade's recent success is its renewed ability to replenish its ranks through new staff recruits from the campus. On this score, Crusade has experienced sharp growth in recent years. After the lull that lasted from the late 1970s through the early 1990s, Crusade has recruited nearly one thousand staff members annually over the past several years. The majority of those recruits have come from the American campus.

A variety of statistics suggests Campus Crusade's contemporary vitality: growing numbers of students involved in campus chapters, expansion to additional campuses, and a massive increase in what Crusade terms "exposures to the Gospel." By "exposures," Crusade means the number of students who have encountered its message of Jesus Christ either at campus events, through conversations with staff and involved students, or through media campaigns, including Crusade's websites. Crusade counted upwards of seven million annual "exposures" between 1998 and 2002. The large majority of those exposures, however, came through media campaigns rather than through personal contacts. Thus, one suspects considerable duplication and superficiality in most recorded "exposures." Indeed, another statistic reveals that Crusade faces great difficulty in its primary mission of "winning the campus for Christ." The organization has recorded between four and ten thousand annual "decisions" for Christ on the campus over the past decade—an infinitesimal percentage of non-Christian collegians. Perhaps this dichotomy of rising participation and staff recruits but fewer converts reflects changes in the collegiate population since the 1950s and the upward mobility experienced by evangelicals in recent decades. Crusade today encounters fewer first-generation white collegians from small-town Protestant backgrounds—students who had grown up in a Protestant culture and who readily articulated "decisions for Christ." At the same time, today's well-educated and affluent suburban evangelicals are sending children to colleges who have grown up in megachurches and parachurch ministries and who seamlessly become part of the evangelical subculture on campus. Contemporary evangelicals are roughly as likely as other Americans to obtain bachelor's degrees, and most evangelical students attend public universities. High school students active in Young Life, Student Venture, and Awana Clubs provide a built-in market share for Campus Crusade, InterVarsity, and other evangelical campus ministries, which may explain the growing numbers of students participating in such groups. Simultaneously, despite its large budget and creative media campaigns, Crusade has struggled to convince non-Christian students to embrace its gospel.[36]

In addition to struggling to convert many nonevangelical students, parachurch evangelicalism makes little impact on academic instruction or the institutional values of university culture. Bright offered a sober assessment of the state of American higher education shortly before his organization's fiftieth year of ministry. "The philosophy of the classroom . . . ," he charged, "is total decadence, total anti-God, anti-Christ, and anti-Bible. Any person who has anything to do with the secular college or university knows that it's a cesspool." George Marsden has with less passion contended that "as long as the prevailing intellectual outlook of universities is built on community standards antithetical to most traditional religious belief, what goes on in the classrooms will be undermining the outlooks presented in campus religious meetings." There are signs that universities are becoming more interested in religion: the increased number of academic articles discussing religion, a proliferation of academic centers studying religion, and the growing willingness of faculty in certain disciplines to articulate their personal religious beliefs. Evangelicals may form a more vocal presence in the ivory tower today than in the late 1960s, but particularly in comparison with Crusade's founding years in the 1950s, the secular academy today is at best no more open to traditional religious beliefs in the classroom or other public settings than it was fifty years ago. Few public universities would host a "religious emphasis" week today, as UCLA did in 1953. Given Bright's repeated incantation of a dictum widely attributed to Abraham Lincoln that "the philosophy of the classroom of one generation becomes the philosophy of government the next," it is surprising that Campus Crusade has never made a concerted attempt to influence "the philosophy of the classroom." The organization has since the mid-1960s operated a small "faculty ministry" and in the 1980s sought to create a national network of evangelical faculty. Such initiatives, however, have never ranked among the organization's top priorities. InterVarsity, by contrast, has devoted greater resources to creating a network of Christian graduate students and faculty. Moreover, Crusade's persistent emphasis on direct evangelism as the primary mission of all Christians hardly encourages Crusade staff and students to pursue the vocation of university teaching and scholarship. Walter

Bradley, a professor of mechanical engineering at Baylor and a longtime associate Crusade staff member, believes Crusade erred in targeting students while leaving the larger culture of the university intact. "The students are the tourists," explains Bradley. "The faculty and the administrations are the permanent residents." The ministry's "win the campus for Christ" slogan aside, Crusade's mission has actually been to win as many collegians for Christ as possible and to recruit Christian students for evangelical ministries at home and abroad.[37]

Several mainline Protestant denominations, including the Presbyterian Church (U.S.A.) and the United Methodist Church, continue to operate hundreds of ministry chapters across the United States. Evangelical parachurch groups, however, have become the most visible face of Protestantism on the American campus. According to the university chaplain at Brown, about four hundred students (about 7 percent of the student body) participate in the three major evangelical organizations on campus, more than the number of students active in all of Brown's mainline ministries combined. The success of evangelical campus ministries in large part mirrors the broader success of evangelical congregations and denominations during an era of mainline numerical decline, but it is hard to know exactly why evangelical ministries in particular have displayed greater vitality than their mainline counterparts. The basic ideals of mainline Protestantism seem more congruent with the regnant philosophies of American academia, and mainline denominations moved more quickly than evangelical organizations to promote civil rights and racial diversity. As recently as the late 1950s, Harvard University's Memorial Chapel would not allow non-Christian wedding ceremonies. Now chapels at many schools welcome Buddhists, Muslims, and an increasingly wide array of student religious groups. It has been evangelicals, however, who have thrived in this new environment of religious diversity and competition. In particular, evangelical organizations have been a major beneficiary of the influx of Asian and Asian American students, a high percentage of whom are Protestants. For instance, as of several years ago Asian American students comprised 90 percent of IVCF's membership at Yale. Most Crusade chapters remain predominantly white, but the organization has attracted growing numbers of racial minorities through its segmented campus ministries. Crusade's international ministries have both directly and indirectly augmented its ability to operate in a multicultural context. Staff who have spent time on overseas mission trips become predisposed to move beyond white American expressions of evangelical Christianity. Given high rates of immigration to the United States from Asia in recent decades, organizations like Campus Crusade are reaping an American campus harvest from decades of mass evangelism in Korea and other Asian countries.[38]

Furthermore, in contrast with most mainline campus ministries, evangelical student organizations transcend denominational boundaries, adapt more quickly to student culture, and market themselves more aggressively. Evangelical ministries, although they affirm many aspects of campus culture (athletics and popular music, for instance), have also adopted a countercultural ethos through their insistence that eternal salvation comes exclusively through Jesus Christ, their commitment to evangelism, and their conservative positions on issues like premarital sex and drinking. Thus, students who join evangelical campus ministries like Campus Crusade enter into a subculture in some critical ways distinct from, yet at the same time not radically at odds with, mainstream campus culture.[39]

Despite its struggles to convert non-Christian students and impact the broader trajectory of American higher education, Campus Crusade has helped reestablish evangelicalism as a permanent fixture at major American universities. At midcentury, the inchoate efforts of Inter-Varsity aside, chapel services and mainline Protestant campus ministries comprised the center of Protestantism at American universities and colleges. Today, a plethora of evangelical organizations form the most visible expression of Protestantism at most universities. For example, more than fifty evangelical groups minister to students at both the University of California at Berkeley and UCLA. Betty DeBerg, in a recent study of campus religion, suggests that religious "supply" may "outstrip" religious "demand" at many universities. With so many different evangelical organizations alone, her observation is probably correct, as a proliferation of religious groups does not necessarily translate into increased student religiosity. At the same time, such qualifications should not obscure the genuine accomplishment of evangelical campus ministries over the past several decades. When Crusade began its work in 1951, evangelicalism was far less prominent on the campus than it is today. By the early twenty-first century evangelicalism had established itself as a visible subculture on most American campuses. Even accepting the limits of Crusade's campus strategy—and that of most other evangelical organizations—evangelicalism's reemergence as an influence at public and private non-church-affiliated universities and colleges is a testimony to decades of patient organizing and evangelizing on the part of parachurch ministries. Evangelicals have found space for their message in university dormitories, fraternity houses, and locker rooms—places that are as, if not more, central to the lives of many students, as academic classrooms.[40]

In a surprising development within the recent history of American higher education, evangelicals have mounted a serious challenge to the secularization, or de-Christianization, of the university. Parachurch organizations like Campus Crusade are only one part of this phenomenon. Evangelical colleges and universities continue to grow rapidly, while established evangelical schools like Wheaton College, Calvin College, and Gordon College enjoy increased prestige. Between 1990 and 2002, enrollment at schools belonging to the Council of Christian Colleges and Universities jumped 60 percent, much more quickly than enrollments at public and other private institutions.[41] There is still no evangelical university with anything approaching the academic pedigree or cultural influence of Harvard or Notre Dame, but evangelical schools now occupy a significant part of the American academic landscape. Alongside the growth of evangelical colleges and universities, parachurch organizations have been the primary vehicle through which evangelicalism has reestablished itself as a thriving subculture at predominantly secular institutions. American higher education has not returned to the heyday of the YMCA at its most evangelical, and few at Yale would predict a reprise of the 1802 revival that swept through a third of the student body. Partly due to the creative and persistent efforts of organizations like Campus Crusade for Christ, however, it is no longer reasonable to conceive of American higher education as moving inexorably toward a secular, or post-Christian, future.

Conclusion

In July 2003, Campus Crusade's staff members gathered at Colorado State University for the organization's biannual staff conference. More than five thousand in attendance, they sang, swayed, and raised their hands to the high-octane praise music that pulsated through the university's basketball arena. A group of contemporary gospel musicians, all African American, led the assembly in worship on several occasions. The vast majority of Crusade staff present were young, white Americans in their twenties and thirties, many of whom looked and dressed like collegians. Several high-profile evangelical speakers motivated staff members to remain passionate about telling other people about Jesus, and Crusade leaders Steve Douglass, Dennis Rainey, and Paul Eshleman reported on the growth of the ministry over the past two years. Veteran Crusaders heartily cheered the entrance of roughly one thousand new colleagues carrying flags representing the countries of the world. "Oh Lord," the assembly sang, "we ask for the nations." The weeklong event provided a snapshot of American evangelicalism in the early years of the twenty-first century: modern, racially sensitive, confident, and affluent.[1]

Crusade's 2003 staff conference also marked an indelible turning point in the organization's history. Shortly before the end of the conference, Bill Bright died in his Orlando condominium. Over the last decade of his life, Bright gradually evidenced his mortality, starting with treatment for prostate cancer in 1993. In 2000, beginning to lose his energy, Bright was diagnosed with pulmonary fibrosis, an incurable disease that slowly diminishes lung capacity. Unlike Billy Graham, Pat Robertson, and Oral Roberts, Bright did not groom one of his sons as his handpicked successor, instead turning over Crusade's presidency to Steve Douglass in 2001.[2]

After her husband died, Vonette Bright flew to Colorado and participated in a memorial service with Crusade's staff. Wearing a bright red outfit, she described her husband's final weeks in detail and told the assembled staff, "I'm exactly where I want to be tonight." The praise band, shelving its more raucous songs, led the assembly in singing Bright's favorite hymns: "Crown Him with Many Crowns," "Rejoice, the Lord Is King," and "Great Is Thy Faithfulness." Paul Eshleman and Steve Douglass, among others, delivered eulogies to Crusade's founder and told stories about the man who had started with a handful of friends in Los Angeles and later presided over one of the evangelical world's largest parachurch ministries.

Over his last two decades at the helm of Campus Crusade, Bill Bright became an evangelical elder statesman. Bright helped steer American evangelicalism away from its heritage of fundamentalist separatism and toward greater ecumenical engagement with theologically like-minded Catholics and Pentecostals. Crusade's ministries in Latin America and Asia often suffered from the mutual hostility between Protestants and Catholics in predominantly Catholic countries. Still, as early as the mid-1970s Crusade formed partnerships with Catholic churches and hierarchies, particularly in Europe. By the 1990s, Crusade's relationship with Catholic authorities had improved considerably, and the *Jesus* film ministry often worked in conjunction with Catholic organizations. In 1994, Bright joined a number of Protestant scholars, pastors, and parachurch leaders in signing "Evangelicals and Catholics Together" (ECT). Spearheaded by Charles Colson and Richard John Neuhaus, ECT articulated shared moral and political beliefs on topics ranging from abortion to free markets, and the signatories expressed a mutual commitment to evangelism while promising to avoid "sheep-stealing."[3]

In 1996, Bright received the Templeton Prize for Progress in Religion, an award created by John Templeton, a Bahamas-based global investor. Prior winners of the Templeton Prize included Mother Teresa, Billy Graham, and Aleksandr Solzhenitsyn. Bright donated his $1 million prize to Campus Crusade's worldwide efforts to promote prayer and fasting. As a sign of Bright's ecumenical attitude toward the Catholic Church, Edward Idris Cardinal Cassidy presided over an award ceremony in Bright's honor in Rome. Cassidy candidly noted that "Campus Crusade has not always been in good relations with the Catholic Church in different parts of the world," and he condemned "an aggressive proselytism," particularly in Latin America. The cardinal, however, praised Bright's contribution to ECT and mentioned that Campus Crusade, through its New Life 2000 initiative, was participating in the Catholic Church's Great Jubilee Year 2000.[4]

In addition to furthering evangelical cooperation with the Catholic Church, Bright also continued his outreach to charismatic and Pentecostal Christians. For example, Bright publicly defended the controversial Pentecostal evangelist Benny Hinn, at whose meetings people "slain in the Spirit" fall to the ground when Hinn touches them. Hinn's flamboyance makes many other evangelicals uneasy, and some evangelicals have questioned his orthodoxy because of his statements about the Trinity, healing, and prosperity. Hinn once claimed that each member of the Trinity was itself a triune being. "If I can shock you . . . ," he stated in a 1990 broadcast, "there's nine of them." Such utterances led James Robison and a number of other evangelicals to publicly rebuke Hinn in 1993. In the midst of such controversies, Hinn sought counsel from Bright. "[Hinn] is widely criticized in some circles," stated Bright in a 2001 interview, "but thank God for the thousands that come to Christ through his ministry." "I think Dad came to the conclusion," comments Bright's son Brad, "that Benny Hinn honestly, truly loves Jesus Christ with his whole heart." Zachary Bright, however, reveals that his father became "frustrated" with Hinn when the latter reiterated unorthodox teachings he had previously repudiated. Despite some theological concerns, Bright allowed Hinn to pray for him following his diagnosis with pulmonary fibrosis.[5]

One reason Bright enjoyed warmer relations with the charismatic movement toward the end of his life was his growing belief in the power of divine healing. In an interview with *Charisma*, Bright told a story about an evangelist in Hong Kong who was healed from a mysterious illness after Bright prayed for him. In 2001, Bright, with coauthor Ted Dekker, published a novel about a young African boy with the gift of healing—a novel that also featured an aging evangelist who accepted that he himself would not benefit from the gift. "[W]e have reported situations," Bright wrote about showings of *Jesus* in the novel's afterword, "where people have actually been raised from the dead, and their communities revolutionized by the message that resulted." Bright's acceptance of divine healing illustrates his wide openness to the supernatural and, along with his endorsement of ECT, his willingness to cross theological boundaries. "I'm a classical Christian," he explained. "By that I mean I'm a New Testament Christian. I'm not an evangelical. I'm not a fundamentalist. I'm not Orthodox. I'm just a follower of Jesus in the traditional New Testament sense." According to Zachary Bright, after his father relinquished the formal leadership of Crusade, he felt more willing to cross ecclesiastical borders and publicly embrace phenomena like faith healing.[6]

Evangelical ecumenism remained very different from mainline Protestant ecumenism. Campus Crusade retained a seventeen-point statement of faith that began with an affirmation of biblical inerrancy and emphasized Jesus Christ as "the only mediator between God and man." Articles in Crusade's *Worldwide Challenge* condemned religious pluralism and detailed stories of individuals converting to Jesus from other religions. In 1985, Bright ignited a firestorm of controversy within the evangelical world by rescinding a speaking invitation for Tony Campolo to a "youth congress" jointly organized with Youth for Christ. Campolo's 1983 book, *A Reasonable Faith*, suggested universal salvation, and Campolo had distressed some socially and politically conservative evangelicals through his outspoken pacifism and social liberalism. The conflict became public, and *Christianity Today* covered a modern-day "heresy trial" at which Campolo defended his beliefs before several evangelical theologians. As the Campolo flap indicated, Bright remained a theological conservative, but he also demonstrated a greater irenicism in his later years. Several years before his death, Bright traveled to a conference in Hawaii at which Campolo was the main speaker. "Bill Bright showed up," recalls Campolo, "and attended all the meetings and told me that he was there for one reason and for one reason alone, to affirm me and to affirm my ministry." In the early 1990s, Bright met with Peter Gillquist and Jon Braun and reminisced about their years together before the bitter conflict of 1967–68. He also invited Dan Fuller to Arrowhead Springs in order to restore a friendship that had broken on the shoals of debates over biblical inerrancy. More than two decades after Jim Wallis generated considerable negative publicity for Bright and Campus Crusade, Bright even reconciled with the *Sojourners* editor. The two met on an Orlando beach, told each other their conversion stories, and affirmed the importance of both evangelism and helping the poor. Shortly before his death, Bright mailed Wallis a $1,000 check for *Sojourners*. Bright never repaired his breach with Jim Taylor, his old business partner, but he left few other rifts unhealed.[7]

Bill Bright was not the most famous American evangelical of his generation. Billy Graham has been "America's Pastor," its foremost evangelist, and the public face of evangelicalism for nearly six decades. Carl Henry was

American evangelicalism's premier theologian during the postwar years. Jerry Falwell and Pat Robertson embody the politicization of evangelicalism. Oral Roberts, Jimmy Swaggart, and Jim Bakker serve as symbols of both the tremendous appeal and instability of televangelist personalities. Bright was not a mass evangelist, the leader of a political movement, or an original theological thinker. Yet especially during the last quarter of the twentieth century, as Crusade grew in size and scope, Bright exerted significant influence in all of these realms. Through the *Four Spiritual Laws* and other booklets, Bright popularized a slimmed-down and easy-to-digest version of evangelical theology that he relentlessly marketed around the world. Alongside the *Jesus* film, the *Four Spiritual Laws* became one of the most widely used evangelistic tools around the world in the late twentieth century. Through his efforts to motivate conservative Christians to involve themselves in grassroots politics, his contacts with national politicians, and his membership in conservative political organizations, Bright quietly contributed to the growth of the Religious Right. An entrepreneurial businessman, Bright ran Campus Crusade like a small business for fifteen years, then created a corporate structure and designated a successor with a Harvard MBA.

Bright's legacy—and the history of Campus Crusade for Christ—reflects many of the changes within American evangelicalism over the decades since World War II. Bright and his organization pushed evangelicalism toward the mainstream of American society. For example, Campus Crusade furthered the evangelical embrace of folk and then rock music in the late 1960s and early 1970s. Bright himself preferred classical music and, according to his son Zachary, owned a complete collection of Beethoven's works. In the early 1970s, Bright temporarily reined in the use of rock music at Crusade functions, and he never felt comfortable with the cutting edge of Christian music. Zachary Bright remembers telling his father, "You can have a conservative view of music and keep what worked for you, or you can win [young people to Christ]." "I'd rather win," Crusade's president responded. Bright recruited young evangelists who entered Greek houses that were anathema to most conservative Protestants, allowed several staff members to dress like hippies (also anathema) in the late 1960s, and hired former executives to evangelize businessmen and politicians. Although Crusade never embraced an egalitarian understanding of gender roles, the organization made practical accommodations on this issue, which remains bitterly contested among evangelicals.

Bright was distinctly pragmatic, often crossing cultural and theological boundaries for the cause of evangelism. There were always limits to such pragmatism, and Bright's brand of evangelism simultaneously remained in tension with certain aspects of American culture. Bright encouraged female staff members to dress modestly, opposed the sexual revolution of the late 1960s and 1970s, and continued to advocate abstinence from alcohol long after social drinking became acceptable in many evangelical circles. Yet Bright's commitment to evangelism mostly kept him on the pragmatic path of cultural adaptation. Alongside Campus Crusade, other parachurch organizations and megachurches participated in this process, driven by a mission to introduce people to Jesus and to their institutions. The evangelistic imperative encourages evangelicals to remain close to the center of mainstream American culture.[8]

Part of evangelicalism's movement toward the mainstream was its accumulation of, and comfort with, material prosperity and wealth. Bright came of age spiritually in the context of "Hollywood evangelicalism," and throughout his career he praised businessmen who accumulated wealth and then dedicated it to the cause of evangelism. Bright was a religious salesman, both for Jesus and for Campus Crusade—he excelled at persuading individuals and groups to follow Jesus and support his organization. It is hard to imagine that Bright once hesitated to ask potential supporters for money. He lacked the flamboyance of Roberts and Bakker, but no one in the evangelical world proved more adept at befriending wealthy evangelicals and persuading them to devote their money to the cause of global evangelism. In recent years, Bright hosted fund-raising events at which he asked his sometimes astonished guests how many millions they would pledge to Campus Crusade.[9] Moreover, Bright required all of Crusade's staff members—there are now roughly five thousand in America and nearly thirty thousand worldwide—to become effective fund-raisers themselves, since they raise their own salaries. Whereas Bright in the early 1950s raised $100 per month for each of his staff, single staff now must raise roughly $45,000 per year and married staff upwards of $70,000. Finally, Bright left behind a fund-raising edifice that was not dependent on his own leadership. Since Bright turned over Crusade's presidency to Steve Douglass, Crusade's revenues have continued to grow rapidly, approaching $500 million in 2005.[10] Campus Crusade's innovative and successful fund-raising initiatives, such as requiring staff to raise their own support, inspired many imitators, and countless parachurch ministries with large budgets now populate the evangelical landscape.

Crusade's primary fund-raising strategy was to persuade evangelical donors that the fulfillment of the Great Commission required money and that Crusade's evangelistic strategies were a cost-effective means of spreading the gospel. Ultimately, like most successful salesmen, Bright succeeded because he believed in his product, and he attracted like-minded Christians to his organization because of that transparent belief. Many colleagues of Bright who were interviewed for this project shared an anecdote about Bright witnessing to people on airplanes, in taxicabs, and in hotel elevators. Similar stories are such a clichéd part of most evangelical leaders' biographies that it is tempting to simply dismiss them. The endless repetition of stories about Bright's devotion to personal evangelism, however, makes it necessary to highlight this facet of his personality and leadership. "You were either saved," comments Tim LaHaye, Bright's friend and the coauthor of the bestselling *Left Behind* series, "or a prospect for Bill Bright."[11] Although political organizations like the Moral Majority and Christian Coalition attracted much more media attention, most parachurch organizations, like Campus Crusade, dedicated themselves to evangelism.

Bright also raised funds by appealing to evangelicals' cultural and political anxieties. In the 1950s, he portrayed Campus Crusade as the solution to communist infiltration of the campus; in later years, he presented his organization as an antidote to student radicalism and secular humanism. Alarmist rhetoric about political threats and moral decay at American universities helped Bright raise funds for campus evangelism, and it also signaled his interest in American politics. Until the end of his life, Bright continued to articulate a Manichaean view of American politics as a battle between good and evil. Shortly before the 2002 midterm elections, he outlined the political landscape for his staff:

On the one side are those who either tolerate or advocate what God hates — the murder of the unborn, the degrading of women by greedy predatory pornographers, militant homosexual behavior, and those who would rewrite the U.S. Constitution to force their godless views upon us all, excluding the God of the Bible from the public square and the marketplace of ideas.

On the other side are those who value life, believe we are created in the image of God, want to protect both mother and baby, and provide real opportunities for ethnic minorities and those who are truly in need of assistance for equality.

"I sincerely believe that NOT VOTING is a sin," warned Bright (emphasis in original). "Be sure to check," he reminded his followers, "what the candidates on your ballot believe and support and vote for those who hold Biblical values." He encouraged his staff to watch a video produced by David Barton entitled *The Role of Pastors and Christians in Civil Government*. Barton runs Wallbuilders, an organization that encourages Christians to become involved in politics and return the United States to the religious values of the "Founding Fathers." Although Bright did not specify the partisan affiliations of the two sides that he discussed, his delineation of the issues encouraged his staff to vote for Republican candidates, who more typically support the moral choices that he outlined. Former *Time* religion writer Richard Ostling once described Bright's "office hallway" as a "Democrat-free zone" featuring photographs of Bright with presidents Ford, Reagan, and George H. W. Bush. By signing a 2002 letter written by Southern Baptist official Richard Land, Bright applauded George W. Bush's "bold, courageous, and visionary leadership" and endorsed his "using military force if necessary to disarm Saddam Hussein."[12]

After Bright's death, the 2004 election confirmed the marriage of evangelicalism with political conservatism. Seventy-two percent of white American voters who identified themselves as "evangelical" or "born-again" voted for George W. Bush, and many powerful Republican politicians openly displayed an evangelical faith. As has been the case since the early 1970s, there is a visible "progressive," or left-leaning, evangelicalism, represented by Jim Wallis of *Sojourners* and Ron Sider of Evangelicals for Social Action. Growing numbers of evangelical intellectuals support policies designed to alleviate national and global poverty and oppose the use of American military power. As evidence of this trend, a large number of Calvin College faculty and students protested Bush's policies on the Iraq War and the environment during the president's 2005 commencement visit to the Grand Rapids bastion of reformed evangelicalism. As Laurence Moore observed two decades ago, the connection between evangelicals "and political conservatism is by no means made of steel." Nonetheless, it has been a strong and durable connection and will probably survive current dissatisfaction with the Iraq War and the Bush administration. In fact, even as journalists in recent years have once again discovered the presence of "the small but growing voice of the Christian left," Americans who describe themselves as evangelical or born-again have been voting Republican in increasingly solid majorities. The evangelical left has attained a measure of visibility over the past few years, but it is premature to opine, as Jim Wallis did in 2007, that "[w]e have now entered the post-Religious Right era." Even if evangelicalism becomes more politically diverse and encompasses a greater number of young progressives, conservative evangelicals will not disappear as a critical Republican voting bloc.[13]

The strong support of evangelical Christians for George W. Bush in 2000 and 2004, however, obscures a long-standing and never resolved debate within politically conservative evangelical ranks about the proper relationship between the spiritual and the political. Evangelicals disagree about the priority of politics and the appropriateness of political advocacy on the part of their leaders. For instance, Cal Thomas and Ed Dobson, two veterans of the Christian right, suggested in 1999 that politics could not produce the needed revival of Christianity and morality in the United States. Paul Weyrich, a conservative Catholic and along with Dobson a seminal figure in the formation of the Moral Majority, conceded, "I do not believe that a majority of Americans actually shares our values." More recently, David Kuo's exposé of the Bush administration's faith-based initiative included a call for Christians to temporarily "fast" from politics. Within Campus Crusade, Bright's political activism—particularly when it generated headlines—caused discomfort to a staff primarily motivated by evangelism. The installation of Steve Douglass as Crusade's president augured a shift away from Bright's political interests. Douglass states that before the 2004 election, he encouraged staff members to vote, but he avoided making any partisan recommendations and even avoided using the "buzzwords" that evangelical leaders often use to implicitly suggest partisan choices. Unlike Douglass, Dennis Rainey, director of Crusade's FamilyLife ministry, sought to galvanize evangelicals to oppose same-sex marriage in the months leading up to the 2004 election. Even Bright and Rainey, however, never assumed a public political posture as forthrightly partisan as Jerry Falwell, Pat Robertson, James Kennedy, and James Dobson. As both Kuo's book and the internal differences within Campus Crusade illustrate, the major debate within conservative evangelical circles is not over substantive political issues but over priorities and the level of explicit partisanship.[14]

In 2003, Steve Douglass outlined his vision for Campus Crusade's next ten years. Douglass commented that initially he believed he needed to launch "another big program"—given the significance of Explo '72, Here's Life, and New Life 2000 to Crusade's history—but "heard nothing from God on the subject." "God finally gave me a clear word," Douglass shared. "No new big program at this time." Instead, Douglass encouraged Campus Crusade's staff members to "help build movements everywhere" so that "everyone will know someone who truly follows Jesus." Despite his choice not to inaugurate a high-profile event or program, Douglass demonstrated that Campus Crusade would not depart from Bill Bright's penchant for audacious goal-setting. "I have a deep sense from the Lord that in the next ten years . . . ," he predicted, "one billion people will indicate decisions for Jesus Christ." Douglass expects those conversions to come mostly through Campus Crusade's "partnerships with others in the body of Christ." However many "decisions for Christ" Campus Crusade records over the next decade, it is safe to assume that the vast majority of such conversions will come from outside the United States. Indeed, a major reason for Crusade's rapid growth since 1980 is the organization's focus on global evangelism during a time when conservative forms of Protestant Christianity have exploded across Latin America, Africa, and Asia.[15]

The situation in the United States is somewhat different. Evangelical Christianity in America is not growing exponentially, but evangelical churches and organizations continue to prosper while mainline denominations continue to stagnate and decline. Although evangelicals remain a minority—perhaps one-fifth to one-quarter of the American population—they now form a visible presence on American campuses, in government, in business, and on the airwaves. The enthusiasm with which evangelicals embraced Mel Gibson's movie about Jesus's crucifixion, the success of the *Left Behind* series and Rick Warren's *The Purpose-Driven Life*, and the current prominence of James Dobson in Republican politics all testify to the broad influence of evangelicalism in American culture. In 1950 or 1970, few scholars of American religion would have predicted that American evangelicals would comprise a powerful Republican voting bloc, present a vocal witness for Jesus Christ on the American campus, or raise billions of dollars each year for evangelistic enterprises at home and abroad. Through its indefatigable marketing of Jesus and ability to mobilize evangelical wealth for evangelism, Campus Crusade for Christ helped ensure the continued presence of Jesus in American dormitories, legislative offices, and conference rooms. There are many followers of Jesus in the United States, but evangelicals constitute his most aggressive and creative sales force.

Notes

Abbreviations

BGCA	Billy Graham Center Archives, Wheaton, Ill.
CCC	Campus Crusade for Christ
Communique	*Campus Crusade Communique*
CT	*Christianity Today*
FF	Fundamentalism File, J. S. Mack Library, Bob Jones University, Greenville, S.C.
FPHC	Thomas Zimmerman Papers, Flower Pentecostal Heritage Center, Springfield, Mo.
FTSA	Fuller Theological Seminary Archives, Pasadena, Calif.
GCAH	General Commission on Archives and History, United Methodist Church, Madison, N.J.
GLA	Gospel Light Archives, Ventura, Calif.
HIA	Walter H. Judd Papers, Hoover Institution Archives, Stanford, Calif.
LAT	*Los Angeles Times*
NYT	*New York Times*
PTSA	Princeton Theological Seminary Archives, Princeton, N.J.
RCP	Russell Chandler Papers, American Religions Collection, University of California at Santa Barbara
WC	*Worldwide Challenge*

Introduction

1. *CT*, 7 July 1972, 31–32.

2. Niebuhr, "Fundamentalism"; *Time*, 8 April 1966; *Newsweek*, 25 Oct. 1976, 68–78.

3. For general treatments, see Carpenter, *Revive Us Again*; Marsden, *Reforming Fundamentalism*; Hart, *That Old-Time Religion*; Balmer, *Blessed Assurance*. For biographical windows into post–World War II evangelicalism, see Harrell, *Oral Roberts*; Martin, *Prophet with Honor*.

4. Board, "Great Evangelical Power Shift," 17. Wuthnow contends that the expansion of government in recent decades has been the single biggest factor responsible

for the proliferation of "special purpose organizations," as Protestants have formed nondenominational agencies "for the express purpose of combating, restraining, or promoting certain types of government action." Wuthnow, *Restructuring of American Religion*, 114. Although evangelicals and liberals have formed countless agencies for partisan purposes in recent decades, the proliferation of fundamentalist/evangelical parachurch organizations began in response to the bitter theological divisions of the early twentieth century and reflected the already weak sense of denominationalism in American religion. Also, despite the prominence of the Christian Coalition and Focus on the Family, the majority of evangelical parachurch groups are evangelistic or humanitarian rather than primarily political in nature.

5. Statistics from 2005–6 annual reports of World Vision, Focus on the Family, Young Life, and Prison Fellowship; Christian Broadcasting Network, "Condensed Financial Information," <http://www.cbn.com/about/annualReports/> (28 Feb. 2007). On parachurch budgets, see Robin Klay, John Lunn, and Michael S. Hamilton, "American Evangelicalism and the National Economy, 1870–1997," and Michael S. Hamilton, "More Money, More Ministry: The Financing of American Evangelicalism since 1945," both in Eskridge and Noll, *More Money, More Ministry*.

6. Stackhouse, *Evangelical Landscapes*, esp. chap. 2.

7. Mead, *Lively Experiment*, 115–21. Mead terms such organizations "inter- or super-denominational societies."

8. There are excellent studies of nondenominational agencies and organizations in earlier eras of American history. For example, see Hopkins, *History of the Y.M.C.A. in North America*. There are many in-house histories of more recent organizations, such as Hunt and Hunt, *For Christ and the University*. Little scholarly work has been done on the history of Campus Crusade itself. Richard Quebedeaux wrote a brief historical overview and analysis in the mid-1970s, and Michael Richardson contributed an authorized biography of Bill Bright. See Quebedeaux, *I Found It!*; Richardson, *Amazing Faith*.

9. Marsden, *Evangelicalism and Modern America*, xiv.

10. T. Smith, "Evangelical Kaleidoscope." See also Sweeney, "Essential Evangelicalism Dialectic." D. G. Hart, in *Deconstructing Evangelicalism*, dubs evangelicalism an "abstraction" and asserts that the term "evangelicalism" has become devoid of scholarly meaning. However, one could make similar complaints about political conservatism, also a network of disparate movements and organizations, yet certainly a phenomenon worthy of scholarly analysis.

11. The formulation here draws on David Bebbington's four-point definition that identifies evangelicals as Protestant Christians who emphasize conversionism, activism, biblicism, and crucicentrism. Bebbington, *Evangelicalism in Modern Britain*, 2–17.

12. CCC, 2005 Annual Report; CCC, *Reaching Our World for Christ* (ca. 2003). Both in author's possession.

13. *Family Manifesto*, 4.

14. On Finney, see Hambrick-Stowe, *Charles G. Finney*. On Whitefield, see Lambert, *"Pedlar in Divinity."* On Moody, see Evensen, *God's Man for the Gilded Age*. On broadcasting pioneers, see Abrams, *Selling the Old-Time Religion*; Hangen, *Redeeming*

the Dial. On the televangelists of the 1970s and 1980s, see Schultze, *Televangelism and American Culture*.

15. Hart, *That Old-Time Religion*, 178. For helpful studies of how American Christians have brought their own products into the marketplace, see Moore, *Selling God*; Wosh, *Spreading the Word*; Hendershot, *Shaking the World*.

16. Stark and Finke, *Acts of Faith*, 196. The phrase "optimum tension" is from Mauss, *Angel and Beehive*. Similarly, Christian Smith suggests "that a religious movement that unites both clear cultural distinction and intense social engagement will be capable of thriving in a pluralistic, modern society." C. Smith, *American Evangelicalism*, 90. Stark and Finke do not persuade me that scholars should discard the now much-maligned secularization thesis, especially outside the American context. Moreover, I am not convinced that faith more readily thrives in religiously pluralistic rather than monolithic environments. See responses to Stark and Finke by Bruce, *God Is Dead*; Carroll, "Upstart Theories." Even if one remains skeptical of their arguments against secularization, however, Stark and Finke's "axis of tension" helps explain the relative performance of different groups in the religious marketplace. See *Acts of Faith*, 143. In environments of competitive religious pluralism, "medium-tension" religious groups tend to outperform highly sectarian and "low-tension" groups.

17. Niebuhr, Pauck, and Miller, *Church against the World*, 123; McLoughlin, *Modern Revivalism*, esp. 523–50; Hart, *Deconstructing Evangelicalism*, 196; Moore, *Selling God*, 272–76. See the discussion of Niebuhr in Prothero, *American Jesus*, 294–97.

18. On the secularization of American colleges and universities, see Marsden, *Soul of the American University*, esp. 408–24. For a different perspective on this process, see Roberts and Turner, *Sacred and Secular University*.

19. On the history of American higher education and student culture since 1945, see Horowitz, *Campus Life*; C. Lee, *Campus Scene*; Lucas, *American Higher Education*; Sperber, *Beer and Circus*; Ehrman, *Eighties*, 193–202.

20. Notable exceptions include Ribuffo, *Old Christian Right*; Martin, *With God on Our Side*; McGirr, *Suburban Warriors*; Dochuk, "From Bible Belt to Sun Belt."

21. On the symbolic importance of gender issues to American religious organizations, see Chaves, *Ordaining Women*.

22. On this topic, see R. Stephen Warner, "The De-Europeanization of American Christianity," in Prothero, *Nation of Religions*, 233–55.

23. Hout, Greeley, and Wilde, "Demographic Imperative in Religious Change."

Chapter 1

1. Quote from interview with Charley Bright, 4 Oct. 2004. I have compiled information about Bill Bright's childhood and youth from several sources: 1955 Bright biography (in all likelihood self-composed), RCP; Richardson, *Amazing Faith*; Quebedeaux, *I Found It!*; interviews with Charley Bright and Roy Curtis Zachary, 4 Oct. 2004.

2. Interview with Brad Bright, 10 Dec. 2004.

3. See Scales and Goble, *Oklahoma Politics*, chaps. 9–12.

4. Bill Bright, *Witnessing without Fear*, 22.

5. Bright undergraduate transcript, Fuller Theological Seminary Registrar's Office, Pasadena, Calif.

6. *Northeastern*, 19 March, 26 March 1941; 1955 Bright biography.

7. *Northeastern*, 20 Nov. 1942, 19 March 1943. On the migration of Oklahomans to California during these years, see Gregory, *American Exodus*.

8. This phrase, playing on the title of C. S. Lewis's *Mere Christianity*, appears in *WC*, April 1979, 26–30.

9. Bill Bright, *Witnessing without Fear*, 22; Quebedeaux, *I Found It!*, 5–7; interview with Esther Brinkley, 12 Sept. 2003.

10. On Trotman and the Navigators, see Skinner, *Daws*; Hoke, "Sketch of the Month." In this and subsequent paragraphs on Bright's early months in Los Angeles, I rely most heavily on Richardson, *Amazing Faith*; Quebedeaux, *I Found It!*; 1955 Bright biography; interviews with Daniel Fuller, 5 Sept. 2003 and 28 June 2004, Esther Brinkley 12 Sept. and 2 Dec. 2003, and Louis H. Evans Jr., 8 Sept. and 15 Oct. 2003.

11. *LAT*, 11 March 1956.

12. *Life*, 10 Jan. 1949, 75–84; interview with Lauralil Deats, 30 Sept. 2003.

13. Interview with Daniel Fuller, 28 June 2004. On Mears, see B. Powers, *Henrietta Mears Story*; Baldwin and Benson, *Henrietta Mears and How She Did It!*; Roe, *Dream Big*; Madden, "Henrietta C. Mears"; J. Turner, "Power behind the Throne." On Riley, see Trollinger, *God's Empire*.

14. Interview with Rose Essick, 9 Sept. 2003; interview with Peggy T. Cantwell, 13 Jan. 2004; interview with Anna Kerr, 25 May 2004; Mears quoted in B. Powers, *Henrietta Mears Story*, 135. Mears's strategy reflects the decades-long attempt of both mainline and evangelical leaders to project a more masculine and robust version of the church. See Bendroth, "Why Women Loved Billy Sunday"; Putney, *Muscular Christianity*; Bederman, "'Women Have Had Charge of the Church Work Long Enough.'" On fundamentalism and gender during the 1940s, see Bendroth, *Fundamentalism and Gender*, chap. 4; Hamilton, "Women, Public Ministry, and American Fundamentalism."

15. Interview with Daniel Fuller, 28 June 2004; Mears to Smith, 2 May 1948, Wilbur Smith Papers, FTSA; Mears, "The Sunday School That Wins the Lost," Henrietta Mears Papers, GLA; *LAT*, 9 Aug. 1953.

16. For detailed accounts of the NAE's founding, see Carpenter, *Revive Us Again*, 141–60; Stone, *On the Boundaries of American Evangelicalism*, 74–86. On the National Sunday School Association, see Murch, *Cooperation without Compromise*, 124–32; Murch, *Adventuring for Christ in Changing Times*, 164–72, 325–26.

17. On Wyrtzen and the early years of Youth for Christ, see Carpenter, *Revive Us Again*, 161–76; Bergler, "Winning America," 104–17; Martin, *Prophet with Honor*, 89–105. For a more general discussion of American fears about juvenile delinquency, see Gilbert, *Cycle of Outrage*.

18. Bill Bright, *Witnessing without Fear*, 26; Bright application to Fuller Theological Seminary, 23 Aug. 1947, Fuller Theological Seminary Registrar's Office.

19. Interview with Daniel Fuller, 5 Sept. 2003.

20. Ibid.

21. Roe, *Dream Big*, 274–80; concerns about divorce, etc., from Henrietta Mears, "1936–1937 Christian Institute: First Seminar Notes of Miss Henrietta C. Mears on Personal Work," Mears Papers, GLA.

22. Morrison quoted in Marty, *Under God, Indivisible, 1941–1960*, 147.

23. Roe, *Dream Big*, 278–80. The Keswick movement, sometimes called the Higher Life movement, began at an 1875 conference held in the northern English town of Keswick. Like Wesleyan holiness teachers, Keswick leaders emphasized the need for individuals to reach the point of "absolute surrender" and commitment to God. That surrender led to the indwelling of the Holy Spirit and effective service, often in foreign missions. Spread across the United States by Dwight Moody, Charles Trumbull, and a wide variety of conferences and speakers, Keswick thought became a fixture among fundamentalist Baptists and Presbyterians in early-twentieth-century America. By the 1940s, there was no longer a very well organized or financed Keswick movement, but Keswick teachings permeated much of midcentury evangelical and fundamentalist spirituality. See Carpenter, *Revive Us Again*, 80–85. I was first made aware of Keswick's influence on Bright by Kathryn Long, "Bill Bright's Theology of Salvation: An Analysis," unpublished class paper, Gordon-Conwell Theological Seminary, 1986. Marsden also makes the connection in *Fundamentalism and American Culture*, 248, n. 24.

24. Interview with Louis H. Evans Jr., 8 Sept. 2003; Bright quoted in Richardson, *Amazing Faith*, 36.

25. Fellowship of the Burning Heart membership pledge, personal papers of Ralph Hamburger, Pasadena, Calif.; "The Fellowship of the Burning Heart," n.d., GLA; Roe, *Dream Big*, 286–87; interview with Jim Halls, 3 Oct. 2003.

26. Brochure excerpted in Roe, *Dream Big*, 285; Bright quoted in *WC*, April 1979. On Northfield, see Robert, *Occupy until I Come*, 145–50; Hopkins, *John R. Mott*, 24–30. On the postwar surge of foreign missionary activity, see Carpenter, *Revive Us Again*, 177–86. In the mid-1980s, IVCF restyled its name to InterVarsity Christian Fellowship.

27. Bright application to Fuller Theological Seminary; Harold Ockenga, "The Challenge to the Christian Culture of the West," *Fuller Seminary Bulletin* 1.1 (ca. 1947), FTSA.

28. Interview with Gary Demarest, 11 Sept. 2003; interview with Daniel Fuller, 5 Sept. 2003; Bill Bright, *Come Help Change the World* (1970), 24.

29. Bright academic transcript, Fuller Theological Seminary Registrar's Office; letter from Carl Henry to author, July 2003; Henry to Ockenga, 15 Dec. 1947, Ockenga Papers, Gordon-Conwell Theological Seminary, South Hamilton, Mass.

30. Interview with Gary Demarest, 11 Sept. 2003; Henry to Bright, 9 July 1948, FTSA. On fundamentalist reactions to the formation of the State of Israel, see Boyer, *When Time Shall Be No More*, 183–93.

31. V. Bright, *For Such a Time*, 19. Background information from interview with Roy Curtis Zachary, 4 Oct. 2004.

32. V. Bright, *For Such a Time*, 20, 44.

33. Interview with Louis Scroggin, 12 May 2004; interview with Esther Brinkley, 2 Dec. 2003.

34. Interview with Esther Brinkley, 2 Dec. 2003; interview with Candy Bayliss, 18 June 2004.

35. Interview with Ted Franzle, 3 Oct. 2003; interview with Gary Demarest, 11 Sept. 2003; interview with Dan Fuller, 5 Sept. 2003.

36. Interview with Anna Kerr, 10 Sept. 2003; interview with Colleen Townsend Evans, 8 Oct. 2003.

37. Orr, *Good News in Bad Times*, 154; Bright quoted in Orr, *Second Evangelical Awakening in America*, 190; *United Evangelical Action*, 1 Dec. 1949, 3. On Graham's experience at Forest Home, see Orr, *Good News in Bad Times*, 152–54; Carpenter, *Revive Us Again*, 222–23; Martin, *Prophet with Honor*, 109–13.

38. See Orr, *Inside Story of the Hollywood Christian Group*; Bill Bright, "Truth about Hollywood." On Graham's Los Angeles campaign, see Martin, *Prophet with Honor*, chap. 7; Orr, *Good News in Bad Times*, chap. 8; Carpenter, *Revive Us Again*, chap. 12.

39. Interview with Louis Evans Jr., 15 Oct. 2003; Richardson, *Amazing Faith*, 57–58. On the conflict between Fuller Seminary and the Presbytery of Los Angeles, see Marsden, *Reforming Fundamentalism*, esp. 96–97.

40. Remarks by Bill Bright at Oral Roberts University faculty luncheon, 12 Nov. 1982, Holy Spirit Research Center, Oral Roberts University, Tulsa, Okla.

41. Interview with Dale Bruner, 13 Sept. 2003; interview with Dan Fuller, 5 Sept. 2003; Graham quoted in Martin, *Prophet with Honor*, 116. On evangelical antipathy toward intellectual life, see Noll, *Scandal of the Evangelical Mind*.

42. Quotes from *Come Help Change the World* (1970), 25; 1955 Bright biography. See also the account in Richardson, *Amazing Faith*, 58–59.

Chapter 2

1. CCC, "Statement of Purpose," enclosed in Bright to John MacKay, 25 April 1951, MacKay Papers, PTSA.

2. Jones quoted in Carpenter, *Revive Us Again*, 62; Riley quoted in Laats, "Roots of the Culture Wars," 114; data on the growth of postwar student populations from U.S. Bureau of the Census, *Historical Statistics of the United States*, 383; Ravitch, *Troubled Crusade*, 14, 183. On earlier fundamentalist worries about American higher education, see Marsden, *Fundamentalism and American Culture*, 141–64; Marsden, *Soul of the American University*, 267–70; Carpenter, *Revive Us Again*, 62–63; Laats, "Roots of the Culture Wars," chap. 4.

3. Buckley, *God and Man at Yale*, xv–xvi. On Buckley, see Marsden, *Soul of the American University*, 10–16. On the use of loyalty oaths in California, see Gardner, *California Oath Controversy*.

4. CCC, "Statement of Purpose" and synopsis of "The Great Adventure," enclosed in Bright to MacKay, 25 April 1951; *Communique* (n.d., ca. 1952).

5. Interview with Donn Moomaw, 11 Sept. 2003; interview with Louis H. Evans Jr., 8 Sept. 2003.

6. CCC, "Statement of Purpose"; Bill Bright, *Come Help Change the World* (1970), 27–28; *WC*, Jan. 1976, 13.

7. *Time*, 5 Nov. 1951, 50–51; *Newsweek*, 22 April 1957, 115–20; *Newsweek*, 2 Nov. 1953, 55; *Daily Bruin*, 8 Oct. 1951, 12 Dec. 1951, 21 March 1953, 12 March 1953.

8. Interview with Roe Brooks, 3 Dec. 2003; *Communique*, Jan. 1955; U.S. Bureau of the Census, *Historical Statistics of the United States*, 383. Crusade's strategy and Brooks's comments illustrate a more widespread postwar anxiety about American manhood, as many pundits and politicians spoke of a crisis of masculinity and reaffirmed robust images of male physicality. See Cuordileone, *Manhood and American Political Culture in the Cold War*.

9. Bill Bright, *Come Help Change the World* (1970), 29; interview with Donn Moomaw, 11 Sept. 2003.

10. *Hour of Decision*, 14 June 1953, Walter F. Bennett & Company Collection, videotape F 60, BGCA; interview with Donn Moomaw, 11 Sept. 2003. See also *Wittenburg Door*, Aug.–Sept. 1975.

11. Interview with Earl Palmer, 23 Feb. 2004; interview with Donn Moomaw, 11 Sept. 2003; interview with Richard Edic, 21 March 2004.

12. V. Bright, *For Such a Time*, 24; *Communique*, Feb. 1953; Bright to Bob Jones Jr., 23 Jan. 1953, CCC File, FF.

13. Bill Bright, *Come Help Change the World* (1970), 30; *Communique*, Jan. 1955.

14. Interview with Daniel Fuller, 5 Sept. 2003; interview with Roy Curtis Zachary, 4 Oct. 2004; interview with Robert Kendall, 7 Feb. 2004; interview with Gordon Klenck, 20 July 2003.

15. Dalhouse, *Island in the Lake of Fire*, 41; *American Mercury* (ca. 1940) quoted in D. Turner, *Standing without Apology*, 73.

16. Interview with Dorothy Graham, 30 Dec. 2003; interview with Roe Brooks, 3 Dec. 2003; letter from Roger Aiken to author, 18 March 2004.

17. Letter from Roger Aiken to author, 18 March 2004; Bettger, *How I Raised Myself*; Harrell, *Oral Roberts*, 115; Graham quoted in McLoughlin, *Modern Revivalism*, 513; Bill Bright, "Christianity on the Campus," 143; interview with Colleen Townsend Evans, 8 Oct. 2003; interview with Esther Brinkley, 12 Sept. 2003; Little to Charles Troutman, 15 March 1961, Troutman Papers, Box 1, Folder 40, BGCA.

18. Interview with Gordon Klenck, 20 July 2003; "Sample Team Clincher," Daniel P. Fuller Papers, Sermons 1951–52, FTSA. On Graham, Liebman, Sheen, and Peale, see Graebner, *Age of Doubt*, 61–62, 103; Ellwood, *Fifties Spiritual Marketplace*, 12–14; D. Miller, "Popular Religion of the 1950s"; Heinze, "*Peace of Mind*."

19. *Campus Crusade Challenger*, n.d. (ca. 1959); copy of religious questionnaire, personal papers of Dorothy Graham, San Diego, Calif.; *Communique*, Jan. 1955.

20. Interview with Daniel Fuller, 5 Sept. 2003; interview with Robert Kendall, 7 Feb. 2004; letter from Aiken to author, 17 March 2004; 1955 Bright biography, RCP.

21. *Communique*, n.d. (ca. 1952), April 1953; interview with Jens Christy, 13 Jan. 2004; interview with Ney Bailey, 5 Oct. 2004.

22. Richardson, *Amazing Faith*, 86; CCC, "Where Are You Going for Christ" (ca. 1964), personal papers of Dorothy Graham.

23. *WC*, May–June 1991, 33; CCC, "Where Are You Going for Christ"; interview with Joanne (Whitworth) McClurkin, 17 May 2004.

24. Interview with Esther Brinkley, 12 Sept. 2003; V. Bright, *For Such a Time*, 26–29, 50. Bright wrote this autobiographical essay in the mid-1970s, well after the publication of Friedan's trailblazing work. Bright's comment indicates that feminist concerns had penetrated the evangelical mind-set by the 1970s and may have colored her interpretation of earlier events.

25. Bendroth, *Fundamentalism and Gender*, 89–113; Graham quoted in *Revival in Our Time*, 96; V. Bright, *For Such a Time*, 24; interview with Lee Etta Dickerson, 15 April 2004; *Women's Manual*, 26, 72. On the broader reaffirmation of domesticity after the war, see May, *Homeward Bound*, 75–91.

26. *Communique*, Sept. 1955.

27. Interview with Robert Kendall, 7 Feb. 2004.

28. *Communique*, June 1955, Special Edition 1957, Special Edition 1957–58; *LAT*, 15 March 1952, 20 April 1952; Bill Bright, "Christianity on the Campus," 142.

29. *Communique*, Special Edition 1959–60, Jan. 1955; interview with Bill Counts, 6 Jan. 2004.

30. *Communique*, Nov. 1953, June 1955; interview with Ney Bailey, 5 Oct. 2004. Other evangelicals, including Youth for Christ and Billy Graham, utilized similar techniques. See Carpenter, *Revive Us Again*, 166; Stackhouse, *Evangelical Landscapes*, 104.

31. Rossinow, *Politics of Authenticity*; Dunn, *Campus Crusade*, 13.

32. *Communique*, Special Edition 1957–58.

33. *Communique*, Feb. 1953, Jan. 1955; Bill Bright, "Christianity on the Campus," 139, 143; interview with Roe Brooks, 3 Dec. 2003.

34. Ockenga quoted in McLoughlin, *Modern Revivalism*, 482; Graham quoted in Whitfield, *Culture of the Cold War*, 80; McLoughlin, *Modern Revivalism*, 510. On Pelley and Winrod, see Ribuffo, *Old Christian Right*. The most comprehensive history of American anticommunism is R. Powers, *Not without Honor*.

35. On communist organizations on campus, see Schrecker, *No Ivory Tower*, 84–93; Ravitch, *Troubled Crusade*, 99–100.

36. Oakley, *God's Country*, 326; Herberg, *Protestant, Catholic, Jew*; Marty, *New Shape of American Religion*, 7. Whitfield's *Culture of the Cold War* suggests that the upsurge of religiosity represented a response to Cold War fears. James Hudnut-Beumler, in *Looking for God in the Suburbs*, makes a helpful distinction between "popular religion" and its elite religious critics, though he offers little discussion of the evangelical branch of the religious revival.

37. *Communique*, Special Edition 1956, April 1955.

38. *Daily Bruin*, 19 March 1956; *Los Angeles Herald*, 6 April 1956; R. B. Allen to John A. Murdy Jr., May 14, 1956, Chancellor's Office, Administrative Files, Box 310, Folder 246, UCLA University Archives.

Chapter 3

1. Ockenga quoted in Carpenter, *Revive Us Again*, 149; Ayer quoted in Carpenter, *New Evangelical Coalition*, 46; Grounds quoted in *Christian Life*, March 1956, 19.

2. Hunt and Hunt, *For Christ and the University*, esp. chap. 2, pp. 81, 141–42.

3. Bright to Keith L. Hunt, 20 June 1989, Records of IVCF, Box 378, Folder 3, BGCA; "terrific clash" from Paul Little to Charles Troutman, 15 March 1961, Troutman Papers, Box 1, Folder 40, BGCA.

4. Woods to Charles Troutman, 29 April 1952, Troutman Papers, Box 1, Folder 40; interview with Gordon Klenck, 10 December 2003; interview with Robert Kendall, 7 Feb. 2004; Woods excerpt from 13 Nov. 1953 letter, Records of IVCF, Box 20, Folder 3; Woods to Bright, 14 Feb. 1957, Records of IVCF, Box 8, Folder 3; *Communique*, June 1955; Hummel, *Campus Christian Witness*, 157, 62, 13; Nyquist to Charles Hummel and Paul Little, 2 Dec. 1960, Records of IVCF, Box 8, Folder 3.

5. Troutman to Bright, 28 May 1961, and Bright 1961 form letter, Troutman Papers, Box 1, Folder 40; Troutman to Ian Burnard, 25 July 1962, Troutman Papers, Box 1, Folder 38; Alexander to IVCF staff, 11 June 1965, Records of IVCF, Box 20, Folder 3.

6. Hunt and Hunt, *For Christ and the University*, 92, 140.

7. Shields to Lon Chesnutt, 23 Aug. 1962, Records of the General Board of Higher Education and Ministry, GCAH; Memorandum included in Hazel Trostel to Robert Davis, 28 Aug. 1962, GCAH; interview with Jim Craddock, 29 March 2004; interview with Jan Lindsey, 6 Jan. 2004; Bright circular, April 1961, Records of IVCF, Box 135, Folder 33.

8. Hammond and Mitchell, "Segmentation of Radicalism"; Shields to Chesnutt, 23 Aug. 1962; "The Church and Higher Education," Synod of Arkansas, Presbyterian Church, U.S., 1966, GCAH.

9. Bright to Jones Jr., 13 March 1953, and 15 March 1957, Bright to Jones Sr., 12 March 1956, and Bright to Jones Jr., 23 Jan. 1953, FF. Stenholm's statistics in D. Turner, *Standing without Apology*, 370, n. 37.

10. On BJU and the NAE, see Dalhouse, *Island in the Lake of Fire*, 62–73; D. Turner, *Standing without Apology*, 161–66. On the theology of new evangelicals in the 1950s, see Marsden, *Reforming Fundamentalism*, 162–65; "Is Evangelical Theology Changing?," *Christian Life*, March 1956, 16–19.

11. D. Turner, *Standing without Apology*, 170; *Evangelical Christian*, May 1955, 215. Upon reading Graham's "neither a fundamentalist nor a liberal" statement, Rice slightly misquoted and lukewarmly defended him in *Sword of the Lord*, 17 June 1955, 10. On Graham's relationship with separatist fundamentalism, see Butler, "Billy Graham and the End of Evangelical Unity."

12. Dalhouse, *Island in the Lake of Fire*, 80; Graham to Jones Sr., 3 June 1952, FF; *Sword of the Lord*, 19 April 1957; Jones Sr. to Al and Lu Bradshaw, 15 Aug. 1958, FF; Martin, *Prophet with Honor*, 222; Jones Jr. to Ralph Mitchell, 7 Nov. 1956, quoted in D. Turner, *Standing without Apology*, 181–82.

13. Jones Jr. to Weniger, 1 May 1958, and Wright to Jones Sr., 17 May 1957, G. Archer Weniger Papers, FF. In 1 Samuel 4, when the Philistines capture the ark of the cove-

nant, the wife of Phinehas gives birth to a son and names him Ichabod, meaning "the glory has departed from Israel." Wright suggested that by opposing Graham, Jones was departing from God's will or that God's blessing would depart from him.

14. Bright to Jones Sr., 15 March 1957 (includes "statement of faith"), CCC File, FF; interview with Roe Brooks, 3 Dec. 2003; Bright to Jones Sr., 12 Sept. 1957, Bright to Stenholm, 10 April 1957, CCC File, FF.

15. Jones Sr. to Bright, 29 March 1957, Jones to Rice, 21 Aug. 1957, Jones to Bright, 22 Oct. 1957, and Stenholm to Bright, 3 May 1958, CCC File, FF.

16. Bright to Jones Sr., 1 July 1958, FF; interview with Dave Coterill, 17 May 2004; Bright to Bell, May 6 1958, Lemuel Nelson Bell Papers, Box 17, Folder 17, BGCA; Bright to Jones Sr., 1 July 1958, FF; interview with Dorothy Graham, 30 Dec. 2003.

17. Bright to Jones Sr., 21 June 1958, Jones to Bright, 23 June 1958, CCC File, FF.

18. Bright to Jones Sr., 1 July 1958, CCC File, FF.

19. Jones Sr. to Bright, 3 July 3 1958, Stenholm to Bright, 23 June 1958, Bright to Jones Jr., 21 July 1958, Jones Jr. to Bright, 10 July 1958, CCC File, FF.

20. Jones Sr. to Lu and Al Bradshaw, 15 Aug. 1958, Jones Sr. to Coterill, 13 Aug. 1958, Jones Sr. to Bright, 28 Aug. 1958, and Jones Jr. to Bright, 5 Sept. 1958, CCC File, FF; Jones Sr. to Dorothy Hauser, 19 Aug. 1958, personal papers of Dorothy Graham, San Diego, Calif.

21. Interviews with William Greig Jr., 1 Oct. 2003, Lee Etta (Lappen) Dickerson, 15 April 2004, Dave Coterill, 17 May 2004, Ray Nethery, 21 Dec. 2003; Stenholm to Glen Rosenberger, 22 July 1963, CCC File, FF. Number of staff (including full- and part-time workers) from Bright circular, 31 March 1958, personal papers of Dorothy Graham.

22. LaHaye to Jones Jr., 30 April 1974, in Bob Jones Jr. Correspondence, FF; interview with Howard Hendricks, 5 Oct. 2004; Dollar, *History of Fundamentalism in America*, 220, 277. Dallas Theological Seminary later came under fire from BJU for inviting "new evangelicals" to speak on its campus.

23. CCC, "Policy Relating to Doctrine and the Church," n.d. (ca. 1960), personal papers of Ted Martin, Crestline, Calif.; Bright to Margie Lou Chapin, 10 Oct. 1962, CCC File, FF.

24. Interview with Jim Craddock, 29 March 2004.

25. Wacker, "Travail of a Broken Family"; Synan, *Holiness-Pentecostal Tradition*, 207–9, 226–33; Harrell, *All Things Are Possible*, 99–116, 230.

26. Harrell, *Oral Roberts*, 17; interview with Deanne Rice, 2 Oct. 2004; *CT*, 13 Sept. 1963, 3–7.

27. Interview with Dale Bruner, 6 March 2004; Orr, *Full Surrender*, 104; Bill Bright, *Believing God for the Impossible*, 62–63. Orr's book contains his 1949 Forest Home talks.

28. Interview with Ray Nethery, 21 Dec. 2003; email from Robert Kendall to author, 12 March, 2004.

29. Bill Bright, *Come Help Change the World* (1970), 49; email from Kendall to author, 12 March 2004; Torrey, *Holy Spirit*, 193; Graham, *Peace with God*, 160.

30. Bill Bright, "Ye Shall Receive Power," mimeograph of typescript, Gilbert Stenholm Papers, FF; revised version of "Ye Shall Receive Power" in *Ten Basic Steps toward*

Christian Maturity, 13. Fundamentalists and evangelicals who made this three-pronged division typically cited 1 Corinthians 2 and 3. In the King James text, Paul complains that he "could not speak unto you [the Corinthian believers] as unto spiritual, but as unto carnal."

31. Interview with Dave Coterill, 17 May 2004; Robert B. Thieme Jr., "Rebound and Keep Moving," audiotape, personal papers of Dorothy Graham; interview with Greg Barnett, 17 March 2004; *Have You Made the Wonderful Discovery of the Spirit-Filled Life?*; Bill Bright, "Walking in the Spirit," n.d., personal papers of Dorothy Graham. On earlier Keswick spirituality (including Murray and Torrey), see Ostrander, "Battery and the Windmill."

32. Bill Bright, "Ye Shall Receive Power"; "Explaining the Ministry of the Spirit to Others" (ca. 1960), personal papers of Ted Martin; Bright to L. Nelson Bell, 6 May 1958, Bell Papers, Box 17, Folder 17, BGCA.

33. Bill Bright, "Ye Shall Receive Power"; interview with Donn Moomaw, 15 March 2004; interview with Gordon Klenck, 8 April 2004; interview with Ted Martin, 6 Sept. 2003; interview with Jan Lindsey, 6 Jan. 2004. When Campus Crusade published a revised version of Bill Bright's "Ye Shall Receive Power" in 1983, it deleted the references to tongues.

34. Bill Bright, *Believing God for the Impossible*, 63; interview with Peter Gillquist, 13 Jan. 2004; interview with Donn Moomaw, 15 March 2004.

35. "Policy Relating to Doctrine and the Church" (n.d.), personal papers of Ted Martin; "Campus Crusade for Christ and the Charismatic Movement" (n.d.), personal papers of Peter Gillquist, Goleta, Calif.

36. CCC, "Policy Relating to Doctrine and the Church"; interview with Ray Nethery, 21 Dec. 2003.

Chapter 4

1. "History of Campus Crusade for Christ," n.d. (ca. 1964), Records of IVCF, Box 135, Folder 3, BGCA.

2. CCC, "Program for Action" (1951), FF; *Communique*, Feb. 1954, May 1954, Sept. 1955.

3. *Communique*, Special Edition 1959–60; Bill Bright, undated circular (ca. 1958–59), personal papers of Dorothy Graham, San Diego, Calif.; *Collegiate Challenge*, March 1965; interview with Kundan Massey, 11 May 2004.

4. Bill Bright, *Witnessing without Fear*, 39–42; *Communique*, Special Edition 1959–60.

5. Bright quoted in *Communique*, Special Edition 1959–60; interview with Ray Nethery, 21 Dec. 2003. On American foreign missions and nationalism during this time period, see Robert, "Shifting Southward."

6. Troutman to Burnard, 25 July 1962, Troutman Papers, Box 1, Folder 38, BGCA; circular to British chapters of IVCF, 27 Nov. 1967, Records of IVCF, Box 20, Folder 3, BGCA; interview with Robert Kendall, 7 Feb. 2004.

7. Bright quoted in Dec. 1960 circular, Records of IVCF, Box 8, Folder 3, BGCA. On the postwar ascendancy of American evangelical missionaries, see Coote, "Uneven

Growth of Conservative Evangelical Missions." On the China lobby, see Patterson, *Grand Expectations*, 170–73; Bachrack, *Committee of One Million*, esp. chaps. 1 and 2.

8. Interview with Bob Horner, 8 April 2004.

9. Bill Bright, *Come Help Change the World* (1970), 43–44; "God's Plan for Your Life" (ca. 1957), CCC Archives, Orlando, Fla.

10. Interview with Joanne McClurkin, 17 May 2004; interview with Bill Counts, 6 Jan. 2004; Bill Bright, *Come Help Change the World* (1970), 45–46; "God's Plan for Your Life (Containing Four Spiritual Laws)" (ca. 1960), personal papers of Ted Martin, Crestline, Calif.

11. Interview with Lois Mackey, 9 Jan. 2004; interview with Gordon Walker, 8 March 2004; Bill Bright, *Have You Heard of the Four Spiritual Laws?*; Watt, *Transforming Faith*, 18, 22.

12. Bright to "Staff and Advisory Committee Members," 26 Nov. 1965, Box 241, Folder 1, HIA.

13. Bill Bright, *Come Help Change the World* (1970), 45; Bill Bright, "Witnessing in the Spirit" (ca. 1965), personal papers of Dorothy Graham; interview with Howard Ball, 9 Feb. 2004; interview with Zachary Bright, 2 Feb. 2005; Hofstadter, *Anti-Intellectualism in American Life*, 48–49, n. 8. See the helpful discussion of Hofstadter in Noll, *Scandal of the Evangelical Mind*, 10–12.

14. *Collegiate Challenge*, March 1965.

15. Richardson, *Amazing Faith*, 82–83; interview with Charley Bright, 4 Oct. 2004; interview with Louis Scroggin, 12 May 2004.

16. Interview with Dale Smith, 12 Dec. 2003; interview with Jim Craddock, 29 March 2004; *Fort Worth Press*, 18 April 1967.

17. Interview with Dorothy Graham, 30 Dec. 2003. See Michael S. Hamilton, "More Money, More Ministry," in Eskridge and Noll, *More Money, More Ministry*, esp. 104–8.

18. Interview with Louis Scroggin, 12 May 2004. On the impact of Crusade's new fund-raising methodology on other parachurch organizations, see Barry Gardner, "Technological Changes and Monetary Advantages," in Eskridge and Noll, *More Money, More Ministry*, 302.

19. Bright circular, June 1957, personal papers of Dorothy Graham; Bright circular, Jan. 1960, Records of IVCF, Box 135, Folder 33, BGCA; Bill Bright, "The Secret of World Evangelism" (ca. 1960), personal papers of Dorothy Graham.

20. Interview with Louis Scroggin, 12 May 2004. Lists of board members found in *Communique*, Special Edition 1957–58, Special Edition 1959–60. Scroggin does not remember the specifics of the plan.

21. Email from Robert Kendall to author, 21 May 2004; interview with John Goodwin, 13 April 2004; Hummel to Charles Troutman, 10 Nov. 1961, Troutman Papers, Box 1, Folder 40, BGCA.

22. Email from Robert Kendall to author, 21 May 2004; interview with Jon Braun, 15 Jan. 2004.

23. Herriott, *It Can Happen Here*; Bright circular, July 1960, Records of IVCF, Box 135, Folder 33, BGCA; Bill Bright, "The Priority of Prayer" (remarks at Governor's

Prayer Breakfast, ca. 1962), personal papers of Dorothy Graham; Bright Thanksgiving 1961 circular, Troutman Papers, Box 1, Folder 40, BGCA.

24. Interview with Dale Bruner, March 6, 2004; interview with Jon Braun, 15 Jan. 2004; interview with Bill Counts, 7 Oct. 2004; interview with Jim Craddock, 29 March 2004. On Protestant opposition to Kennedy, see Martin, *Prophet with Honor*, 269–83; Massa, "A Catholic for President?"

25. Bright to Bell, 4 Nov. 1961, Bell Papers, Box 17, Folder 17, BGCA; undated endorsement letter, Bright to von Frellick, Box 241, Folder 2, HIA; *Denver Post*, 1 April 1962.

26. Lisa McGirr and Darren Dochuk have documented the vitality of evangelical and fundamentalist anticommunist movements in the Sunbelt during the 1950s and early 1960s. See McGirr, *Suburban Warriors*; Dochuk, "From Bible Belt to Sunbelt." Earlier generations of historians documented links between fundamentalists and right-wing political "extremism." For example, see Hofstadter, *Paranoid Style in American Politics*, chap. 3; Ribuffo, *Old Christian Right*.

27. Rough draft of the "Precinct Primer," and Christian Citizen brochure, Box 241, Folder 2, HIA; interview with Gene Edwards, 15 Dec. 2004.

28. *NYT*, 1 Feb. 1962; *Christian Citizen*, June 1962, Box 241, Folder 2, HIA; Bright to Bell, 4 Nov. 1961, Bell Papers, BGCA.

29. Interview with Peter Gillquist, 13 Jan. 2004; interview with Frank Kifer, 24 July 2004; interview with Jon Braun, 15 Jan. 2004. On Bunker Hunt, see Hurt, *Texas Rich*. On Welch, see R. Powers, *Not without Honor*, 286–96.

30. Interview with Peter Gillquist, 13 Jan. 2004; interview with Jon Braun, 15 Jan. 2004; interview with Gordon Klenck, 8 April 2004; interview with Jim Craddock, 29 March 2004; interview with Gene Edwards, 15 Dec. 2004. By the 1964 election, Crusade had established its headquarters at Arrowhead Springs, near San Bernardino.

31. Interview with Bill Counts, 7 Oct. 2004; interview with Frank Kifer, 24 July 2004. On Southern evangelicals and the civil rights movement, see Chappell, *Stone of Hope*; S. Miller, "Politics of Decency," esp. chaps. 2 and 4.

32. Starr, *Embattled Dreams*, 29; *LAT*, 25 May 1963; Bill Bright, *Come Help Change the World* (1970), 20–22.

33. Bill Bright, *Come Help Change the World* (1970), 21–23; interview with Arlis Priest, 14 May 2004.

34. Email from Robert Kendall to author, 21 May 2004; interview with Arlis Priest, 14 May 2004.

35. Bill Bright, *Come Help Change the World* (1970), 53; interview with Gene Edwards, 15 Dec. 2004; interview with Robert Kendall, 7 Feb. 2004.

36. Interview with Gordon Klenck, 8 April 2004; interview with Arlis Priest, 14 May 2004.

37. Interview with Ray Nethery, 21 Dec. 2003; Richardson, *Amazing Faith*, 114–15; *Fort Worth Press*, 18 April 1967.

38. Bill Bright, "In Memorium," Mears Papers, GLA.

39. Interview with Curt Mackey, 9 Jan. 2004.

Chapter 5

1. Reagan quoted in Kurt Schuparra, "'A Great White Light': The Emergence of Ronald Reagan," in Farber and Roche, *Conservative Sixties*, 101. On Reagan, Kerr, and Berkeley, see Kerr, *Gold and Blue*, vol. 2, chaps. 15 and 16; Rorabaugh, *Berkeley at War*, esp. chaps. 1–3.

2. Jo Anne Butts, "Report on Campus Crusade Invasion," 29 Jan. 1967, Records of IVCF, Box 20, Folder 3, BGCA; interview with Jon Braun, 15 Jan. 2004; interview with Peter Gillquist, 13 Jan. 2004.

3. My understanding of the New Left and the counterculture has been most influenced by Gitlin, *Sixties*; Lyons, *People of This Generation*; Rorabaugh, *Berkeley at War*.

4. On the YAF, see Schneider, *Cadres for Conservatism*; Andrew, *Other Side of the Sixties*. See also the collection of essays in Farber and Roche, *Conservative Sixties*.

5. Two prominent exceptions are McGirr, *Suburban Warriors*; and Dochuk, "From Bible Belt to Sunbelt."

6. In *Direct Action*, for example, James Tracy explicates the role of radical pacifists in 1960s protest and discusses their influence on the formation of the New Left.

7. Notable exceptions are Flowers, *Religion in Strange Times*; Oppenheimer, *Knocking on Heaven's Door*.

8. *CT*, 31 July 1970, 20–21; Martin, *Prophet with Honor*, 370–71.

9. Bill Bright, *Come Help Change the World* (1970), 97; Bright circular, March 1967, CCC File, FF; interview with Peter Gillquist, 13 Jan. 2004. On the "be-in," see Gitlin, *Sixties*, 208–14. William Martin provides a brief account of Crusade's weeklong campaign at Berkeley in *With God on Our Side*, 93–94.

10. *NYT*, 28 Jan. 1967; memorandum from Berney to Paul Little, Records of IVCF, Box 135, Folder 33, BGCA; *Crusade in Action* (1967 CCC newspaper).

11. Bill Bright, "Walking in the Spirit," typescript of address at staff training event (ca. 1965), personal papers of Dorothy Graham, San Diego, Calif. On parietal protests, see Wynkoop, *Dissent in the Heartland*, 137–41.

12. *Collegiate Challenge*, Spring 1968, Summer 1967; *Crusade in Action*.

13. *Daily Californian*, 26 Jan. 1967; Jeff Porro memorandum, 5 Feb. 1967, and Paul Griffith, "The Campus Crusade for Christ Convention in Review," Records of IVCF, Box 20, Folder 3, BGCA; Butts, "Report on Campus Crusade Invasion," BGCA.

14. *Daily Californian*, 27 Jan. 1967; *Crusade in Action*; Bill Bright, *Come Help Change the World* (1970), 99–100; Butts, "Report on Campus Crusade Invasion," BGCA; Braun and Gillquist quoted in Martin, *With God on Our Side*, 94.

15. *Los Angeles Herald-Examiner*, 28 Jan. 1967; *Crusade in Action*; Bill Bright, *Come Help Change the World* (1970), 98; Griffith, "Campus Crusade Convention," BGCA. On the People's Park protests, see Rorabaugh, *Berkeley at War*, 155–66.

16. Interview with Beverly Counts, 6 Jan. 2004; interview with Jimmy Williams, 22 Jan. 2004; interview with Jim Green, 9 Sept. 2003. Charles Woodbridge charged that Crusade's "folk-singing groups" with "mini-skirted young ladies" were "a travesty of the Holy Gospel." Woodbridge, *Campus Crusade*, 6. Woodbridge, formerly a professor at Fuller Seminary, attended Crusade's founding banquet in 1951 but later

became an inveterate fundamentalist opponent of "new evangelicalism." See Marsden, *Reforming Fundamentalism*, 174–75.

17. Interview with Jim Green, 9 Sept. 2003. On other conservative groups borrowing tactics from the New Left (and the civil rights movement), see Schneider, *Cadres for Conservatism*, 110–26; Formisano, *Boston against Busing*.

18. On McDowell, see Musser, *Josh*; interview with Alan Scholes, 16 Sept. 2003; interview with Glenn Plate, 9 Sept. 2003.

19. Interview with Glenn Plate, 9 Sept. 2003; interview with Conrad Koch, 11 Nov. 2003; *CT*, 5 Dec. 1969, 35.

20. Email from Jack Sparks to author, 24 Sept. 2004; *CT*, 8 May 1970, 40. On the CWLF, see Sparks, *God's Forever Family*, Heinz, "Christian World Liberation Front."

21. Interview with Bob Horner, 14 April 2004. The analysis here is contrary to the sketch given by Isserman and Kazin in *America Divided*, 254. For a suggestive portrait of the diverse types of students present at antiwar protests at the University of Wisconsin–Madison, see Maraniss, *They Marched into Sunlight*. On the diverse nature of campus life more broadly, see Lyons, *People of This Generation*, esp. 195–96.

22. Oppenheimer, *Knocking on Heaven's Door*, 6; Bright's comments from *LAT*, 8 Aug. 1971. Similar to the argument here, Oppenheimer suggests that much of the religious establishment's engagement with the counterculture was more aesthetic than substantive. Unlike the organizations studied in Oppenheimer's book, Crusade appears to have been more impacted by the New Left and the student counterculture than the civil rights movement and feminism.

23. Interview with Jan Lindsey, 6 Jan. 2004. See the account of Smith's ministry in McGirr, *Suburban Warriors*, 243–46.

24. Port Huron Statement quoted in Isserman and Kazin, *America Divided*, 177.

25. Hayden quoted in ibid.; Bill Bright, *Come Help Change the World* (1970), 18; *Student Action* (CCC periodical), 1969. In *A Generation Divided*, Rebecca Klatch identifies generational characteristics shared by members of SDS and YAF. On the Left's quest for authenticity, see Rossinow, *Politics of Authenticity*; Lyons, *People of This Generation*; Tracy, *Direct Action*.

26. Gitlin, *Sixties*, 417; Gallup, *Gallup Poll*, 3:2250; *Esquire*, Dec. 1970, 135; interview with Jim Wallis, 22 July 2004; Ellwood, *One Way*, 117. On the role of denominational campus ministers on the left at the University of Pennsylvania, see Lyons, *People of This Generation*, 107–10.

27. Interview with Jan Lindsey, 6 Jan. 2004; copy of blank weekly report, personal papers of Frank Kifer, Hay Market, Va.; interview with Jim Craddock, 29 March 2004; interview with Peter Gillquist, 13 Jan. 2004; interview with Bill Counts, 7 Oct. 2004.

28. Interview with Jon Braun, 15 Jan. 2004; interview with Peter Gillquist, 13 Jan. 2004; interview with Bruce Cook, 30 July 2004. After Braun and Gillquist left Crusade, they intended to form "first-century-type church" groups in homes and colleges. *CT*, 16 Aug. 1968, 40. On Witness Lee, Watchman Nee, and the origins of the local church movement, see J. Lee, "Watchman Nee and the Little Flock Movement."

29. Interview with Gordon Walker, 8 March 2004; interview with Bill Counts, 7 Oct. 2004; interview with Jan Lindsey, 6 Jan. 2004.

30. Interview with Bailey Marks, 11 Feb. 2004; interview with Jon Braun, 15 Jan. 2004; interview with Peter Gillquist, 13 Jan. 2004.

31. Interview with Swede Anderson, 11 April 2005; Musser, *Josh*, 117; emails to author from Kent Hutcheson, 2 July 2006, 9 July 2006.

32. Interview with Bailey Marks, 11 Feb. 2004; interview with Peter Gillquist, 13 Jan. 2004; interview with Jon Braun, 15 Jan. 2004; *CT*, 12 April 1968, 712. See Gillquist and Walker, *Arrowhead Springs to Antioch*.

33. Bill Bright, *How to Love by Faith*; interview with Gordon Walker, 8 March 2004; Hal Lindsey, "Seven Signs of the Times" (1966), audio recording, personal papers of Jerry Regier, Tallahassee, Fla.; interview with Bill Counts, 7 Oct. 2004.

34. Several interviewees, including Gordon Walker, 8 March 2004, and Jimmy Williams, 22 Jan. 2004, remembered the exact quote.

35. Interview with Gene Edwards, 15 Dec. 2004; interview with Ron Jenson, 3 April 2005. Jenson's anecdote confirmed by interview with Alan Hlavka, 27 Jan. 2005. On the authoritarian ethos of other conservative organizations such as YAF, see Hijiya, "Conservative 1960s."

36. Interview with Peter Gillquist, 13 Jan. 2004; *LAT*, 11 March 1956; *Cincinnati Enquirer*, 27 June 1971. For early accounts of the Jesus movement, see Plowman, *Jesus Movement in America*; Enroth, Erickson Jr., and Peters, *Jesus People*; Ellwood, *One Way*.

37. Interview with Swede Anderson, 21 July 2003.

38. Ibid.; Bill Bright, *Believing God for the Impossible*, 37.

39. Interview with Jimmy Williams, 5 Oct. 2004; interview with Jim Green, 9 Sept. 2003; interview with Bruce Cook, 30 July 2004.

40. Interview with Bruce Cook, 30 July 2004; interview with Alan Scholes, 16 Sept. 2003; interview with Swede Anderson, 11 April 2005.

41. Howard to Parker, 4 Aug. 1971, Folder RM 2-1 "Religious Services in White House 9/1/71–9/30/71," SF RM Box 15, White House Central Files, Nixon Presidential Material, National Archives and Records Administration, College Park, Md.; Parker to Haldeman, 1 Feb. 1971, Folder "HRH Chronological," Box 199, Haldeman Files, White House Special Files, Nixon Presidential Material; email from Paul Eshleman to author, 26 April 2007; "stormy session" from Haldeman notes, 2 Feb. 1972, Box 45, White House Special Files, Nixon Presidential Material. I would not have pursued this story without the painstaking research of William Martin in *Prophet with Honor*, 394–96.

42. Since Crusade seated thousands of additional participants on the field and pictures show the 68,000-seating-capacity stadium nearly full, the organization's report of 85,000 delegates appears credible.

43. *Dallas Morning News*, 15 June 1972, 18 June 1972; Eshleman and Rohrer, *EXPLO Story*, 10. For a fundamentalist critique of Explo '72, see Russell, *Untold Explo Story*.

44. *Dallas Times Herald*, 8 June 1972, 13 June 1972; *Dallas Morning News*, 18 June 1972; *NYT*, 16 June 1972; *Saturday Review*, 8 July 1972, 15. On Graham's embrace of the Jesus movement, see Eskridge, "'One Way.'" By the early 1970s, the new fashions of dress and rhetoric associated with the late 1960s were no longer meaningfully countercul-

tural, having been appropriated by everyone from evangelists to advertising executives. For a helpful discussion of the latter relationship, see Frank, *Conquest of Cool*.

45. *Dallas Times Herald*, 11 June 1972; *Dallas Morning News*, 18 June 1972; *Military Chaplain*, March–April 1972, 5; *Worldwide Impact*, July 1972; *Reformed Journal*, July–Aug. 1972, 16; Nixon quoted in *Dallas Times Herald*, 18 June 1972; Wallis banner reported in Eshleman and Rohrer, *EXPLO Story*, 47; interview with Skinner, *Wittenburg Door*, Aug.–Sept. 1972.

46. *Dallas Morning News*, 20 June 1972, 18 June 1972.

Chapter 6

1. *NYT*, 16 Jan. 1977; Harrell, *Pat Robertson*, chap. 8. On Lindsey and Morgan, see Jorstad, *Evangelicals in the White House*, 88, chap. 10; *Time*, 14 March 1977, 62–70. Denominational statistics from Carroll, Johnson, and Marty, *Religion in America*, 15.

2. Martin, *Prophet with Honor*, 463; *Washington Post*, 16 Aug. 1976; *NYT*, 6 June 1976; *LAT*, 30 May 1976; *Newsweek*, 25 Oct. 1976, 68–78.

3. Scott Flipse contends that abortion was the key catalyst for evangelical political involvement. See Flipse, "Below-the-Belt Politics," in Farber and Roche, *Conservative Sixties*, 127–41. On conflict over the ERA, see Mathews and De Hart, *Sex, Gender, and the Politics of ERA*; Critchlow, *Phyllis Schlafly and Grassroots Conservatism*. Both the conservative strategist Paul Weyrich and the former vice president of the Moral Majority, Ed Dobson, contend that the threat of government regulation of Christian schools in the late 1970s pushed evangelicals and fundamentalists toward political mobilization. See Cromartie, *No Longer Exiles*, 26, 52. In *Religion and Politics in the United States*, Kenneth Wald sketches a multifactorial explanation for the emergence of the Religious Right, pointing to evangelical socioeconomic gains, status anxieties, institutional growth, and the fact that the civil rights movement, Vietnam, Watergate, and the Carter campaign itself injected a concern for morality into American politics. Along with the growth of evangelical institutions, Wald's emphasis on evangelical socioeconomic gains—which enabled larger contributions to political campaigns—deserves more scholarly attention.

4. Richard Pierard, "The New Religious Right in American Politics," in Marsden, *Evangelicalism and Modern America*, 164, 166.

5. *Bright Side* (internal CCC newsletter for staff and supporters), 15 Dec. 1973, personal papers of Frank Kifer, Hay Market, Va.

6. Interview with Bailey Marks, 11 Feb. 2004; Marks, *Ordinary Businessman*, 43–49.

7. Kim to Marks, 31 Dec. 1971, personal papers of Frank Kifer; *Worldwide Impact*, Sept. 1974. On Korean evangelicalism, see T. Lee, "Born-Again in Korea."

8. *CT*, 13 Sept. 1974, 76; email from Plowman to author, 5 March 2005; Bright to Plowman, 8 Nov. 1974, Records of *CT*, Box 22, Folder 16, BGCA.

9. Letter from Bright to staff and advisory committee members, 26 Nov. 1965, Box 241, Folder 1, HIA; Bright to Graham, 7 Oct. 1971, Records of the Billy Graham Evangelistic Association, Box 98, Folder 1, BGCA; Park, *Protestantism and Politics in Korea*, 184; *CT*, 13 Sept. 1974, 75.

10. *NYT*, 19 Aug. 1974; *Washington Post*, 19 Aug. 1974; Bill Bright, draft of an undated press release, sent to Harold Lindsell, Records of *CT*, Box 22, Folder 16, BGCA.

11. Campus Crusade, like most evangelical organizations, defined "family" as rooted in a marriage relationship between a man and a woman.

12. Interview with Howard Hendricks, 5 Oct. 2004; interview with Ney Bailey, 5 Oct. 2004.

13. Letha Scanzoni, "Christian Perspective on Alternative Styles of Marriage," in Collins, *Make More of Your Marriage*, 166; Scanzoni, "Conservative Christians and Gay Civil Rights"; *WC*, Dec. 1975, 40–41.

14. Interview with Ney Bailey, 5 Oct. 2004; interview with Dennis Rainey, 6 Oct. 2004.

15. *Campus Ministry Manual*, 525, 533, 542.

16. Bright quoted in *WC*, July 1978, 41; *WC*, May 1977, 42–43.

17. *WC*, April 1978, 36, July 1978, 9, May 1979, 35.

18. Bill Bright, *Movement of Miracles*, 39; Richardson, *Amazing Faith*, 161; interview with Howard Ball, 9 Feb. 2004; interview with Glenn Plate, 9 Sept. 2003.

19. Interview with Bruce Cook, 30 July 2004; Carter endorsement in *WC*, Jan. 1976, 56.

20. *WC*, Jan. 1976, 57.

21. Interview with Bruce Cook, 30 July 2004.

22. Ibid.; Bill Bright, "The Countdown to '76" (ca. fall 1975), in Wilbur Smith Papers, "Bright, Bill, Correspondence 1971–1976," Trinity International University Archives, Deerfield, Ill.; *Washington Post*, 27 Feb. 1976. Twenty-five million goal is from *WC*, Nov. 1975, 50.

23. Pierard, "Evangelicals and the Bicentennial," 19; *WC*, July 1976, 49–50.

24. *WC*, Jan. 1976, 17; Bill Bright, *Your Five Duties as a Christian Citizen*, 10, 14, 15; *CT*, 24 Sept. 1976, 22.

25. *WC*, May 1975; *Washington Post*, 13 March 1975; concerns over the purchase from interview with Bruce Bunner, 16 Jan. 2004. Several years later, Crusade was forced to sell the building when it learned that the property's current zoning did not permit its operation by a nonprofit organization.

26. McCollister quoted in Wallis and Michaelson, "Plan to Save America," 9; interviews with Swede Anderson, 21 July 2003, 11 April 2005.

27. Bright to Hoover, 2 July 1970, "William R. Bright" File, FBI, obtained under the Freedom of Information Act; Bright to Judd, 9 June 1975, Box 241, Folder 1, HIA. On Judd, see Edwards, *Missionary for Freedom*. Quotations and information about Conlan from Conlan, *From the Pews to the Polls* (ca. 1976); *Washington Post*, 7 Sept. 1976; *CT*, 24 Sept. 1976, 20.

28. *Moody Monthly*, May 1976, 8–11; "Jewish Telephone Presentation" (1976), personal papers of Jerry Regier, Tallahassee, Fla.; interview with Robert Pittenger, 9 March 2005.

29. Wallis and Michaelson, "Plan to Save America"; interview with Jim Wallis, 22 July 2004. On Wallis and *Sojourners*, see Bivins, *Fracture of Good Order*, chap. 2.

30. DeVos quoted in Wallis and Michaelson, "Plan to Save America"; interview with Jerry Hagee, 6 March 2005; *NYT*, 1 Aug. 1976.

31. *Newsweek*, 6 Sept. 1976, 49–50; interview with Brad Bright, 10 Dec. 2004.

32. Undated circular in RCP; *CT*, 24 Sept. 1976, 22; *Time*, 3 Jan. 1977; Bright to Henry Anatole Grunwald, 4 Jan. 1977, Box 241, Folder 1, HIA; interview with Brad Bright, 10 Dec. 2004.

33. Bright quoted in *Wittenburg Door*, Feb.–March 1977, 15, 22; Quebedeaux quoted in *Wittenburg Door*, June–July 1978, 22; interview with Jim Wallis, 22 July 2004. Ron Sider, who also attended the gathering, remembers Bright's public denunciation of Wallis but does not recall Skinner's response.

34. Alan Nagel and eight other staff members to Bright, 10 Sept. 1976; Spencer and Sherman Brand to Bright, n.d. (ca. fall 1976), both in personal papers of Spencer Brand, Annandale, Va.; interview with Bruce Cook, 30 July 2004.

35. Interview with Swede Anderson, 11 April 2005.

36. *NYT*, 17 April 1977; *Christian Century*, 24 Nov. 1976, 1031; *Chicago Tribune*, 19 Nov. 1976; *Wittenburg Door*, Feb.–March 1977, 12.

37. Conway and Siegelman, *Snapping*, 46; *People*, 4 Dec. 1978, 94; "Backgrounder on *People* Magazine Interview and Campus Crusade Position," personal papers of Dorothy Graham, San Diego, Calif.

38. Bill Bright, *Movement of Miracles*, 73, 159; *WC*, Dec. 1976, 31–32, Feb. 1977, 50, Oct. 1981, 10; Bright to Grunwald, 4 Jan. 1977, HIA.

39. Wagner, "Who Found It?"; interview with Bruce Cook, 30 July 2004; interview with Conrad Koch, 11 Nov. 2003.

40. *Wittenburg Door*, Feb.–March 1977, 13; *In This Generation* (Explo '74 Souvenir Program), personal papers of Kent Hutcheson, Aurora, Colo.

41. Regier quoted in Martin, *With God on Our Side*, 152; Harrell, *Pat Robertson*, 176; Bright inscription in copy of *Movement of Miracles* sent to Carter, 14 Aug. 1977, White House Central Files, "Bill Bright," Jimmy Carter Presidential Library, Atlanta, Ga.; Bright to Carter, 27 June 1977, White House Central Files, "Campus Crusade for Christ," Carter Presidential Library. Using National Election Studies data, political scientist John Green estimates that Carter garnered 48 percent of the 1976 evangelical vote, compared to Ford's 52 percent. This represented a major shift from 1972, when Nixon attracted 80 percent of evangelical votes. Green, "Estimates of Evangelical Voting Behavior, 1960–2004," unpublished analysis, photocopy in author's possession.

Chapter 7

1. Interview with Howard Hendricks, 5 Oct. 2004; *WC*, Jan. 1976, 17.

2. Interview with Tim LaHaye, 29 March 2005.

3. On Lausanne, see Martin, *Prophet with Honor*, 439–55; *Time*, 5 Aug. 1974, 48–50.

4. Bill Bright, *Movement of Miracles*, 154; *WC*, Dec. 1976, 33, Jan. 1977, 10.

5. *WC*, Aug. 1979, 50; interview with Alan Scholes, 16 Sept. 2003; CCC, 1981 Annual Report, personal papers of Frank Kifer, Hay Market, Va.

6. *Cincinnati Enquirer*, 27 June 1971; *NYT*, 15 Nov. 1977; *Wall Street Journal*, 26 Nov. 1975; Carter, *Politics of Rage*, 336; AP article, 3 June 1980, RCP. Hunt's connection with CFF from interview with Jerry Hagee, 6 March 2005.

7. "Campaign Master Plan for Development," Records of the Billy Graham Evangelistic Association, Collection 17, Box 224, Folder 8, BGCA; *NYT*, 15 Nov. 1977; interview with Ron Blue, 29 July 2004.

8. Harrell, *Oral Roberts*, 141–42; Schultze, *Televangelism and American Culture*, 142–43, 172.

9. Bill Bright, *As You Sow*; letter quoted in *National and International Religion Report*, 9 May 1988, 5; Bill Bright, *Believing God for the Impossible*, 102–3, 105; *WC*, June 1980, 50.

10. Alan Nagel et al., to Bright, 13 Jan. 1983, personal papers of Spencer Brand, Annandale, Va.; interview with Ron Blue, 29 July 2004; *WC*, Sept.–Oct. 1991, 56.

11. Hubbard quoted in *Newsweek*, 25 Oct. 1976, 78; *LAT*, 1 June 1981.

12. Interview with Robbie Gowdey, 21 May 2005.

13. CCC, 1981 Annual Report, in author's possession; Bill Bright, preface to Marks and Newhinney, *Awakening in Asia*, 9; *WC*, April 1979, 34; Bill Bright, *Come Help Change the World* (1985), 200, 207; *WC*, May 1981; Marks, foreword to *Awakening in Asia*, 7; *WC*, Nov. 1980, 50.

14. Coote, "Uneven Growth of Conservative Evangelical Missions"; *CT*, 19 Sept. 1980, 44. SBC statistic from "Our History," <http://www.imb.org> (29 July 2007).

15. Interview with John Heyman, 15 March 2005.

16. *Christian Century*, 6 June 2001, 26; Eshleman, *I Just Saw Jesus*, 40–43; Richardson, *Amazing Faith*, 168.

17. Interview with Daniel Fuller, 5 Sept. 2003; Bill Bright, "Message to Staff," 7 Feb. 1983, personal papers of Spencer Brand; *Chosen People*, Feb. 1967, 7, 18; *LAT*, 22 March 1967. On fundamentalist anti-Semitism, see Marsden, *Fundamentalism and American Culture*, 210.

18. *CT*, 24 Sept. 1976, 21; Eshleman, *I Just Saw Jesus*, 48. On the Jerusalem conference, see Boyer, *When Time Shall Be No More*, 188.

19. Eshleman, *I Just Saw Jesus*, 43; interview with John Heyman, 15 March 2005; *Christian Century*, 6–13 June 2001, 31.

20. *Washington Post*, 1 April 1980; *CT*, 21 Dec. 1979, 28–29.

21. Eshleman, *I Just Saw Jesus*, 70–72; *Christian Century*, 6 June 2001, 26–31; interview with John Heyman, 15 March 2005.

22. *NYT*, 8 Feb. 2004; interview with John Heyman, 15 March 2005.

23. Bright memorial service, 21 July 2003, tape in author's possession.

24. *Christian Life*, Feb. 1987, 17; Pierson quoted in Barrett and Reapsome, *Seven Hundred Plans*, 22. On Pierson's plan, see Robert, *Occupy until I Come*, 150–56.

25. Interview with Bailey Marks, 28 March 2005; *Baptist Standard*, 3 Dec. 1997, 15.

26. Zimmerman to Rev. James Swanson, 20 Aug. 1974, FPHC.

27. Interview with Zachary Bright, 2 Feb. 2005; interview with Brad Bright, 10 Dec. 2004.

28. Bright, remarks at faculty luncheon, 12 Nov. 1982, Holy Spirit Research Cen-

ter, Oral Roberts University, Tulsa, Okla.; Eshleman quoted in *Charisma*, Oct. 2001, 45. On the rapid growth of global Pentecostalism, see Jenkins, *Next Christendom*, esp. 60–78; Cox, *Fire from Heaven*.

29. Interview with Bailey Marks, 28 March 2005; *Jesus Film Project Update* (newsletter published by CCC's *Jesus* film ministry) (2001), 6; *NYT*, 8 Feb. 2004.

30. Interview with Jim Wallis, 22 July 2004; interview with Wes Michaelson, 15 June 2004; interview with Arlis Priest, 14 June 2004; interview with Pat Robertson, 23 June 2005.

31. Maddox, *Preacher at the White House*, 161.

32. Interview with Pat Robertson, 23 June 2005; *WC*, Dec. 1979, 32.

33. Interview with James Robison, 12 April 2005; Martin, *With God on Our Side*, 205–6; interview with Robbie Gowdey, 21 May 2005; Hadden and Shupe, *Televangelism*, 24.

34. *CT*, 2 Nov. 1979, 81; Martin, *With God on Our Side*, 209; interview with Robert Pittenger, 9 March 2005.

35. Martin, *With God on Our Side*, 209; interview with James Robison, 12 April 2005.

36. *NYT*, 22 Jan. 1980, 28 Jan. 1980; Maddox, *Preacher at the White House*, 162; Martin, *With God on Our Side*, 189–90; interview with Tim LaHaye, 29 March 2005.

37. Interview with John Gilman, 17 March 2005; interview with John Gimenez, 10 March 2005.

38. *Rock Church Proclaims*, in Richard C. Halverson Papers, Box 40, PTSA; Hadden and Swann, *Prime Time Preachers*, 4; Manuel, *Gathering*, 64–70, 82; *Washington Post*, 15 March 1980; *CT*, 23 May 1980, 46.

39. Interview with Robert Pittenger, 9 March 2005; Hadden and Shupe, *Televangelism*, 22–23; *CT*, 23 May 1980, 46; *Christian Herald*, Nov. 1980, 88; *Sojourners*, June 1980, 10.

40. *WC*, July 1980, 41; *NYT*, 30 April 1980; *Sojourners*, June 1980, 11; *CT*, 23 May 1980, 47.

41. Interview with John Gimenez, 10 March 2005.

42. Interview with Jerry Regier, 27 July 2004; *CT*, 18 July 1980, 64. For more background on debates over the WHCF, see Martin, *With God on Our Side*, 173–89.

43. *NYT*, 7 June 1980; *CT*, 18 July 1980, 64; *NYT*, 13 July 1980; *WC*, Sept. 1980.

44. *Washington Post*, 25 Jan. 1980, 3 July 1980, 31 July 1980.

45. *Washington Post*, 18 July 1980; *NYT*, 21 Aug. 1980; *Wall Street Journal*, 17 Sept. 1980; *NYT*, 23 Aug. 1980; interview with Robert Pittenger, 9 March 2005. Contrary to the *Post*'s report, Bright did not speak at the event.

46. Bright telegram to Thomas Zimmerman, 3 May 1980, FPHC; interview with John Gimenez, 10 March 2005. Reagan won 60 percent of evangelical votes in 1980, compared to Ford's 52 percent in 1976. John Green, "Estimates of Evangelical Voting Behavior, 1960–2004," unpublished analysis, photocopy in author's possession. Several researchers question whether evangelicals and fundamentalists comprised a significant portion of "New Republican" voters in 1980. See Himmelstein and McRae, "Social Conservatism." Much of the difficulty in assessing the evangelical impact in

the 1980 election stems from definitional confusion and the difficulty obtaining data that consistently compare the evangelical vote in the 1976 and 1980 elections, respectively. See Wilcox, "Fundamentalists and Politics." Wilcox, however, concludes that a majority of "denominational fundamentalists" voted for Carter in 1976 but for Reagan in 1980. Without comparing the two elections, Jeffrey Brudney and Gary Copeland suggest that "evangelical" turnout was especially high in 1980 and strongly favored Reagan. See Brudney and Copeland, "Evangelicals as a Political Force." Brudney and Copeland, like most other researchers, contend that evangelical support contributed to but was not decisive for Reagan's victory.

47. Interview with Tim LaHaye, 29 March 2005.

Chapter 8

1. *LAT*, 7 March 1996; interview with Bill Armstrong; interview with Ron Jenson, 3 April 2005; Bright and Jenson, *Kingdoms at War*, 42.

2. *LAT*, 7 March 1996; Bright to Thomas Zimmerman, 2 Nov. 1982, FPHC; *Washington Post*, 12 Feb. 1983; interview with Bill Armstrong, 9 March 2005.

3. Bright and Jenson, *Kingdoms at War*, 16; Vonette Bright to Richard C. Halverson, 20 July 1990, Halverson Papers, Box 39, PTSA; *CT*, 4 April 1986, 43.

4. Bright to Zimmerman, 17 Jan. 1987, FPHC; *NYT*, 21 July 1988, 12 Aug. 1988; *LAT*, 13 July 1988.

5. Bright to Halverson, 10 April 1990, Halverson Papers, Box 6; Bright and Damoose, *Red Sky in the Morning*, 174; Bill Bright, foreword to Brad Bright, *God Is the Issue*, 9. On the ADF, see *New Yorker*, 21 March 2005, 62–71.

6. "September: Road to Victory Watch—Day Two," <http://www.pfaw.org/pfaw/general/default.aspx?oid=3936> (26 July 2006); Boston, *Close Encounters with the Religious Right*, 60. On the CNP, see *NYT*, 20 May 1981; *Baton Rouge State-Times*, 8 Jan. 1987.

7. Bill Bright, *Come Help Change the World* (1985), 236–37; *WC*, Aug. 1978, 9–11; interview with Ted Martin, 6 Sept. 2003.

8. Donovan, *Pat Robertson*, 156–60; Noll, *Scandal of the Evangelical Mind*, 17; Lucas, *American Higher Education*, 316; email from Kathryn Long to author, 27 June 2006.

9. *WC*, Nov. 1977, 29–30; Bill Bright, *Come Help Change the World* (1985), 235; *WC*, Aug. 1978, 35. On the influence of Schaeffer, see Martin, *With God on Our Side*, 195–97.

10. Interview with Pat MacMillan, 29 July 2004; interview with Howard Hendricks, 5 Oct. 2004; *WC*, Dec. 1979, 43–44; *LAT*, May 10, 1983; interview with Robbie Gowdey, 21 May 2005.

11. Information on emergency meeting from interview with Conrad Koch, 11 Nov. 2003; interview with Bob Horner, 14 April 2004; *Campus Ministry Manual*, 542; Bill Bright, "Message to Staff," 7 Feb. 1983, personal papers of Spencer Brand, Annandale, Va.

12. Bill Bright, *Come Help Change the World* (1985), 239; *CT*, 3 Feb. 1984; interview with Brad Bright, 10 Dec. 2004; *San Diego Union*, 30 Aug. 1984.

13. *CT*, 19 Oct. 1984; *San Diego Tribune*, 12 Sept. 1984, 26 Sept. 1985.

14. *LAT*, 6 Nov. 1985; interview with Brad Bright, 10 Dec. 2004; *LAT*, 4 June 1987; interview with Bailey Marks, 28 March 2005.

15. Bright letter to staff, 11 Dec. 1986, FPHC; interview with Conrad Koch, 11 Nov. 2003.

16. *Chronicle of Higher Education*, 17 June 2005, A17.

17. "Danvers Statement," <http://www.cbmw.org/about/danvers.php> (7 Nov. 2006); *Family Manifesto*.

18. Interview with Dennis Rainey, 6 Oct. 2004.

19. *Journal for Biblical Manhood and Womanhood*, Spring 1999, 5–6; Hankins, *Uneasy in Babylon*, chap. 7; interview with Dennis Rainey, 6 Oct. 2004.

20. Rainey and Bright quoted in *Journal for Biblical Manhood and Womanhood*, Spring 1999, 3, 5; interview with Dennis Rainey, 6 Oct. 2004. On the symbolic importance of gender issues within the evangelical community, see Chaves, *Ordaining Women*; Hankins, *Uneasy in Babylon*, chap. 7.

21. Wilcox, *Soft Patriarchs*, 9; Watt, *Transforming Faith*, 131–36; demographics of board in CCC, 2004 Annual Report, in author's possession; interview with Gwen Martin, 6 Sept. 2003; interview with Steve Sellers, 11 Feb. 2004. On the symbolism of evangelical gender rhetoric, see also Gallagher and Smith, "Symbolic Traditionalism and Pragmatic Egalitarianism."

22. Addendum quoted in *Journal for Biblical Manhood and Womanhood*, Spring 1999; Bright quoted in *World*, 11 Sept. 1999, 32.

23. *CT*, 22 June 1992, 70; interview with Steve Sellers, 11 Feb. 2004; interview with Gwen Martin, 6 Sept. 2003; interview with Dennis Rainey, 6 Oct. 2004.

24. Bill Bright, *Coming Revival*, 32, 59; *National Religious Broadcasters*, Nov. 2000, 22, 24; *Montgomery Journal*, 7 Feb. 2000. On the conflicts at Tufts and Middlebury, see *CT*, 12 June 2000, 24; *Washington Times*, 16 May 2000.

25. Interview with Dennis Rainey, 6 Oct. 2004; FamilyLife press release, 19 Nov. 2003, <http://www.familylife.com>, in author's personal collection.

26. *Family Room*, March 2004, Sept. 2004, Oct. 2004; *Washington Post*, 15 Oct. 2004; "Dennis Rainey at Mayday for Marriage," <http://www.familylife.com/vote/mayday _notes.asp> (20 July 2006).

27. On gay marriage and the 2004 election, see Green, Rozell, and Wilcox, *Values Campaign?*, introduction, chaps. 3 and 4.

28. FamilyLife, 2005 Annual Report, <http://www.familylife.com/donations/ 2005_Ministry_Report.pdf> (7 Nov. 2006); interview with Dennis Rainey, 6 Oct. 2004.

29. *National Religious Broadcasters*, Nov. 2000, 22.

30. Interview with Steve Sellers, 11 Feb. 2004; *Philadelphia Inquirer*, 31 Dec. 1984; *CT*, 7 March 1986, 44–45. On changes in campus culture during these years, see Horowitz, *Campus Life*, chaps. 11 and 12; Sperber, *Beer and Circus*, 3–11.

31. *LAT*, 26 Dec. 1981; interview with Crawford Lorritts, 19 April 2005; *CT*, 27 May 1991, 62.

32. Interview with Steve Sellers, 11 Feb. 2004; Chen quoted in *CT*, April 2006, 70.

On white discomfort with ministries that attract large numbers of Asian American students, see Kim, *God's New Whiz Kids?*, chap. 6.

33. *Chronicle of Higher Education*, 18 May 2001, A42; *Virginian-Pilot*, 17 June 2001; *Would You Like to Know God Personally?*; Bright quoted in *National Religious Broadcasters*, Nov. 2000, 24.

34. *CT*, 4 March 1996, 69. The campaigns can be viewed at <http://www.escmedia. org/campaigns/index.html>.

35. *Lantern* (Ohio State University newspaper), 3 March 2005; *Boston Globe*, 30 Nov. 2003.

36. Statistics provided by CCC, courtesy of Mike Nyfeller. On levels of educational attainment by religion, see Beyerlein, "Specifying the Impact of Conservative Protestantism on Educational Attainment." On the growing affluence of evangelicals, see Schmalzbauer, *People of Faith*, chap. 2; *NYT*, 22 May 2005.

37. Bright quoted in *National Religious Broadcasters*, Nov. 2000, 22–23; Marsden, *Soul of the American University*, 441–42, n. 7; interview with Walter Bradley, 21 July 2003. For recent statistics on the religious affiliation and beliefs of university professors in the natural and social sciences, see Elaine Howard Ecklund and Christopher P. Scheitle, "Religious Differences between Natural and Social Scientists: Preliminary Results from a Study of 'Religion among Academic Scientists,'" conference paper, 2005 Annual Meeting of the Association for the Sociology of Religion; Neil Gross and Solon Simmons, "How Religious Are America's College and University Professors?," working paper, 5 Oct. 2006. According to Gross and Simmons, 17 percent of faculty at secular institutions describe themselves as "born-again Christians," compared to roughly 40 percent of the general population. John Schmalzbauer suggests that the number and visibility of faculty with strong religious convictions has risen in recent decades. See Schmalzbauer, *People of Faith*. For other aspects of the revival of academic interest in religion, see Schmalzbauer and Mahoney, "Return of Religion in the Academy."

38. John Schmalzbauer, "Campus Ministry: A Statistical Portrait," <http://www. religion.ssrc.org/reforum/Schmalzbauer/> (27 April 2007); *NYT*, 22 May 2005; Marsden, *Soul of the American University*, 411; Kim, *God's New Whiz Kids?*, 1; Busto, "Gospel according to the Model Minority?," 173.

39. The conclusion of this paragraph reflects the argument of Christian Smith in *American Evangelicalism*.

40. Kim, *God's New Whiz Kids?*, 1; Cherry, DeBerg, and Porterfield, *Religion on Campus*, 282.

41. Riley, *God on the Quad*, 7.

Conclusion

1. Details on the 2003 staff conference and Bright memorial service from author's own notes and tapes of the conference.

2. Bill Bright, *Journey Home*, 5.

3. "Evangelicals and Catholics Together." On Crusade's partnerships with Catho-

lics in Eastern Europe, see Scott, "Evangelicals and Catholics Really Together." On broader trends, see Rausch, *Catholics and Evangelicals*, esp. chap. 2, "Catholic-Evangelical Relations: Signs of Progress."

4. *NYT*, 7 March 1996; *Ecumenical Trends*, July–Aug. 1996, 15–16.

5. *CT*, 28 Oct. 1991, 44, 16 Aug. 1993, 38–39; *Charisma*, Oct. 2001, 46; interview with Brad Bright, 10 Dec. 2004; interview with Zachary Bright, 2 Feb. 2005. For background on Hinn, see the *Globe and Mail* (Toronto), 15 Feb. 1978.

6. *Charisma*, Oct. 2001, 46–47; Bright and Dekker, *Blessed Child*, 350; interview with Zachary Bright, 2 Feb. 2005.

7. CCC, "Statement of Faith," <http://www.ccci.org/statement_of_faith.html> (27 April 2007); *WC*, "A Separate Peace" (1991 special issue), 19–25; *WC*, Sept.–Oct. 2003; interview with Tony Campolo, 17 May 2005; Campolo, *Reasonable Faith*; interview with Peter Gillquist, 13 Jan. 2004; interview with Daniel Fuller, 5 Sept. 2003; interview with Jim Wallis, 22 July 2004; Wallis, "Power of Reconciliation." On the rift with Campolo, see *CT*, 20 Sept. 1985, 30–38; *CT*, 13 Dec. 1985.

8. Interview with Zachary Bright, 2 Feb. 2005.

9. Interview with Louis Scroggin, 12 May 2004.

10. CCC, 2005 Annual Report, in author's possession.

11. Interview with Tim LaHaye, 29 March 2005.

12. Bright, memo to staff, 1 Nov. 2002, personal collection of author; AP State and Local Wire, 14 July 2001 (10 Nov. 2006); Richard C. Land, Chuck Colson, Bill Bright, D. James Kennedy, and Carl D. Herbster to George W. Bush, 3 Oct. 2002, <http://www.erlc.com/article/the-so-called-land-letter> (16 July 2007).

13. Estimate of 2004 evangelical vote from John Green, "Estimates of Evangelical Voting Behavior, 1960–2004," unpublished analysis, photocopy in author's possession; Moore, *Religious Outsiders*, 157; Wallis article, *Time*, 16 Feb. 2007, <http://www.time.com/time/nation/article/0,8599,1590782,00.html> (27 April 2007). On Bush's visit to Calvin, see *NYT*, 23 May 2005.

14. Dobson and Thomas, *Blinded by Might*; Joseph L. Conn, "Rift on the Right," *Church and State*, April 1999, 4–6; Kuo, *Tempting Faith*; conversation with Steve Douglass, 21 Nov. 2005.

15. Douglass, *Our Future Direction* (CCC, 2003); "A Message from Our President" (Steve Douglass), <http://www.lakehart.org/president_letter.shtm> (30 July 2006). On the growth of Christianity in the developing world, see Jenkins, *Next Christendom*.

Bibliography

Archival Collections

Bob Jones University, J. S. Mack Library, Fundamentalism File, Greenville, S.C.
  Campus Crusade for Christ File
  Bob Jones Jr. Correspondence
  Gilbert Stenholm Papers
  G. Archer Weniger Papers
Spencer Brand Personal Papers. Annandale, Va.
Campus Crusade for Christ Archives. Orlando, Fla.
Jimmy Carter Presidential Library. Atlanta, Ga.
  White House Central Files
Federal Bureau of Investigation. Washington, D.C.
  "William R. Bright" File
Flower Pentecostal Heritage Center, Assemblies of God. Springfield, Mo.
  Thomas Zimmerman Papers
Fuller Theological Seminary Archives. Pasadena, Calif.
  Daniel P. Fuller Papers
  Wilbur Smith Papers
General Commission on Archives and History, United Methodist Church.
    Madison, N.J.
  Records of the General Board of Higher Education and Ministry
Peter Gillquist Personal Papers. Goleta, Calif.
Gospel Light Archives. Ventura, Calif.
  Henrietta Mears Papers
Billy Graham Center Archives. Wheaton, Ill.
  Lemuel Nelson Bell Papers
  Walter F. Bennett & Company Collection
  Christianity Today records
  Billy Graham Evangelistic Association records
  Inter-Varsity Christian Fellowship records
  Charles Troutman Papers
Dorothy Hauser Graham Personal Papers. San Diego, Calif.
Ralph Hamburger Personal Papers. Pasadena, Calif.

Holy Spirit Research Center, Oral Roberts University. Tulsa, Okla.
    Oral Roberts University Records
Hoover Institution Archives. Stanford, Calif.
    Walter H. Judd Papers
J. Kent Hutcheson Personal Papers. Aurora, Colo.
Frank Kifer Personal Papers. Hay Market, Va.
Ted Martin Personal Papers. Crestline, Calif.
National Archives and Records Administration. College Park, Md.
    Nixon Presidential Material
Ockenga Institute, Gordon-Conwell Theological Seminary. South Hamilton, Mass.
    Harold J. Ockenga Papers
Princeton Theological Seminary Archives. Princeton, N.J.
    Richard C. Halverson Papers
    John MacKay Papers
Jerry Regier Personal Papers. Tallahassee, Fla.
Trinity International University Archives. Deerfield, Ill.
    Wilbur Smith Papers
University of California at Los Angeles, University Archives. Los Angeles, Calif.
    Chancellors Office, Administrative Files
University of California at Santa Barbara, Special Collections. Santa Barbara, Calif.
    American Religions Collection, Russell Chandler Papers

Interviews Conducted by the Author

Swede Anderson, 21 July 2003, Fort Collins, Colo.
Swede Anderson, 11 April 2005, telephone
Bill Armstrong, 9 March 2005, telephone
Ney Bailey, 5 Oct. 2004, Frisco, Tex.
Howard Ball, 9 Feb. 2004, Orlando, Fla.
Greg Barnett, 17 March 2004, telephone
Candy Bayliss, 18 June 2004, telephone
Ron Blue, 29 July 2004, Atlanta, Ga.
Walter Bradley, 21 July 2003, Fort Collins, Colo.
Jon Braun, 15 Jan. 2004, telephone
Brad Bright, 10 Dec. 2004, Orlando, Fla.
Charley Bright, 4 Oct. 2004, Porter, Okla.
Zachary Bright, 2 Feb. 2005, Irwindale, Calif.
Esther Brinkley, 12 Sept. 2003, Pasadena, Calif.
Esther Brinkley, 2 Dec. 2003, telephone
Roe Brooks, 3 Dec. 2003, telephone
Dale Bruner, 13 Sept. 2003, Pasadena, Calif.
Dale Bruner, 6 March 2004, telephone
Bruce Bunner, 16 Jan. 2004, Weston, Conn.
Tony Campolo, 17 May 2005, telephone

Peggy T. Cantwell, 13 Jan. 2004, telephone
Jens Christy, 13 Jan. 2004, telephone
Bruce Cook, 30 July 2004, Atlanta, Ga.
Dave Coterill, 17 May 2004, telephone
Beverly Counts, 6 Jan. 2004, telephone
Bill Counts, 6 Jan. 2004, telephone
Bill Counts, 7 Oct. 2004, Dallas, Tex.
Jim Craddock, 29 March 2004, telephone
Lauralil Deats, 30 Sept. 2003, telephone
Gary Demarest, 11 Sept. 2003, Pasadena, Calif.
Lee Etta Dickerson, 15 April 2004, telephone
Richard Edic, 21 March 2004, telephone
Gene Edwards, 15 Dec. 2004, telephone
Rose Essick, 9 Sept. 2003, Burbank, Calif.
Colleen Townsend Evans, 8 Oct. 2003, telephone
Louis H. Evans Jr., 8 Sept. 2003, Bakersfield, Calif.
Louis H. Evans Jr., 15 Oct. 2003, telephone
Ted Franzle, 3 Oct. 2003, telephone
Daniel Fuller, 5 Sept. 2003, Pasadena, Calif.
Daniel Fuller, 28 June 2004, telephone
Peter Gillquist, 13 Jan. 2004, telephone
John Gilman, 17 March 2005, telephone
John Gimenez, 10 March 2005, telephone
John Goodwin, 13 April 2004, telephone
Robbie Gowdey, 21 May 2005, telephone
Dorothy Graham, 30 Dec. 2003, telephone
Jim Green, 9 Sept. 2003, San Clemente, Calif.
William Greig Jr., 1 Oct. 2003, telephone
Jerry Hagee, 6 March 2005, telephone
Jim Halls, 3 Oct. 2003, telephone
Howard Hendricks, 5 Oct. 2004, Dallas, Tex.
John Heyman, 15 March 2005, telephone
Alan Hlavka, 27 Jan. 2005, telephone
Bob Horner, 8 April 2004, telephone
Bob Horner, 14 April 2004, telephone
Ron Jenson, 3 April 2005, Rancho Bernardo, Calif.
Robert Kendall, 7 Feb. 2004, New Port Richey, Fla.
Anna Kerr, 10 Sept. 2003, Hollywood, Calif.
Anna Kerr, 25 May 2004, telephone
Frank Kifer, 24 July 2004, Vienna, Va.
Gordon Klenck, 20 July 2003, Fort Collins, Colo.
Gordon Klenck, 10 Dec. 2003, telephone
Gordon Klenck, 8 April 2004, telephone
Conrad Koch, 11 Nov. 2003, Avon, Conn.

Tim LaHaye, 29 March 2005, telephone
Barry Leventhal, 1 Dec. 2004, telephone
Jan Lindsey, 6 Jan. 2004, telephone
Crawford Lorritts, 19 April 2005, telephone
Curt Mackey, 9 Jan. 2004, telephone
Lois Mackey, 9 Jan. 2004, telephone
Pat MacMillan, 29 July 2004, Atlanta, Ga.
Bailey Marks, 11 Feb. 2004, Orlando, Fla.
Bailey Marks, 28 March 2005, telephone
Gwen Martin, 6 Sept. 2003, Crestline, Calif.
Ted Martin, 6 Sept. 2003, Crestline, Calif.
Kundan Massey, 11 May 2004, telephone
Joanne McClurkin, 17 May 2004, telephone
Wes Michaelson, 15 June 2004, telephone
Donn Moomaw, 11 Sept. 2003, Los Angeles, Calif.
Donn Moomaw, 15 March 2004, telephone
Ray Nethery, 21 Dec. 2003, telephone
Earl Palmer, 23 Feb. 2004, telephone
Robert Pittenger, 9 March 2005, telephone
Glenn Plate, 9 Sept. 2003, San Diego, Calif.
Arlis Priest, 14 May 2004, telephone
Arlis Priest, 14 June 2004, telephone
Dennis Rainey, 6 Oct. 2004, Little Rock, Ark.
Jerry Regier, 27 July 2004, Tallahassee, Fla.
Deanne Rice, 2 Oct. 2004, Tulsa, Okla.
Pat Robertson, 23 June 2005, telephone
James Robison, 12 April 2005, telephone
Alan Scholes, 16 Sept. 2003, Fallbrook, Calif.
Louis Scroggin, 12 May 2004, telephone
Steve Sellers, 11 Feb. 2004, Orlando, Fla.
Ronald Sider, 26 July 2004, telephone
Dale Smith, 12 Dec. 2003, telephone
Thomas Trask, 7 July 2004, telephone
Gordon Walker, 8 March 2004, telephone
Jim Wallis, 22 July 2004, Washington, D.C.
Jimmy Williams, 22 Jan. 2004, telephone
Jimmy Williams, 5 Oct. 2004, Dallas, Tex.
Ralph Winter, 12 Sept. 2003, Pasadena, Calif.
Roy Curtis Zachary, 4 Oct. 2004, Tulsa, Okla.

Periodicals Consulted

Campus Crusade Communique. Los Angeles, Calif.
Charisma. Altamonte Springs, Fla.

Christian Century. Chicago, Ill.
Christianity Today. Carol Stream, Ill.
Christian Life. Wheaton, Ill.
Collegiate Challenge. San Bernardino, Calif.
Daily Bruin. Los Angeles, Calif.
Daily Californian. Berkeley, Calif.
Dallas Morning News. Dallas, Tex.
Dallas Times Herald. Dallas, Tex.
Evangelical Christian. Willowdale, Ont.
Journal for Biblical Manhood and Womanhood. Libertyville, Ill.
Los Angeles Times. Los Angeles, Calif.
Northeastern. Tahlequah, Okla.
San Diego Tribune. San Diego, Calif.
San Diego Union. San Diego, Calif.
Sojourners. Washington, D.C.
Sword of the Lord. Dallas, Tex.
United Evangelical Action. Wheaton, Ill.
Washington Post. Washington, D.C.
Wittenburg Door. San Diego, Calif.
Worldwide Challenge. San Bernardino, Calif., and Orlando, Fla.
Worldwide Impact. San Bernardino, Calif.

Articles

Bederman, Gail. "'The Women Have Had Charge of the Church Work Long
    Enough': The Men and Religion Forward Movement of 1911–1912 and the
    Masculinization of Middle-Class Protestantism." *American Quarterly* 41 (Sept.
    1989): 432–65.
Bendroth, Margaret. "Why Women Loved Billy Sunday: Urban Revivalism and
    Popular Entertainment in Early Twentieth-Century American Culture."
    Religion and American Culture 14 (Summer 2004): 251–71.
Beyerlein, Kraig. "Specifying the Impact of Conservative Protestantism on Edu-
    cational Attainment." *Journal for the Scientific Study of Religion* 43 (Dec. 2004):
    505–18.
Board, Stephen. "The Great Evangelical Power Shift." *Eternity*, June 1979, 17–21.
Bright, Bill. "Christianity on the Campus." *American Mercury*, Dec. 1956, 137–43.
———. "The Truth about Hollywood." *Christian Life*, July 1950, 10–12, 40, 42.
Brudney, Jeffrey L., and Gary W. Copeland. "Evangelicals as a Political Force:
    Reagan and the 1980 Religious Vote." *Social Science Quarterly* 65 (Dec. 1984):
    1072–1079.
Busto, Rudy V. "The Gospel according to the Model Minority? Hazarding an In-
    terpretation of Asian American Evangelical College Students." In *Spiritual
    Homes: Religion and Asian Americans*, edited by David Yoo and Russell Leong,
    169–87. Honolulu: University of Hawaii Press, 1999.

Carroll, Michael P. "Upstart Theories and Early American Religiosity: A Reassessment." *Religion* 34 (April 2004): 129–43.

Coote, Robert T. "The Uneven Growth of Conservative Evangelical Missions." *International Bulletin of Missionary Research* 6 (July 1982): 118–23.

Eskridge, Larry. "'One Way': Billy Graham, the Jesus Generation, and the Idea of an Evangelical Youth Culture." *Church History* 67 (March 1998): 83–106.

"Evangelicals and Catholics Together: The Christian Mission in the Third Millennium." *First Things* 43 (May 1994): 15–22.

Gallagher, Sally K., and Christian Smith. "Symbolic Traditionalism and Pragmatic Egalitarianism: Contemporary Evangelicals, Family, and Gender." *Gender and Society* 13 (April 1999): 211–33.

Hamilton, Michael S. "Women, Public Ministry, and American Fundamentalism, 1920–1950." *Religion and American Culture* 3 (Summer 1993): 171–96.

Hammond, Phillip E., and Robert E. Mitchell. "Segmentation of Radicalism: The Case of the Protestant Campus Minister." *American Journal of Sociology* 71 (Sept. 1965): 133–43.

Heinz, Donald. "The Christian World Liberation Front." In *The New Religious Consciousness*, edited by Charles Y. Glock and Robert N. Bellah, 143–61. Berkeley: University of California Press, 1976.

Heinze, Andrew R. "*Peace of Mind* (1946): Judaism and the Therapeutic Polemics of Postwar America." *Religion and American Culture* 12 (Winter 2002): 31–58.

Henry, Carl F. H. "American Evangelicals in a Turning Time." *Christian Century*, 5 Nov. 1980, 1058–62.

Hijiya, James A. "The Conservative 1960s." *Journal of American Studies* 37 (Aug. 2003): 201–27.

Himmelstein, Jerome L., and James A. McRae Jr. "Social Conservatism, New Republicans, and the 1980 Election." *Public Opinion Quarterly* 48 (Autumn 1984): 592–605.

Hoke, Don. "Sketch of the Month." *Youth for Christ Magazine*, Jan. 1950, 24–27.

Hout, Michael, Andrew Greeley, and Melissa J. Wilde. "The Demographic Imperative in Religious Change in the United States." *American Journal of Sociology* 107 (Sept. 2001): 468–500.

Lee, Joseph Tse-Hei. "Watchman Nee and the Little Flock Movement in Maoist China." *Church History* 74 (March 2005): 68–96.

Massa, Mark S., S.J. "A Catholic for President?: John F. Kennedy and the 'Secular' Theology of the Houston Speech, 1960." *Journal of Church and State* 39 (Spring 1997): 297–317.

Miller, Douglas T. "Popular Religion of the 1950s: Norman Vincent Peale and Billy Graham." *Journal of Popular Culture* 9 (Summer 1975): 66–76.

Niebuhr, H. Richard. "Fundamentalism." In *Encyclopaedia of the Social Sciences*, edited by Edwin R. A. Seligman, vol. 6, 526–27. New York: Macmillan, 1930–34.

Ostrander, Richard. "The Battery and the Windmill: Two Models of Protestant Devotionalism in Early-Twentieth-Century America." *Church History* 65 (March 1996): 42–61.

Pierard, Richard V. "Evangelicals and the Bicentennial." *Reformed Journal*, Oct. 1976, 19–23.

Robert, Dana L. "Shifting Southward: Global Christianity since 1945." *International Bulletin of Missionary Research* 24 (April 2000): 50–58.

Scanzoni, Letha. "Conservative Christians and Gay Civil Rights." *Christian Century*, 13 Oct. 1976, 857–62.

Schmalzbauer, John, and Kathleen A. Mahoney. "The Return of Religion in the Academy." Forthcoming.

Scott, David Hill. "Evangelicals and Catholics Really Together in Poland, 1975–1982." *Fides et Historia* 34 (Winter–Spring 2002): 89–109.

Shelley, Bruce. "The Rise of Evangelical Youth Movements." *Fides et Historia* 18 (Jan. 1986): 47–63.

Smith, Timothy. "The Evangelical Kaleidoscope and the Call to Christian Unity." *Christian Scholar's Review* 15 (1986): 125–40.

Sweeney, Douglas A. "The Essential Evangelicalism Dialectic: The Historiography of the Early Neo-Evangelical Movement and the Observer-Participant Dilemma." *Church History* 60 (March 1991): 70–84.

Turner, John G. "The Power behind the Throne: Henrietta Mears and Post–World War II Evangelicalism." *Journal of Presbyterian History* 83 (Fall–Winter 2005): 141–57.

Wacker, Grant. "Travail of a Broken Family: Evangelical Responses to Pentecostalism in America, 1906–1916." *Journal of Ecclesiastical History* 47 (July 1996): 505–28.

Wagner, C. Peter. "Who Found It?" *Eternity*, Sept. 1977, 12–19.

Wallis, Jim. "The Power of Reconciliation." *Sojourners*, Nov. 2004, 5–6.

Wallis, Jim, and Wes Michaelson. "The Plan to Save America." *Sojourners*, April 1976, 4–12.

Wilcox, Clyde. "Fundamentalists and Politics: An Analysis of the Effects of Differing Operational Definitions." *Journal of Politics* 48 (Nov. 1986): 1041–51.

Books

Abrams, Douglas Carl. *Selling the Old-Time Religion: American Fundamentalists and Mass Culture, 1920–1940.* Athens: University of Georgia Press, 2001.

Andrew, John A. *The Other Side of the Sixties: Young Americans for Freedom and the Rise of Conservative Politics.* New Brunswick, N.J.: Rutgers University Press, 1997.

Bachrack, Stanley D. *The Committee of One Million: "China Lobby" Politics, 1953–1971.* New York: Columbia University Press, 1976.

Baldwin, Ethel May, and David V. Benson. *Henrietta Mears and How She Did It!* Glendale, Calif.: Regal Books, 1966.

Balmer, Randall. *Blessed Assurance: A History of Evangelicalism in America.* Boston: Beacon Press, 1999.

Barrett, David B., and James W. Reapsome. *Seven Hundred Plans to Evangelize the*

World: The Rise of a Global Evangelization Movement. Birmingham, Ala.: New Hope, 1988.

Bebbington, D. W. *Evangelicalism in Modern Britain: A History from the 1730s to the 1980s.* London: Unwin Hyman, 1989.

Bendroth, Margaret Lamberts. *Fundamentalism and Gender: 1875 to the Present.* New Haven: Yale University Press, 1993.

Bergler, Thomas E. "Winning America: Christian Youth Groups and the Middle-Class Culture of Crisis, 1930–1965." Ph.D. diss., University of Notre Dame, 2000.

Bettger, Frank. *How I Raised Myself from Failure to Success at Selling.* Englewood Cliffs, N.J.: Prentice-Hall, 1949.

Bivins, Jason. *The Fracture of Good Order: Christian Antiliberalism and the Challenge to American Politics.* Chapel Hill: University of North Carolina Press, 2003.

Boston, Robert. *Close Encounters with the Religious Right: Journeys into the Twilight Zone of Religion and Politics.* Amherst, N.Y.: Prometheus Books, 2000.

Boyer, Paul. *When Time Shall Be No More: Prophecy Belief in Modern America.* Cambridge, Mass.: Harvard University Press, 1992.

Bright, Bill. *As You Sow.* San Bernardino, Calif.: Here's Life, 1989.

———. *Believing God for the Impossible: A Call to Supernatural Living.* San Bernardino, Calif.: Here's Life, 1979.

———. *Come Help Change the World.* Old Tappan, N.J.: Fleming H. Revell, 1970.

———. *Come Help Change the World.* San Bernardino, Calif.: Here's Life, 1985.

———. *The Coming Revival: America's Call to Fast, Pray, and "Seek God's Face."* Orlando: NewLife Publications, 1995.

———. *Have You Heard of the Four Spiritual Laws?* San Bernardino, Calif.: Campus Crusade for Christ, 1965.

———. *How to Love by Faith.* San Bernardino, Calif.: Campus Crusade for Christ, 1971.

———. *The Journey Home: Finishing with Joy.* Nashville: Thomas Nelson, 2003.

———. *A Movement of Miracles.* San Bernardino, Calif.: Campus Crusade for Christ International, 1977.

———. *Witnessing without Fear.* San Bernardino, Calif.: Here's Life, 1987.

———. *Your Five Duties as a Christian Citizen.* San Bernardino, Calif.: Christians Concerned for More Responsible Citizenship, 1976.

Bright, Bill, and John N. Damoose. *Red Sky in the Morning.* Orlando: NewLife, 1998.

Bright, Bill, and Ted Dekker. *Blessed Child.* Nashville: Word, 2001.

Bright, Bill, and Ron Jenson. *Kingdoms at War.* San Bernardino, Calif.: Here's Life, 1986.

Bright, Brad. *God Is the Issue: Recapturing the Cultural Initiative.* Peachtree City, Ga.: NewLife, 2003.

Bright, Vonette Z. *For Such a Time as This.* Old Tappan, N.J.: Fleming H. Revell, 1976.

Bruce, Steve. *God Is Dead: Secularization in the West.* Malden, Mass.: Blackwell, 2002.

Buckley, William F., Jr. *God and Man at Yale: The Superstitions of Academic Freedom.* Chicago: Henry Regnery, 1951.

Butler, Farley Porter, Jr. "Billy Graham and the End of Evangelical Unity." Ph.D. diss., University of Florida, 1976.

Campolo, Anthony. *A Reasonable Faith: Responding to Secularism.* Waco, Tex.: Word, 1983.

Campus Ministry Manual. San Bernardino, Calif.: Campus Crusade for Christ International, 1974.

Carpenter, Joel A. *Revive Us Again: The Reawakening of American Fundamentalism.* New York: Oxford, 1997.

———, ed. *A New Evangelical Coalition: Early Documents of the National Association of Evangelicals.* New York: Garland, 1988.

Carroll, Jackson W., Douglas W. Johnson, and Martin E. Marty. *Religion in America: 1950 to the Present.* San Francisco: Harper & Row, 1979.

Carter, Dan T. *The Politics of Rage: George Wallace, the Origins of the New Conservatism, and the Transformation of American Politics.* New York: Simon & Schuster, 1995.

Chappell, David L. *A Stone of Hope: Prophetic Religion and the Death of Jim Crow.* Chapel Hill: University of North Carolina Press, 2004.

Chaves, Mark. *Ordaining Women: Culture and Conflict in Religious Organizations.* Cambridge, Mass.: Harvard University Press, 1997.

Cherry, Conrad, Betty A. DeBerg, and Amanda Porterfield. *Religion on Campus.* Chapel Hill: University of North Carolina Press, 2001.

Collins, Gary, ed. *Make More of Your Marriage.* Waco, Tex.: Word, 1976.

Conlan, John. *From the Pews to the Polls.* N.p., n.d.

Conway, Flo, and Jim Siegelman. *Snapping: America's Epidemic of Sudden Personality Change.* Philadelphia: Lippincott, 1978.

Cox, Harvey. *Fire from Heaven: The Rise of Pentecostal Spirituality and the Reshaping of Religion in the Twenty-First Century.* Reading, Mass.: Addison-Wesley, 1994.

Critchlow, Donald T. *Phyllis Schlafly and Grassroots Conservatism: A Woman's Crusade.* Princeton, N.J.: Princeton University Press, 2005.

Cromartie, Michael, ed. *No Longer Exiles: The Religious New Right in American Politics.* Washington, D.C.: Ethics and Public Policy Center, 1992.

Cuordileone, K. A. *Manhood and American Political Culture in the Cold War.* New York: Routledge, 2005.

Dalhouse, Mark Taylor. *An Island in the Lake of Fire: Bob Jones University, Fundamentalism, and the Separatist Movement.* Athens: University of Georgia Press, 1996.

Dobson, Ed, and Cal Thomas. *Blinded by Might: Can the Religious Right Save America?* Grand Rapids: Zondervan, 1999.

Dochuk, Darren T. "From Bible Belt to Sunbelt: Plain Folk Religion, Grassroots Politics, and the Southernization of Southern California, 1939–1969." Ph.D. diss., University of Notre Dame, 2005.

Dollar, George W. *A History of Fundamentalism in America.* Greenville, S.C.: Bob Jones University Press, 1973.

Donovan, John B. *Pat Robertson: The Authorized Biography*. New York: Macmillan, 1988.

Douglass, Steve. *Our Future Direction*. Campus Crusade for Christ, 2003.

Dunn, Charles W. *Campus Crusade: Its Message and Methods*. Greenville, S.C.: Bob Jones University Press, 1980.

Edwards, Lee. *Missionary for Freedom: The Life and Times of Walter Judd*. New York: Paragon House, 1990.

Ehrman, John. *The Eighties: America in the Age of Reagan*. New Haven: Yale University Press, 2005.

Ellwood, Robert S. *The Fifties Spiritual Marketplace: American Religion in a Decade of Conflict*. New Brunswick, N.J.: Rutgers University Press, 1997.

———. *One Way: The Jesus Movement and Its Meaning*. Englewood Cliffs, N.J.: Prentice-Hall, 1973.

Enroth, Ronald M., Edward E. Ericson Jr., and C. Breckinridge Peters. *The Jesus People: Old-Time Religion in the Age of Aquarius*. Grand Rapids: Eerdmans, 1972.

Eshleman, Paul. *I Just Saw Jesus*. San Bernardino, Calif.: Here's Life, 1985.

Eshleman, Paul, with Norman B. Rohrer. *The EXPLO Story: A Plan to Change the World*. Glendale, Calif.: G/L Regal Books, 1972.

Eskridge, Larry, and Mark A. Noll, eds. *More Money, More Ministry: Money and Evangelicals in Recent North American History*. Grand Rapids: Eerdmans, 2000.

Evensen, Bruce J. *God's Man for the Gilded Age: D. L. Moody and the Rise of Modern Mass Evangelism*. New York: Oxford University Press, 2003.

The Family Manifesto: A Declaration of Timeless Principles. Little Rock, Ark.: FamilyLife, 2000.

Farber, David, and Jeff Roche, eds. *The Conservative Sixties*. New York: Peter Lang, 2003.

Flowers, Ronald B. *Religion in Strange Times: The 1960s and 1970s*. Macon, Ga.: Mercer University Press, 1984.

Formisano, Ronald. *Boston against Busing: Race, Class, and Ethnicity in the 1960s and 1970s*. Chapel Hill: University of North Carolina Press, 1991.

Frank, Thomas. *The Conquest of Cool: Business Culture, Counterculture, and the Rise of Hip Consumerism*. Chicago: University of Chicago Press, 1997.

Gallup, George H., ed. *The Gallup Poll: Public Opinion, 1935–1971*. 3 vols. New York: Random House, 1972.

Gardner, David P. *The California Oath Controversy*. Berkeley: University of California Press, 1967.

Gilbert, James. *A Cycle of Outrage: America's Reaction to the Juvenile Delinquent in the 1950s*. New York: Oxford University Press, 1986.

Gillquist, Peter, and Gordon Walker. *Arrowhead Springs to Antioch: Odyssey to Orthodoxy*. N.p., 1987.

Gitlin, Todd. *The Sixties: Years of Hope, Days of Rage*. New York: Bantam, 1987.

Graebner, William. *The Age of Doubt: American Thought and Culture in the 1940s*. Boston: Twayne, 1991.

Graham, Billy. *Peace with God.* Garden City, N.Y.: Doubleday, 1953.

Green, John C., Mark J. Rozell, and Clyde Wilcox. *The Values Campaign? The Christian Right and the 2004 Elections.* Washington, D.C.: Georgetown University Press, 2006.

Gregory, James N. *American Exodus: The Dust Bowl Migration and Okie Culture in California.* New York: Oxford University Press, 1989.

Hadden, Jeffrey K., and Anson Shupe. *Televangelism: Power and Politics on God's Frontier.* New York: Henry Holt, 1988.

Hadden, Jeffrey K., and Charles E. Swann. *Prime Time Preachers: The Rising Power of Televangelism.* Reading, Mass.: Addison-Wesley, 1981.

Hambrick-Stowe, Charles E. *Charles G. Finney and the Spirit of American Evangelicalism.* Grand Rapids: Eerdmans, 1996.

Hangen, Tona J. *Redeeming the Dial: Radio, Religion, and Popular Culture in America.* Chapel Hill: University of North Carolina Press, 2002.

Hankins, Barry. *Uneasy in Babylon: Southern Baptist Conservatives and American Culture.* Tuscaloosa: University of Alabama Press, 2002.

Harrell, David Edwin, Jr. *All Things Are Possible: The Healing and Charismatic Revivals in Modern America.* Bloomington: Indiana University Press, 1975.

———. *Oral Roberts: An American Life.* Bloomington: Indiana University Press, 1985.

———. *Pat Robertson: A Personal, Religious, and Political Portrait.* San Francisco: Harper & Row, 1987.

Hart, D. G. *Deconstructing Evangelicalism: Conservative Protestantism in the Age of Billy Graham.* Grand Rapids: Baker Academic, 2004.

———. *That Old-Time Religion in Modern America: Evangelical Protestantism in the Twentieth Century.* Chicago: Ivan R. Dee, 2002.

Have You Made the Wonderful Discovery of the Spirit-Filled Life? San Bernardino, Calif.: Campus Crusade for Christ International, 1966.

Hendershot, Heather. *Shaking the World for Jesus: Media and Conservative Evangelical Culture.* Chicago: University of Chicago Press, 2004.

Henry, Carl F. H., ed. *Prophecy in the Making: Messages Prepared for the Jerusalem Conference on Biblical Prophecy.* Carol Stream, Ill.: Creation House, 1971.

Herberg, Will. *Protestant, Catholic, Jew: An Essay in American Religious Sociology.* Garden City, N.Y.: Doubleday, 1955.

Herriott, C. Calvin. *It Can Happen Here.* Oradell, N.J.: American Tract Society, n.d.

Hofstadter, Richard. *Anti-Intellectualism in American Life.* New York: Knopf, 1966. Originally published in 1963.

———. *The Paranoid Style in American Politics, and Other Essays.* New York: Knopf, 1965.

Hopkins, C. Howard. *History of the Y.M.C.A. in North America.* New York: Association Press, 1951.

———. *John R. Mott, 1865–1955: A Biography.* Grand Rapids: Eerdmans, 1979.

Horowitz, Helen Lefkovitz. *Campus Life: Undergraduate Cultures from the End of the Eighteenth Century to the Present.* New York: Knopf, 1987.

Hudnut-Beumler, James. *Looking for God in the Suburbs: The Religion of the American Dream and Its Critics, 1945–1965*. New Brunswick, N.J.: Rutgers University Press, 1994.

Hummel, Charles E. *Campus Christian Witness: An Inter-Varsity Christian Fellowship Manual*. Chicago: Inter-Varsity Press, 1958.

Hunt, Keith, and Gladys Hunt. *For Christ and the University: The Story of InterVarsity Christian Fellowship of the U.S.A., 1940–1990*. Downers Grove, Ill.: InterVarsity Press, 1991.

Hurt, Harry, III. *Texas Rich: The Hunt Dynasty from the Early Oil Days through the Silver Crash*. New York: W. W. Norton, 1981.

Isserman, Maurice, and Michael Kazin. *America Divided: The Civil War of the 1960s*. New York: Oxford University Press, 2000.

Jenkins, Philip. *The Next Christendom: The Coming of Global Christianity*. New York: Oxford University Press, 2002.

Jorstad, Erling. *Evangelicals in the White House: The Cultural Maturation of Born Again Christianity, 1960–1981*. New York: Edwin Mellen, 1981.

Kerr, Clark. *The Gold and the Blue: A Personal Memoir of the University of California, 1949–1967*. 2 vols. Berkeley: University of California Press, 2001–3.

Kim, Rebecca Y. *God's New Whiz Kids? Korean American Evangelicals on Campus*. New York: New York University Press, 2006.

Klatch, Rebecca E. *A Generation Divided: The New Left, the New Right, and the 1960s*. Berkeley: University of California Press, 1999.

Kuo, David. *Tempting Faith: An Inside Story of Political Seduction*. New York: Free Press, 2006.

Laats, Adam. "Roots of the Culture Wars: Fundamentalism and American Education in the 1920s." Ph.D. diss., University of Wisconsin, 2006.

Lambert, Frank. *"Pedlar in Divinity": George Whitefield and the Transatlantic Revivals, 1737–1770*. Princeton, N.J.: Princeton University Press, 1994.

Lee, Calvin. *The Campus Scene, 1900–1970: Changing Styles in Undergraduate Life*. New York: McKay, 1970.

Lee, Timothy S. "Born-Again in Korea: The Rise and Character of Revivalism in (South) Korea, 1885–1988." Ph.D. diss., University of Chicago Divinity School, 1996.

Lucas, Christopher J. *American Higher Education: A History*. New York: St. Martin's, 1994.

Lyons, Paul. *The People of This Generation: The Rise and Fall of the New Left in Philadelphia*. Philadelphia: University of Pennsylvania Press, 2003.

Madden, Andrea V. B. "Henrietta C. Mears, 1890–1963: Her Life and Influence." M.A. thesis, Gordon-Conwell Theological Seminary, 1997.

Maddox, Robert L. *Preacher at the White House*. Nashville: Broadman, 1984.

Manuel, David. *The Gathering*. Orleans, Mass.: Rock Harbor Press, 1980.

Maraniss, David. *They Marched into Sunlight: War and Peace, Vietnam and America, October 1967*. New York: Simon & Schuster, 2003.

Marks, Bailey. *An Ordinary Businessman*. San Bernardino, Calif.: Here's Life, 1979.

Marks, Bailey, with Shirley Mewhinney. *Awakening in Asia*. San Bernardino, Calif.: Here's Life, 1981.

Marsden, George. *Fundamentalism and American Culture: The Shaping of Twentieth-Century Evangelicalism, 1870–1925*. New York: Oxford University Press, 1980.

———. *Reforming Fundamentalism: Fuller Seminary and the New Evangelicalism*. Grand Rapids: Eerdmans, 1987.

———. *The Soul of the American University: From Protestant Establishment to Established Unbelief*. New York: Oxford University Press, 1994.

———, ed. *Evangelicalism and Modern America*. Grand Rapids: Eerdmans, 1984.

Martin, William C. *A Prophet with Honor: The Billy Graham Story*. New York: William Morrow, 1991.

———. *With God on Our Side: The Rise of the Religious Right in America*. New York: Broadway, 1996.

Marty, Martin E. *The New Shape of American Religion*. New York: Harper & Brothers, 1959.

———. *Under God, Indivisible, 1941–1960*. Vol. 3 of *Modern American Religion*. Chicago: University of Chicago Press, 1996.

Mathews, Donald G., and Jane Sherron De Hart. *Sex, Gender, and the Politics of the ERA: A State and a Nation*. New York: Oxford University Press, 1990.

Mauss, Armand L. *The Angel and the Beehive: The Mormon Struggle with Assimilation*. Urbana: University of Illinois Press, 1994.

May, Elaine Tyler. *Homeward Bound: American Families in the Cold War Era*. New York: Basic Books, 1988.

McGirr, Lisa. *Suburban Warriors: The Origins of the New American Right*. Princeton, N.J.: Princeton University Press, 2001.

McLoughlin, William G., Jr. *Modern Revivalism: Charles Grandison Finney to Billy Graham*. New York: Ronald Press, 1959.

Mead, Sydney. *The Lively Experiment: The Shaping of Christianity in America*. New York: Harper & Row, 1963.

Miller, Steven P. "The Politics of Decency: Billy Graham, Evangelicalism, and the End of the Solid South, 1950–1980." Ph.D. diss., Vanderbilt University, 2006.

Moore, R. Laurence. *Religious Outsiders and the Making of Americans*. New York: Oxford University Press, 1986.

———. *Selling God: American Religion in the Marketplace of Culture*. New York: Oxford University Press, 1994.

Murch, James DeForest. *Adventuring for Christ in Changing Times*. Louisville, Ky.: Restoration Press, 1973.

———. *Cooperation without Compromise: A History of the National Association of Evangelicals*. Grand Rapids: Eerdmans, 1956.

Musser, Joe. *Josh: Excitement of the Unexpected*. San Bernardino, Calif.: Here's Life, 1981.

Niebuhr, H. Richard, Wilhelm Pauck, and Francis P. Miller. *The Church against the World*. Chicago: Willett, Clark, 1935.

Noll, Mark. *The Scandal of the Evangelical Mind*. Grand Rapids: Eerdmans, 1994.

Oakley, J. Ronald. *God's Country: America in the Fifties*. New York: Dembner, 1986.

Oldfield, Duane Murray. *The Right and the Righteous: The Christian Right Confronts the Republican Party*. Lanham, Mass.: Rowman & Littlefield, 1996.

Oppenheimer, Mark. *Knocking on Heaven's Door: American Religion in the Age of Counterculture*. New Haven: Yale University Press, 2003.

Orr, J. Edwin. *Full Surrender*. London: Marshall, Morgan & Scott, 1951.

———. *Good News in Bad Times: Signs of Revival*. Grand Rapids: Zondervan, 1953.

———. *The Inside Story of the Hollywood Christian Group*. Grand Rapids: Zondervan, 1955.

———. *The Second Evangelical Awakening in America: An Account of the Second World-wide Evangelical Revival Beginning in America in the Mid-19th Century*. London: Marshall, Morgan & Scott, 1952.

Park, Chung-Shin. *Protestantism and Politics in Korea*. Seattle: University of Washington Press, 2003.

Patterson, James T. *Grand Expectations: The United States, 1945–1974*. New York: Oxford University Press, 1996.

Plowman, Edward. *The Jesus Movement in America: Accounts of Christian Revolutionaries in Action*. Elgin, Ill.: David C. Cook, 1971.

Powers, Barbara Hudson. *The Henrietta Mears Story*. Westwood, N.J.: Fleming H. Revell, 1957.

Powers, Richard Gid. *Not without Honor: The History of American Anticommunism*. New York: Free Press, 1995.

Prothero, Stephen. *American Jesus: How the Son of God Became a National Icon*. New York: Farrar, Straus and Giroux, 2003.

———, ed. *A Nation of Religions: The Politics of Pluralism in Multireligious America*. Chapel Hill: University of North Carolina Press, 2006.

Putney, Clifford. *Muscular Christianity: Manhood and Sports in America, 1880–1920*. Cambridge, Mass.: Harvard University Press, 2001.

Quebedeaux, Richard. *I Found It! The Story of Campus Crusade for Christ*. New York: Harper & Row, 1979.

Rausch, Thomas P., ed. *Catholics and Evangelicals: Do They Share a Common Future?* New York: Paulist, 2000.

Ravitch, Diane. *The Troubled Crusade: American Education, 1945–1980*. New York: Basic Books, 1983.

Revival in Our Time: The Story of the Billy Graham Evangelistic Campaigns, Including Six of His Sermons. Wheaton: Van Kampen Press, 1950.

Ribuffo, Leo. *The Old Christian Right: The Protestant Far Right from the Great Depression to the Cold War*. Philadelphia: Temple University Press, 1983.

Richardson, Michael. *Amazing Faith: The Authorized Biography of Bill Bright*. Colorado Springs, Colo.: WaterBrook, 2000.

Riley, Naomi Schaefer. *God on the Quad: How Religious Colleges and the Missionary Generation Are Changing America*. New York: St. Martin's, 2005.

Ro, Bong-Rin, and Marlin L. Nelson. *Korean Church Growth Explosion*. Seoul: Word of Life Press, 1983.

Robert, Dana L. *Occupy until I Come: A. T. Pierson and the Evangelization of the World.* Grand Rapids: Eerdmans, 2003.

Roberts, Jon H., and James Turner. *The Sacred and the Secular University.* Princeton, N.J.: Princeton University Press, 2000.

Roe, Earl O., ed. *Dream Big: The Henrietta Mears Story.* Ventura, Calif.: Regal Books, 1990.

Rorabaugh, W. J. *Berkeley at War: The 1960s.* New York: Oxford University Press, 1989.

Rossinow, Douglas. *The Politics of Authenticity: Liberalism, Christianity, and the New Left in America.* New York: Columbia University Press, 1998.

Russell, John. *The Untold EXPLO Story; or, What the Official EXPLO Story Has Concealed.* Greenville, S.C.: Bob Jones University Press, 1973.

Scales, James R., and Danney Goble. *Oklahoma Politics: A History.* Norman: University of Oklahoma Press, 1982.

Schmalzbauer, John. *People of Faith: Religious Conviction in American Journalism and Higher Education.* Ithaca, N.Y.: Cornell University Press, 2003.

Schneider, Gregory L. *Cadres for Conservatism: Young Americans for Freedom and the Rise of the Contemporary Right.* New York: New York University Press, 1999.

Schrecker, Ellen W. *No Ivory Tower: McCarthyism and the Universities.* New York: Oxford University Press, 1986.

Schultze, Quentin J. *Televangelism and American Culture: The Business of Popular Religion.* Grand Rapids: Baker, 1991.

Skinner, Betty Lee. *Daws: The Story of Dawson Trotman, Founder of the Navigators.* Grand Rapids: Zondervan, 1974.

Smith, Christian. *American Evangelicalism: Embattled and Thriving.* Chicago: University of Chicago Press, 1998.

Sparks, Jack. *God's Forever Family.* Grand Rapids: Zondervan, 1974.

Sperber, Murray. *Beer and Circus: How Big-Time College Sports Is Crippling Undergraduate Education.* New York: Henry Holt, 2000.

Stackhouse, John G., Jr. *Evangelical Landscapes: Facing Critical Issues of the Day.* Grand Rapids: Baker, 2002.

Stark, Rodney, and Roger Finke. *Acts of Faith: Explaining the Human Side of Religion.* Berkeley: University of California Press, 2000.

Starr, Kevin. *Embattled Dreams: California in War and Peace, 1940–1950.* New York: Oxford University Press, 2002.

Stoll, David. *Is Latin America Turning Protestant? The Politics of Evangelical Growth.* Berkeley: University of California Press, 1990.

Stone, Jon R. *On the Boundaries of American Evangelicalism: The Postwar Evangelical Coalition.* New York: St. Martin's Press, 1997.

Synan, Vinson. *The Holiness-Pentecostal Tradition: Charismatic Movements in the Twentieth Century.* Grand Rapids: Eerdmans, 1997.

Ten Basic Steps toward Christian Maturity. San Bernardino, Calif.: Campus Crusade for Christ, 1964.

Torrey, R. A. *The Holy Spirit: Who He Is and What He Does, and How to Know Him in*

All the Fulness of His Gracious and Glorious Ministry. New York: Fleming H. Revell, 1927.

Tracy, James. *Direct Action: Radical Pacifism from the Union Eight to the Chicago Seven*. Chicago: University of Chicago Press, 1996.

Trollinger, William Vance. *God's Empire: William Bell Riley and Midwestern Fundamentalism*. Madison: University of Wisconsin Press, 1990.

Turner, Daniel L. *Standing without Apology: The History of Bob Jones University*. Greenville, S.C.: Bob Jones University Press, 1997.

U.S. Bureau of the Census. *Historical Statistics of the United States, Colonial Times to 1970*. Washington, D.C.: Government Printing Office, 1975.

Wald, Kenneth. *Religion and Politics in the United States*. 4th ed. Lanham, Md.: Rowman & Littlefield, 2003.

Watt, David Harrington. *A Transforming Faith: Explorations of Twentieth-Century Evangelicalism*. New Brunswick, N.J.: Rutgers University Press, 1991.

Whitfield, Stephen J. *The Culture of the Cold War*. 2nd ed. Baltimore: Johns Hopkins University Press, 1996.

Wilcox, W. Bradford. *Soft Patriarchs, New Men: How Christianity Shapes Fathers and Husbands*. Chicago: University of Chicago Press, 2004.

Women's Manual: Campus Crusade for Christ. San Bernardino, Calif.: Campus Crusade for Christ, 1971.

Woodbridge, Charles J. *Campus Crusade: Examined in the Light of Scripture*. Greenville, S.C.: Bob Jones University Press, 1970.

Wosh, Peter J. *Spreading the Word: The Bible Business in Nineteenth-Century America*. Ithaca, N.Y.: Cornell University Press, 1994.

Would You Like to Know God Personally? Orlando: Campus Crusade for Christ, 2000.

Wuthnow, Robert. *The Restructuring of American Religion: Society and Faith since World War II*. Princeton, N.J.: Princeton University Press, 1988.

Wynkoop, Mary Ann. *Dissent in the Heartland: The Sixties at Indiana University*. Bloomington: Indiana University Press, 2002.

Index

Bright, Charley, 14

Bright, Forrest Dale, 13–16

Bright, Mary Lee Rohl, 13–14

Bright, Roy Curtis, 15

Bright, Sam, 13, 16

Bright, Vonette Zachary, 34, 37–38, 50, 56, 80–81, 87, 95, 116–17, 164, 174, 186, 194; marries Bill Bright, 31–33; role in Campus Crusade ministries, 47, 48–49, 51, 57–58, 100, 106–7, 212–13; and feminist movement/gender roles, 57, 156, 209, 209–12, 244 (n. 24); at Bill Bright's memorial service, 228

Bright, William ("Bill"): and Explo '72, 1, 139–46; development of *Four Spiritual Laws*, 6, 99–103, 231; political beliefs and activities, 9, 15, 16, 63–65, 67, 93–94, 97–98, 107–12, 141, 149, 152–54, 160–68, 171–72, 174, 179, 187–97, 199–203, 214, 231, 233–35; commitment to evangelism, 10–11, 24, 27, 29–30, 37, 48, 139, 174, 175, 179–80, 220, 233; style of leadership, 10–11, 53–54, 106–7, 113, 134–35, 138, 139–40, 158, 160, 173, 203, 208; early years in Oklahoma, 13–17; moves to California, 16, 17–18; business enterprises, 18, 24–25, 33–34, 104; conversion, 19, 23; at Princeton Theological Seminary, 24–25; joins Fellowship of the Burning Heart, 25–29; at Fuller Theological Seminary, 29–31, 36–38, 182; marries Vonette Zachary, 31–33; founds Campus Crusade for Christ, 37–39, 41, 43–45; relationship with Bob Jones University, 49–50, 75–84; and gender roles, 55, 209, 211–13; fund-raising, 63–64, 83–84, 92, 93, 95, 104–6, 107–8, 112–16, 176–81, 205–6, 232–33; conflict with InterVarsity leaders, 70–72; theological beliefs, 78, 81, 84, 87–90, 91, 229–30; and charismatic/Pentecostal Christianity, 89–91, 114, 145, 186, 191, 228–30; and Christian Citizen movement, 109–12, 148, 162; and Berkeley Blitz, 121–26, 138–39; conflicts with staff members, 133–38, 140–41, 151, 158, 160, 230; and Explo '74, 151–54, 167; and Here's Life, America, 158–61, 163–64, 167–71, 173;

conflict with Jim Wallis, 164–67, 230, 255 (n. 33); and Judaism, 166, 182–83; and *Jesus* film, 181–85; and New Life 2000, 185, 229; and Washington for Jesus (WFJ), 191–92, 195, 196–97, 200; and International Christian Graduate University, 203–8; stance on homosexuality, 207, 214, 233; 2003 death of, 227–28; wins Templeton Prize, 228–29

Bright, Zachary, 103, 186, 229–30, 231

Brom, Hugh, 38

Brown University, 223

Bruner, Dale, 37, 108

Bryant, Anita, 157–58

Buckley, William F., 43

Bundy, Edgar C., 110

Bush, George H. W., 195, 234

Bush, George W., 84, 215, 234–35

California Institute of Technology (Caltech), 30

Calvary Chapel, 131, 186

Calvin College, 225, 234

Campolo, Tony, 230

Campus Associates, 116

Campus Crusade for Christ: use of *Four Spiritual Laws*, 1, 99–103, 120, 123, 131, 142, 151, 159, 163, 219–20, 231; and popular culture/music, 1–2, 50, 62–63, 82–84, 93–94, 119–20, 123–24, 126–27, 129–30, 132, 139, 142–43, 145–46, 217, 224, 227, 231–32, 250 (n. 16), 252–53 (n. 44); Explo '72, 1–2, 121, 139–46, 150–51, 152, 164, 171, 235, 252 (n. 42); campus ministry, 8, 43–49, 53–57, 59–63, 66–67, 70–75, 98–100, 126–34, 175, 217–25; and homosexuality, 9, 157–58, 172, 214–15, 220; and gender roles, 9–10, 46, 55–59, 61–62, 123–24, 155–58, 209–13, 231; founding of, 38–39, 43–45; and race, 59, 112, 121, 141, 145, 218–19, 220, 223–24, 227; fund-raising, 63–64, 83–84, 89, 92, 93, 96, 104–6, 113–16, 147, 176–81, 190, 205, 232, 248 (n. 18); and charismatic/Pentecostal Christianity, 69, 84–92, 93, 114, 141, 145, 185–87, 228; conflict with InterVarsity Christian Fellowship,

70–75, 97; international ministries, 94–98, 151–54, 175, 180–81, 184–87, 208, 216–17, 228–29, 236; acquisition of Arrowhead Springs, 112–17; Berkeley Blitz, 119–20, 121–28, 129, 142; and New Left, 119–20, 121–33, 138; and Catholic Church, 145, 184, 187, 228–29; and Explo '74, 151–54; and Here's Life, America, 158–61, 163–64, 167–71, 173, 175, 180; Christian Embassy, 162–64; and Judaism, 163, 182–83; and Here's Life, World, 175–77, 179–81, 190; development of *Jesus* film, 181–85, 187; and New Life 2000, 185, 229; and International Christian Graduate University, 203–8

Carlson, Frank, 149

Carr, John, 193–94

Carter, Jimmy, 159; and 1976 election, 148–49, 171, 253 (n. 3), 255 (n. 41), 258 (n. 46); and 1980 election, 188–96, 258 (n. 46)

Cash, Johnny, 1, 140

Cassidy, Edward Idris, Cardinal, 228–29

Catholicism, 26, 41, 43, 65, 108–9, 153, 157, 162, 200, 201, 220, 235. *See also* Campus Crusade for Christ: and Catholic Church; Evangelicalism: and Catholic Church

Chambers, Oswald, 51

Charismatic movement, 4, 205; relationship with evangelicalism, 69, 85, 90–92, 93, 114, 141, 145, 185–87, 191–92, 228–30

Chen, Dennis, 219

Chi, Daniel, 152

Children of God, 141–42, 169

Christian Broadcasting Network, 3, 178. *See also* Robertson, Pat

Christian Citizen, 109–12, 138, 148, 162, 164

Christian Coalition, 150, 202, 233, 238 (n. 4)

Christian Embassy, 162–64, 167, 171, 193, 195, 199, 254 (n. 25)

Christian Freedom Foundation (CFF), 110, 164–65, 167, 176, 183, 187, 195

Christianity Today, 152, 181, 183–84, 193, 218, 230

Christians Concerned for More Responsible Citizenship, 167

Christians for Biblical Equality (CBE), 209

Christian World Liberation Front (CWLF), 129, 131, 139

Church of the Nazarene, 84

Cleaver, Eldridge, 147

Clinton, Bill, 210

Coalition for the First Amendment, 194

Coffin, William Sloane, 120, 200

Cohen, Gerson, 200

Coker, Sam, 159

Colorado State University, 227–28

Colson, Charles, 3, 141, 147, 159, 165, 210, 228

Conlan, John, 110, 162–63, 179, 189–90; and Christian Freedom Foundation, 164–66

Connally, John, 189–90

Continental Congress on the Family, 154–55

Conway, Flo, 168–69

Cook, Bruce, 140–41, 150–51; and Here's Life, America, 158–60, 163, 167, 170, 171

Coote, Robert, 180

Council for National Policy (CNP), 202

Council on Biblical Manhood and Womanhood (CBMW), 209

Counterculture, 120–21, 123, 126, 129–31, 139, 142–43, 145–46, 251 (n. 22), 252–53 (n. 44)

Counts, Beverly, 126

Counts, Bill, 61, 99, 109, 112, 126, 133, 135, 137

Cox, Harvey, 187

Craddock, Jim, 73, 84, 104, 109, 111, 133

Crane, Philip, 194

Dallas Theological Seminary (DTS), 20, 83, 105, 154, 173, 246 (n. 22); influence on Campus Crusade for Christ, 5, 87–88, 90

Damoose, John, 201

Danvers Statement, 209, 213

Davenport, Bob, 46, 66

Deacon, Brian, 183

DeBerg, Betty, 224

Dekker, Ted, 229
Demarest, Gary, 29–31, 34
DeMille, Cecil B., 181–82
DeMoss, Arthur, 147, 218
Destino movement, 219
DeVos, Richard, 164
Dispensationalism, 90
Dobson, Ed, 235, 253 (n. 3)
Dobson, James, 3, 84, 154, 194, 201, 202, 210, 235–36
Douglass, Judy Downs, 156–57, 212
Douglass, Steve, 140, 150–51, 160, 184; assumes presidency of Campus Crusade for Christ, 227–28, 231, 232, 235–36
Downs, Judy. *See* Douglass, Judy Downs
Dunn, Charles, 63

Edwards, Gene, 110–11, 114, 138
Edwards, Jonathan, 203
Ellwood, Robert, 132
Epic movement, 219
Equal Rights Amendment (ERA), 149–50, 154, 158, 188, 190, 193–94, 196–97
Eshleman, Paul, 150, 155, 160, 187, 227–28; leadership of Explo '72, 140, 151; leadership of *Jesus* film, 182–84, 187
Evangelicalism: defined, 4, 238 (nn. 10, 11); and popular culture/music, 6–7, 22, 23, 50, 82–84, 121, 132–33, 139, 142–43, 145–46, 224, 227, 231; and higher education, 8, 27–29, 37–39, 42–43, 45–46, 61–63, 73–75, 102–3, 130–33, 203–8, 217–25, 260 (n. 37); and anticommunism, 8–9, 25–27, 35, 41–43, 63–66, 97–98, 108–11, 127–28, 149, 152–54, 160, 162, 171, 178–79, 188–89, 193, 196, 200; and conservative politics, 8–9, 107–12, 141, 144, 147–50, 157–58, 160–61, 164–68, 171, 173–74, 187–97, 199–203, 214–15, 233–36, 253 (n. 3), 255 (n. 41), 257–58 (n. 46); and gender roles, 9–10, 20, 46, 55–59, 61–62, 154–58, 209–13, 231, 240 (n. 14); and homosexuality, 10, 149, 154, 155, 157–58, 190, 192–94, 202, 209, 213–15; divergence from fundamentalism, 22–23, 29, 50, 62–63, 69, 75–84, 145, 211, 228; and Catholic Church, 26, 108–9, 145, 187, 200, 228–29; and Judaism,

26, 163, 182–83, 200; and foreign missions, 27–28, 70, 94–98, 162, 174–75, 180–81, 184–87, 236; and postwar religious boom, 34–36, 45, 52, 65–68, 244 (n. 36); and race, 59, 112, 121, 141, 145, 218–19, 223–24, 227; and Pentecostalism/charismatic movement, 84–85, 89–92, 141, 145, 185–87, 191–92, 228–30
Evangelical Orthodox Church, 137
Evangelicals and Catholics Together (ECT), 228–29
Evangelicals for Social Action, 234
Evans, Colleen Townsend, 34, 36
Evans, Dale, 36
Evans, Louis, Jr., 27, 34, 36, 44
Evans, Louis, Sr., 18–19, 33, 38, 44, 45, 48, 74
Explo '72, 1–2, 121, 139–46, 150–51, 152, 164, 171, 235, 252 (n. 42)
Explo '74, 151–54, 164

Falwell, Jerry, 2, 83, 181, 192; political activities, 173, 188, 195, 196–97, 200, 202, 231, 235
FamilyLife, 7, 150, 158, 171–72, 174, 208–16, 217, 235; and gender roles, 9, 155–56, 209–11; founding of, 155; and homosexuality and gay marriage, 214–15
Family Research Council, 194, 214–15
Farmer, James L., 193
Federal Council of Churches (FCC), 22, 174
Fellowship of Christian Athletes (FCA), 8, 74–75
Fellowship of the Burning Heart, 27–28, 34, 35, 45
Feminism: and American evangelicalism, 7, 57, 149–50, 154–58, 172, 210–12, 244 (n. 24)
Finke, Roger, 7, 239 (n. 16)
Finney, Charles, 6–7
First Presbyterian Church of Hollywood, 18–30, 33, 34–35, 37, 43, 44–45, 46, 50, 52, 75, 80, 85, 99, 104, 105, 106, 108, 117, 139
Flipse, Scott, 253 (n. 3)
Focus on the Family, 3, 155, 210, 214–15, 238 (n. 4)

National Association of Evangelicals
(NAE), 4, 22–23, 69, 75–76, 77, 78, 84, 92, 174
National Council of Churches (NCC), 77, 193
National Day of Prayer, 200
National Religious Broadcasters (NRB), 188, 190, 194
National Sunday School Association, 22
Navigators, 18, 60, 74–75, 130–31
Nethery, Ray, 82, 86, 91, 96, 113–14, 116, 151
Neuhaus, Richard John, 228
New Folk, 119–20, 127, 130, 250 (n. 16)
New Left, 120–22, 126–33, 250 (n. 6)
Niebuhr, H. Richard, 2, 7
Nixon, Richard, 111, 149, 159, 165, 255 (n. 41); and Explo '72, 1, 121, 141, 144
Noll, Mark, 204, 248 (n. 13)
Northeastern State College, 15–16

Oakes, J. Stanley, 208
Oakley, J. Ronald, 65
Occidental College, 30
Ockenga, Harold J., 17, 22, 25, 29, 30, 64, 69
O'Donnell, John W., 179
Ohio State University, 220
Oppenheimer, Mark, 130, 251 (n. 22)
Oral Roberts University, 186
Orr, J. Edwin, 35, 86–87
Ostling, Richard, 234
Oxford University, 28, 203

Page, Eleanor, 161–62
Parachurch organizations, 2–7, 8, 11, 44, 46, 69, 106, 217–18, 221–25, 228, 232–33, 238 (n. 8); significance to American evangelicalism, 2–7, 11, 67–68, 237–38 (n. 4); competition and conflict between, 4, 70–75
Park, Chung Hee, 152–53
Pelley, William Dudley, 64
Pentecostalism, 4, 84–85, 160, 200, 205; relationship with evangelicalism, 69, 84–85, 89–92, 114, 141, 145, 185–87, 191–92, 228–30
Peterson, J. Allan, 154–55, 158
Pew, J. Howard, 109

Pierce, Bob, 3, 95
Pierson, Arthur T., 185
Pittenger, Robert, 163, 189–90, 195–96, 197
Plate, Glenn, 128, 158
Plowman, Edward, 152, 193
Port Huron Statement, 131
Priest, Arlis, 113–16, 187–88
Princeton Theological Seminary, 21, 24–25, 29, 37, 48
Princeton University, 24
Promise Keepers, 210
Protestantism, mainline, 8, 22, 25–26, 85, 97, 109, 132, 147, 180, 236, 251 (n. 26); relationship with evangelicalism, 4, 26, 36, 44, 73–74, 76–78, 83–84, 174, 193, 223–24

Quebedeaux, Richard, 17–18, 166, 238 (n. 8)

Rainey, Dennis: leadership of FamilyLife, 155, 209–16, 227; and gender roles, 209–13; on homosexuality and gay marriage, 214–15, 235
Reagan, Ronald, 36, 119, 148, 200, 234; and 1980 election, 189–90, 193, 195–97, 257–58 (n. 46)
Regier, Jerry, 171; and White House Conference on Families, 193–94, 197
Religious Coalition for a Moral Defense Policy, 200
Religious Right. See Evangelicalism: and conservative politics
Religious Roundtable, 195
Republican Party, 14–15; and evangelicalism, 9, 107, 109, 144, 148–49, 159, 162, 171, 173, 189–90, 195–96, 202, 206, 214, 234–36, 257–58 (n. 46)
Rice, John R., 76–77, 79, 83, 245 (n. 11)
Rice University, 88
Richardson, Michael, 55, 116, 182, 238 (n. 8)
Riffe, Jerry, 79–80, 82
Riley, William B., 19, 42, 105, 182
Ringer, Bob, 99
Roberts, Oral, 2, 16, 51, 85, 89, 141, 148, 227, 231; fund-raising, 177–78, 205
Robertson, Pat, 2, 3, 17, 84, 147, 148, 181,